Don Daniels
Grammatical Reconstruction

Studies in Language Change

Edited by
Cynthia Allen
Harold Koch
Malcolm Ross

Volume 16

Don Daniels
Grammatical Reconstruction

―

The Sogeram Languages of New Guinea

DE GRUYTER
MOUTON

ISBN 978-3-11-077713-0
e-ISBN (PDF) 978-3-11-061621-7
e-ISBN (EPUB) 978-3-11-061656-9
ISSN 2163-0992

Library of Congress Control Number: 2019956246

Bibliographic information published by the Deutsche Nationalbibliothek
The Deutsche Nationalbibliothek lists this publication in the Deutsche Nationalbibliografie;
detailed bibliographic data are available on the Internet at http://dnb.dnb.de.

© 2021 Walter de Gruyter GmbH, Berlin/Boston
This volume is text- and page-identical with the hardback published in 2020.
Cover image: iStockphoto/thinkstock
Typesetting: Integra Software Services Pvt. Ltd.
Printing and binding: CPI books GmbH, Leck

www.degruyter.com

Contents

List of Abbreviations —— XI

Chapter 1   Introduction —— 1
1.1   The Sogeram languages —— 2
1.2   Madang and Trans New Guinea —— 8
1.3   Previous research —— 9
1.4   My fieldwork —— 11

Chapter 2   Methodology —— 13
2.1   Can syntax be reconstructed? —— 13
2.1.1   What is reconstruction? —— 14
2.1.2   What is syntax? —— 19
2.1.3   Are reconstruction and syntax compatible? —— 22
2.2   How syntax can be reconstructed —— 24
2.3   Other perspectives on syntactic reconstruction —— 28
2.3.1   Formal approaches to syntactic reconstruction —— 29
2.3.2   Functional approaches to syntactic reconstruction —— 33
2.3.2.1   Arbitrariness —— 34
2.3.2.2   Regularity —— 35
2.3.2.3   Borrowing —— 37
2.4   Other methodological issues —— 38
2.4.1   External and internal evidence —— 39
2.4.2   The subgrouping of the Sogeram languages —— 39

Chapter 3   Phonology —— 45
3.1   Proto-Sogeram phonological inventory —— 45
3.1.1   Proto-Sogeram phonotactics —— 51
3.2   The Greater West Sogeram languages and Apalɨ —— 54
3.2.1   West and Greater West Sogeram innovations —— 54
3.2.1.1   Word-initial consonant deletion —— 55
3.2.1.2   Loss of final *a from prosodic units —— 56
3.2.1.3   Palatalization of word-final *Ki —— 57
3.2.1.4   Word-initial plosive lenition in Manat and Apalɨ —— 58
3.2.2   Mand innovations —— 58
3.2.2.1   Sporadic *k and *kw lenition —— 59
3.2.2.2   Stop denasalization —— 59
3.2.2.3   *a-centering —— 59
3.2.2.4   Word-final *a loss —— 60

3.2.2.5	Nasal fortition and final *ŋ > h	60
3.2.2.6	Glide fortition	61
3.2.3	Nend innovations	61
3.2.3.1	Plosive voicing	62
3.2.3.2	Word-final *i loss	63
3.2.3.3	Word-final *n-rhotacization	63
3.2.3.4	Sporadic word-initial *a loss	63
3.2.3.5	Sporadic vowel harmony	63
3.2.3.6	*f lenition	63
3.2.4	Manat innovations	64
3.2.4.1	Sporadic word-initial vowel loss with *u metathesis	64
3.2.5	Apalɨ innovations	65
3.2.5.1	Word-final nasal velarization	66
3.2.5.2	Merger of *ñ and *n	66
3.2.5.3	Palatalization of *k and *s	67
3.2.5.4	Epenthesis and paragoge	67
3.2.5.5	Plosive voicing and *[β] > f	67
3.2.5.6	*ai > e	68
3.2.5.7	Palatalization of *z in Apalɨ and possibly Mum	68
3.3	The North Sogeram languages	68
3.3.1	Broader innovations	68
3.3.1.1	Voicing of prenasalized stops and *z	69
3.3.1.2	Labiovelar loss	69
3.3.1.3	Word-final nasal deletion with ɨ-deletion in Manat, Mum, and Sirva	69
3.3.1.4	*w fortition in Manat, Mum, and Sirva	70
3.3.2	North Sogeram innovations	70
3.3.2.1	Word-initial *f fortition	71
3.3.2.2	*u fortition	72
3.3.2.3	Word-final *r deletion	72
3.3.2.4	Sporadic *i-loss	72
3.3.2.5	Sporadic plosive lenition	73
3.3.3	Mum innovations	73
3.3.3.1	Word-final labiovelar creation	74
3.3.3.2	Word-initial *i fortition	74
3.3.3.3	Sporadic vowel centering	75
3.3.4	Sirva innovations	75
3.3.4.1	Word-initial *i and *u breaking	75
3.3.4.2	*h-loss	75

3.4	The East Sogeram languages —— 76
3.4.1	East Sogeram innovations —— 76
3.4.1.1	Voicing of prenasalized stops —— 76
3.4.1.2	Word-final nasal loss in Aisian and Kursav —— 77
3.4.1.3	*ɨ harmonization —— 77
3.4.1.4	Lowering of *i and *u in Kursav and Gants —— 78
3.4.2	Aisian innovations —— 78
3.4.2.1	Word-final *i deletion —— 79
3.4.2.2	Stop denasalization —— 80
3.4.2.3	Word-internal *r loss —— 80
3.4.2.4	Word-final *a centering —— 81
3.4.2.5	Simplification of vowel sequences —— 81
3.4.2.6	Merger of *ñ and *n —— 81
3.4.3	Magɨ innovations —— 81
3.4.3.1	*r vocalization —— 82
3.4.4	Aisi innovations —— 82
3.4.4.1	*i and *u lowering —— 83
3.4.4.2	Labiovelar loss and *a rounding —— 83
3.4.4.3	*d lenition —— 83
3.4.4.4	Glide formation —— 84
3.4.5	Kursav innovations —— 84
3.4.5.1	Sporadic word-initial *t lenition —— 84
3.4.5.2	*e lowering —— 85
3.4.5.3	Merger of *ñ and *n —— 85
3.4.5.4	Word-initial *u breaking —— 85
3.4.6	Gants innovations —— 85
3.4.6.1	Sporadic word-final *m loss —— 86
3.4.6.2	Non-initial *t lenition —— 86
3.4.6.3	Merger of *p and *f —— 86
3.4.6.4	Syllable-final *r vocalization —— 87
3.5	Orthographic conventions —— 87
Chapter 4	**Verbs and Verb Morphology —— 89**
4.1	The Proto-Sogeram verb —— 89
4.1.1	Root vowels and vowel elision —— 90
4.1.2	Dual and plural number —— 92
4.1.3	The third person plural —— 93
4.2	Serial verb constructions —— 96
4.2.1	The form of serialized verbs —— 96

4.2.2	Aspectual serial verbs —— 102
4.2.3	Orientation serial verbs —— 108
4.2.4	Causative and manner serial verbs —— 116
4.3	Final morphology —— 119
4.3.1	Immediate past —— 121
4.3.2	Today past —— 123
4.3.3	Recent and far past —— 125
4.3.4	Historic past —— 126
4.3.5	Future —— 128
4.3.6	Habitual —— 129
4.3.7	Imperative —— 132
4.3.8	Prohibitive —— 133
4.3.9	Counterfactual —— 134
4.3.10	Irrealis —— 136
4.4	Medial morphology —— 140
4.4.1	Same-subject —— 140
4.4.2	Different-subject realis —— 141
4.4.3	Different-subject simultaneous —— 144
4.5	Other morphology —— 148
4.5.1	Nominalization —— 148
4.5.2	Participle —— 153
4.5.3	Irrealis infinitive —— 155

Chapter 5	**Nominal Morphology** —— 159
5.1	Inalienably possessed nouns —— 159
5.1.1	Possessive prefixes —— 159
5.1.2	Plural marking —— 160
5.2	Pronouns and noun phrase enclitics —— 162
5.2.1	Subject pronouns —— 162
5.2.2	Object pronouns and enclitic —— 165
5.2.3	Oblique pronouns and enclitic —— 169
5.2.4	Possessive pronouns —— 175
5.2.5	Emphatic pronouns and enclitic —— 177
5.2.6	Interrogative pronoun —— 182
5.3	Demonstratives —— 183
5.3.1	Demonstrative roots —— 184
5.3.2	Bare roots —— 186
5.3.3	Contrastive root reduplication —— 195
5.3.4	Object and oblique —— 198
5.3.5	Topic/object —— 200

5.3.6	Locative 1 —— 204	
5.3.7	Locative 2 —— 208	
5.3.8	Focus —— 209	

Chapter 6 Syntactic Constructions —— 213
6.1	Word classes —— 213	
6.1.1	Adjectives —— 213	
6.1.2	Adverbs —— 216	
6.2	The noun phrase —— 217	
6.2.1	Attributive noun —— 218	
6.2.2	Adjective —— 219	
6.2.3	Possessor —— 220	
6.3	Clause structure —— 223	
6.3.1	Negation —— 223	
6.3.2	Interrogatives —— 228	
6.3.3	Nonverbal predicates —— 230	
6.4	Clause combining —— 238	
6.4.1	Switch reference —— 238	
6.4.2	Clause chain nominalization —— 240	
6.4.3	Quoted speech —— 247	

Chapter 7 Lexical Reconstructions —— 251
7.1	Proto-Sogeram lexemes —— 253	
7.2	Inalienably possessed nouns —— 291	
7.3	English – Proto-Sogeram finderlist —— 300	

Chapter 8 Conclusion —— 305
8.1	Proto-Sogeram grammar sketch —— 306	
8.1.1	Phonology (Chapter 3) —— 306	
8.1.1.1	Vowel elision (§4.1.1) —— 307	
8.1.2	Parts of speech —— 308	
8.1.2.1	Nouns —— 308	
8.1.2.2	Verbs (Chapter 4) —— 309	
8.1.2.3	Adjectives (§6.1.1) and adverbs (§6.1.2) —— 309	
8.1.2.4	Pronouns (§5.2) —— 309	
8.1.2.5	Demonstratives (§5.3) —— 310	
8.1.3	Noun phrase structure (§6.2) —— 311	
8.1.3.1	Enclitics and demonstratives —— 312	
8.1.4	Verb morphology (Chapter 4) —— 313	
8.1.4.1	Immediate past (§4.3.1) —— 314	

8.1.4.2	Today past (§4.3.2) —— **314**	
8.1.4.3	Recent past (§4.3.3) —— **315**	
8.1.4.4	Far past (§4.3.3) —— **315**	
8.1.4.5	Historic past (§4.3.4) —— **315**	
8.1.4.6	Future (§4.3.5) —— **316**	
8.1.4.7	Habitual (§4.3.6) —— **316**	
8.1.4.8	Imperative (§4.3.7) —— **316**	
8.1.4.9	Prohibitive (§4.3.8) —— **317**	
8.1.4.10	Counterfactual (§4.3.9) —— **317**	
8.1.4.11	Irrealis (§4.3.10) —— **317**	
8.1.4.12	Same-subject (§4.4.1) —— **318**	
8.1.4.13	Different-subject realis (§4.4.2) —— **318**	
8.1.4.14	Different-subject simultaneous (§4.4.3) —— **318**	
8.1.4.15	Nominalization and participle (§4.5.1, §4.5.2) —— **318**	
8.1.4.16	Irrealis infinitive (§4.5.3) —— **319**	
8.1.5	Clause structure —— **319**	
8.1.5.1	Verbal clauses —— **319**	
8.1.5.2	Serial verb constructions (§4.2) —— **319**	
8.1.5.3	Nonverbal clauses (§6.3.3) —— **320**	
8.1.6	Clause combining (§6.4) —— **321**	
8.1.6.1	Clause chaining and switch reference (§6.4.1) —— **322**	
8.1.6.2	Clause chain nominalization (§6.4.2) —— **322**	
8.1.6.3	Quoted speech (§6.4.3) —— **323**	
8.2	Texts —— **323**	
8.2.1	Schleicher's Fable —— **323**	
8.2.2	How the Ancestors Got Sago —— **325**	

References —— **329**

Index —— **341**

List of Abbreviations

1	first person
1/2	first or second person
2	second person
2/3	non-first person
3	third person
ACC	accusative
ADJZ	adjectivizer
ADVZ	adverbializer
AJTZ	adjunctivizer
BEN	benefactive
CAUS	causative
CHAR	characterized by
COM	comitative
COMP	completive
CONT	continuous
CPR	comparison
CTR	contrastive
CTRF	counterfactual
DEF	definite
DELAY	delayed relative tense
DESID	desiderative
DIM	diminutive
DS	different subject
DU	dual
EMPH	emphatic
EXCL	exclamative
EXST	existential
FAR	far (tense)
FD	far deictic distance
FFUT	far future
FOC	focus
FPST	far past
FUT	future
GEN	genitive
HAB	habitual
HIS	historic (tense)
HPST	historic past
IFUT	immediate future
ILOC	location of item
IMP	imperative
INDF	indefinite
INF	infinitive
INS	instrumental
INT	intensifier

IPST	immediate past
IRR	irrealis
LI	locative/instrumental
LNK	linking morpheme
LOC	locative
MD	middle deictic distance
MPST	middle past
ND	near deictic distance
NEG	negative
NFUT	non-future
NMLZ	nominalizer
NMPT	nominalizer/participle
NOM	nominative
OBJ	object
OBL	oblique
PL	plural
POSS	possessive
PRAG	pragmatically salient
PRED	predicate
PROH	prohibitive
PRS	present
PTCP	participle
PURP	purposive
Q	interrogative particle
QD	interrogative demonstrative
QUOT	quotative particle
RPST	recent past
SEQ	sequential
SET	setting
SIM	simultaneous
SG	singular
SPEC	specific
SS	same subject
TEMP	temporal
TOP	topic
TPST	today past
UFUT	uncertain future
VOC	vocative
YPST	yesterday past

Chapter 1
Introduction

How much of a language can be reconstructed? Certainly we can reconstruct phonology and lexicon. Morphology is also fairly uncontroversial. But what about syntax—can we reconstruct that? If so, how? And how certain can we be about the outcome? When we put it all together, how complete a picture of a proto-language can we hope to attain?

These questions are old. A century and a half ago Schleicher (1868) tried to reconstruct the grammar of Proto-Indo-European, and twenty years ago Gildea hoped "to reconstruct a reasonable grammar sketch of Proto-Carib" (1998: 44). This book is another entry in that conversation, inspired by the desire to know what proto-languages were like. I argue that we can reconstruct a great deal of a proto-language and arrive at a respectable picture of its overall structure, but that there are serious difficulties that require methodological adaptation and that sometimes prevent us from achieving the level of certainty we might wish for. Nevertheless, I am convinced that syntactic reconstruction is possible, and that when it is combined with more established processes of lexical, phonological, and morphological reconstruction, we really can get a sense for what proto-languages were like.

My argument takes the form of a demonstration: I reconstruct the lexicon, phonology, morphology, and syntax of the ancestor to the Sogeram languages of Papua New Guinea. The result is an 18-page sketch of Proto-Sogeram grammar and—a tribute to Schleicher's initial foray into the field—two constructed Proto-Sogeram texts. But the path there is long, and there are several things to do along the way.

The first, and most important, is to develop a method for reconstructing syntax. There is, as yet, no consensus about how to do this, although there have been several recent efforts (Willis 2011; Barðdal 2013, 2014; Walkden 2014). Indeed, some linguists believe it is not possible (Lightfoot 2002a, 2002b). So I devote the second chapter to my methodology, outlining what language is, how it changes, and what that means for how we can reconstruct it.

Another goal is to broaden our theoretical understanding of language structure and change. Most of the Sogeram languages are almost completely undescribed, so the reconstruction of their common ancestor makes a contribution to our typology of language change, enlarging the storehouse of data against which our theories ought to be measured.

In my view, syntactic reconstruction relies heavily on phonological reconstruction, so after describing my method, I begin with phonology. In Chapter 3 I reconstruct the phonology of Proto-Sogeram (PSoG) and describe how that system changed in each daughter branch. Then in Chapters 4 and 5 I reconstruct the morphology and syntax associated with verbs and nouns, and in Chapter 6 I address more abstract syntactic constructions. Chapter 7 contains the reconstructed Proto-Sogeram lexicon, and in Chapter 8 I present some concluding thoughts, along with the Proto-Sogeram grammar sketch and texts.

Much of the book employs a standard version of the comparative method. There are few methodological refinements we can make anymore to the processes by which we reconstruct phonology, morphology, and lexicon, so those sections employ orthodox methods. But whenever our exploration of Proto-Sogeram grammar takes us into syntactic waters, I use the methodological ideas from Chapter 2 to see what can be reconstructed.

In this chapter I first introduce the Sogeram languages (§1.1) and then the family they belong to (§1.2). I present previous research on these languages in §1.3, and describe my own fieldwork in §1.4.

1.1 The Sogeram languages

The Sogeram family consists of ten languages spoken along the Ramu and Sogeram Rivers in inland Madang Province, Papua New Guinea. Their location is shown in Figure 1. Four of the languages—Mand, Manat, Magɨ, and Kursav—are each spoken in only one village. Others, such as Gants, Apalɨ, and Mum, are spoken across much larger territories. The largest languages are Gants and Mum, with two to three thousand speakers each. The smallest is Mand, with only eight remaining speakers; Kursav is a close second with ten. Language shift to Tok Pisin is in general quite advanced in central Madang (Kulick 1992), and all of the Sogeram languages (with the possible exception of Gants) are endangered. In none of my fieldwork did I ever hear a child speaking one of the languages I was investigating.

The genealogical relationships among the Sogeram languages are shown in the family tree in Figure 2, although I defer a more comprehensive discussion of the internal relationships within the family to §2.4.2 below.

The issue of language names is somewhat complicated. The names used in the current edition of the *Ethnologue* (Eberhard, Simons, and Fennig 2019) are generally taken from Z'graggen's pioneering work in the Madang area (Z'graggen 1971, 1975a). In these works Z'graggen "used important and well known village names as language names, because such names are a handy reference to the location". He also noted that people in Madang often have no name for their language and declared that "the speakers of a language themselves are invited to give their own language name to replace the proposed name" (Z'graggen 1975a: 5). Because

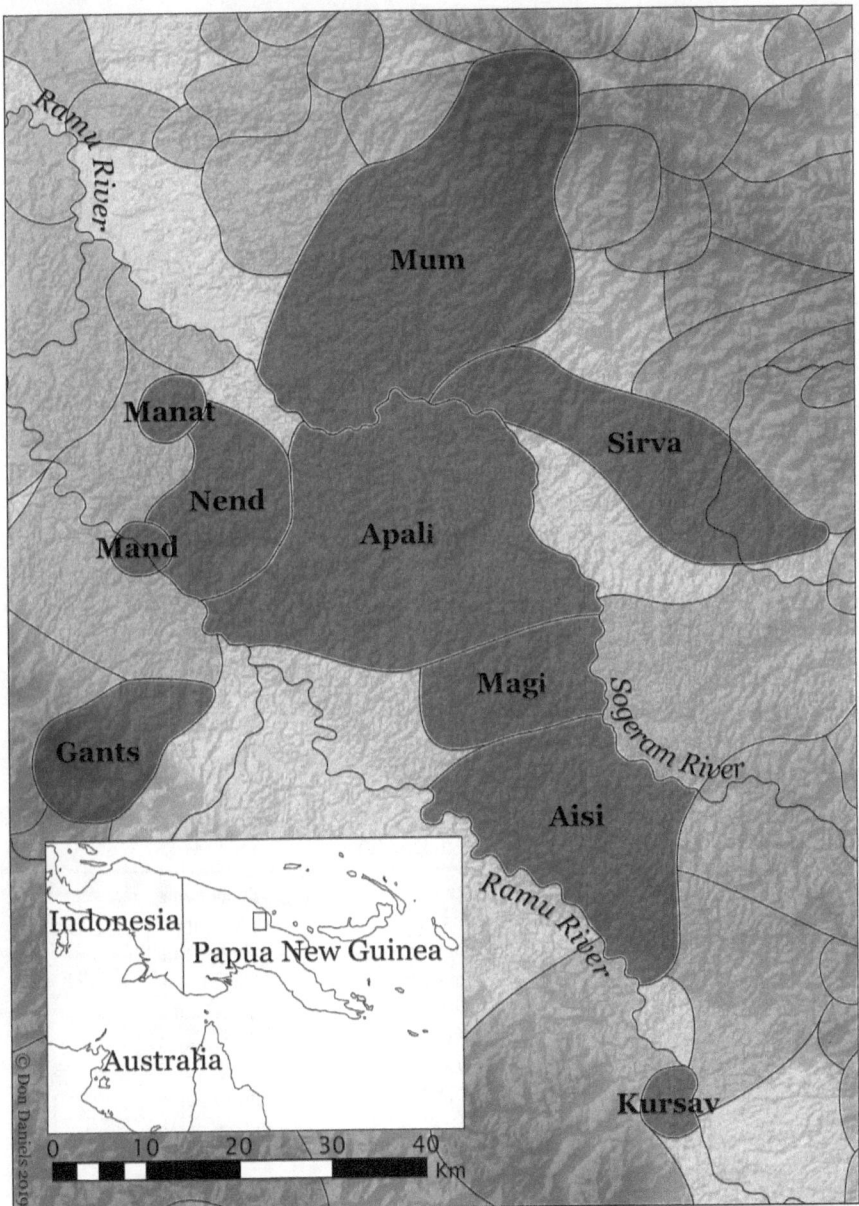

Figure 1: Map of the Sogeram languages.

languages in the Sogeram area generally *do* have a name by which they are known, I have decided, at the risk of further multiplying the number of language names in the Papuanist literature, to use the names by which speakers refer to

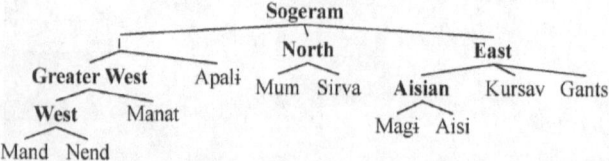

Figure 2: Sogeram family tree.

their languages instead of the names by which Z'graggen originally referred to them. The names he used, with the exception of Gants, are village names that do not refer to a language or a kind of speech. Rather, when speakers wish to refer to a language, they often refer to it by means of a salient word in that language, often "no". Thus Mand, Nend, Manat, Apalɨ, and Magɨ are named after the word for "no" in each of those respective languages. Similarly, Mum and Aisi are named after the words for "what" and "why". And sometimes a language has a name that does not appear to have any meaning apart from its use as a language name; this is the case for Sirva, Kursav, and Gants. Table 1 shows the language names that I (and speakers) use, what they mean, the names Z'graggen used, and what they mean. It should be noted that in three cases—Nend, Apalɨ, and Mum—the *Ethnologue* name of the language had been changed by missionaries with Pioneer Bible Translators well before my arrival on the scene.

Table 1: Language names.

Name used here	meaning	Z'graggen's name	meaning
Mand	'no'	Atemple	village name
Nend	'no'	Angaua	demonym
Manat	'no'	Paynamar	village name
Apalɨ	'no'	Emerum	village name
Mum	'what'	Katiati	village name
Sirva	language name	Sileibi	village name?
Magɨ	'no'	n/a	
Aisi	'why'	Musak	village name
Kursav	language name	Faita	village name
Gants	language name	Gants	language name

Matters become somewhat complicated with the Aisian languages, Magɨ and Aisi. These are two closely related languages that are not mutually intelligible. In Z'graggen's work, though, only Aisi was surveyed, so it was, until recently, the only one of these languages recognized in sources like the *Ethnologue*. Magɨ is spoken in the single village of Wanang, which is not contained in Z'graggen's list of villages (1975a: 68–94). Z'graggen referred to the language he surveyed as Musak, but as that is the name of a village, it will not do as a name for the language. Speakers of Aisi refer to their language as Aisi, which is their word for 'why' (composed of the word for 'what,' *ai*, with the benefactive enclitic *=si*), and I follow their usage. Speakers of Magɨ refer to their own language as *magɨ*, their word for 'no'. This, then, serves as a convenient label for that language. But the word for 'why' in Magɨ is also *aisi*, and speakers of Magɨ consider themselves speakers of "an" Aisi, although they consider their own language different from the other Aisi. For this reason I use the name Aisian for the genetic unit that contains Magɨ and Aisi.[1]

One other entity has been renamed, and that is the Sogeram family itself. In Z'graggen's original classification (1971, 1975b), the closest thing to the Sogeram subgroup was his Wanang stock, which contained Mand, Nend, Manat, Apalɨ, and Aisi. Subsequent research has added Kursav from Z'graggen's Brahman group (Pawley 2001); Gants from the East New Guinea Highlands group (Pawley 2006a); and Mum and Sirva from Z'graggen's Josephstaal group (Daniels 2010). The addition of the previously un-surveyed Magɨ was noted above. The Sogeram group is thus substantially different from Z'graggen's Wanang group, so a new name is justified. It may also be that Z'graggen intended to name the group "Sogeram" in the first place. He says that his Wanang group is "named after the Wanang River, which in turn is one of the main tributaries of the Ramu River" (Z'graggen 1971: 61), but the Wanang flows into the Sogeram; the Sogeram flows into the Ramu. So it is not clear which river Z'graggen had in mind when he named the Wanang group—the Wanang is still, technically, a tributary of the Ramu—but it is possible that it was the Sogeram. Given, then, that the family under discussion here differs substantially from Z'graggen's Wanang, that "Sogeram" is more appropriate geographically, and that Z'graggen may have intended the name to be "Sogeram" all along, I consider the relabeling of this genetic unit justified.

A few words about orthography are also in order. Orthographies have been developed for Bible translation projects in Nend, Apalɨ, and Mum, and I employ those orthographies when citing data from these languages. For the rest, I have developed my own orthography. In general, prenasalization on voiced stops is not written, so <b d g> represent /mb nd ŋg/. The exceptions to this are Nend, where the prenasalization is written even though it is not phonemic; and Aisian,

---

[1] In Daniels (2015) I refer to Aisi as Mabiŋ because the Aisi word for 'no' is *mabiŋ*. However, speakers of Aisi do not refer to their own language that way so in later work (Daniels 2016) I changed my usage.

where prenasalized stops lost prenasalization and now contrast with nasal–stop clusters, so single-unit phonemes <b d g> contrast with clusters <mb nd ŋg>. The Sogeram languages have at most one liquid, although a couple have no phonemic liquid (only an allomorph of /d/ or /t/). The symbol for this liquid is <r> in every language except Apalɨ, where it is <l>. The presence of fricatives /ɸ/, /β/ and /ɣ/ is common, and these are represented by the symbols <f>, <v>, and <h> in every language. The palatal nasal /ɲ/ is written <ñ>, and the palatal consonants /c/ and /tʃ/, since they are not contrastive in any language, are both written <c>. The symbol <z> has perhaps the most confusing range of uses. In Mand it represents a voiced post-alveolar fricative /ʒ/; in Nend it represents the alveolar /z/; and in Manat, Mum, and Sirva it represents a prenasalized alveolar fricative /nz/.

Finally, it is worth saying a little about the internal diversity of the Sogeram family, and what that might mean for its age. Z'graggen (1971: 62–68) conducted a lexicostatistical analysis of some of the languages, the results of which are presented in Table 2. Unfortunately, he did not group Kursav or Gants with the other Sogeram languages, and he had not yet discovered Sirva, so he presents no figures for those languages.

Table 2: Z'graggen's cognacy rates.

	Mand	Nend	Manat	Apalɨ	Mum	Aisi
Mand	100	47	12	14	6	11
Nend		100	17	15	9	11
Manat			100	12	12	10
Apalɨ				100	17	36
Mum					100	13
Aisi						100

This table suggests that Sogeram languages from different subgroups are quite distantly related. Mum and the West Sogeram languages share 6–9% cognate vocabulary; Aisi shares 10–11% with the West Sogeram languages and Manat. These figures are extraordinarily low. Per Z'graggen's own methodology (1971: 6) this level of shared vocabulary indicates that the languages are related at the level of the "phylum" or "microphylum". The percentages suggest that Sogeram is as old as Indo-European: Dyen, Kruskal, and Black (1992) give similar cognate percentages between Irish and Afghan (9.3%), Catalan and Albanian (11.0%), Frisian and Bengali (12.8%), and Latvian and Armenian (13.1%).

But in fact Z'graggen's figures are artificially low, owing to his not understanding the phonological history of the Sogeram languages. Several cognates, such as Mand *bi-* ~ Mum *kimu-* 'die,' look so different today that Z'graggen could not have spotted them. I have conducted brief cognacy counts of my own on three of the Sogeram languages—Mand, Sirva, and Gants—and I present the results in Table 3. These percentages were calculated using a 103-item wordlist based on the one used by Boerger and Zimmerman (2012). The figures are not absolute; even given a solid understanding of the phonological relationships among languages, generous scoring and stringent scoring can yield differences of about 3%. In other words, the figures in Table 3 can be understood to be valid ±1.5%.

Table 3: Cognacy rates for three Sogeram languages.

	Mand	Sirva	Gants
Mand	100	21	18
Sirva		100	28
Gants			100

These percentages, ranging from 18–28%, are significantly higher than Z'graggen's. But they still suggest that Sogeram is older than most Indo-European subgroups. The figures are consistent with the view that the most distantly related Sogeram languages are as closely related to one another as members of geographically adjacent subgroups of Indo-European. For example, Dyen, Kruskal, and Black (1992) give similar cognate percentages between Italic and Celtic (e.g., Spanish and Welsh at 19.0%), Italic and Slavic (French and Polish at 21.9%), Germanic and Slavic (German and Czech at 25.9%), Baltic and Slavic (Latvian and Bulgarian at 30.6%), Greek and Armenian (18.7%), Indo-Aryan and Iranian (Punjabi and Persian at 20.2%), and distantly related Indo-Aryan languages (Sinhalese and Bengali at 27.9%). While the limitations of the lexicostatistical method are well known, this quick count and comparison with Indo-European will hopefully help readers form an intuition about the internal diversity of the Sogeram languages. If some of the suggested ages of the primary Indo-European branches are to be believed (as found in, for example, Chang et al. 2015), the Sogeram family may be on the order of 2,500 or 4,000 years old. However, it must be borne in mind that prehistoric social situations in New Guinea were in all likelihood very different from those in Eurasia, and rates of linguistic diversification may have been quite different too. For this reason I prefer a more conservative estimate of the age of the Sogeram family, and suggest that 3,000 years ago is the best guess for when Proto-Sogeram may have been spoken.

1.2 Madang and Trans New Guinea

The Sogeram subgroup belongs to the Madang family, which is generally recognized as the "largest well-defined branch" of Trans New Guinea (Pawley 2006a: 429). Madang contains some 108 languages (Eberhard, Simons, and Fennig 2019) which belong to four primary subgroups: Kalam–Kobon, Croisilles, Rai Coast, and South Adelbert. An additional pair of languages, Korak and Waskia, may belong to the South Adelbert group (Ross 2000), or to the North Adelbert branch of the Croisilles group (Z'graggen 1975b: 577), or to a fifth first-order subgroup of Madang (Pawley 2006a). Sogeram belongs to the South Adelbert group, which also contains the Josephstaal subgroup, consisting of five languages.

The Madang group belongs to the Trans New Guinea (TNG) family, a large genetic grouping that has been argued to contain most of the Papuan languages across the central cordillera of New Guinea as well as many others (Pawley 2005; Ross 2005; Pawley and Hammarström 2018). The position of the ten Sogeram languages within this large family is shown in Figure 3.

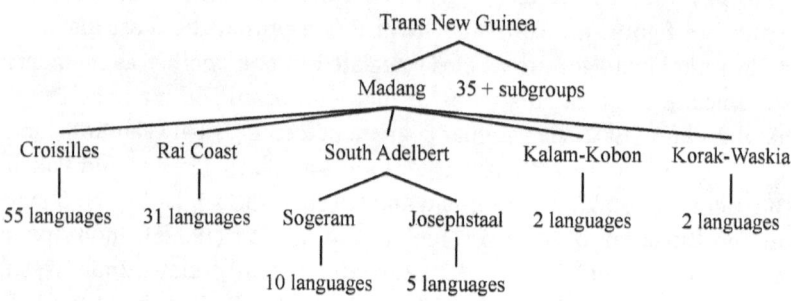

Figure 3: The position of Sogeram within Trans New Guinea.

The history of the Trans New Guinea hypothesis has been documented in detail by Pawley (1998a, 2005), so I provide only a brief overview here. Trans New Guinea was first proposed by McElhanon and Voorhoeve (1970) and was expanded on significantly in an edited volume five years later (Wurm 1975). However, these early attempts at classification were marred by serious methodological weaknesses (Haiman 1979; Lang 1976), and historical-linguistic work on the Papuan languages of New Guinea lost steam. Some two decades later, researchers at the Australian National University reinvigorated the research program by arguing that although Wurm and his colleagues had overreached in many respects, the core of Trans New Guinea was indeed a valid genetic grouping. These researchers offered reconstructions and subgroupings based on a more traditional application of the comparative method (Pawley 1995, 1998a, 2001, 2005, 2012; Ross 1995, 2000, 2005), and their findings have as a consequence been regarded more positively.

In the history of Trans New Guinea studies, Madang's place in the family has not been in doubt since Z'graggen first argued for its inclusion (Z'graggen 1975b). The boundaries of the Madang branch are well defined, as it is characterized by the innovation of the Proto-Madang 1SG, 2SG, and 3SG pronouns *ya, *na, and *nu from Proto-TNG *na, *ŋga, and *ya (Pawley 1998a: 683). And its relationship to other secure Trans New Guinea subgroups is not in doubt, as cognacy can be established for other pronouns, verbal morphology, and core vocabulary (Suter 1997; Pawley 2005; Ross 2005).

1.3 Previous research

Research into the history of the Sogeram family, as well as into the synchronic structure of the Sogeram languages, has been extremely limited. The first surveys into the area were conducted by E. R. Stanley (1923), Aloys Kaspruś (1942), and Arthur Capell (1951, 1952). Stanley's expedition collected a Mand wordlist, and Kaspruś collected wordlists for Mand, Nend, Apali, and Aisi which I have not located (Kaspruś n.d.). Capell, as far as I can tell, never surveyed a Sogeram language during his fieldwork.

The seminal work on the languages of Madang was done by John Z'graggen (1971, 1975a, 1975b, 1980a, 1980b, 1980c, 1980d), who conducted fieldwork on the vast majority of the over 150 languages in the Province. He also did extensive bibliographic work to compile and summarize previous research that had been conducted in the area. (It is due to his efforts that I am aware of the survey by Kaspruś.) A significant aspect of this pioneering work was establishing what languages existed in Madang. Thus, in his 1971 work, Z'graggen listed Mum and Manat as "previously unrecorded" (1971: 59, 63). Sirva was not discovered until later fieldwork had been done; in 1975 it is described as "a new entry" (1975b: 584). Kursav was not surveyed until 1973 (Z'graggen 1975b: 628), and also appears to have been previously unrecorded. As mentioned above, Stanley and Kaspruś had collected wordlists for Mand, Nend, Apali, and Aisi, but Z'graggen placed those languages in a wider comparative and geographic context, and made the material that he collected widely available. He collected wordlists and basic grammatical information for each of the Sogeram languages, although his wordlist for Gants was "very brief" (1971: 95). He published the Sogeram material (except for Gants, which he considered a member of the East New Guinea Highlands group) in his South Adelbert wordlist (1980a).

I am unaware of other research since then on any of the Sogeram languages, with three exceptions. In the 1980's Pioneer Bible Translators, a missionary organization, started Bible translation projects among the Nend, Mum, and Apalɨ people, and the missionaries working on these projects have produced some descriptive materials.

The Nend project has changed hands a few times, but the linguistic work was done by Kyle Harris. He produced a collection of texts (n.d.) and published a grammar sketch (1990).

The Mum project has also undergone some transformation, but the linguistic work was done by Michael Sweeney. He produced a phonological description (1994a), an ethnographic sketch (1994b), and a collection of texts (n.d.).

The most productive project, in linguistic terms, has been the Apalɨ one with Martha Wade. She has produced a phonological description (1987), a 256-page grammar sketch (1989), an ethnographic sketch (1991), a dictionary (n.d.a), a collection of texts (n.d.b), and two journal articles (1993, 1997).

Aside from these materials, I am unaware of any other research on the Sogeram languages. There has been more research in the areas surrounding the Sogeram languages, and on the other languages in the Madang group. It is not feasible to provide an exhaustive survey of all the work that has been done in Madang province, but I provide a brief overview (a more complete bibliography can be found in Carrington 1996).

There are five non-Sogeram languages in the South Adelbert branch of Madang. These are called the Josephstaal languages, and for two of them there is material available outside of Z'graggen's wordlists. Capell (1951: 143–147) published some grammatical notes and a brief text on Moresada (which he called Murusapa). Andrew Ingram worked on Anamuxra, writing a grammar (2001) and papers describing the classifier system (2003) and serial verbs (2010).

Outside of South Adelbert, I am aware of 17 Madang languages that have received significant grammatical or lexical documentation and analysis, out of a total of 93 non-South Adelbert languages. Most of this work takes the form of documentary and descriptive materials produced by members of SIL International (formerly the Summer Institute of Linguistics). This body of work includes grammars and a few dictionaries on 14 languages: Amele (Roberts 1987), Anjam (Rucker 1983), Bargam (Hepner 2002, 2006), Girawa (Gasaway, Lillie, and Sims 1992; Lillie 1999), Kesawai (Priestley 1986, 2008, 2018), Kobon (Davies 1981), Maia (Hardin 2002; Hardin et al. 2007), Mauwake (Järvinen and

Kwan 2007; Berghäll 2015), Ogea (Colburn n.d.), Pamosu (Tupper 2012), Saep (Voltmer 1998), Siroi (Wells 1979; Kleef 2007), Usan (Reesink 1987), and Waskia (Barker and Lee 1985). There has also been some work done by other scholars, including work on Kalam (Pawley 1966; Lane 2007; Pawley and Bulmer 2011), Tauya (MacDonald 1990, 2013), and Waskia (Ross and Paol 1978). Finally, there is one grammar written by a German colonial-era missionary on Bongu (Hanke 1909).

1.4 My fieldwork

Fieldwork for this project was carried out over four separate trips to Madang Province between 2006 and 2014. The first was conducted in January and February 2006. During this trip I collected wordlists on Nend, Manat, Mum, Sirva, Aisi, and Kursav, aimed at conducting lexical and phonological reconstruction that was eventually published in Daniels (2010). Grammatical research was limited to the collection of a few verb paradigms. The second trip took place in July and August of 2010, during which I conducted three weeks of intensive fieldwork on Manat. The third trip lasted seven months, from December 2011 to July 2012. During that time I conducted two to three weeks of fieldwork on each of Mand, Sirva, Aisi, Kursav, and Gants. This fieldwork was conducted in the village for every language except Gants; Gants fieldwork was conducted in Madang town. During this trip I also conducted a few days of fieldwork on Magɨ and one week of follow-up fieldwork on Manat. The final field trip took place in July and August 2014. I conducted two weeks of follow-up fieldwork on each of Mand and Kursav, and also conducted brief follow-up elicitation sessions on Manat, Sirva, and Aisi.

For each language I focused on recording transcribing naturalistic speech—primarily monologue, with a little conversation—with the goal of creating a small corpus for each language that could serve as the basis for analysis. During the transcription process I often conducted on-the-spot elicitation whenever I encountered an unfamiliar verb form or construction, which was often. These spontaneous elicitation questions were not audio recorded, but only transcribed in my field notebooks. I also conducted more structured elicitation sessions that were recorded. This data is summarized in Table 4: the average corpus size (not counting Magɨ) is 71 minutes. This data, in combination with the Nend, Mum, and Apalɨ materials described above, serves as the primary basis for the analysis in this book.

Table 4: Summary of Sogeram data.

Language	Transcribed speech (h:mm:ss)	Recorded elicitation (h:mm:ss)
Mand	1:12:04	13:16:45
Manat	1:31:32	9:48:54
Sirva	0:56:07	9:41:30
Magɨ	0:08:41	6:05:50
Aisi	1:18:17	9:18:33
Kursav	1:28:17	13:04:53
Gants	0:42:28	8:06:18
Total	**7:17:26**	**69:22:43**

Chapter 2
Methodology

In this chapter I argue for a method by which we can reconstruct syntax. There have been linguists for a long time who have held that this is possible—150 years ago August Schleicher claimed "that cohesive sentences can ... be constructed in Proto-Indo-European" (1868: 206)[2]—but there have also been plenty of linguists who held that it is not. Today we still find widespread disagreement about all aspects of the issue: what the primary obstacles are, how to overcome them, whether they are even surmountable, what the result of overcoming them would represent, and so on. There is sometimes even confusion about basic points, much of it attributable to the different theoretical assumptions that scholars bring to the table.

For this reason I start my own contribution with the basics. Too often the role of ontology in this debate has been overlooked, and scholars have instead argued about the "utility" or "viability" of their preferred theoretical approaches. But linguistic theories are not tools, they are hypotheses. Whether a linguistic theory appears useful or viable to a historical linguist is irrelevant if that theory is wrong about the nature of language.

So in order to evaluate the proposition "syntax can be reconstructed," we must answer four questions. First, what is reconstruction? Second, what is syntax? Third, what kinds of objects, ontologically speaking, can be reconstructed? And fourth, is syntax such an object? If we can answer those four questions—and I try my hand at it in §2.1—we can establish that syntax can be reconstructed.

Only then can we safely move from ontology to method. In §2.2 I address the *how* of it: how do we reconstruct syntax? I then compare my method with other approaches in §2.3, and address some methodological issues related to subgrouping in §2.4.

2.1 Can syntax be reconstructed?

In this section I argue that syntax can be reconstructed. As described above, this enterprise requires answering four separate, but related questions. I discuss the first question, "What is reconstruction?" in the next section, followed by "What is syntax?" in §2.1.2. I then address the final two questions, about the relationship between syntax and reconstruction, in §2.1.3.

---

[2] My translation from the German "Dass ... zusammenhangende sätze in indogermanischer ursprache gebildet werden können".

2.1.1 What is reconstruction?

I answer this question by examining reconstruction in its more traditional guise of lexical reconstruction. By examining what this process is, and how it manages to produce reliable results, we can begin to evaluate how appropriate it is to extend it to syntax.

However, even here we must examine the nature of lexical signs in order to understand what it means to reconstruct them. Therefore it will be helpful to begin with a linguistic token which will serve as an example below. Figure 4 is a spectrogram of me saying the word *tree*. This is as synchronic as language gets: it was a speech event that began sometime in the afternoon of January 23, 2015, and ended half a second later. It is not cognate with anything. It is nonsensical to even try to apply the notion of cognacy to it, because it is an event, and as we will see below, events cannot be cognate. Examining the spectrogram, we can make several observations—that I affricated /t/ before /r/, that during the /r/ F3 shifted from 2406 Hz to 2563 Hz, that the vowel lasted 250ms and had an F1 of 215 Hz and an F2 of 2170 Hz—and none of these observations are particularly relevant for the comparative method. They are facts about a *token* of speech, and the comparative method does not deal in tokens. They simply are not made of the right ontological stuff for it to operate on them. The comparative method deals in *types*, as presented in (1).

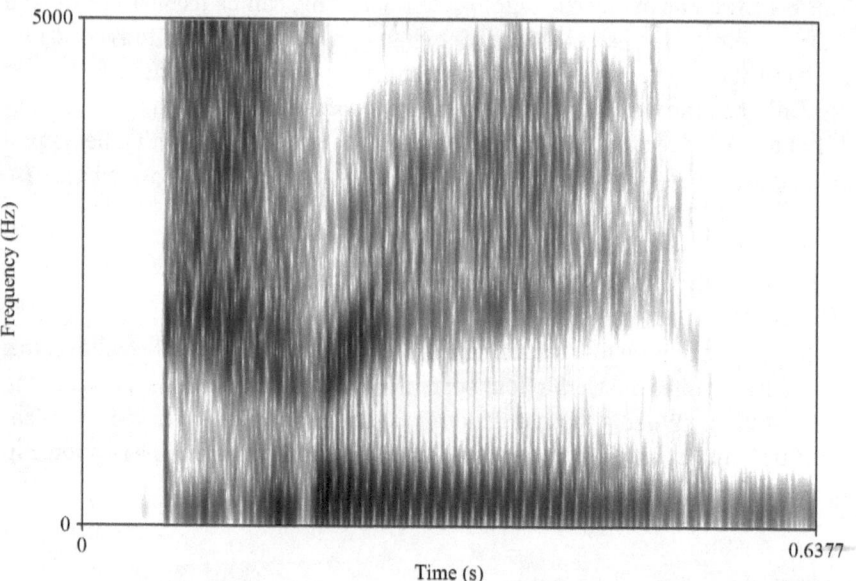

Figure 4: A token of *tree*.

(1) /tri/

This is the word *tree* in phonemic transcription. It represents a linguistic *sign*, in the Saussurean sense, and now we have something that the comparative method can use. Specifically, (1) represents the part of the sign known as the *signifier*, which combines via a process of reference with a *signified*—in this case, the concept of trees—to form the complete sign. I will examine the signifier, the signified, and the referential link in turn.

The first observation we can make about the signifier is that it is structured: it is composed of a specific set of phonemes in a specific chronological order. Changing this structure changes the signifier: thus *bat* and *pat* are different words, as are *bat* and *tab*.

Another feature is that the signifier is a generalization over a number of real-world tokens of experience that are stored in the language user's memory. These tokens are obviously not distributed at random, but cluster around certain phonetic sequences that are meaningful in the language user's speech community. Thus I have many tokens of /tri/ stored in my lexicon, but not of /tro/ or /træ/ because those are not English words. Importantly, these meaningful token clusters are clusters, not points; in other words, speakers store "detailed phonetic knowledge of a type which is not readily modelled using the categories and categorical rules of phonological theory" (Pierrehumbert 2001: 137). Mental representations of words, and the phonemes that compose them, emerge from this collection of tokens so that "words are represented in the lexicon as a range of phonetic variation" (Bybee 2001a: 137) which displays these clustering properties. This means that phonemes exhibit more gradience than traditional phonological theory has typically admitted (Hooper 1976). But speakers do form generalizations about the token clusters they store, and the central parts of any cluster, being more frequent, can replace less frequent representations (Bybee 2001a: 143). Thus the concept of the phoneme should be retained on empirical grounds as well as for analytic convenience (see also Nguyen, Wauquier, and Tuller 2009).

Each such signifier has a meaning: it refers to a signified. These meanings have been shown to exhibit a prototype structure in the mental lexicon (Rosch 1978). This mental representation is also embedded in a network of related concepts, called a *frame* (Fillmore 1982; Petruck 1997), and each individual token of use emphasizes a subset of those related concepts. Thus in the range of meanings expressible by any particular item, there are "differences in structural weight" (Geeraerts 1999: 94) between the prototypical meanings at the center of the range and those at the periphery. As a result of these facts about the structure of meaning, individual lexemes exhibit a high degree of semantic inertia but are also able to shift their meanings through gradual shifts in the prototypical core or the periphery of their meaning (Geeraerts 1997).

Turning to the referential link that binds the signifier to the signified, we observe that it is usually arbitrary. (This is not the case for onomatopoetic words, and I return to this point later.) The particular arrangement of phonemes in the signifier is not motivated by any real-world properties of the signified. The tokens that compose the signifier are also arbitrary, in that the particular phonetic facts about any token of *tree* do not correlate in any way with the specific meaning of *tree* that was intended by that token. That is, a token of *tree* with a particularly long vowel would not be expected to refer to a particularly tall tree.

The sign, then, is composed of two generalizations—one phonemic, one semantic—bound by a referential link. As such it is a linguistic type, an abstraction from a number of linguistic experiences. And because it is abstracted from multiple experiences, a type is an inherently diachronic entity, although at a shallow enough time depth that it is generally used to make synchronic statements and is best conceived of synchronically. (It would be odd, at the very least, to say that English *tree* and Proto-Indo-European *dréwo-, its etymological source, are the same lexical type.) To see how types behave over longer stretches of time, and to see why the comparative method works, I will employ Henning Andersen's concept of a "tradition of speaking" (Andersen 2001, 2006: 65–66). A sign is a linguistic tool that is traditionally used within a particular community to express a certain concept. Every new use of that sign participates in, and is informed by, that tradition, while simultaneously extending it and thereby changing it. Thus English *tree* and Proto-Indo-European *dréwo- are a part of the same tradition of speaking, connected by an uninterrupted chain of usage, token after token of people making alveolar and rhotic gestures with their tongues to convey ideas of tree-ness to their interlocutors. From this perspective, a linguistic type is simply any reasonably circumscribed collection of tokens in a given tradition of speaking, such that the collection's phonological and semantic properties are sufficiently homogeneous. This relationship between token, type, and tradition is illustrated in Figure 5. The horizontal dimension represents time, running from left to right, and each dot along the line is a linguistic token. This diagram makes explicit the relationship between Proto-Indo-European *dréwo-, Proto-Germanic *trewa-, and English *tree* (Kroonen 2013: 522).

We also know that traditions of speaking extend across space as well as time, and that they can split up for a variety of reasons. Bearing this in mind, we can define cognacy as descent from the same tradition of speaking.

And now we can see why the comparative method deals only in types, not tokens: types are diachronic, while tokens are not. Types are capable of being cognate because they extend along a tradition of speaking. To use the visual

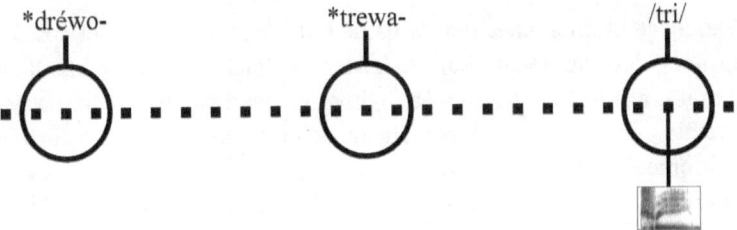

Figure 5: A tradition of speaking. (Not to scale.)

metaphor of Figure 5, types exist along the horizontal dimension. This means that they not only participate in the tradition, they *are* the tradition, in a very meaningful sense. The difference between a type and a tradition is one of degree: how long a time span are we dealing with? The difference between a type and a token, though, is one of kind: types are generalizations, tokens are events. They are points on the timeline, not lines, and therefore they cannot be cognate.

Any token is, of course, an *expression* of some linguistic type, but it itself is not that type. In fact, it depends wholly on that type for its interpretation; nobody would be able to make sense of me saying *tree* if there were not already a rich tradition of people saying *tree* to mean "tree". For this reason it may strike readers as unintuitive to say that linguistic tokens are incapable of cognacy, but this is only because the way we think about tokens is mediated by types. We use the types we have stored in our lexicon to decode the tokens we encounter, and when we encounter a new token, we assign it to its proper type. So a token (like Figure 4) participates in a type (*tree*), and a type may be cognate (i.e., descended from the same tradition of speaking) with a type in another language, like Danish *træ*. If we then find a token of *træ*, we can establish a relationship between tokens in the two languages. But this relationship is not profitably understood as a relationship of cognacy, only as *mediated* by a relationship of cognacy. This distinction is less apparent when considering prototypical tokens, because prototypical tokens, by definition, closely resemble their types. But our two hypothetical tokens may be non-prototypical in many ways—they may contain disfluencies, or abnormal vowel height, or mistimed articulators of various kinds—and they would still be tokens of their respective types. But we would not want to say that *this* disfluency or *that* abnormally low vowel in the token of *tree* is "cognate" with the corresponding part of the token of *træ*. We would only say that we have a non-prototypical token of *tree* on our hands, and that the type it represents is still cognate with the Danish type *træ*.

Now that we have established how signs are capable of cognacy, it is time to turn to the comparative method and establish how they are reconstructed. For this discussion I focus on reconstructing the form, the signifier, since reconstruction of the meaning is less systematic. We have seen that the signifier is a structured sequence of phonemes that is passed along in a tradition of speaking, but this alone does not mean that it needs to be diachronically stable. It is conceivable that it would change often enough, or in a sufficiently random way, that reconstruction would be impossible. The question then becomes, why is the signifier diachronically stable? There are two answers.

The first answer has to do with the structure of the collection of tokens from which the lexical type emerges. Recall that the collection of tokens is a cluster, with more tokens in the center than around the periphery. The center of the cluster is the prototype, and unless there is a reason to produce non-prototypical tokens (such as articulatory ease, which I discuss below), new tokens will tend strongly to be prototypical. They thereby reinforce the strength of the center of the cluster, further increasing the likelihood that future tokens will also be prototypical. So we see that inertia is built into the very structure of the system, and change is thereby rendered unlikely. This fact is obscured by the fact that most linguistic research focuses on the dynamic aspects of the linguistic system, which are perhaps more inherently interesting, but the fact remains that at any given time most parts of most languages are not changing.

The other factor that contributes to the diachronic stability of the sign is the arbitrariness of the referential link between the signifier and the signified. There is no reason for the particular sequence of phonemes /tri/ to signify "tree," and because of that there is also no reason for that sequence of phonemes to change or resist change. This becomes particularly apparent when we attempt to reconstruct onomatopoetic words, which *are* motivated and which therefore either change, or fail to change, in unpredictable ways. Attempting to reconstruct the Proto-Oceanic (POc) term for 'chicken,' Clark (2011: 284) is able to observe only that a "pattern of consonants occurs which could represent POc *k-k-r-k, though the vowels are not consistent and one or other of the consonants may not appear". He also notes "that *k in this term is never lenited (to ɣ, ʔ etc) in the many languages where this is a regular change. This presumably reflects its onomatopoetic origin" as an imitation of the rooster's crow. He hesitantly offers the reconstruction *kokorako. On the other hand, the POc word for 'starling,' *pusiRa, is much easier to reconstruct in spite of having far fewer reflexes (Clark 2011: 348).

These two factors—the inertia inherent in the collection of tokens and the arbitrariness of the sign—explain why the sign is diachronically stable, and therefore why reconstruction is valid in cases of identity. We reason that, if we see identical signs in two different traditions of speaking, both had their origin in the same tradition of speaking, which has been inherited unchanged in each one. This is plausible because the sign is diachronically stable.

However, change does happen, and for our purposes we can divide it into two categories: unmotivated and motivated. Many examples of vowel change can be conceived of as the former, such as the oft-cited hypothetical where the historical linguist is presented with reflexes *a* and *o* of some proto-vowel. This kind of unmotivated change is rare for the reasons stated above. This means that when it does occur, it will usually only take place in one or two daughter traditions of the original tradition of speaking, allowing the historical linguist to posit that the more common reflex is the original one. In a scenario where this is not the case, such as *a changing to *o* independently in two out of three daughter languages, the comparative method fails.

Motivated change can take many forms. The motivation can be the impetus towards articulatory ease, based on the physiological composition of the vocal tract (assimilation, word-final devoicing, etc.); the creation by another change of a new, easier articulatory possibility (pull chains); encroachment into phonetic space by some other segment (push chains); extension of predominant patterns in the lexicon (analogy); and so on. The key to reconstruction in all of these cases is an understanding of the motivation behind the change. The historical linguist simply posits a proto-form that can be accounted for by motivated changes and then lists those changes. This principle, which has been called the directionality principle (cf. Walkden 2014: 48), accounts for the fact that, when presented with cognate words like, say, *apa* and *aba*, we know to reconstruct *apa and posit intervocalic voicing. But note that the reasoning behind that reconstruction is the same as the reasoning behind reconstruction in cases of analogical change: we have two forms, one of which can be explained by a common motivating factor (voicing assimilation or analogy), the other of which cannot. We posit that the unexplainable form is archaic, and that the other form changed in an explainable way as a result of the motivating factor.

And that is how, and why, the comparative method works when applied to lexical signs. To review: signs are generalizations over two sets of tokens—one phonetic, one semantic—bound by a (usually arbitrary) referential link. They are resistant to change because the composition of the collections of tokens encourages future tokens to be prototypical, that is, not innovative. When they do change, it is usually for a reason. A linguist who understands these reasons can reconstruct earlier stages of language by positing a scenario in which a plausible proto-stage is followed by plausible changes to give an internally consistent, reasonable account of the data.

2.1.2 What is syntax?

Syntax, like the lexicon, is made up of signs. This is the fundamental hypothesis of construction grammar (Hoffmann and Trousdale 2013a: 1), and I consider it correct. Syntax and the lexicon are thus essentially the same thing, existing at opposite ends of a continuum of schematicity (Croft 2001). At one end, lexical signs have signifiers that contain only phonological material, as with *tree*. At the other end, the signifiers of maximally schematic constructions contain only other constructions, like the English ditransitive construction [S V O O] (Goldberg 1995). And in between there is a wide range of variation, with different constructions specifying various amounts of phonological and constructional material. Importantly, like lexical signs, grammatical signs[3] are types that are generalized over a number of tokens of experience.

These points are not conceived of as analytic devices or notational conventions: they are claims about objective (primarily cognitive) reality. Language is not *viewed as* constructions or *treated constructionally*. The claim is that "language *is* the inventory of its constructions" (Fried and Östman 2004: 13, emphasis in original; see also Fillmore 1988: 37, 2013: 112).

This is the basic claim of construction grammar, although it remains at this point a hypothesis. But it is a hypothesis with a considerable body of evidence to support it, and below I present some of this evidence from child language acquisition, adult language use, and diachronic observations. More information can be found in the chapters in Hoffmann and Trousdale's volume (2013b).

The original motivation for construction grammar was a desire to account for certain idiosyncratic constructions in English, and these constructions remain some of the primary theoretical evidence that grammar is composed of signs and that these signs exist on a continuum of schematicity with words. They are construction grammar's favorite examples, and any comprehensive theory of grammar must be able to explain them. How does an idiosyncratic construction like the *let alone* construction (Fillmore, Kay, and O'Connor 1988) or [*what's* X *doing* Y], as in "What am I doing reading this book?" (Kay and Fillmore 1999) work? Where do the semantics of transfer come from in *I'll bake you a cake*, or the semantics of caused motion in *She sneezed the foam off the cappuccino* (Goldberg 2006)?

But there is also empirical evidence for constructions, especially from child language acquisition. Children first learn only single words, including complex constructions that they treat as single words, such as *all-gone*. Next, they begin to produce 'pivot constructions,' forms consisting of a 'pivot word' and productive empty slot (Braine 1976). These can be arrived at either by analyzing a previously unanalyzed holophrase (thus *all-gone* may become [*all* X], as in *all done* and *all broke*) or by adding a productive slot to a single word (so *more* might

---

[3] In this discussion I use *construction*, in its technical, construction-grammatical sense, and *grammatical sign* interchangeably to highlight the parallel between constructions and lexical signs.

become [*more* X], as in *more cereal* and *more cookie*). Tomasello (1992) makes a similar observation about children's early verb-argument constructions, which are usually tied to particular verbs. This pattern also holds for questions, which are learned as formulae that gradually become more flexible: [*what's* X *doing*] becomes [*what's* X Y-*ing*] and eventually [*what* AUX NP V] (Dąbrowska 2000). Even the acquisition of the most schematic constructions, like the argument structure constructions [S V O O] and [S V O Obl], proceeds along lexical lines. In child language input, tokens of these constructions occur most frequently with certain semantically basic verbs—in our examples, *give* for [S V O O] and *put* for [S V O Obl]. The meanings of these verbs are then associated with the constructions, and as children acquire more verbs that occur in these positions, the constructional meaning emerges. That is, the generalization that unifies all tokens of [S V O O] in the child's mind (something like, "This arrangement of elements means 'X causes Y to receive Z'") becomes stronger as the instantiating tokens become more diverse (Goldberg 1999; Goldberg, Casenhiser, and Sethuraman 2004).

So we see that children acquire language via gradual increases in the productivity of individual constructions, which begin on the lexical end of the spectrum of schematicity and slowly become more abstract. And this pattern continues into adult language use: certain lexemes continue to prefer certain constructions and vice versa (Stefanowitsch and Gries 2003). Ungrammaticality—the unacceptability of certain forms—can then be explained as extremely low frequency or non-occurrence of similar forms in a given person's language experience (Bybee and Eddington 2006). In other words, there continues to be an important interaction between types and tokens at every stage of language use. This can be seen particularly clearly when one examines the emergence of particular constructions over longer stretches of time in what is known as grammaticalization.

There are several facts about long-term grammatical change that seem to support a usage-based view of the emergence of grammar. First, grammatical reanalysis is often gradual (Haspelmath 1998). For example, in the creation of English *gonna*, the verb *go* was originally the main verb in the construction *be going to V*, but no longer is. It is difficult to pinpoint a single moment or generation when this reanalysis took place. Rather, the process is better explained by suggesting a gradual change in the composition of the cluster of tokens that underlie the construction (Bybee 2006: 721). The gradualness of reanalysis implies a second, related fact: constituency is gradient. The English complex preposition *in spite of* behaves in some ways like a complex phrase composed of *in*, *spite*, and *of*, and in some ways like a simple preposition. There is thus no clear-cut answer to the question whether *of*, in this case, heads a prepositional phrase that is a constituent of another prepositional phrase headed by *in* (see Bybee 2010: 138ff. for a more detailed discussion of *in spite of*).

Multiple strands of evidence thus converge on the conclusion that our language faculty is composed of constructions, and that these constructions are signs in the traditional sense of ordered strings of linguistic material that convey meaning. We have not yet established, however, that one can apply the comparative method to grammar in the same way as the lexicon. There is a very important ontological difference between words and grammar: lexemes are signs made out of phonemes, while grammatical constructions are signs made out of other signs. This difference has far-reaching implications for diachrony, as we will see below.

2.1.3 Are reconstruction and syntax compatible?

It is now time to consider what sorts of objects the comparative method requires, which is a point that has sometimes been overlooked in the literature on syntactic reconstruction. But we must remember that any method can only be appropriately applied to certain kinds of objects. You can't fry your lab results, and you can't do statistics on an egg. If we are aware of what the comparative method requires, we can determine whether syntax fits the bill.

First, though, I must introduce five "problems" that have framed a good deal of the debate around this question. These are the correspondence problem, the regularity problem, the arbitrariness problem, the directionality problem, and the borrowing problem. Each represents a difficulty, whether real or perceived, with applying the traditional methods of comparative reconstruction to syntax, and a successful method of syntactic reconstruction will have to grapple with each of them.

The correspondence problem has perhaps received the most attention, as for many linguists it is the most serious (Lightfoot 1979, 2002a, 2002b; von Mengden 2008; Willis 2011; Walkden 2013, 2014). The view is that linguistic entities "in sister languages correspond if (and only if) they go back to one and the same item in the parent language" (von Mengden 2008: 103). But if "sentences are not transmitted as whole units from generation to generation" (Willis 2011: 411), then no diachronic correspondence between sentences is possible, either between two chronologically separated varieties of the same language, or, consequently, between two related languages.[4] If such correspondence is impossible, then reconstruction, at least via the comparative method, is also impossible.

---

[4] Campbell & Harris (2002: 606) note that there is a potential exception to this principle in the case of "formulaic language". For an attempt at the reconstruction of a linguistic formula, see Slade (2008).

The regularity problem is the observation that phonological correspondences—like English *f* to Latin *p*—are confirmed by their regular occurrence throughout the lexicon of each sister language, while no such confirmation is possible for syntactic correspondences. In other words, while a sound change is regular in the sense that it applies throughout the lexicon of the affected language, a grammatical change would not be expected to be regular in the same way.

For the arbitrariness problem, the key observations are that (i) words are usually arbitrary pairings of form and meaning, (ii) this arbitrariness has diachronic consequences that are important for the comparative method, and (iii) it is not clear that grammar possesses this particular kind of arbitrariness. Therefore, grammar may exhibit different diachronic behavior and be unsuitable for reconstruction via the comparative method.

The directionality problem presupposes that a satisfactory resolution to the correspondence problem has been reached. Once we have established a correspondence between linguistic items in sister languages, then, if those items are not identical, we need a theory of directionality to tell us what innovations are most plausible, and therefore what to reconstruct to the protolanguage (Balles 2008: 179–180). Several authors, particularly within the generative tradition, have argued that syntactic change does not exhibit this kind of directionality, and that syntactic reconstruction is therefore impossible (see especially Lightfoot 1979, 2002a, 2002b).

Finally there is the borrowing problem. Scholars of all persuasions agree that grammatical borrowing is a serious obstacle to syntactic reconstruction (Bowern 2008; Willis 2011; Walkden 2013; Seržant 2015; Ross 2015; Daniels 2017a), because grammatical borrowing often happens without accompanying lexical borrowing. This means that it cannot be spotted via the observation of irregular sound correspondences, which is normally sufficient to spot borrowings in the case of lexical reconstruction. Because grammatical patterns can be borrowed from one language into another without the borrowing of morphology (Epps 2007, 2013; Heine and Kuteva 2003, 2005; Næss and Jenny 2011; Ross 2007, 2008), the question arises of how we can ever be reasonably certain that they did not spread via contact after the breakup of the proto-language.

With these concepts in mind, we now return to the question at hand: are syntax and the comparative method compatible? As discussed above, the comparative method operates on linguistic types, as opposed to tokens. Linguistic types are culturally transmitted patterns of behavior that perpetuate themselves by virtue of serving some function in a community. If their fulfilment of that function is not necessarily linked to any of their inherent properties—basically, if they are arbitrary signs—they can be expected to change in more or less predictable ways.

Under those circumstances, cognate signs can be recognized because they exhibit similarity in both form and function. Any discrepancies between cognate signs can be accounted for by positing a plausible proto-sign and a plausible series of changes that led to the creation of all attested daughter signs.

Is syntax this sort of linguistic sign? Mostly. It is learned and transmitted in the right way, for starters. Each syntactic construction in a language's inventory is a conventionalized cultural behavior that serves a useful communicative function. As such, syntactic signs are the kind of inherently diachronic entity that the comparative method needs. But it is not clear that they possess the kind of arbitrariness that would ensure their unhindered transmission from generation to generation. Certain aspects of syntax, such as the strong cross-linguistic preference for subject-initial word order, are clearly motivated. And we would expect this iconic motivation to interfere with the diachronic transmission of syntactic signs in much the same way that we observe it interfering with lexical signs like Proto-Oceanic *kokorako 'chicken': by promoting changes that strengthen the iconic link and by inhibiting changes that weaken it.

However, as I argue below, this observation does not mean that syntax cannot be reconstructed. In lexical and morphological reconstruction we must be aware of several factors that could motivate a particular change, such as articulatory pressures, analogy, and so on. Recognizing that syntax may be influenced by iconicity simply means that in reconstructing syntax, we must be aware of an additional possible motivator for linguistic changes. This makes syntactic reconstruction more difficult and somewhat less certain than lexical or morphological reconstruction, but it is still possible.

2.2 How syntax can be reconstructed

Given the considerations discussed above, I propose the following methodology for reconstructing syntax. First, correspondences must be set up. Because of the lack of regularity in syntactic change, more care must be used in this step than is necessary in lexical reconstruction. In particular, the historical linguist must be more conservative when it comes to semantic innovations. Note also that the more fillers a construction has, the less likely another construction is to resemble it by chance, so correspondences involving longer, more complex constructions are more secure. Finally, to mitigate the problem of borrowing, the grammatical constructions in the correspondence must specify some amount of phonological material that can be tested for cognacy. In other words, only partially schematic constructions can be directly reconstructed; fully schematic constructions cannot. Since phonological borrowings can be spotted with some confidence due to the regularity of phonological change, restricting ourselves to the reconstruction of partially schematic constructions reduces the risk of reconstructing constructions that have actually spread through contact.

Once correspondences have been set up, the historical linguist can use an understanding of grammaticalization and other grammatical change to posit a proto-form and a set of innovations deriving the modern forms from it. This is possible even in the absence of regularity because the directionality of the changes we might expect in many cases of grammatical change is quite clear. When the direction of a change is less apparent, the reconstruction is obviously less secure. The comparativist must also remain aware that potentially iconic structures could influence directional tendencies.

This methodology is not flawless, though. It can fail when the amount of phonological material contained in the construction is so little that it is not diagnostically useful, or when the particular sequence of phonemes in the construction is not expected to reflect diagnostic sound changes. There is also the possibility that irregular phonological attrition, which is often part of grammaticalization, has affected the relevant phonological material. The methodology can also fail in some instances of parallel grammaticalization. Suppose, for example, that Proto-AB breaks into Language A and Language B, and that Language A then innovates a new construction employing its reflex of the Proto-AB word *aka, which is *a?a*. If Language B then borrows this construction but employs its own reflex of *aka, *aga*, then this method also fails. If Language B had borrowed the Language A form *a?a*, we could spot the borrowing, as it would not exhibit the expected reflex of Proto-AB *k. But if Language B copies the Language A pattern *with its own cognate word*, this method is not capable of discovering that this innovative construction does not date to Proto-AB.

These limitations, while real, are not crippling. The comparativist must simply use appropriate judgment when applying the method to particular data sets. It must be decided on a case-by-case basis whether the amount of phonological material specified in a particular construction is sufficient for secure reconstruction. The possibility of parallel grammaticalization must also be kept in mind, appropriate discussion of geographical proximity and known contact histories must be made, and the likelihood that two constructions resemble each other by chance—given the number of potential constructions that could serve a similar communicative function—must also be assessed.

When applied judiciously, this method is in fact capable of reconstructing wholly schematic constructions, due to the structure that constructions are observed to exhibit in the mental lexicon (more discussion on this point can be found in Daniels 2017a). The caveat is that these wholly schematic constructions cannot be reached directly. Construction grammarians have long observed that the constructions that speakers store in their memory are organized into a default inheritance hierarchy—a structure in which more general parent constructions are instantiated by more specific daughter constructions. These daughter constructions inherit the properties of their parent by default but often specify additional idiosyncratic properties of their own (Langacker 1987; Goldberg and van der Auwera 2012). An example is the English prepositional phrase construction [P NP] . This is a very general phrasal construction that takes two fillers, a preposition (P) and a noun phrase (NP). English also possesses a [P N] construction exemplified by expressions like *at church*, *to work*, and *in prison*. The [P N] construction is obviously a daughter of the [P NP] construction, as it exhibits many of the same distributional properties and is composed of a preposition plus a nominal element. These properties are said to be inherited by the [P N] construction from its parent, the [P NP] construction. But the [P N] construction also stipulates some of its own properties. For example, it takes a noun (N) as the second filler, not a noun phrase. It also expresses a meaning that cannot be predictably derived from the lexical semantics of the fillers, and that can be described as "stereotypical activity associated with N" (Goldberg 2013: 21). Thus being *at church* or *in prison* means that you are performing (or undergoing) a particular activity associated with churches or prisons—that is, worshiping or being incarcerated. (A warden who is in a prison is not said to be *in prison*.) And when we examine the daughters of the [P N] construction, we again observe the same pattern: they inherit their parent's properties by default, but some specify their own additional information. For example, *at home* does not refer to any particular activity associated with the home but is rather interpreted as a simple locative expression.

Because constructions exhibit this behavior with relation to one another, it is possible, after reconstructing sufficient partially schematic constructions, to posit a more schematic parent construction that accounts for a set of its less schematic daughters. This is essentially an act of synchronic descriptive linguistics, performed on the reconstructed set of proto-constructions. It is the same process by which we move from the observation of phonological expressions like *at church*, *to work*, and *in prison* to the analytic generalization of a [P N] construction.

An example will help illustrate this process. In §6.4.2 I argue for the reconstruction of three related subordination constructions that employed demonstrative forms to subordinate clause chains. These subordinate clause chains functioned as noun phrases in their matrix clauses, and their matrix functions were signaled by the form of the demonstrative that was used as a subordinator. These constructions are shown in (2)–(4); the demonstrative forms used in these constructions are the topic/object suffix *-n, the locative enclitic *=ñ, and the bare middle demonstrative *ka. Each of these is securely reconstructed in §5.3.

(2) *[S DEM-n]$_{NP}$ Syntax: noun phrase in topic or object position

(3) *[S DEM=ñ]$_{NP}$ Syntax: locative noun phrase

(4) *[S ka]$_{NP}$ Syntax: left-peripheral topic noun phrase

Based on these three reconstructions, we can generalize a broader, more schematic construction, illustrated in (5).

(5) *[S DEM=CASE]$_{NP}$ Syntax: noun phrase with function indicated by CASE

The schematic construction in (5) is generalized based on other reconstructions; it is not itself directly reconstructed. But because we know that constructions are organized hierarchically in the mental lexicon, we can posit a generalization over (2)–(4) that accounts for their similarities. This analysis leads to a question: can we, based on (5), posit that other reconstructed Proto-Sogeram demonstratives also functioned as subordinators? For example, can we claim that focus demonstratives with the focus suffix *-kw (§5.3.8) could be used in this construction, even though such a construction cannot be directly reconstructed? The inference that, if topic/object, locative, and bare demonstratives could function as subordinators, then focus demonstratives in *-kw probably could too, can certainly be made. But the conclusion that, since we cannot directly reconstruct a subordinating function for *-kw, we cannot reliably know whether it existed in Proto-Sogeram, is also reasonable. I find the latter position more compelling, in part because it is more conservative. Therefore if there is not direct attestation of a construction in sufficiently diverse witnesses, I refrain from reconstruction.

As mentioned, it is also important to bear in mind the potential influence of iconicity on grammatical patterns. To illustrate this issue I present the orientation serial verb construction, which is reconstructed in §4.2.3. In this construction, shown in (6), an intransitive serialized verb precedes the other serialized verbs, which may take objects of their own. The initial intransitive verb, which is usually a verb of motion or posture, orients the subject of the clause to the action expressed by the other verbs in the clause. This construction is exemplified in the Gants example (7), where the intransitive serial verb *aŋa* 'go' is separated from the other verbs by the object *kɨmna yue* 'seeds of food'.

(6) (NP$_{SBJ}$) *V$_{INTR}$ [(NP$_{OBJ}$) V-INFL]$_{VP}$

Gants

(7) Ya   op-idiŋ   aŋa kimna yue   ada mai-ci-niŋ   wa-m-ek.
    1SG   garden-DEF.SG   go   food   seed do   bring-PRS-1SG   say-FPST-3SG
    '"I'm going to the garden and bringing seeds," he said.'

This construction is potentially iconic in that the intransitive verb is located to the left of any objects, which places it next to the subject. Because the subject is the only argument of the intransitive verb, it is conceivable that the verb would be drawn towards the subject over time, and that its location to the left of the object does not date to Proto-Sogeram but is rather an innovation that has taken place independently in several daughter languages. This parallel innovation may have been motivated by the real-world relationship between an intransitive event and its single argument. A potential scenario might play out as follows. Suppose orientation serial verbs in Proto-Sogeram were located where all the other verbs are: at the end of the clause, after all the arguments (8).

(8) †(NP$_{SBJ}$) (NP$_{OBJ}$) V$_{INTR}$ V-INFL

But orientation serial verbs have a natural affinity for their subjects, so they were moved to the left of the object in multiple daughter languages. This process would have been helped by intransitive clauses, where the intransitive verb was already next to the subject due to the fact that there was no object. It would also have been helped by the affinity between a transitive verb and its object, which are also separated in the hypothetical reconstruction in (8).

This is a plausible scenario, and although I am not proposing that it actually took place, its plausibility casts doubt on my actual reconstruction, given in (6). In cases like this, where a reconstructed construction is not wholly arbitrary, the historical linguist must acknowledge that fact, discuss the potential ways iconicity could have interfered with the construction, and propose a reconstruction with appropriate caution.

2.3 Other perspectives on syntactic reconstruction

In much of the preceding discussion I have neglected to situate my own ideas among those of other scholars. This omission was deliberate, as I believe that comparison with other methods will be more fruitful now that my whole framework has been presented. In this section I provide a comparison with the two main approaches to syntactic reconstruction: formal ones in the following section, and functional ones in §2.3.2.[5]

2.3.1 Formal approaches to syntactic reconstruction

Formal (or generative, or Chomskyan, or Minimalist) syntacticians have approached syntactic reconstruction in a few different ways. The view of language that is common from within the Minimalist Program obviously differs from my own, and generative theoreticians consequently see a slightly different set of problems besetting the enterprise of comparative syntax. For them, the correspondence and directionality problems are more serious, while the arbitrariness problem is almost nonexistent. They also see an additional problem, the "radical reanalysis" problem, although they differ about how serious it is.

There is an interesting tension in the formal literature on syntactic reconstruction because in some sense, syntactic reconstruction is impossible for a Minimalist. If all humans share the same innate grammar, then there is nothing to say about speakers of proto-languages except that they also had the same grammar. And though generative scholars occasionally acknowledge this difficulty, they also claim, rightly, that saying there is nothing to reconstruct about proto-languages is taking matters a bit too far. The question, then, is what it actually means for them to reconstruct syntax.

This is where their understanding of reanalysis comes in. Because they assume that an individual's grammar does not change significantly during adult life, the locus of language change must be in child language acquisition. When a child hears the utterances produced around it, it forms its own mental grammar on the basis of that input, and in the process may analyze some strings in a new way. For formalists, this is what it's all about, since this is basically the only mechanism available in their theory for changing syntax.

A key question for reconstruction, then, is whether this process of reanalysis is constrained in any way, and especially whether it has any directional tendencies. If not, then presumably it operates in too random a way for its effects to be undone by a historical linguist; this is the position taken by Lightfoot (1979, 1980, 2002a, 2002b). However, others have observed that, whatever the theoretical possibilities are, in practice the observed range of reanalysis is much more limited.

---

[5] In what follows I forego a discussion of the entire history of syntactic reconstruction, referring the reader instead to Walkden's capable summary of earlier attempts (2013: 96–99).

Willis (2011) notes that any syntactic innovation must produce an analysis that is as good a fit for the data as the original grammar, and this principle, which he calls 'local directionality', will severely constrain the possibilities for reanalysis in any given case. Walkden (2014) makes a similar point, remarking that acquisition is normally quite successful, and reanalysis is never so radical as to affect mutual intelligibility between successive generations in a speech community.

However, although the reanalysis issue can be dealt with in their framework—both Willis and Walkden provide plausible, motivated accounts for the directionality of syntactic change—the generative view of language still leads them to commit errors. Most notable is the continual confusion of types and tokens in their discussion of what it might mean to reconstruct syntax. One frequently encounters comments to the effect that, in syntactic reconstruction "it is collections of 'cognate' sentences containing a particular feature rather than sets of lexical items" that would be the object of reconstruction, followed by statements that this is of course impossible because "sentences are not transmitted as whole units from generation to generation" (Willis 2011: 411; see similar comments in Lightfoot 2002a: 119; Pires and Thomason 2008: 44; Walkden 2013: 103, 2014: 51). Of course it is true that sentences are not transmitted from generation to generation, because they are linguistic tokens, not types. And as I discussed above, tokens are not transmitted diachronically—only the types they participate in are.

Others have raised these objections before. The responses from formalists vary somewhat, but they all maintain that the correspondence problem is real. Walkden (2013: 104) and von Mengden (2008: 103) contend that correspondences cannot be set up because the combinatorial possibilities are too large: while the productivity of any language's phonological system is relatively constrained, a syntactic system must be able "to account for the discrete infinity of sentences that are grammatical in any language" (Walkden 2014: 104). This is, however, a *non sequitur*. How rich the combinatorial possibilities are has no bearing on whether two constructions exist in a relationship of correspondence to one another. My English prepositional phrase construction [P NP] is directly descended from earlier English [P NP] constructions, because it is a linguistic type that is transmitted in a tradition of speaking in the way described above. The fact that English allows an infinite number of possible prepositional phrases is neither here nor there.

Willis, by contrast, argues that it is still impossible to establish correspondence sets because while "in phonology, each affected lexical item is independent evidence of a prior sound change, in syntax, there is only really a single observation" (2011: 413). He is right, but this is a statement about the regularity problem, not the correspondence problem. We cannot establish correspondence *sets* in syntactic reconstruction (much as in morphological reconstruction; cf. Koch

1996: 222), but we can establish individual correspondences, because diachronic relations of cognacy do hold between successive stages of a construction in a tradition of speaking.

But formalists discussing comparative syntax continually return to the correspondence problem, which they consistently articulate as an inability on the part of sentences (syntactic tokens) to enter into relations of cognacy. And of course it's easy to see why they do this: in generative theory, there is no such thing as a syntactic type. Or rather, there is only one syntactic type, namely our shared, innate syntactic apparatus. And reconstructing that is not an insightful exercise.

So they reconstruct something else. Not syntax *per se*, but the idiosyncratic expression of a universal syntax in some particular proto-langauge. And this is where, in my view, the weakness of Minimalist ontology begins creating real problems for them. I have found very little discussion, in the formal literature on syntactic reconstruction, of what language *is*, and what implications that ontological claim has for diachrony and therefore for reconstruction. If they made such an ontological claim, we could treat it as the premise to their argument, and then evaluate their conclusions in light of the soundness of both their premise and their argument. But in the absence of such a claim, we are left with arguments that proceed from very hazy premises, via usually sound argumentation, to conclusions that cannot be evaluated because it was never made very clear what it is we're actually talking about.

I will take George Walkden's work as an example. This is not to single him out for derision—rather the opposite. Though I frankly admit I am an outsider to Minimalism, he seems to me to have made the most progress in solving the relevant problems, and his approach, with its understanding that "syntactic reconstruction is lexical reconstruction" (2014: 113) is in spirit very similar to my own. Thus I hope the comparison can illuminate some of the differences that arise when a similar methodological idea is applied in our respective frameworks.

Walkden assumes the Borer-Chomsky Conjecture, which states that "all parameters of variation are attributable to the features of particular items (e.g. the functional heads) in the lexicon" (2014: 19, citing Baker 2008). So if syntactic variation is actually lexical, then reconstructing the syntax of a particular variety means reconstructing the relevant parts of its lexicon. This insight inspires Walkden to reach for an analogy between phonology and syntax that will allow for syntactic reconstruction (2013: 108, 2014: 54). He observes that, at least in some theories, phonemes have features that can be represented in an attribute–value matrix. He gives the example of /t/, which is [+coronal], [–voice], [–continuant], and so on. In the Borer-Chomsky view of language, the same is true of functional heads. In English, for example, the tense head T has feature values [tense:past], [*u*Case:nom], [*u*Num:], and [*u*Pers:]. Walkden then comments that this analogy "enables units of syntactic variation, lexical items, to be seen as analogous to the units of phonological variation" (2013: 109, 2014: 55). But this is explicitly not an ontological claim. He does not say that functional lexical heads *actually resemble* phonemes, only that they *can be seen* in similar ways; and he never explains why it might be more accurate to see them in such a way, only why it might be convenient.

The analogy is rendered even more problematic by the fact that Walkden never tells us what a functional head is. He describes, briefly, what functional heads do in the Minimalist architecture (2014: 7), but not what their ontological status is. As far as I can tell, they are simply descriptive devices, useful for accounting for a variety of linguistic facts but not necessarily reflective of any external reality.

The phonological side of Walkden's analogy is similarly short on ontological substance. He does not claim that phonemes are composed of feature values, only that certain theories "represent variation" this way (2013: 108, 2014: 54). Again we must ask: is this how things really are? And is this how things really change? In this case I can say with more authority that no, it is not. The fact that phonemes can be represented with features is purely an analytical device. It has nothing to do with how phonological structure is acquired or passed on in a tradition of speaking, and is consequently irrelevant for reconstruction. What matters for reconstruction is the arbitrary association between certain meanings and certain sequences of articulatory gestures. These gestures are a learned behavior that is diachronically stable enough to be reconstructed, and that is what the comparativist reconstructs.[6]

Perhaps tellingly, Walkden actually makes relatively little use of his own methodology in the reconstructions he proposes. He argues for the 'cognacy' of phonologically null functional heads in the clausal left periphery of the Northwest Germanic languages (2014: 89); he reconstructs the word order of Northwest Germanic *wh*-questions based on identity among daughter languages (2014: 115); he reconstructs Proto-Northwest Germanic as a "partial null argument" language, also based on identity (2014: 215); and he reconciles this with Gothic, a "full null argument" language, with a dubious directional claim that change from full to partial is more likely than the reverse, so the Gothic type should be reconstructed

---

[6] Astute readers will infer that this way of representing things means that I also reject claims by some historical linguists (such as von Mengden 2008: 99) that phonological reconstruction is the reconstruction of abstract contrastive relations between phonemes, and not the reconstruction of phonetic substance. Phonetic substance is, in fact, central to phonological reconstruction. Postulating a phonetic realization for proto-phonemes is what gives us criteria of directionality for resolving non-identical correspondences, and reconstruction is not possible without directionality.

to Proto-Germanic (2014: 226). Most of these reconstructions make little use of his methodological proposals, leaving the non-Minimalist reader to wonder what utility those proposals have.

He certainly does have his moments, though. He's at his best when dealing with the syntactic properties of individual lexemes,[7] and he offers interesting reconstructions of a Proto-Northwest Germanic exclamative construction with *hʷat 'what' (2014: 143) and an interrogative word *hʷaþeraz (or *hʷeþeraz) 'which of two', which became a question-introducing form (2014: 154–155). Interestingly, these reconstructions—in spirit and in outcome, if not in method—strongly resemble Jóhanna Barðdal's reconstruction of the 'woe is me' construction to Proto-Indo-European, in that the cognacy of a particular lexical item is leveraged to reconstruct the construction it participated in (Barðdal 2013; Barðdal et al. 2013).

Formal approaches can thus produce valuable results when they are focusing on lexemes, which are entities that all linguistic theories agree are real. But when they are dealing with null functional heads or other theoretical constructs, the existence of which other theories reject, their proposals would benefit from greater explicitness about what those constructs actually represent.

2.3.2 Functional approaches to syntactic reconstruction

Since the present work is couched in Construction Grammar, it will not surprise readers to find that I have a greater affinity for work in the functional tradition. However, I do not agree with other practitioners on all points, and it will be instructive to point out areas where we differ so that we can sharpen our methods.

A key insight—perhaps *the* key insight—for syntactic reconstruction is that syntax is, like the lexicon, composed of signs. It is this that allows for a theory of inheritance and change that is compatible with reconstructive methods. And because syntactic constructions can be partially schematic—that is, they can contain a combination of morphological and non-morphological material—the relationship between a reconstructed morpheme (say, a case suffix) and the more abstract syntactic construction it participates in (such as a particular clause type) is made explicit. In much non-constructional functional work this relationship, between a morpheme and the construction it is found in, is left under-theorized, although plenty of work has claimed that syntactic reconstruction needs pho-

---

[7] For what it's worth, Walkden seems to agree with this assessment, since he summarizes one of his chapters with the comment that "syntactic reconstruction is at its most believable when dealing with the syntactic properties of those lexical items that have overt phonological forms traceable via lexical-phonological reconstruction" (2014: 156).

nological correspondences, or at least would benefit from them (Hamp 1976; A. Harris 1985, 2008; Gildea 1998, 2000). Some of this work even uses the notion of a "construction" in its older, more general usage—that is, not in the technical sense used in Construction Grammar—to argue that "when one reconstructs the morphology of a given construction, one is often able to reconstruct some of the associated syntactic constituency relationships as well" (Gildea 2000: 97). Generally speaking, a good deal of this non-constructional work is straightforwardly interpretable in constructional terms, as Barðdal and Gildea (2015: 6–7) point out for Alice Harris's work on Kartvelian (1985, 1990, 2008). In general I follow their lead and interpret work constructionally when it seems appropriate, instead of repeatedly criticizing other functional scholars for insufficiently availing themselves of the blessings of Construction Grammar.

What, then, are my main points of disagreement with current constructional thinking on syntactic reconstruction? They center on three issues: arbitrariness, regularity, and borrowing. In what follows I describe how my understanding of the role of these issues in syntactic reconstruction differs from the understanding of other functional scholars. I focus to some degree on the work of Jóhanna Barðdal and her colleagues, but as with Walkden's work in the previous section, this is not because I consider her work poor. Rather it is because she has made significant progress in developing a methodological framework for syntactic reconstruction that is based on an understanding of the linguistic sign that matches my own. Consequently illuminating those areas where we do see things differently should prove instructive.

2.3.2.1 Arbitrariness

Not much has been said about the role arbitrariness might play in syntactic change or syntactic reconstruction. For formalists it appears to be a non-issue, presumably since syntax is an innate genetic endowment with no iconic relationship to external reality, and all syntactic variation is encoded in (presumably arbitrary) lexemes.

The fact is, though, that syntax is often iconic (Haiman 1980, 1985, 2008; Newmeyer 1992; Croft 2008). One need not look far for confirmation of this fact. The cross-linguistic preponderance of subject-initial word order is difficult to interpret as anything other than iconic: in languages that have subjects, those subjects will usually be the originators of the events of their clauses. So because real-world events usually begin with their subjects, there is iconic motivation for abstract word-order constructions to also begin with their subjects.

This fact has consequences for diachrony, and therefore reconstruction. The existence of an iconic link between syntactic constructions and the events they describe can be expected to interfere with normal processes of language inheritance, as we saw in the case of Proto-Oceanic *kokorako 'chicken' above. We must reckon with this fact in our reconstructions.

Unfortunately, few scholars have acknowledged this. Barðdal and Eythórsson offer brief treatments of the arbitrariness issue in a number of their papers, concluding that "the arbitrariness requirement is simply not needed for syntactic reconstruction" (Barðdal 2013: 446; cf. also Barðdal and Eythórsson 2012a: 367, Barðdal and Eythórsson 2012b: 267). They offer two arguments in support of this claim. First, arbitrariness is only needed to establish the genetic relatedness of languages, which has usually already been established by the time anyone starts trying to reconstruct syntax. Second, syntactic constructions can be arbitrary because their meaning can be (and often is) non-compositional.

The first point is well taken: arbitrariness is, in fact, required to demonstrate genetic relatedness, and I agree that it would be foolhardy to attempt syntactic reconstruction on a language family whose relatedness is disputed.

But the second argument misses the point. They take the arbitrariness of a sign to stand in opposition to its non-compositionality, and consider the meaning of a construction to be arbitrary when the meaning of the whole cannot be predictably derived from the meanings of the parts (Barðdal and Eythórsson 2012b: 367; Barðdal 2013: 446). This conception fails to capture why arbitrariness is important in reconstruction: it is important because it can affect the ways signs change. The conception of arbitrariness that is important in reconstruction is opposed to iconicity, not non-compositionality. We must ask whether the *arrangement* of component signs in a grammatical sign is arbitrary, not whether the meanings of the component signs have a predictable relationship to the meaning of the parent sign.

It is important to note, though, that although I concede that iconicity in syntax may interfere with the diachronic transmission of some grammatical signs, this does not mean that they are not still transmitted from generation to generation. It only means that expected patterns of change may not manifest themselves, that unexpected changes may crop up, and that languages may undergo similar changes independently of one another. There is still diachronic identity between successive manifestations of constructions, and therefore correspondences can still exist between signs inherited into sister languages. Iconicity just adds noise to the signal: it means that, in reconstructing grammar, we face potentially "onomatopoetic" forms—forms that behave in unexpected ways because they are iconic—more often.

2.3.2.2 Regularity

The regularity problem (Pires and Thomason 2008: 52; Barðdal and Eythórsson 2012b: 367) is the observation that the analogy between phonological and syntactic reconstruction breaks down in the following way. Sound changes are hypothesized (and often seen) to be regular: when we propose a rule *t > *d* in a particular environment, we expect *t to change to *d* consistently whenever it occurs in that environment (Osthoff and Brugmann 1878). This regularity assures us that two languages under examination really are related. It also allows us, under favorable circumstances, to identify borrowed vocabulary by recognizing that a particular sound change is not reflected where it should be or vice versa. This is not possible with syntactic constructions, though, for two reasons. First, wholly schematic constructions, by definition, do not contain phonemes so nothing can be tested for cognacy. Second, even constructions that specify phonological material often—but not always—display unexpected sound changes because individual constructions change on their own. For example, when *going to* changed to *gonna* in the purpose construction (Bybee 2006), it did not undergo a similar change in any other construction. Thus the change from *going to* to *gonna* was not regular in the historical-linguistic sense of the word, and the same can be said, in general, of grammatical change as a whole. Each change to a grammatical construction is irregular because it affects that, and only that, construction.

It should be noted that this understanding of regularity puts me at odds, once again, with Barðdal and her colleagues. They state that "the perceived lack of regularity in syntactic change, i.e. the perceived lack of directionality, is not crucial ... for syntactic reconstruction. First of all, not all sound changes are regular, in the sense that their directionality is known" (Barðdal and Eythórsson 2012b: 367). Here they use *regular* in its more everyday sense of "ordinary," rather than its technical historical-linguistic sense of "complete". That is, for them sound changes are regular if they are typologically "normal" and their directionality can therefore be inferred. This is similar to the usage found in Harris and Campbell, who understand *regular* to mean "not 'exceptionless,' but 'rule-governed and not random'" (1995: 326).

But the sense of *regular* typically used by historical linguists is very different, as Harris and Campbell implicitly acknowledge. A sound change is regular if it affects a particular phoneme regularly in a given environment in every instance, whether or not the change at hand displays the typologically expected directionality. The concept to which these authors refer also has its place, but it is more properly conceived of as pertaining to the directionality of change, not the regularity of change. That is, if changes are found to be *regular* in the sense of "normal" or "rule-ordered," then we will be able to determine what forms are innovative because they reflect regular changes.

But regularity in the sense of exceptionlessness also matters, and this kind of regularity cannot occur in grammatical constructions because they take a different kind of filler. Rather than phonemes, grammatical constructions take other constructions as fillers. And when a particular filler or sequence of fillers undergoes a change in some construction, in general that same sequence *does not* undergo the same change in other constructions, although of course it may. This is true with phonological fillers such as *going to*, as well as constructional ones. For example, when main clauses undergo changes that affect their constructional fillers (such as the order of subject, object, and verb), subordinate clauses often do not (Bybee 2001b).

In spite of the fact that syntactic change is technically irregular, though, the diachronic identity between successive stages such as purposive *going to* and *gonna* is obvious. The expressions are part of the same tradition of speaking; they are cognate. This situation is analogous to what we find when dealing with irregular phonological change (Blust 1996). Even when sound changes do not live up to the Neogrammarian ideal—and the fact is that sometimes they don't—there is still diachronic identity between the relevant forms. Identity has just been obscured by irregular phonological change. Thus establishing correspondence, and therefore cognacy, is still possible in cases of irregular lexical or grammatical change where we have only one attestation of a given change.

So while I acknowledge that syntactic change is, in general, not regular, I maintain that diachronic identity still obtains between successive iterations of a construction undergoing change. If we can spot that identity, then we can set up correspondences. And once these have been set up, we can, assuming we have a good theory about the directionality of change, begin to reconstruct. We see then that regularity is not actually essential to the comparative method. This is an important point and is one of the main ways that syntactic reconstruction differs from lexical reconstruction. Regularity is widespread in phonological change and has been a well-known feature of comparative reconstruction for a long time, and has proven itself quite useful for confirming cognacy and uncovering borrowings. But the fact that it has been a feature of the comparative method since its inception does not mean that it has ever been essential to it. In fact, regularity is also not generally found in morphological reconstruction (Koch 1996: 222), which has not prevented that field from achieving considerable success. The only truly essential ingredients for the comparative method are correspondence and directionality.

2.3.2.3 Borrowing

Another issue where I disagree with some of the functional literature is the matter of borrowing (for more extensive discussion, see Daniels 2017a). While it has occasionally been acknowledged as serious, it has not often received a thorough treatment. For example, Harris and Campbell (1995: 372–374) discuss it only enough to say that sometimes, the effects of contact on a lower-order subgroup can be recognized by examining languages from other branches of a family. But of course, this only works if we are fortunate enough to have contact affect only languages from lower-order subgroups, to say nothing of contact among related languages.

Other authors generally treat syntactic borrowing as something that is always accompanied by lexical borrowing; it is quite common to find statements to the effect that "a contact situation that entails mutual [syntactic] borrowing should result in a number of [lexical] cognates across the languages in contact, and their form should be easily recognizable as borrowed" (Barðdal et al. 2012: 524; see similar statements in Gildea 1998: 38; Barðdal and Smitherman 2013: 61; Barðdal and Eythórsson 2012a: 366). But the fact is that grammatical borrowing without accompanying lexical borrowing happens quite frequently (Epps 2007, 2013; Heine and Kuteva 2003, 2005; Næss and Jenny 2011; Ross 2007). For example, Ross (2007) describes the wholesale copying of syntactic patterns from a Papuan language into an Austronesian one on Karkar Island off the coast of Madang. Importantly, the process was accompanied by very little lexical or morphological borrowing. Rather, the borrower language, Takia, has copied the donor language patterns with native Austronesian morphology. This means that even when identical syntactic patterns are found in two languages, we cannot be sure that they existed in the common ancestor of those languages, as the pattern could have been innovated after the breakup of the proto-language and then spread via contact among sister languages (Ross 2008).

If we acknowledge that syntactic borrowing can happen in this way, we must concede that fully schematic grammatical constructions—that is, constructions that contain no phonological material, only constructional material—cannot be directly reconstructed for the simple reason that "we have no set of principles for how to identify a loan construction or piece of syntax from an inherited one" (Bowern 2008: 201; see also Willis 2011: 414; Walkden 2013: 106). Nevertheless, the reconstruction of schematic patterns without phonological substance is fairly common (Barðdal and Eythórsson 2012b; Barðdal et al. 2012; Klamer and Schapper 2012).

2.4 Other methodological issues

In this section I discuss two methodological issues which are not unique to syntactic reconstruction per se, but which still require attention. Both have to do with subgrouping. The first is the issue of how to weigh Sogeram-external evidence against Sogeram-internal evidence in reconstructing Proto-Sogeram; the second is the issue of how best to understand Sogeram-internal subgroups and what bearing that has on our reconstruction.

2.4.1 External and internal evidence

What should be done when the evidence from Sogeram languages appears to conflict with evidence from outside the family? In general I have given preference to the evidence from Sogeram languages, since it is often unclear how to interpret external evidence. The phonological (morphological, syntactic, etc.) history of the Josephstaal languages is not known, so the question of how Josephstaal data bears on Sogeram questions is tricky. The issue is even murkier when one goes farther afield. For example, the Sogeram languages show evidence for two possible reconstructions of an interrogative pronoun 'who': *uña and *ani (§5.2.6). In neither case is the internal evidence quite sufficient to warrant reconstruction, but an external cognate could secure either reconstruction. Pawley (2005: 87) reconstructs PTNG *wani 'who,' but this could be interpreted as evidence for both reconstructions. Did the *wa sequence simplify to PSoG *u, was a final *a added, and was the *ni sequence actually a palatal nasal? If so, PTNG *wani could give PSoG *uña. But if, instead, word-initial liquids were lost, then *wani could give *ani. At present we simply do not know enough about the history of the parents to Proto-Sogeram to reach a judgment, so I remain agnostic.

However, there are also cases where the internal evidence is inconclusive, and external evidence can be used to resolve the difficulty. For example, in the case of the future tense suffix *-ɨba (§4.3.5) the only Sogeram reflexes are found in Apalɨ and Aisian, which is not sufficient for reconstruction. But similar suffixes are found in two languages of the Josephstaal group, the sister to Sogeram: Moresada *-mba* and Anamuxra *-ba* (with prenasalized *b*). Since these suffixes are fairly clearly cognate, I propose the Proto-Sogeram reconstruction *-ɨba.

In general, however, the former situation is more common: I usually do not know how to interpret the external evidence because of our lack of knowledge about the history of the relevant Trans New Guinea subgroups. But where the external evidence is straightforwardly interpretable, I try to use it whenever it is available.

2.4.2 The subgrouping of the Sogeram languages

How a linguist understands the internal subgrouping of a family has significant implications for how that linguist will reconstruct the family's proto-language. Consequently, historical linguists have devised a variety of methods for modeling the often complex historical relationships between languages, in an effort to "get it right" and arrive at the best reconstruction. The most popular is the family tree model, proposed by August Schleicher (1853) to capture the way "that one people, the Proto-Indo-Europeans, split up, over time, into those eight peoples, each of which then later differentiated in a similar way until the diversity of our era eventually developed".[8] For Schleicher, family trees were principally a representation of population history, depicting a process in which people groups split up into discrete subgroups, which later split up themselves.

We now know, however, that matters are rarely so simple. The split-ups implied by Schleicher's model are hardly ever punctual events, but rather take place over generations or centuries. And as populations gradually disperse, linguistic innovations can continue to spread through them unevenly, producing overlapping isoglosses that are difficult for the family tree model to capture (Ross 1988; François 2015; Kalyan and François 2018). Because of this shortcoming, Johannes Schmidt proposed the wave model as an alternative to the family tree model (1872). In this model, linguistic innovations are conceived of as waves rippling out from a central point of innovation, spreading geographically some distance through a speech community and eventually stopping. Waves can overlap, but as they accumulate, speech varieties gradually become less mutually intelligible.

Although the family tree and wave models were initially put forward as mutually exclusive conceptualizations, later generations of linguists have recognized that they are in fact compatible with one another: a perfect family tree is simply what arises when waves happen not to overlap (Pawley 1999). While this formulation can be understood as a concession that the wave model is the correct one, as it can model family tree situations as well as others, it is better to think of the difference between family trees and wave models in terms of the level of abstraction employed. A wave diagram attempts to capture the messiness of overlapping isoglosses and represent the linguistic history of a family fairly accurately. A tree diagram, on the other hand, abstracts away from the mess to give a simpler, more easily understood picture of the history of a family.

When they are conceptualized this way, it is easy to see that family trees and wave diagrams both have their place, as do intermediate ways of diagramming language relationships like Ross's (1988) device for drawing dialect linkages in family trees.

The Sogeram family is what Pawley calls an "imperfect subgroup," a chain of lects in which some innovations "spread over the whole chain, in contrast to

---

[8] My translation from the German "... dass eine Nation, das indogermanische Urvolk, sich mit der Zeit in jene acht Völker geteilt habe, von denen jedes in ähnlicher Weise sich später wieder differenzierte, bis endlich die Mannigfaltigkeit unserer Epoche entstand". The "eight peoples" to which Schleicher refers are the recognized Indo-European subgroups of his day: speakers of Celtic, Germanic, Baltic, Slavic, Italic, Greek, Iranian, and Indic languages.

other innovations which spread only over parts of the chain" (Pawley 1999: 130). While Proto-South Adelbert, the immediate parent of Proto-Sogeram, has not been reconstructed in much detail (but see Pawley 1998b), it is clear that Sogeram is defined by at least three innovations (see Daniels 2017b: 85–87).

The first is a semantic innovation to a lexeme. Proto-Trans New Guinea *kin(i,u) 'sleep' (Pawley 2012: 113) is reflected in other Madang languages with its reconstructed meaning. Anamuxra (a member of the Josephstaal branch of South Adelbert; Ingram 2003: 161) has kn- 'sleep', as does Kalam (a member of the Kalam-Kobon branch; Pawley and Bulmer 2011: 301); and Jilim (a member of the Rai Coast branch) has kñ- 'sleep'. But in Proto-Sogeram the cognate *kɨña or *kɨñɨ- meant 'stay', and this innovative meaning is reflected in every daughter language.

The second and third innovations both concern the loss of plural marking and the semantic extension of the dual. This happened both with the free pronouns and with the verbal subject agreement suffixes. The dual pronominal formative was *-ra in Proto-Madang (Ross 2000), as can be seen in Anamuxra -r (Ingram 2001: 198), Kalam -t (Pawley and Bulmer 2011: 41), and Kobon -l(e) (Davies 1981: 154). But pronouns in *-ra developed plural meaning in Proto-Sogeram, and retain that meaning in all daughter languages, while the older plural forms were lost.

Similarly, the dual subject agreement suffixes, which Pawley (2005: 90) reconstructs as *-uL '1DU' and *-iL '2/3DU', are retained in Kalam (Pawley and Bulmer 2011: 66), Kobon (Davies 1981: 166), and Anamuxra (Ingram 2001: 210) as dual suffixes, but in Proto-Sogeram as plural suffixes. The erstwhile plural suffixes, meanwhile, have been lost in Proto-Sogeram.

So the Sogeram languages seem like a genuine clade in the Trans New Guinea family, although we have to acknowledge that we know very little about most of the Josephstaal languages, the group most closely related to Sogeram, so it may turn out that some of them actually belong in the Sogeram group.

The understanding of the internal subgrouping of the Sogeram languages has evolved considerably in the last few years, primarily due to the findings reported in Daniels, Barth, and Barth (2019). They took the innovations in Daniels (2015) and subjected them to the methods of historical glottometry (François 2015; Kalyan and François 2018), which resulted in some revisions to the subgrouping scheme Daniels had first proposed. The outcome is summarized in the glottometric diagram in Figure 6. This diagram can be read in much the same way as a wave diagram. Each dot represents a language,[9] and each line represents a set of

---

[9] The abbreviations in this figure are as follows: Mnd = Mand; Nen = Nend; Mnt = Manat; Apa = Apalɨ; Sir = Sirva; Mag = Magɨ; Ais = Aisi; Kur = Kursav; Gaj = Gants.

innovations shared by the languages it surrounds. The thickness of that line represents the strength of that subgroup, measured in terms of how often and how strongly it is attested in the data, and also how often it is contradicted in the data. Thus the method does not represent relative chronology, but it does distinguish shared innovations (on the inside of an isogloss) from retentions (on the outside).

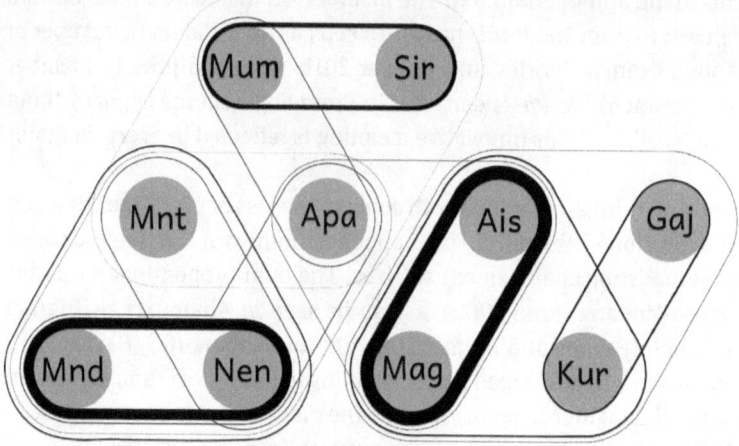

Figure 6: Glottometric diagram of the Sogeram languages.

The diagram in Figure 6 can be summarized in the family tree given in Figure 7 (reproduced from Figure 2 in Chapter 1). This is, of course, a simplification, but it serves as a useful, and more easily remembered, condensation of the information in Figure 6.

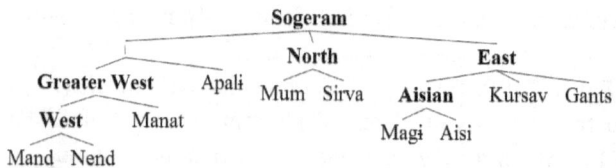

Figure 7: Sogeram family tree.

This comparison between a glottometric diagram and a family tree brings up an important methodological discussion: what is the proper way to understand subgrouping in the comparative method? Some historical linguists believe that the family tree model of language diversification is an essential component of comparative reconstruction (Fox 1995: 232). But this seems contradictory. The comparative method is grounded in observed facts about how languages change, and a theoretical understanding of language change that allows the analyst to undo those changes and reconstruct prior language states. If the comparative method is empirically grounded, then how can a theoretical construct like the family tree—which historical linguists almost universally agree is "a vast oversimplification" (Matisoff 2002: 292)—be an essential component to it? Of course it cannot. The family tree model is only useful to a comparativist insofar as it corresponds to the actual facts of language diversification and change in the family at hand. To the extent that it abstracts away from these actual messy facts—cross-cutting innovations and overlapping patterns of inheritance and all the rest—the family tree model can lead to errors.

For example, it is possible for two languages, A and B, to form a subgroup in a family, while Language B also shares innovations with Language C. The fact that Language B shares more innovations with Language A (which is why they are subgrouped together) does not mean that its innovations in common with C are the result of borrowing; this is simply the outcome of a normal dialect continuum. In such a situation, innovations to B and C are found in separate "branches" of the family, and an overly strict application of the family tree model would result in incorrect reconstructions.

What we need in order to reconstruct is simply a reasonable assurance of independent development, that is, assurance that the forms we are examining are not the result of a shared development that took place after the breakup of the proto-language. This kind of assurance is possible in a more nuanced theory of language diversification, such as Ross's linkage model (first proposed in 1988 and more fully developed in 1997), but it is more difficult to obtain. For a comparativist working in this kind of model, the set of language groups that may show evidence of shared development after the breakup of the proto-language is greater. Therefore this kind of model requires more conservatism when deciding what languages must exhibit reflexes of a given item in order to reconstruct it to the proto-language.

Let us examine the case of Apalɨ to see how this kind of method can be applied. In the Sogeram family tree, Apalɨ groups most closely with the Greater West Sogeram branch, suggesting that a form found in Apalɨ and a North Sogeram or East Sogeram language could be reconstructed to Proto-Sogeram. But an examination of the glottometric diagram shows that this is unwarranted, since Apalɨ also shares innovations with the North Sogeram languages, especially Mum, and the Aisian languages. As such, if I have a cognate set involving Apalɨ and one other Sogeram language, I only treat it as reliably dating to the Proto-Sogeram stage if the other language is Kursav or Gants. If the other language is Mand I sometimes suggest that it may date to a later stage of Proto-Sogeram, but do not treat the reconstruction as secure.

Readers will note that this process is circular. These guidelines for reconstruction presuppose the existence of a subgrouping scheme, but of course that very subgrouping scheme must be based on some reconstruction, which of course required a subgrouping scheme, and so on. This circularity is an inescapable part of comparative reconstruction, but that does not make the process unsound. Rather it is best understood as a process of abductive reasoning (as Givón 2000 points out for internal reconstruction). Given a set of observations about a language family, the researcher posits a reconstruction. This is a hypothesis, a theory that can plausibly account for the observed facts. Based on that reconstruction the researcher then proposes a subgrouping that fits the reconstruction. But subsequent reconstructions may require modifications to the subgrouping, and those may impact established reconstructions. At each stage in this process the linguist is making abductive inferences: positing the combination of proto-language and subgrouping schema that she thinks best fits the data. As this process goes on, the knowledge it produces becomes increasingly more reliable.

We have now laid out a method for reconstructing syntax; we have discussed how it interacts with subgrouping; and we have prepared our data for reconstruction. The stage is set, all the actors at their stations. The excited reader may now turn the page, ready to be thrilled by subordinate clauses and nonverbal predicates, only to be disappointed at the sight of a chapter on phonological reconstruction. I implore the reader not to lose heart. This is how it must be. Before we can reconstruct syntax, we must reconstruct morphology, because we need cognate morphological material in our syntactic cognate sets in order to safeguard against borrowing. And before we can reconstruct morphology, we must reconstruct phonology, because how can anything be reconstructed without phonology? So that is where our drama begins, in the next chapter. It then advances, through verbal and nominal morphology (Chapters 4 and 5), and reaches its climax in Chapter 6, on syntax. The denouement consists of the reconstructed lexicon (Chapter 7) and a concluding summary, which includes a grammar sketch of Proto-Sogeram (Chapter 8).

Chapter 3
Phonology

In this chapter I present the phonological reconstruction of Proto-Sogeram (PSoG) and discuss the phonological innovations that have taken place in each daughter language. I have already discussed Proto-Sogeram phonology in some detail in previous work (Daniels 2010, 2015), although the present study involves significantly better data than the 2010 paper and some smaller improvements on the 2015 analysis. I begin below by presenting the reconstructed phonological inventory and discussing phonotactic patterns. The rest of the chapter then covers phonological developments in the daughter branches.

3.1 Proto-Sogeram phonological inventory

The reconstructed Proto-Sogeram phonological inventory is given in (9) below. It differs from Daniels (2010) in the addition of two additional phonemes, *ñ and *f, and from both Daniels (2010) and Daniels (2015) in the addition of prenasalized consonants and the glides *w and *y.

(9) *p   *t   *k   *kʷ \<kw\>   *i   *ɨ   *u
  *ᵐp \<b\>   *ⁿt \<d\>   *ᵑk \<g\> *ᵑkʷ \<gw\>
  *ɸ \<f\>   *s   *a
              *ⁿs \<z\>
  *m   *n   *ɲ \<ñ\>   *ŋ
              *r
              *j \<y\>   *w

Where the orthographic symbol I use differs from the phonetic character that I posit for a reconstructed phoneme, I present the orthographic symbol in \<angled brackets\> on the right. The orthographies that I use for Proto-Sogeram and for modern Sogeram languages are phonemic, and sometimes correspondences can be hard to keep track of. For this reason, throughout this chapter I give phonetic transcriptions in [square brackets] next to phonemic, orthographic representations when appropriate—for example, *tagwa [taⁿkʷa] 'step on'. I provide a comparison of orthographies at the end of this chapter.

Five aspects of the reconstruction in (9) merit special discussion: the prenasalized consonants, the reconstruction of *kw and *gw, the reconstruction of *f, the status of the glides *w and *y, and the status of *ɨ.

In earlier work I did not reconstruct prenasalized stops, opting instead to reconstruct frequent nasal–stop clusters, as in *ampɨŋ 'wing,' *kɨntɨr 'root,' *mɨŋka 'come down,' and *iŋkwa 'give', which I now represent as *abɨŋ, *kɨdɨr, *mɨga, and *igwa. I also reconstructed a nasal–sibilant sequence, as in *punsɨŋ 'bone', which I now represent as *puzɨŋ. It is important that the phonetic character of the reconstructions I propose is not different than before: what has changed is rather my phonological analysis of Proto-Sogeram. My analysis still posits, as before, that each of these consonants was composed of a nasal phase followed by a voiceless obstruent. But I now consider them single-segment phonemes rather than consonant clusters. Two things effected this change in analysis.

First, I became aware of similar phoneme inventories in modern languages. It had not occurred to me to reconstruct voiceless prenasalized consonants without also reconstructing voiced ones, because I did not think that was an attested kind of phoneme inventory. But Ngkolmpu, a Yam language of southern New Guinea (Carroll 2016), and Phola, a Tibeto-Burman language of Yunnan Province, China (Pelkey 2011) both exhibit such phoneme inventories, which for me raised the possibility that Proto-Sogeram was similar.

The second consideration was that the reflex of these consonants is a single segment in every daughter language, never a cluster. The only possible exception is Nend, but even there Harris lists ŋk as a separate consonant (1990: 80), and sequences of a nasal and a voiceless stop behave as a single segment in reduplication processes (1990: 82). So the reconstruction of voiceless prenasalized stops was rendered plausible by typological considerations, and then rendered preferable by phonological ones. It also helps conform the Proto-Sogeram reconstruction to what has been proposed for earlier proto-stages: prenasalized stops have been tentatively reconstructed for Proto-South Adelbert (Pawley 1998b) and Proto-Trans New Guinea (PTNG; Pawley 1998a, 2001, 2012).

It still remains for me to establish that these segments were, in fact, voiceless. Here the key evidence is the West Sogeram (WS) reflexes, particularly the Mand ones, and an external witness. Table 5 gives several correspondences involving the Proto-Sogeram prenasalized consonants. Note that in Mand, the nasality was lost (§3.2.2.2), giving a consistent reflex of a simple voiceless obstruent. In Nend, the original voicelessness was sometimes retained (as in, for example, 'wing' and 'come down') and sometimes not (as in 'walk' and 'give'). In every other language, the reflex is a voiced, prenasalized consonant—except Aisi, where prenasalization was lost and *d has a reflex of r (§3.4.2.2).

We are then faced with a classic problem of the comparative method: whether to posit one unusual change or several normal ones. We can reconstruct voiced

3.1 Proto-Sogeram phonological inventory

Table 5: Word-medial obstruent correspondences.

GWS				NS		ES			PSoG
Mand	Nend	Manat	Apalɨ	Mum	Sirva	Aisi	Kursav	Gants	
apɨh	mpɨŋ	(v)ab	abɨŋ	abɨ	abɨ				*abɨŋ [aᵐpɨŋ] 'wing'
ipi(a)			ibi	ñibi	ib	ib	-(n)ibe	ibe	*ibi [iᵐpi] 'name'
tɨr	ntɨr		hɨdɨlɨ	kɨdɨ		kɨrɨr	-kɨdɨr	kɨdɨ	*kɨdɨr [kɨⁿtɨr] 'root'
ta-	nda-	da-	hɨda-	kɨda-	kɨda-	kr-		kɨda	*kɨda [kɨⁿta] 'walk'
ka(jɨ)-	ŋka-	mɨga-	mɨga-	mɨga-	mɨga-	mɨga		mɨga	*mɨga [mɨⁿka] 'come down'
kɨñ	ŋkɨñ		lɨgɨŋ				rigi	tigin	*tɨgɨñ [tɨⁿkɨŋ] 'black'
ikw-	eŋgwa-	igu-	igu-	gu-	gu-	igw-		gw-	*igwa [iⁿkʷa] 'give'
asɨn					maz			majɨm	*mazɨn [maⁿsɨn] 'bowstring'
asɨh(ɨd)	ansɨŋ	azɨ	hajɨŋ	kaz					*kazɨŋ [kaⁿsɨŋ] 'decoration'

consonants, which requires positing a single unusual change in West Sogeram, namely devoicing these stops in every environment, even intervocalically. Or we can reconstruct voiceless consonants, which requires positing multiple voicing changes, namely in Manat, Apalɨ, Proto-North Sogeram (PNS) and Proto-East Sogeram (PES). I prefer the latter analysis for two reasons: (i) we do not actually have to posit multiple separate changes, but can rather posit a very early change that affected the dialects of Proto-Sogeram that eventually became Manat, Apalɨ, Proto-North Sogeram, and Proto-East Sogeram; and (ii) even if this change happened multiple times, it is a very natural change, and positing that it happened a few times is still preferable to positing a single instance of devoicing in Proto-West Sogeram (PWS).

This reconstruction is also supported by Sogeram-external evidence. Capell (1951) surveyed some languages of the Bogia district, including Moresada [msx], which he called Murusapa. This language belongs to the Josephstaal group, which is a sister to Sogeram. Capell gives several sentences and a short text, and some brief analysis reveals the following forms. A verb *ntarɛmbiŋ* seems to mean 'they will hear,' with the likely morphological breaks *ntarɛ-mb-iŋ* [hear-FUT-3PL] (Capell 1951: 146). A further verb *ŋkɛrga* 'see' appears several times on pages 146–147. These forms suggest two things. First, they appear cognate with the Proto-Sogeram reconstructions *idar [iⁿtar] 'hear' and *iga [iⁿka] 'see,' suggesting that *d [ⁿt] and *g [ⁿk] were voiceless in Proto-South Adelbert, and were then inherited as such into both Proto-Sogeram and Moresada. Second, they suggest that Moresada regularly lost word-initial *i. This conclusion is supported by another apparent cognate: *saman* 'brother' (Capell 1951: 146), which resembles PSOG *isaŋ 'same-sex older sibling (1.POSS)'.[10]

For now, then, I consider it most likely that Proto-Sogeram had voiceless prenasalized stops and no voiced ones. The reconstruction of the voiceless prenasalized fricative *z [ⁿs] is less secure, as it rests on only four forms: *kazɨŋ 'festival decoration', *kuza 'yam', *mazɨn 'bowstring', and *puzɨŋ 'bone'. But these reveal essentially the same pattern of inheritance for *z as the stops: a voiceless s in Mand and a single-segment voiced prenasalized z in most other languages. (A complicating factor is the occasional reflex of a prenasalized affricate or palatal stop, in Apalɨ, Mum, and Gants. This remains to be worked out in future research.)

The reconstruction of the labiovelar stops *kw [kʷ] and *gw [ⁿkʷ] faces a similar problem in that it pits the West Sogeram reflexes against others. In both West Sogeram languages, Mand and Nend, the labiovelar obstruents *kw*, *gw*, and *hw* [kʷ, ⁿgʷ, ɣʷ] are clearly single phonemes. In Mand, for example, they have a distribution similar to other obstruents, occurring in complex onsets like *kwrih* [kʷriɣ] 'arrow, spear' and complex codas like *arhw* [arɣʷ] '1PL'. And for some Southern Nend speakers, the lip rounding approaches full closure, so that *kw* could be considered a coarticulated [k͡p]. In other languages, though, the reflexes of *kw and *gw are more ambiguous, and are perhaps most easily analyzed as two segments, a stop and *w* (or an allophone of *u*). This is especially the case in Manat, Apalɨ, and North Sogeram (NS), where many sequences of *kwV became *ku (§3.3.1.2). The situation in East Sogeram is similar, though; reflexes in Kursav, for example, include *kwaka 'cut, chop' > *kwaka-* and *mirkwa 'cordyline' > *merkwa*. In both of these cases the *kw* is phonetically a [kw] sequence and, at the present state of research, there is little to suggest that an analysis as a single phoneme is preferable.

As this discussion makes clear, the question of whether to reconstruct single-segment *kw and *gw also involves other questions, such as whether to reconstruct *w as a separate phoneme or as an allophone of *u, and what the permitted Proto-Sogeram vowel sequences were and how they were syllabified. So we must either reconstruct the phonemes *kw [kʷ] and *gw [ⁿkʷ] and posit that they became two in most languages, or reconstruct clusters of velar stop + *w and posit that they became single phonemes in Proto-West Sogeram. In this case considerations of naturalness are of little help: both changes are equally plausible, as are both

---

[10] Note that the Moresada future tense suffix -*mb*, probably cognate with the PSOG future tense suffix *-ɨba, appears to contain a voiced prenasalized stop. It may be that only word-initial prenasalized stops remained unvoiced in Moresada, and that word-medial ones behaved differently. But at present not enough is known about the language to be sure.

proposed Proto-Sogeram consonant inventories. I reconstruct a separate series of labiovelar stops, citing three deciding factors: (i) the reflexes of the sequence of PSoG *k, *u, and *a in the North Sogeram languages (§3.3.1.4), (ii) the behavior of labiovelar-final verbs in a morphophonemic vowel elision process, and (iii) a labiovelar-conditioned vowel-rounding change in Aisi (§3.4.4.2).

The first point hinges on the only reconstructed *kua sequence in the lexicon, *kuar 'garden'. As I discuss below, this would have been pronounced as two syllables, with an epenthetic *[w]: *[ku.war]. Epenthetic *w, along with the consonantal allophone *[w] of *u (see below), underwent fortition in Manat, Mum, and Sirva (§3.3.1.4), giving the reflex *kiva* [kɨβa] in the latter two languages. This reflex clearly differs from reflexes of *kwa and *gwa sequences, like *kwaka 'cut, chop' > Sirva *kwaha-* [kwaɣa] and *igwa 'give' > Sirva *gwa-* [ⁿgwa]. These divergent reflexes show that the labiovelars in forms like *kwaka and *igwa are not composed of *k or *g plus the consonantal allophone of *u, because *k plus *u develops as in *kuar. This leaves us with two possible explanations. First, we can posit a new phoneme that was distinct from *u—say, *w—and propose that clusters of *k and *w behaved differently before *a than sequences of *k and *u. Or second, we can reconstruct a single segment *kw instead of a cluster, and say that this segment developed differently than *ku. The latter hypothesis is to be preferred, because if we adopt the former, we are pressed into explaining why *w only occurs in one environment, namely after velars, since there is no evidence of a *w-like consonant that is distinct from *u occurring anywhere else in the language.

The second piece of evidence for reconstructing labiovelar consonants comes from patterns of verbal morphophonemics. The final vowel of a verb root was often elided in the presence of vowel-initial suffixes. So for example the *a of *miŋa- 'get' was elided in the presence of the *i in *-in '1SG.IPST': *miŋ-in. This also applied to verbs that ended in *u, such as *kɨmu- 'die,' which became *kɨm-in with this suffix. This elision process still occurs in most Sogeram languages—for example, the reflex of *kɨm-in is *him-in* in Manat and *kum-eniŋ* in Gants. But verbs that ended in labiovelars did not undergo this process. For example, when *igw- 'give' was combined with *-in, the result was *igw-in, with no elision. This can still be seen in multiple reflexes like Mand *ikw-in*, Apalɨ *igu-in*, Sirva *gw-in*, Aisi *igw-eŋ*, and Gants *go-iniŋ*. This difference in behavior between verbs that ended in *u and verbs that ended in labiovelars demonstrates that labiovelar-final verbs ended in a consonant, not a vowel. And as above, we can say that the consonant was a *w that followed a velar stop, or we can say that it was a single labiovelar segment. For the reasons I have stated, the latter analysis is preferable.

The last piece of support for reconstructing labiovelars comes from a sound change in Aisi (§3.4.4.2). In this change, reflexes of Proto-Sogeram labiovelars raised and rounded a preceding *a, so *yakw- 'go up' > *yok-* and *tagw- 'step on' > *tog-*, which suggests that a significant amount of coarticulatory lip rounding still occurred with the velar closure as late as Proto-Aisian (PAIS). This development only took place in these two forms, which is admittedly scanty evidence on which to base this conclusion—and it is not even clear from this evidence that the labiovelars were single-segment phonemes in Proto-Aisian, since such a change could also have taken place with a cluster of a velar stop and *w. But the evidence is suggestive, and, taken together with the evidence from North Sogeram and morphophonemics discussed above, I believe that it renders the reconstruction of labiovelar consonants preferable to any alternatives.

I turn now to the reconstruction of *f [ɸ]. It seems best to reconstruct a non-nasal bilabial consonant in addition to *p, and to posit that it was a bilabial fricative. Reflexes of this consonant are shown in Table 6, and they include *u*, *w*, *v* [β], *f* [ɸ], *b*, and *p*. Reflexes of *p are also given for comparison.

Table 6: Reflexes of PSoG *f and *p.

GWS			NS			ES			PSoG
Mand	Nend	Manat	Apalɨ	Mum	Sirva	Aisian	Kursav	Gants	
v	w	v	v, f	p, v	p, v	b, u	v	p	*f [ɸ]
p	p, v	p, v	v	p, v	p, v	p	p	p	*p

In Daniels (2010) I accounted for some of these reflexes by positing sporadic unusual developments to *p, but it seems now that the costs of positing an additional Proto-Sogeram phoneme, in terms of the economy of the reconstruction, are outweighed by the benefits. Apalɨ *f* can now be accounted for as a reflex of *f, although it occasionally voiced to *v* (§3.2.5.5). In Aisi *f regularly became [w] (probably an allophone of *u*) in onset position and remained [β] (which became an allophone of *b*) in coda position (§3.4.2.2 and §3.4.4.4), while *p remained *p*. The contrast between *f and *p is preserved almost unchanged in Kursav, where *v* [β] today has the word-initial allophone [ɸ]. And in Gants *f merged with *p, which is usually pronounced [ɸ] word-initially and [β] elsewhere.

As regards the phonetic quality of this phoneme, I prefer to reconstruct the allophonic distribution current in Kursav: *[ɸ] word-initially and *[β] elsewhere. (The choice of <f> as the orthographic symbol instead of <v> is thus essentially arbitrary, and differs from Daniels 2015.) This accounts for the fact that in Apalɨ, the voiceless reflex is most common word-initially while the voiced reflex is most common word-medially (although the distribution is not perfect). It also helps explain the word-initial fortition that took place in Proto-North Sogeram

(§3.3.2.1) and the merger between *f and *p that took place in Gants (§3.4.6.3). Lenition to *w* in Nend (§3.2.3.6) and Aisi (§3.4.4.4) could then be explained by positing that the *[ɸ] allophone became voiced, and *[β] then underwent deaffrication to [w].

Another issue to address is the status of *w and *y [j], which I did not include in earlier Proto-Sogeram phoneme inventories. This change, however, is more orthographic than analytic. I remain agnostic on the question of whether *[w] and *[j] were allophones of *u and *i or separate phonemes, but writing the glides makes it clearer to an uninitiated reader how a form like *waka 'maybe' (formerly *uaka) was pronounced.

The final issue is the status of *ɨ. This segment may not always have been phonemic in Proto-Sogeram—in many other Madang languages, including closely related Anamuxra (Ingram 2001), epenthetic central vocoids are inserted to break up illicit consonant clusters. In the Sogeram languages, the vowel *ɨ often does not trigger lenition processes when other vowels do, and sometimes a sequence of *ɨ plus sonorant seems to behave as a syllabic sonorant. Nevertheless, PSoG *ɨ did sometimes trigger vowel elision at morphological boundaries, so for example *tama 'put' plus *-ɨba 'irrealis infinitive' was realized as *tamɨba [tamɨᵐpa]. For this reason I treat *ɨ as a phoneme, while recognizing that it may not always have been phonemic.

3.1.1 Proto-Sogeram phonotactics

Several phonotactic generalizations can be made about Proto-Sogeram based on the words that have been reconstructed. Prenasalized stops tended to occur word-medially. They never occurred word-initially and occurred word-finally only in three morphemes, all of which have problematic correspondence sets: *ibɨd [iᵐpɨⁿt] 'good', *-(na)b [naᵐp] 'daughter-in-law', and the oblique enclitic *=d [ⁿt] (§5.2.3, §5.3.4).

The phoneme *r also did not occur word-initally, meaning that the contrast between *t and *r was restricted to non-initial position. However, the contrast is securely reconstructed by the minimal pair *mita 'leave' and *mira 'firelight'. The only other phonemes that do not appear to have occurred word-initially are *ŋ and *ɨ.

Non-homorganic nasal–stop clusters of also occasionally occurred, although they were uncommon and show irregular development in most cases. Almost all of the reconstructed non-homorganic clusters include *k: *tamkan 'eye,' *kwɨmka 'stomach,' *-mku 'nephew, niece,' and *-ñki 'paternal grandfather'. The only exception is *-ŋti 'father (2.POSS)'.

Word-initially, the corpus only contains the onset clusters *kr (*kra- 'roast') and *fr (*frɨ- 'scratch'), although *pr was probably also allowed, as the cluster is contained as an onset in many forms, like *kupra 'jump' and *upri 'dog' (Daniels 2019). There are also two examples that are reconstructed with a *kwr cluster, so this may also have been allowed word-initially: *akwra 'carry' and *añɨkwrɨñ 'the day before yesterday'. Both of these correspondence sets have problems, though.

The nasals and *r were the only consonants that occurred word-finally with any regularity. Word-final examples of the oral stops, *s, and *f can be seen, though, in forms like *kap 'just,' *kut 'back,' *-muk 'brother of female ego,' *yakw '1SG.POSS', *kwɨŋkɨs 'armpit,' and *karif 'flying fox'.

Various sequences of two vowels were allowed in Proto-Sogeram, although none of them included *ɨ. The most common was the sequence *ai, and reconstructing it is fairly straightforward in a form like *umai 'bean' (cf. Manat *mai*, Mum *umai*, and Kursav *wamai*). The other rising sequence, *au, also occurred, although its reflexes are somewhat more complicated. It became *av [aβ] in Proto-North Sogeram (§3.3.2.2), but otherwise reflexes are not numerous enough to describe patterns with confidence. These two sequences were syllabified together, although it is unclear whether they should be treated as a diphthong—a single complex nucleus—or as a sequence in which the *a was the nucleus and the high vowels took their consonantal allophones *[j] and *[w]. Two reconstructed forms, *kaur 'unripe' and *naudi 'woman,' suggest that analyzing them as a diphthong is preferable because the alternative analysis requires positing complex codas, which are not attested elsewhere. It is, of course, possible that Proto-Sogeram only allowed this kind of complex coda. Moreover, both correspondence sets have problems, so I consider the question unresolved.

Falling vowel sequences require a little more discussion, as *ia and *ua were syllabified differently depending on the context. When they were preceded by a consonant, the first vowel in the sequence was realized as a vowel, an epenthetic glide was pronounced between the vowels, and the *a was pronounced in a separate syllable. That is, they were pronounced *[Ci.ja] and *[Cu.wa]. For example, *kia 'speech' is still two syllables in Apalɨ *ciaŋ*, Kursav *-kia* 'festival,' and Gants *kia*, although in other languages this has changed (such as Mand, Nend *ya* and Sirva *kya*). Similarly, *kuar is still two syllables in Apalɨ *hualɨ*, and the epenthetic glide has changed to *v* in Mum and Sirva *kɨva*.[11]

---

[11] There is a bit of evidence for considering *[j] and *[w] allophones of *i and *u, which involves the resyllabification that took place in some forms after Proto-Greater West Sogeram initial consonant deletion (§3.2.1.1). Forms like *kuar 'garden' and *kia 'speech' originally contained the vocalic allophones of these vowels, as evidenced by the forms cited above. But when the initial consonant of these forms was lost, the following vowel became a consonant, as reflected in

When *ia and *ua were not preceded by a consonant, the first vowel was realized as a consonant, *[j] or *[w]. It was affected by West Sogeram initial consonant deletion (§3.2.1.1), so for example *yakw- 'go up' > Mand ako-, Nend akwɨ-, Manat aku-, and *waka 'maybe' > Manat aka(d).

The sequences *iu and *ui behaved in similar ways. The first of these only occurs once in the reconstructed lexicon, and it is a difficult form to interpret. PSOG *iwi 'nephew, niece (1.POSS)' > Apalɨ iui, Gants yue. The Apalɨ form is syllabified [i.wi], while the Gants form is syllabified [ju.we], with epenthetic [w] inserted between the second and third vowels. Unfortunately, these reflexes do not allow us to reconstruct a syllabification pattern to Proto-Sogeram, since Apalɨ apparently parses from right to left while Gants parses from left to right. So while we can reconstruct the *iu sequence in *iwi 'nephew, niece (1.POSS),' we cannot reconstruct how it behaved, and it may have been pronounced *[juj].

The sequence *ui appears three other times in the reconstructed lexicon: *muyam 'cassowary,' *kuimaŋ 'coconut,' and *kui 'shoot, pierce'. The first of these is straightforward, since it would have been parsed *[mu.jam], leaving the two vowels in different syllables. This vowel sequence gives expected reflexes in every language (except for Mand, where *[j] does not undergo fortition to †z; cf. §3.2.2.6). The second form, *kuimaŋ 'coconut,' appears to have been parsed disyllabically as *[kuj.maŋ], not trisyllabically as †[ku.wi.maŋ]. This is suggested by unexpected reflexes in several languages. The *ui sequence became oi in Mand (koim, with unusual final nasal loss) and Gants (koimaŋ, where the lowering of *u can be ascribed to a regular process of harmony with the following *a; cf. §3.4.1.4). In Manat the sequence was simplified to u (huma), while in Apalɨ it became i (himaŋ). And in Proto-North Sogeram the *i became the nucleus and the *u became a glide (Mum, Sirva kwima). These reflexes are quite different from the Apalɨ and Gants reflexes of *iwi, suggesting that *ui was only disyllabic when it was not followed by a consonant.

Armed with this analysis, we can turn to *kui 'shoot, pierce,' which turns out to be quite a difficult form. As will be shown in the next chapter, Proto-Sogeram verbs occurred in three importantly different environments: as an unbound root (used in serial verb constructions), as a bound root followed by a consonant, and as a bound root followed by a vowel. The unbound form would probably have been *kui, pronounced [ku.wi], or possibly *kuia [ku.ja]. The bound form

---

Mand var, Nend war, and Manat var 'garden' (< *kuar) and in Mand, Nend ya 'speech' (< *kia). However, this fact is more properly understood as reflective of the status of *[j] and *[w] in Proto-Greater West Sogeram, and can be just as easily explained by positing a very ordinary change that made *i and *u glides before vowels.

followed by a consonant would have been, for example, *kui-na 'shoot-2SG.IPST,' pronounced [kuj.na]. And the bound form with a following vowel would have been, for example, *kui-in 'shoot-1SG.IPST,' probably pronounced either [ku.win] or [kujn], although this is not certain. These different root shapes would have influenced each other analogically, which makes analysis difficult, especially given the rarity of correspondence sets for *ui.

A few other patterns appear to occur in the Proto-Sogeram lexicon, but they are not numerous or regular enough to describe in detail—although hopefully someday they will be. I now turn to a discussion of the phonological developments in each of the Sogeram subgroups and languages, beginning with Greater West Sogeram and Apalɨ.

3.2 The Greater West Sogeram languages and Apalɨ

The Greater West Sogeram (GWS) branch is composed of Manat and the two West Sogeram (WS) languages, Mand and Nend (Daniels, Barth, and Barth 2019). Because Apalɨ shares some innovations with these languages, I also discuss it in this section.

The Greater West Sogeram languages share only one phonological innovation, word-initial consonant deletion (§3.2.1.1), and that change was sporadic in Manat. The West Sogeram languages also underwent word-final *ki palatalization (§3.2.1.3), and Manat and Apalɨ share word-initial plosive lenition (§3.2.1.4). Manat and Apalɨ also share some innovations with other languages, such as prenasalized stop voicing, *kw-loss, word-final nasal deletion, and *u fortition. These are discussed in §3.2.4 on North Sogeram languages, where they seem to be centered. Bear in mind that the subgrouping scheme I use, developed in Daniels, Barth, and Barth (2019), is based on more than sound change, so some of the subgroups are not strongly supported based on phonological innovations alone.

3.2.1 West and Greater West Sogeram innovations

The Proto-Greater West Sogeram (PGWS) phoneme inventory was identical to that of Proto-Sogeram, and Proto-West Sogeram (PWS) added only the palatal affricates *c and *j, which are bolded in (10) below. There may also have been an innovation which changed PSOG *f > PWS *w, although it is unclear whether that change happened in Proto-West Sogeram or only in Nend (see §3.2.3.6).

(10) *p   *t   *k   *kʷ <kw>   *i   *ɨ   *u
              *tʃ <c>
     *ᵐp <b> *ⁿt <d>   *ᵑk <g> *ᵑkʷ <gw>   *a
              *ⁿtʃ <j>
     *β <v> *s
              *ⁿs
     *m   *n   *ɲ <ñ>   *ŋ
              *r

3.2.1.1 Word-initial consonant deletion

Word-initial consonants were lost from almost all polysyllabic words in Proto-West Sogeram, along with any following *ɨ. This change had a sweeping effect on the appearance of the lexicon, and affected all consonant types, including plosives (*takam 'vulva' > PWS *akam > Mand akam, Southern Nend aham; *faŋan 'bag' > PWS *aŋan > Mand, Nend aŋan), nasals (*mɨda [miⁿta] 'sword grass' > PWS *da > Mand ta, Nend nta), fricatives (*sɨgi [sɨᵑki] 'pot' > PWS *gi > Nend ncɨ), and glides (*yaka 'come up' > PWS *akai- > Mand akai-, Nend akay-).

Manat also participated in this change, albeit sporadically. However, the fact that the sound change is reflected several items of basic vocabulary makes it clear that it was an indigenous Manat change and not the result of borrowed vocabulary from Nend. Manat basic vocabulary items that lost initial consonants include *kɨñɨ- 'stay' > ñɨ-, *tadam 'leg' > adam, *yakw- 'go up' > aku, *kɨda 'walk' > da-, and many others.

The only consonant that appears to have been affected unusually is *ñ. Although initial *ñ appears to have been rare in Proto-Sogeram, a few correspondence sets shed light on its behavior. The 1.POSS form of the term for 'same-sex younger sibling,' *ñama, has retained the *ñ in Mand ñam, but changed it to n in Nend nam. Positing a subsequent *ñ > n development in Nend is problematic, because word-initial consonant loss created some instances of word-initial *ñ that are retained in Nend as ñ, such as *kɨñɨ- 'stay' > ñɨ-. It seems, then, that this change proceeded somewhat differently in two dialects of Proto-West Sogeram: in one, initial *ñ was simply retained; this state of affairs is retained in Mand. In the other, initial *ñ became *n at the same time as the loss of initial consonants; this state of affairs is retained in Nend.

As mentioned, this change did not affect monosyllabic words: *pam 'one' > PWS *pam > Mand vam, Nend pam; and *tɨm 'piece' > PWS *tɨm > Mand, Southern Nend tɨm. Verbs usually underwent this change even if they were monosyllabic, because they would often have occurred with suffixes that would make them polysyllabic. Thus *fai 'come' > PWS *ai- > Mand ai-, Nend ay-. But some very short

verbs, particularly those that could combine with common suffixes like *-in '1SG.
IPST' or *-i '3SG.IPST' and remain monosyllabic, kept their initial consonants:
*kra 'roast' > PWS *kra- > Mand, Nend kra-. One of these verbs also reflects the
changes to *ñ discussed above: *ña 'eat' > PWS *ña > Mand ja-, Nend na-.

3.2.1.2 Loss of final *a from prosodic units

The innovation I discuss in this section is not really a sound change, but its effect
on the lexicon of the Greater West Sogeram languages was similar enough to a
sound change that this is the most sensible place to discuss it. The development
is discussed in more detail in Daniels and Brooks (2019), but the general outline is
as follows. Proto-Greater West Sogeram borrowed an enclitic *=a from a neighboring, unrelated Ramu language, possibly an ancestor to Chini (see Brooks 2018).
This enclitic attached to the right edge of a prosodic unit and had two distinct
functions: one was as a linking morpheme that indicated the non-finality of
its utterance, and the other was as an exclamative marker on final utterances.
The linking function of this enclitic can be seen in the Mand (11), Nend (12), and
Manat (13) examples below.

    Mand

(11) Akac   kur   **ka-g=a,**   uhra~hɨr   vivi   cɨ-rd.
       intestine 3PL.POSS **FD-NOM=LNK** grow~NMPT pain be-FPST
       'Their guts would swell up and hurt.'

    Nend

(12) O-e-m   mɨra   **ikɲɨ-z=a**   nti   na-ma-r.
       go-SS-CONT pig   **shoot-3SG.DS=LNK** blood eat-HPST-3SG
       'He went and shot a pig and it drank the blood.'   (K. Harris n.d.)

    Manat

(13) Akai **ñɨŋ-ura-s~ñɨŋuras=a,** rum inɨ-b   inɨ-ba   da-ma-g.
       okay **stay-PL-3.DS~SIM=LNK** man ND-NOM ND-LOC walk-PST-3SG.FAR
       'While they were there, this man was wandering around here.'

Its exclamative function is shown in (14)–(16) below.

    Mand

(14) *Yo=a,*   *iku-ŋar-in=a.*
       yes=**EXCL** give-FUT-1SG=**EXCL**
       'Yes, I'll give (it to you).'

Nend

(15) **Caw=a,** ke-n w-in ha-n avizay-v.
brother.i.l=VOC FD-ACC see-1SG.IPST MD-ACC throw.towards-2SG.IMP
'Brother-in-law, throw the ones I see there here.' (K. Harris 1990: 98)

Manat

(16) **Manat=a amɨŋ=a,** ŋar-in **ai-s=a,**
no=EXCL mother.1.POSS=EXCL speak-2SG.DS **come-3SG.IMP=EXCL**
ara-ma-g.
say-pst-3SG.FAR
'"No way Mom! Tell it to come back!" he said.'

As a result of this borrowing event, Nend and Manat lost word-final *a, but only from those parts of speech that commonly occurred at the right edge of a prosodic unit. (Mand lost word-final *a from all words (§3.2.2.4), which may or may not be a related change.) This is a kind of what Round (2010) calls edge-aligned reconstruction, in which the existence of a unit in a proto-language—in this case, a prosodic unit—is inferred from observing sound changes that occurred at the edge of that unit. The reanalysis would have taken the following form: for any word that ended in *a and that occurred at the right edge of a prosodic unit, word-final *a was reanalyzed as the newly borrowed prosodic clitic. For example, the Proto-Greater West Sogeram 3SG pronoun *ba (< PSOG *nɨba '3SG.EMPH') was reanalyzed as *b=a '3SG=EXCL'. Once that reanalysis had taken place, speakers began to produce the "underlying" pronoun *bɨ, with an epenthetic *ɨ.

In Nend and Manat, word-final *a loss is seen in pronouns and verbs but generally not in nouns, adjectives, or adverbs. For example, the pronoun *nɨba [nɨᵐpa] '3SG.EMPH' yields Nend mbɨ '3SG.SBJ' and Manat bɨ '3SG.SBJ', and the 2SG prohibitive suffix *-ɨmɨ-na becomes Nend -mɨn and Manat -imin. However, the noun *abra [aᵐpra] 'place' becomes Nend ampɨra and Manat abra; the adjective *pɨta becomes Nend (yambɨ)ta and Manat vɨta; and the adverb paka 'only' becomes Manat vaca.

3.2.1.3 Palatalization of word-final *Ki

PSOG *ki and *gi were palatalized to c and j in Proto-West Sogeram when they were word-final. Three such sequences have survived into each language: *-pɨki 'paternal grandmother' > Mand -pic, Nend -pij; *-ñki 'paternal grandfather' > Mand -ca(ñ), Nend nca; *-ɨk-i '-DS.SEQ-3SG' > Mand -c 'DS'; and *sɨgi [sɨⁿki] 'pot' > Nend ncɨ. The forms for 'paternal grandfather' are somewhat problematic, as the reflex of *i is a, not †∅ or †ɨ as expected. The 'pot' form illustrates that this change followed word-initial consonant loss (§3.2.1.1), as palatalization would have rendered *sɨgi monosyllabic (ᶜsɨj) and would have blocked deletion of the *s.

It is possible that word-final *ti and *di behaved similarly: *naudi 'woman' > Mand *aca*, Nend *ancɨ*. But since this is the only such reflex that is retained in West Sogeram, we cannot be sure.

3.2.1.4 Word-initial plosive lenition in Manat and Apalɨ

This somewhat unusual change took place in Manat and Apalɨ. (In Manat, it can obviously only be seen in those words that did not undergo word-initial consonant loss; §3.2.1.1) In this change, the stops *p *t *k were lenited to *v *r *h [β ɾ/l ɣ] in word-initial position. Recall that PSOG *r did not occur word-initially, so this change did not affect any phonemic distinctions. It affected *p (*pat 'center' > Manat *vat*, *pubɨŋ 'sweat' > Apalɨ *vubɨŋ*), *t (*tɨbu 'tie' > Manat *rɨbu-*, Apalɨ *lɨbu-*), and *k (*kɨmu 'die' > Manat *hɨmu-*, Apalɨ *hɨma-*). In Apalɨ initial PSOG *kw gives initial *hu*, as in *kwɨmka 'stomach' > *humɨgaŋ*. There are no Proto-Sogeram reconstructions that begin with *kw and have Manat reflexes that have not lost their initial consonant (like *kwɨgɨs 'armpit' > *gɨsɨ*).

3.2.2 Mand innovations

The Mand phoneme inventory is presented in (17). Mand has added a voiceless fricative *f* and voiced fricatives *z*, *h* [ɣ], and *hw* [ɣʷ] (PSOG *f [ɸ] is retained as *v* [β]). It has also added mid vowels, including possibly a mid central ə.

(17)	p	t		k	kʷ \<kw\>		i	ɨ	u
			tʃ \<c\>				e	(ə)	o
	ᵐb \<b\>	ⁿd \<d\>		ᵑg \<g\>	ᵑgʷ \<gw\>			a	
			ⁿdʒ \<j\>						
	ɸ \<f\>	s							
	β \<v\>		ʒ \<z\>	ɣ \<h\>	ɣʷ \<hw\>				
	m	n	ɲ \<ñ\>	ŋ					
		ɾ \<r\>							
	w		j \<y\>						

The prenasalized stops were created by nasal fortition (§3.2.2.5), which also created the prenasalized affricate *j* by fortition of PSOG *ñ. It is unclear how *f* arose; it is very rare in Mand, and none of my Proto-Sogeram cognate sets contain it. The alveopalatal fricative *z* arose via fortition of *y (§3.2.2.6). The velar fricatives were formed by lenition of *k and *kw (§3.2.2.1) as well as from word-final *ŋ (§3.2.2.5). The schwa was created as a non-initial allophone of *a, and may still be best considered an allophone. But loanwords with non-initial [a] have complicated matters, and ə could also be considered a separate phoneme today.

3.2.2.1 Sporadic *k and *kw lenition

Some word-medial instances of *k and *kw were lenited to h [ɣ]. This change appears to have been sporadic, although it affected every instance of these consonants before *r (for example, *kikra 'watch' > ihra [iɣra], *akwra 'carry' > ahwro [aɣʷro] 'take away'). But it also affected some reflexes without a following *r (*-kun 'co-wife' > -(i)hun 'sister-in-law,' *-muk 'brother of female ego > -(i)moh), although it did not affect every such reflex (*kwaka 'cut, chop' > aka-, *yaka 'come up' > akai-). In fact, one word exhibits synchronic variation: during my fieldwork, I recorded 'chicken' as both ikɨkar and ikɨhar.

The fact that this change never affects a k that is a reflex of a Proto-West Sogeram prenasalized stop suggests that it preceded stop denasalization: *igɨn [iⁿkɨn] 'ground possum' > (bor)ikɨn, *magra [maⁿkra] 'pull' > akra- 'fish with a net,' not †ahra- (although the semantic innovation in the second form makes it less than perfectly reliable, and it is the only example of a PSOG *gr sequence with a Mand reflex).

3.2.2.2 Stop denasalization

The Proto-Sogeram and Proto-West Sogeram voiceless prenasalized stops lost their prenasalization in Mand, yielding plain voiceless stops. This applied to all places of articulation regardless of environment: bilabial (*kayabra [kajaᵐpra] 'village' > azapɨr), alveolar (*kɨdɨr [kɨⁿtɨr] 'root' > tɨr), velar (*tɨgɨñ [tɨⁿkɨɲ] 'black' > kiñ), and labiovelar (*igwa [iⁿkʷa] 'give' > ikw-). Even in words where Nend exhibits an irregularly voiced form, such as nda- 'walk' (< *kɨda [kɨⁿta]), Mand consistently has a voiceless stop: ta- 'walk'.

It is unclear how this change affected non-homorganic clusters of nasal and stop. It seems, for example, that *mk was retained (*-mku 'nephew, niece' > ñamku 'female ego's brother's child'), but that *ñk gave c (*-ñki 'paternal grandfather' > -ca), presumably after perseverative place assimilation palatalized the *k (cf. Nend nca 'grandfather'). But these are only single examples, not consistent patterns in the lexicon, so we cannot yet make firm generalizations.

3.2.2.3 *a-centering

Mand occasionally centered *a to ɨ when it occurred in the middle of a longer word. Because most reconstructed words are only one or two syllables, this change only applied to three forms: *apapara 'butterfly' > *apɨpar*, *ikakara 'chicken' > *ikɨkar*, and *kukasa 'frog' > *ukɨs*. The last of these forms suggests this change took place before word-final *a-loss, as the pre-Mand form *ukas probably would not have undergone this change.

It is worth noting that two forms which appear to match the criteria for undergoing this change did not: *kayabra 'village' > *azapɨr*, and PGWS *akwasa 'betelnut' > *ahwas*. Further research into the stress systems of the Sogeram languages might reveal a consistent pattern.

3.2.2.4 Word-final *a loss

Mand lost most instances of word-final *a. When the preceding segments were a vowel plus a sonorant or sibilant, the *a was simply lost, as in *ñama 'same-sex younger sibling (1.POSS)' > *ñam*, and PGWS *akwasa 'betelnut' > *ahwas*. When the *a followed a single segment, it became ɨ, as in *ña 'son' > *ñɨ*. This also happened when the preceding consonant was a plosive: *maga [maᵑka] 'egg' > *akɨ*. There are a few exceptions to this change, such as *mɨda [mɨⁿta] 'sword grass' > *ta*, *kia 'speech' > *ya*, and *kuza [kuⁿsa] 'yam' > *usa* 'taro'. A possible motivation for this change—the borrowing of a pragmatic enclitic from neighboring Ramu languages—is discussed in Daniels and Brooks (2019).

3.2.2.5 Nasal fortition and final *ŋ > h

Many nasals became prenasalized stops in Mand. This change was regular, and affected nasals at all points of articulation: bilabial (*tama 'put' > PWS *ama- > *aba-* [aᵐba]), alveolar (*ina 'sun' > *ida* [iⁿda]), palatal (*ña 'eat' > *ja-* [ⁿdʒa]), and velar (*miŋra 'vomit' > *igra-* [iᵑgra]). It did not affect word-final nasals, so *uram 'house' > *uram*, and *mazɨn 'bowstring' > *asɨn*. When a word-final nasal was present, the change also did not affect any preceding nasals, so *aman 'breast' > *aman* and *faŋan 'bag' > *aŋan*. This patterning created a few suppletive alternations in the lexicon when certain verb suffixes allowed nasal fortition and others blocked it. For example, *kɨmu 'die' > PWS *ma- (with change of verb class) > *bɨ-*, but this verb has retained the root *ma-* with the adjunctivizing suffix -m: *ma-m*. Similarly, *kɨñɨ- 'stay' > PWS *ñɨ- > *jɨ-*, but this verb now has an irregular reduplicated nominalizer/participle *ñɨ~ñ*. This pattern is also visible in one tense suffix, the middle past. This suffix was *-iamɨ > PWS *-emɨ, with the coalescence of *ia > *e*. With the 2SG person agreement suffix -n (< *-na), the suffix remains -*emɨ-n*. But with the 3SG suffix -*i* (< *-i), *-emɨ underwent fortition to become -*eb-i*.

Nasal fortition followed word-final *a-loss, because nasals that were rendered final by that change did not become stops. This is illustrated by the patterning of the 2SG agreement suffix above, as well as by forms like *ñama 'same-sex younger sibling (1.POSS)' > ñam, not ⁺jab or ⁺jabɨ. Note that the behavior of the monosyllabic form *ña 'son' > ñɨ suggests that the final ɨ, created by word-final *a loss (§3.2.2.4), was not phonemic when nasal fortition took place because the ñ did not become ⁺j.

A related change is the fricativization of word-final *ŋ > h [ɣ]. This also appears to have been regular: *abɨŋ 'wing' > apɨh, *kazɨŋ 'festival decoration' > asɨh, and *pubɨŋ 'sweat' > upɨh. However, one would expect this change to either bleed or feed nasal fortition: if this change came first, preceding nasals in a word-final *NVŋ sequence would become stops, while if this change came later, preceding nasals would remain nasals. Unfortunately, the corpus of reconstructed Proto-Sogeram forms only contains two words that contain such a sequence and have reflexes in Mand, and they contradict each other. The first is *kinaŋ 'axe' > idaŋ 'bamboo,' which is semantically problematic, and the second is *nɨ-mɨŋ '3SG.POSS-mother' > mɨŋ. These two forms are not sufficient evidence for any analysis.

3.2.2.6 Glide fortition

The Proto-West Sogeram glides *y and *w, possibly allophones of *i and *u, became the voiced fricatives z and v in Mand. These changes were fairly regular, and affected most instances of these sounds in onset position. Thus *kayabra 'village' > azapɨr, *kui 'shoot, pierce' > PWS *uyɨ- > uz-, and *kuar 'garden' > PWS *war > var. A few instances of *i did not change (*kia > PWS *ya > ya, *muyam > PWS *uyam > uyam), suggesting that this sound change was not completely regular. But the only instance of *w that did not undergo the change to v can be accounted for by pointing out that it was *u in Proto-Sogeram, and could still have been *u when this change took place (*wa 'go' > wa-). It should be mentioned that this change may have interacted with the change *f > *w (§3.2.3.6), which is reflected in Nend forms like wan 'father' (< *-fan), because it is possible that *f > *w actually took place in Proto-West Sogeram, not Nend. It may just as easily have taken place only in Nend, though, so it is unclear whether PSOG *f became PWS *w and then became Mand *v again or not. In any case, it is clear that glides that were formed by Proto-West Sogeram word-initial consonant loss (§3.2.1.1), such as *kuar 'garden' > PWS *war > Mand var, were also strengthened to v.

3.2.3 Nend innovations

The Nend phoneme inventory is presented in (18) below. The Nend inventory is very similar to that of Mand, differing only in that Nend lacks f and ə, and that

Nend *z* is alveolar, not alveopalatal. Phonemes that have been innovated since Proto-West Sogeram are shown in bold.

(18)

p	t		k	kʷ <kw>	i	ɨ	u
		tʃ <c>			e		o
ᵐb <mb>	ⁿd <nd>		ᵑg <ng>	ᵑgʷ <ngw>		a	
		ⁿdʒ <j>					
	s						
β <v>	z		ɣ <h>	ɣʷ <hw>			
m	n	ɲ <ñ>	ŋ				
	ɾ <r>						
w		j <y>					

Nend voiced some of the Proto-Sogeram prenasalized stops (§3.2.3.1), creating voiced prenasalized stops. Some prenasalized stops remained voiceless, though, and Harris (1990) analyzes these as consonant clusters. The voicing change also produced the voiced fricatives *v*, *h* [ɣ], and *hw* [ɣʷ], as well as more tokens of *r*, from oral stops. More tokens of *c* were created by palatalization of *s before *i, as suggested by *isi 'fetch water' > *ici̵-*. The mid vowels were created by a process of harmony triggered by a nearby *a (§3.2.3.5). The voiced alveolar fricative *z* was created by apparently irregular voicing of *s, primarily in the Northern dialect.

The dialect situation in Nend appears to be complex, and the fact that I have data from different villages complicates analysis. I conducted research in the southern village of Kwaringri, but Kyle Harris, whose data I use considerably, was based in the northern village of Pasinkap. My analysis is based primarily on Harris's northern data, of which I have more, but I note the use of southern forms, and possible phonological differences between the two dialects, where appropriate.

3.2.3.1 Plosive voicing

Nend underwent a sporadic plosive voicing process. In this change, voiceless oral stops (*p *t *k *kw) became voiced fricatives (*v r h hw* [β ɾ ɣ ɣʷ]), and voiceless prenasalized stops became voiced. This voicing change happened intervocalically, but not before *i̵, only *i, *a, and *u. Thus *takam 'vulva' > *aham* [aɣam] and *tadam [taⁿtam] 'leg' > *andam*, but *tuti̵m 'salt' > *uti̵m* and *madi̵n [maⁿti̵n] 'side' > *anti̵n*. This change affected labiovelars as well: *igwa [iⁿkʷa] 'give' > Northern *eŋgwa-*, Southern *iŋgwa-* and PGWS *akwasa 'betelnut' > Southern *ahwas*. As stated, however, this change was sporadic, and sometimes plosives did not voice even though they occurred in the triggering environment: *kapa 'bird' > *apa* and *tagwa [taⁿkʷa] 'step on' > *aŋkwa-*.

3.2.3.2 Word-final *i loss

Nend lost most reflexes of word-final *i. This loss often resulted in a syllabic resonant, such as the syllabic *r* in *imɨr* 'cold' (< *kɨmri), and it did not affect *i when it was preceded by a vowel: *sakai 'bamboo' > *ahai*. Final *i-loss followed plosive voicing (§3.2.3.1), as evidenced by *upri 'dog' > Southern *ovɨr*, not †*opɨr*, and by *kakri 'axe' > *kahɨr*, not †*kakɨr*.

3.2.3.3 Word-final *n-rhotacization

Word-finally, many instances of PWS *n became *r* in Nend. This change may also have affected other alveolar consonants, as there is one example of final *d (*ibɨd [iᵐpɨⁿt] 'good' > *imbɨr*) that appears to have undergone this change. (But it should be noted that the voicing of the *b [ᵐp] suggests this form was borrowed from Manat *ibɨd* 'good') This change was blocked if the preceding consonant was a nasal, so *kuman 'arm, hand' > *oman* and *faŋan 'bag' > *aŋan*. Otherwise, it is reflected in only two Proto-Sogeram reflexes (*igɨn 'ground possum' > *iŋkɨr* and *mɨgɨn 'penis' > *ŋgɨr*), but is reflected fairly consistently in multiple West Sogeram correspondences (such as PWS *uban 'top' > Mand *upan*, Nend *ompar* and PWS *in 'now, today' > Mand *in*, Nend *ɨr*).

3.2.3.4 Sporadic word-initial *a loss

There are a few correspondence sets in which Nend lost initial *a, although this change appears to have been quite infrequent. Thus *ataŋ 'far' > *taŋ(opɨr)* and *amɨr 'yesterday' > *mɨr*, but *apar 'mountain' > *apar*. There are no examples of an *a being lost after West Sogeram word-initial consonant deletion, but this is probably only because of the rarity of word-initial *a-loss.

3.2.3.5 Sporadic vowel harmony

Several instances of *i and *u were lowered to *e* and *o* in Nend when they preceded an *a. Thus *ika 'cut, chop' > *eka-*, *mira 'firelight' > *era*, *kuman 'arm, hand' > *oman*, and *uram 'house' > *oram*. This change is distributed unevenly through the Nend dialect area. For example, Northern Nend has *eŋgwa-* 'give' (< *igwa [iⁿkʷa]), while Southern Nend has *iŋgwa-*. But both varieties have un-harmonized *unsa* 'yam' (< *kuza [kuⁿsa]) as well as harmonized *oyam* 'cassowary' (< *muyam). It appears that the change is more common in the north, but that it is not fully regular anywhere.

3.2.3.6 *f lenition

The Proto-Sogeram fricative *f [ɸ] probably became a glide *w in Nend. This analysis is rather tentative, as the change is only reflected in one Nend form today

(*-fan 'father' > Nend *wan*), and suggested by another (*mafra 'crocodile' > Pre-Nend *mawr > *mor*). The change may in fact be reflected only in Northern Nend; I collected a Southern form *irivir* 'straight' (< *sirifir) that may indicate that *f is retained as *v* in Southern Nend, although this form is problematic. The paucity of Nend reflexes appears to be a result of the rarity of this phoneme in Proto-Sogeram, and the fact that it frequently occurred word-initially and was thus deleted from many forms (§3.2.1.1).

It should also be noted that it is equally possible that this change took place in Proto-West Sogeram, as it is clear that Mand underwent a glide fortition change of its own that changed *w > *v* (§3.2.2.6). At present, there is little to indicate which analysis should be preferred, as they both posit the same number and type of changes; the only difference is whether *f > *w happened in Proto-West Sogeram or Nend.

3.2.4 Manat innovations

The phoneme inventory of Manat is presented in (19).

(19)
p	t		k		i	ɨ	u
		tʃ <c>				e	
ᵐb <b>	ⁿd <d>		ᵑg <g>				a
	s						
β <v>			ɣ <h>				
	ⁿz <z>						
m	n	ɲ <ñ>	ŋ				
	ɾ <r>						

Manat has voiced the Proto-Sogeram prenasalized stops and *f, and also added *h* [ɣ]—and merged many instances of *p with *f and *t with *r—via word-initial lenition, which it shared with Apalɨ (§3.2.1.4). It also added *c*, although it is unclear how since the phoneme does not occur in any cognate sets except *paka 'only' > *vaca* 'one,' which probably reflects an irregular development. Manat also has *e*, although it is a very rare vowel in the language and it is also unclear how it arose. It does not appear to have come from PSOG *ai, which is regularly retained as *ai* (*fai 'come' > *ai-*, *umai 'bean' > *mai*).

3.2.4.1 Sporadic word-initial vowel loss with *u metathesis
This is a change that Manat appears to be currently undergoing. Often a word will be pronounced differently from speech act to speech act, sometimes eliding

the initial vowel, and sometimes retaining it. The change appears to have progressed somewhat in the last fifty years, as Z'graggen (1980a) transcribed many word-initial vowels that had disappeared by the time I conducted my fieldwork. However, the variation clearly existed when he collected his wordlist, since he transcribed *ubram* 'arm, hand' as *brʌm*, a pronunciation that I also heard far more often than *ubram*. This change may be facilitated by the prevalence of word-final stress in Manat.

In cases where the vowel being lost was *u, the *u would sometimes metathesize with the following consonant and become a *w*, as in *kukasa 'frog' > *ukasa > kwasa. I also observed this variation in a few synchronic forms (such as *utaya ~ twaya* 'cockatoo' and *uzam ~ zwam* 'father's sister (1.POSS)'). The metathesized *w* may have replaced *ɨ, as seems to have happened in *mukɨr 'white hair' > kur(umɨn).

This change clearly follows word-initial plosive lenition. This can be inferred because the latter is an old change, being shared with Apalɨ, while the former is currently underway. But the inference is also supported by the data, since plosives that are rendered word-initial by vowel loss are not lenited: *ipra 'hide' > pra(vu)-, *kukasa 'frog' > kwasa.

3.2.5 Apalɨ innovations

The Apalɨ phoneme inventory is presented in (20).

(20)

p	t		k		i	ɨ	u
		tʃ <c>			e		o
ᵐb <b>	ⁿd <d>		ᵑg <g>			a	
		ⁿdʒ <j>					
ɸ <f>	s						
β <v>			ɣ <h>				
m	n		ŋ				
	ɾ <l>						

Apalɨ retains the Proto-Sogeram series of voiceless stops, adding a voiceless affricate *c* by palatalizing *k and *s (§3.2.5.3). It also turned the prenasalized fricative *z into a prenasalized affricate *j* (§3.2.5.7), although it also created some tokens of *j* by affrication of other consonants. Apalɨ added a contrast between voiceless *f* [ɸ] and voiced *v* [β] by devoicing some medial tokens of *f (§3.2.5.5). Some tokens of medial *f remained [β], while others were created, along with tokens of *r* and the new phoneme *h* [ɣ], by word-initial (§3.2.1.4) and word-medial (§3.2.5.5) lenition.

Apalɨ lost *ñ [ɲ], merging it with *n (§3.2.5.2) and creating some tokens of the new vowel *e* in the process. More tokens of *e* were also created from the sequence *ai (§3.2.5.6). The vowel *o* is extremely rare, and may not be native to Apalɨ (Martha Wade p.c.).

Apalɨ has two quite divergent dialects, named after their words for 'what': Akɨ and Acɨ. The latter appears to be more closely related to the North Sogeram languages, and Wade has suggested that Apalɨ was formed by the convergence of these two lects, rather than by the divergence of a putative Proto-Apalɨ (Wade 1993). This suggestion comports with a lot of the data, as Acɨ forms often reflect North Sogeram developments which Akɨ forms do not. Acɨ is also interesting in that /c/ and /j/ are realized phonetically as dental stops in that dialect, although the phonemic system appears to be largely the same (Martha Wade p.c.). Where relevant, I point out which dialect a particular form is from, although since Wade works primarily with the Akɨ dialect, I primarily focus on it. There has also been extensive inter-dialect borrowing and many forms, particularly for basic vocabulary, are the same in both dialects.

3.2.5.1 Word-final nasal velarization

Most word-final nasals in Apalɨ were changed to *ŋ*, so that this is now by far the most common word-final nasal. This change affected *m (*muyam 'cassowary' > muiaŋ), *n (*tamkan 'eye' > lamɨgaŋ), and *ñ (*kasɨñ 'sand' > hacɨŋ). However, it also occasionally left the nasals *m and *n unaffected, as in *tutɨm 'salt' > lulɨm and *iman 'louse' > iman. There are no examples of final *ñ failing to undergo velarization, which suggests this change may have affected this consonant regularly before *ñ > n (§3.2.5.2), but after the fronting of vowels preceding *ñ.

However regular this change was, it created many instances of word-final *ŋ*, such that this consonant was so common word finally that it has often been inserted, presumably by analogy, into words that did not originally have it. Wade (p.c.) remarks that "there is often variation between the two main dialects on the presence and absence of /ŋ/, and sometimes within a dialect there is disagreement about it," and there are numerous examples of spontaneous *ŋ*-genesis, such as *kia 'speech' > ciaŋ, *kamɨŋawa 'millipede' > hamɨŋauaŋ, and *kapa 'bird' > havaŋ. Compare these forms to the West Sogeram reflexes, where word-final nasals are generally unaffected: Mand, Nend *ya* 'speech,' Mand *amɨŋau* 'millipede,' and Nend *apa* 'bird'.

3.2.5.2 Merger of *ñ and *n

Apalɨ lost the palatal nasal, changing it to an alveolar one as in *ña 'eat' > na-. Before the distinction was lost, however, *ñ often fronted a preceding vowel, either *a > e (*kañaŋ 'bone' > henaŋ) or *ɨ > i (*sumɨñ 'vine' > sumiŋ). Word-final examples like this last one demonstrate that this vowel fronting took place before word-final nasal velarization (§3.2.5.1).

3.2.5.3 Palatalization of *k and *s

PSoG *k and *g [ⁿk] were palatalized to c [tʃ] and j [ⁿdʒ] before *i, as in *kinaŋ 'axe' > Acɨ cinan, *kia 'speech' > ciaŋ, and *sɨgi 'pot' > siji. This change appears to have affected both dialects equally—or at least, innovative forms do not appear to be predominant in one dialect today—which raises the question of how it interacted with word-initial (§3.2.1.4) and word-medial (§3.2.5.5) lenition of *k > h. It is also worth mentioning that a similar change has happened in Sirva, although in that language [tʃ] and [ⁿdʒ] remain allophones of /k/ and /g/ before /i/.

Another innovation that appears to have happened with much less regularity is the palatalization of *s > c, which sometimes took place before *i (*sikɨñ 'three days away' > cihen) and sometimes before *ɨ (*kasɨñ 'sand' > hacin). Note that both of these forms also contained other palatal consonants, which is common, although not universal, among words that undergo this change. The innovation appears to have originated in the Acɨ dialect, as shown in the variation in words for 'navel': *sibirɨm > Akɨ sibilim, Acɨ cibilim.

3.2.5.4 Epenthesis and paragoge

Apalɨ has inserted epenthetic ɨ to break up every consonant cluster. Thus, *abra 'place' > abɨla, *kaŋra- 'run' > haŋɨla-, and *kukra- 'grow' > huhɨla-. It also paragogically added ɨ after every word-final non-nasal coda: *kɨsar 'spear' > hisalɨ, *mukɨr 'white hair' > muhɨlɨ.

Sometimes, the paragogic vowel was i instead of ɨ, although this was not very common: *amɨr 'yesterday' > amili 'one day away,' *tar 'tree' > lali, *fɨr 'ground, land' > fili.

3.2.5.5 Plosive voicing and *[β] > f

After epenthetic and paragogic insertion of ɨ, the Akɨ dialect of Apalɨ lenited all intervocalic stops—that is to say, all non-word-initial stops. In combination with the word-initial lenition that took place in Apalɨ and Manat (§3.2.1.4), this change had the effect of voicing every voiceless stop in Akɨ. And indeed, Wade states that in Akɨ, voiceless stops "are so infrequent that they could have been imported into the phonology from another language" (1993: 79).

How *f interacted with this change is unclear. Clearly some word-medial instances of *f, articulated as *[β], underwent devoicing to f [ɸ], which preserved the phonemic contrast between erstwhile *f and *p: *kɨfɨr 'night' > *hifɨlɨ* and *ifu 'hit, kill' > *ifa-*. But others did not, such as *ufia 'evening star' > *uvia* and *ya-fan '1.POSS-father' > *iavaŋ*. There has probably been a good deal of inter-dialect borrowing as well as irregular phonetic change, and the interplay between these factors has rendered analysis difficult.

3.2.5.6 *ai > e

Apalɨ simplified the sequence *ai > e in almost all environments. When *ai was split between two syllables this change did not take place: *kayabra 'village' > *haiabɨla*. Otherwise, this change was regular, although PSOG *ai has not been reconstructed in closed syllables: *kusai 'first' > *huse*, *nabai 'daughter-in-law (1.POSS)' > *nabe*, *umai 'bean' > *ume*.

3.2.5.7 Palatalization of *z in Apalɨ and possibly Mum

There are a few cognate sets that suggest Apalɨ and Mum palatalized PSOG *z [ⁿs] to *j* [ⁿdʒ]. These are *kuza 'yam' > Apalɨ *huja*, Mum *kuja*; *kazɨŋ 'festival decoration' > Apalɨ *hajɨŋ*; and *puzɨŋ 'bone' > Mum *puj*. But note that the palatal pronunciation of these sounds in Mum was recorded during my own fieldwork, and that Sweeney transcribes them with <z>, suggesting the dialect or speaker he was working with did not reflect this change. For example, his reflex of *kazɨŋ 'festival decoration' is *kaz*.

3.3 The North Sogeram languages

The North Sogeram (NS) languages are Mum and Sirva. These languages share several innovations, and also share some with other languages. The voicing of prenasalized obstruents is reflected in all non-West Sogeram languages (§3.3.1.1, §3.4.1.1); the loss of the labiovelars is shared with Manat and Apalɨ (§3.3.1.2); and word-final nasal loss (§3.3.1.3) and *u fortition (§3.3.1.4) are shared with Manat.

3.3.1 Broader innovations

In this section I discuss those innovations that Proto-North Sogeram (PNS) shared with other languages, beginning with the most broadly reflected sound change in the family: the voicing of prenasalized obstruents.

3.3.1.1 Voicing of prenasalized stops and *z

The Proto-Sogeram voiceless prenasalized consonants became voiced in all languages except Mand and Nend. This innovation was shared with Proto-East Sogeram (§3.4.1.1). This took place with *b [ᵐp] (*ibi 'name' > Apalɨ *ibi* [iᵐbi], Mum *ñibi* [ɲiᵐbi], Sirva *ib* [iᵐb]), *d [ⁿt] (*kɨda 'walk' > Manat *da-* [ⁿda], Apalɨ *hɨda-* [ɣɨⁿda], Mum, Sirva *kɨda-* [kɨⁿda]), *g [ᵑk] (*mɨga 'come down' > Manat, Apalɨ, Mum, Sirva *mɨga-* [mɨᵑga]), and *gw [ᵑkʷ] (*igw- 'give' > Manat, Apalɨ *igu-* [iᵑgu], Mum, Sirva *gu-* [ᵑgu]). It took place regardless of the nature of the surrounding vowels, and also when the stop was part of a larger consonant cluster (*kugra 'cook' > Apalɨ *hugɨla-* [ɣuᵑgɨra], Mum *kugra-* [kuᵑgra], Sirva *kwagra-* [kwaᵑgra]).

The voiceless prenasalized fricative *z [ⁿs] underwent a similar change, becoming a voiced prenasalized fricative: *kuza 'yam' > Manat *huza* [ɣuⁿza] 'kind of yam,' Apalɨ *huja* [ɣuⁿdʒa], Mum *kuja* [kuⁿdʒa]; *puzɨŋ 'bone' > Mum *puj* [puⁿdʒ], Sirva *puzu* [puⁿzu].

Voiceless stops in non-homorganic clusters of nasal and stop were also voiced in what was probably part of the same development. These stops retained their original place of articulation, and an epenthetic *ɨ was later inserted in some circumstances to break up the cluster. So *tamkan 'eye' > Manat *amiga*, Apalɨ *lamɨgaŋ*, Mum *tamga*; *-mku 'nephew, niece' > Mum *-mɨgw*, Sirva *-mugu*.

3.3.1.2 Labiovelar loss

The Proto-Sogeram labiovelar stops *kw and *gw were lost as unit phonemes in Manat, Apalɨ, and Proto-North Sogeram, becoming a sequence of velar stop and *u. So *igwa 'give' > Sirva *gwa-*, *yakwa 'go up' > Apalɨ *iahua*. (Recall that *u had a consonantal allophone *[w] that became a phoneme in some languages.) When the following vowel was *ɨ, it was lost and the newly created *u became the new nucleus of the syllable: *kwɨgɨs 'armpit' > Apalɨ *huji*, Mum *kugɨs*, Sirva *kugus*; *tɨkwɨ 'area under' > Apalɨ *lɨhu*, Mum *tuhw*, Sirva *tuhu*. For this reason verb-final labiovelars usually became sequences of velar plus *u in bound forms of verb roots, as with the two examples cited above: the bound form of *igwa 'give' was *igw- > Manat, Apalɨ *igu-*, Mum, Sirva *gu-*. Similarly *yakw- > Mum *yahu-*. When the vowel following the labiovelar was *a, it was sometimes lost (*mirkwa 'cordyline' > Apalɨ *milɨhu*) and sometimes retained (*kwaka 'cut, chop > Sirva *kwaha-*).

3.3.1.3 Word-final nasal deletion with ɨ-deletion in Manat, Mum, and Sirva

This change probably originated in Proto-North Sogeram and spread to Manat as well as Proto-East Sogeram (§3.4.1.2). In Mum and Sirva, word-final nasals—and also resonants (§3.3.2.3)—are consistently lost. The only exceptions appear to be short monosyllables like *pɨm 'weight' (> Mum *pɨm* 'heavy') and *tam 'tail'

(> Sirva *tam*). Otherwise, word-final nasals were all lost, including *m (*muyam 'cassowary' > Mum, Sirva *muya*), *n (*faŋan 'bag' > Mum, Sirva *paŋa*), *ñ [ɲ] (*kasiñ 'sand' > Mum, Sirva *kas*), and *ŋ (*mikuŋ 'brain' > Mum *miku* 'head,' Sirva *miku*). The process did not apply recursively: *maniŋ 'banana' > Mum, Sirva *man*.

In Manat, it appears to have primarily affected the non-labial nasals *n (*tamkan 'eye' > *amiga*), *ñ [ɲ] (*kasiñ 'sand' > *has*), and *ŋ (*kaziŋ > *azɨ*), while *m was usually retained (*tadam 'foot, leg' > *adam*, *sagam 'fight' > *agam*). However, sometimes non-labial nasals also remained unaffected (*migin 'penis' > *migin*, *-min 'mother' > *-min*) and sometimes *m was lost (*mɨrɨm 'sap' > *mɨr* > *mɨrmɨr*).

As the examples above illustrate, the deletion of a final nasal was accompanied by the deletion of any preceding *ɨ. (The final ɨ in Manat *azɨ* 'festival decoration' [< *kaziŋ] was probably added later; cf. *kwɨŋkɨs 'armpit' > *gɨsɨ*.)

3.3.1.4 *w fortition in Manat, Mum, and Sirva

The glide *w became *v [β] in these languages, as illustrated by *ir wara 'exceed' > Sirva *irvara-*; *waka 'maybe' > Sirva *vaha*, and *wa 'go, say' > Manat *vu-*, Mum, Sirva *va-* 'say'.

Two forms suggest that the epenthetic *[w] that sometimes followed *u before *a also became *v, while the *u became *ɨ. Recall that the sequence *ua was sometimes pronounced with an epenthetic *[w] as *[u.wa], which means that this change involved two changes: the centering of the *u to *ɨ, and the fortition of the epenthetic *[w] to *v. The two forms in question are *kuar 'garden' > *kɨvar > Manat *var*, Mum, Sirva *kɨva*; and *tua 'burn (intr.)' > Manat *rɨva-*.

This change had the effect of merging word-medial *w and *f as *[β]. But recall that *f had the word-initial allophone *[ɸ], so the distinction between *w and *f was preserved word-initially in these languages (as reflected in Sirva, for example, by *faga 'leaf' > *paga* and *waka 'maybe' > *vaha* 'when').

3.3.2 North Sogeram innovations

Mum and Sirva have undergone several sound changes together and form a relatively distinct subgroup apart from the other Sogeram languages. These were the loss of *ɨ at word boundaries, plosive lenition, *f fortition, *au fortition, and word-final resonant deletion. The last of these may have spread to Manat (§3.3.1.3) and East Sogeram (§3.4.1.2) as word-final nasal deletion, but two features suggest that it applied differently to Mum and Sirva than these other groups. First, it applied much more regularly in North Sogeram than elsewhere, and second, in North Sogeram this change also deleted word-final *r, which is why I term it word-final resonant deletion. (Alternatively, these may simply have been two separate changes: a nasal deletion rule that spread outside of North Sogeram, and an *r deletion rule that did not.)

Two of the other changes, *i-loss (§3.3.2.4) and plosive lenition (§3.3.2.5), show unusual patterns of inheritance into the two North Sogeram languages: sometimes Mum reflects a change while Sirva does not, sometimes vice versa, sometimes both languages reflect it, and sometimes neither does. These patterns are difficult to explain, but suggest that later in its history, Proto-North Sogeram formed a rather diffuse dialect network, and that these changes moved geographically through the speech community, as well as through the lexicon, irregularly. This patchwork of isoglosses means that sound changes cannot easily be assigned to one language (or Proto-North Sogeram dialect). The situation is clearly quite complex, and calls for further investigation. It does suggest, however, that those changes that are consistently reflected in both Mum and Sirva preceded these irregular changes, since they probably took place before Proto-North Sogeram became such a diffuse dialect network.

The Proto-North Sogeram phoneme inventory is shown in (21). Proto-North Sogeram voiced the Proto-Sogeram prenasalized stops and *z [ⁿs], but this did not have a structural impact on the phoeneme inventory. It also lost the labiovelar place of articulation, and added the voiced fricative *h [ɣ], which was created from *k via an irregular lenition process (§3.3.2.5). It merged the initial allophone of *f [ɸ] with *p (§3.3.2.1), leaving only voiced *v [β]. Proto-North Sogeram may also have had a mid front vowel *e, but this is only reflected in one cognate set: *karif 'flying fox' > PNS *ḳarev > Mum, Sirva karev. It is unclear how to interpret this set, so for now I only posit *e to Proto-North Sogeram tentatively.

(21) *p   *t   *k   *i   *ɨ   *u
     *ᵐb <b>   *ⁿd <d>   *ᵑg <g>   (*e)
               *s   *a
     *β <v>   *ɣ <h>
               *ⁿz <z>
     *m   *n   *ɲ <ñ>   *ŋ
               *ɾ <r>

3.3.2.1 Word-initial *f fortition

Word-initially, *f [ɸ] became *p. Examples of this change include *fai- 'come' > PNS *pai- > Mum pai-, Sirva pi-; *fika 'slice, cut' > Mum, Sirva piha-; *fri- 'scratch' >

Mum *prɨ*-; and *fɨr 'land' > Mum *pɨr*. Word-medially, *f remained *[β], orthographically *v: *-fan 'father' > Mum, Sirva -*va*; *ifu 'hit, kill' > Mum *yɨvu*-. Word-finally, it vocalized to *u in one form (*af 'fire' > PNS *au > Mum *ahu/awu*,[12] Sirva *au*) and remained *v in another (*karif 'flying fox' > Mum, Sirva *karev*).

3.3.2.2 *u fortition
The *u in the sequence *au appears to have become *v in Proto-North Sogeram. While PSOG *au was fairly rare, this change is reflected in every instance that has a North Sogeram reflex, suggesting it was regular: *naudi 'woman' > Mum *navudi*; *kaura 'loincloth' > Sirva *kavɨr*; and *tauka 'buy' > Mum *tavha*-, Sirva *tavɨha*-. The vowel following *v* in these examples, either *u*, *ɨ*, or nothing, may reflect inconsistent transcription, sporadic change, or differing developments in as yet undetermined phonological environments.

3.3.2.3 Word-final *r deletion
Word-final resonants were lost from Mum and Sirva. The deletion of nasals was discussed in §3.3.1.3, but in the North Sogeram languages *r was also lost, as in *amur > Mum, Sirva *amu* and *kuar 'garden' > Mum, Sirva *kɨva*. As with nasal deletion, monosyllabic words appear to have been exempt from this process: *mir 'tongue' > Mum, Sirva *mir*, *tar 'tree' > Sirva *tar*. Syllabic *r (i.e., a final *ɨr sequence) was completely lost when preceded by a nasal (*amɨr 'yesterday' > Mum *am*), but it left a *ɨ* behind when preceded by an obstruent (*kɨfɨr 'night' > Mum *kɨvɨ*; *kɨdɨr 'root' > Mum *kɨdɨ*).

3.3.2.4 Sporadic *i-loss
Many instances of word-initial and word-final *i were lost in Mum and Sirva, although the loss in both environments shows irregular patterns of inheritance.

Word-initially, we see *iga 'see, perceive' > Mum, Sirva *ga* and *igwa 'give' > Mum *gu*-, Sirva *gwa*-. Unusually, sometimes Mum loses initial *i while Sirva retains it (*isa 'bite' > Mum *sa*-, Sirva *isa*-), while other times the reverse is the case (*idar- 'hear' > Mum *idar*-, Sirva *dari*-).

Word-final *i shows the same pattern. Some cognate sets show the change applying in Mum but not in Sirva (for example, *sɨgi 'pot' > Mum *sɨg*, Sirva *sɨgi* and *kɨmi 'bow' > Mum *kɨm*, Sirva *kɨmi*), while others show the reverse (*ibi 'name' > Mum *ñibi*, Sirva *ib* and *-si 'same-sex older sibling' > Mum -*si*, Sirva -*s*). Note that

---

[12] Sweeney (n.d.) contains both transcriptions, which may be two permitted variants or two different transcriptions of the same form.

this change was shared with Proto-Aisian, where it was regular, and it may have spread to Proto-North Sogeram from Proto-Aisian (§3.4.2.1).

It is clear from forms like *ina 'sun' (> Mum, Sirva *ina*) and *upri 'dog' (> Mum *upri*, Sirva *uvri*) that the change was not fully regular, so it may possible to explain these unusual patterns of inheritance by positing different patterns of application in the dialects of Proto-North Sogeram.

3.3.2.5 Sporadic plosive lenition

The plosives *p *t *k were lenited to *v *r *h [β ɾ ɣ] intervocalically. As with *i-loss, this change is sometimes reflected in Mum (*kapra 'throw' > PNS *kapara > Mum *kavara-*, Sirva *kapara-*), sometimes in Sirva (*mita 'leave' > Mum *mita-*, Sirva *mira-*), sometimes in neither (*sɨku 'very' > Mum *sɨku*, Sirva *suku*), and sometimes in both (*kaka 'fasten' > Mum, Sirva *kaha-*).

This change represents the same intervocalic lenition process that the Akɨ dialect of Apalɨ underwent (§3.2.5.5), and the two changes are probably related in some way, although it is not clear how. In fact, the other dialect of Apalɨ, Acɨ, also underwent this sound change sporadically, much like Mum and Sirva did. As noted, it has been suggested that the dialects of Apalɨ were formed by the convergence of two distinct language varieties rather than the divergence of a Proto-Apalɨ, and that Acɨ shows signs of a closer affinity with Mum (Wade 1993). Given this complicated state of affairs, it seems likely that this sound change originated in Akɨ and spread irregularly through the speech community that was a parent to Acɨ, Mum, and Sirva.

3.3.3 Mum innovations

The Mum phoneme inventory is shown in (22).

(22)
p	t		k	(kʷ <kw>)		i	ɨ	u
ᵐb <b>	ⁿd <d>		ᵑg <g>	(ᵑgʷ <gw>)				
		(ⁿdʒ <j>?)						
	s							a
β <v>			ɣ <h>	(ɣʷ <hw>)			(e)	
	ⁿz <z>							
m	n	ɲ <ñ>	ŋ					
	ɾ <r>							

Mum has changed little since the Proto-North Sogeram stage. The uncertain status of *e* remains, as it is only attested in a few forms and may be the result of regular phonemic processes—that is, it may not be a phoneme. Mum may also have re-created a labiovelar series of obstruents (§3.3.3.1), although it is unclear whether the labiovelars created by this process should be considered phonemic. Another possible change is that *z [ⁿz] may have become a prenasalized affricate *j* [ⁿdʒ] in some dialects. In this respect Sweeney (n.d.) and I differ in our transcriptions: he prefers *z* while I prefer *j*. I defer to his superior knowledge of the language, although it is possible that [ⁿz] and [ⁿdʒ] are two permissible (or phonetically conditioned) pronunciations of the same phoneme, in which case perhaps Mum underwent an affrication process similar to that seen in Apalɨ (§3.2.5.7).

3.3.3.1 Word-final labiovelar creation

Word-final sequences of a velar obstruent (*k, *g [ᵑg], or *h [ɣ]) plus *u became *kw, gw,* and *hw*, which are sometimes pronounced with a following epenthetic *ɨ*. For example, *aku 'sleep (n.)' > *akw*, *-mku 'nephew, niece' > PNS *-mgu > *-mɨgw*, and *tɨkwɨ 'area under' > PNS *tɨhu > *tuhwɨ*. This change followed word-final nasal deletion (§3.3.1.3), as illustrated by forms like *takun 'moon' > *takw* and *nagum 'neck' > *nagw*, in which the final nasal was lost first, creating the environment for this change to operate.

3.3.3.2 Word-initial *ɨ fortition

Word-initial *ɨ was sometimes strengthened to *ñ* [ɲ] if the following consonant was nasal—that is, if it was a nasal or a prenasalized consonant. If the *ɨ was vocalic, it became *ñi*, as in *ibi [iᵐpi] 'name' > *ñibi* and *iman 'louse' > *ñima*. If the *ɨ was consonantal (i.e., if it was *y), it became *ñ*, as in *yagum [jaᵑkum] 'red' > *ñagw* and *iŋar 'sun' > *yaŋari (probably borrowed from pre-Sirva; cf. §3.3.4.1) > *ñaŋari* 'moon'. This change never affected initial *ɨ in a non-nasal environment, although one possibly related unusual development was the breaking of initial *ɨ in *ifu 'hit, kill' > *yɨvu-*. And even in nasal environments, not every initial *ɨ was strengthened: *ina 'sun' > *ina* and *idar [iⁿtar] 'hear, perceive' > *idar-*. Recall also that several instances of word-initial *ɨ were lost (§3.3.2.4).

There is the possibility that this change did not actually affect vocalic *ɨ, but only *y, and that it was regular, affecting all tokens of *y before nasal consonants. This analysis requires invoking the word-initial vowel breaking change that took place in Sirva (§3.3.4.1) and positing that it spread irregularly to pre-Mum, affecting some *y-initial words but not others. On this analysis, cases like *ibi 'name' > *ñibi* and *iman 'louse' > *ñima* actually involve an intermediate stage where the initial vowel had begun to break but had not yet fully changed to ⁺*ya*. For example, *ibi 'name' > *yɨbi > *ñibi*, and *iman 'louse' > *yɨma > *ñima*. This analysis comports with the fact that Sweeney (n.d.) sometimes transcribes 'name' *ñibi* and sometimes *ñɨbi*—if *ɨ became *yɨ, we might expect the *ɨ to remain when the *y nasalizes to *ñ*.

3.3.3.3 Sporadic vowel centering

Some vowels occasionally centered to *ɨ in Mum. This only happened when they were not word-initial and were in the penultimate syllable, and even then the change was far from regular. Examples include *miŋra 'vomit' > *mɨhra-* and *fumra 'fly' > *pɨmra*. Because of the rarity of this change I leave a fuller investigation for future research.

3.3.4 Sirva innovations

The Sirva phoneme inventory is shown in (23). It is identical to the Proto-North Sogeram inventory in terms of consonants. Sirva has not added palatal affricates, although [tʃ] and [ⁿdʒ] are allophones of *k* and *g* before *i*. The vowel *e* is clearly a phoneme in Sirva, having arisen from *ai (*umai 'bean' > *ume*). Similarly, *au sometimes created *o* (*kaur 'unripe' > *kor* 'young'), although this sequence more frequently underwent fortition in Proto-North Sogeram (§3.3.2.2). While *e* and *o* are clearly phonemes in Sirva, they are still quite rare. Sirva also often harmonized *ɨ to *i* or *u* when that vowel came in the next syllable, as in *kɨmi 'bow' > *kimi* and *kɨmu 'die' > *kumu-*. This change is shared with Proto-East Sogeram and is described in more detail in §3.4.1.3.

(23)

p	t		k		i	ɨ	u
ᵐb \<b\>	ⁿd \<d\>		ᵑg \<g\>		e		o
	s					a	
β \<v\>			ɣ \<h\>				
	ⁿz \<z\>						
m	n	ɲ \<ñ\>	ŋ				
	ɾ \<r\>						

3.3.4.1 Word-initial *i and *u breaking

Sirva often broke initial *i and *u to *ya* and *wa*, as in *iŋar 'sun' > *yaŋari*, *ika 'cut, chop' > *yaha-*, *uram 'house' > *wara*, and *ura 'yell' > *warwar* 'yelling' (with reduplication) . This change was not fully regular, and many word-initial instances of these vowels remain, such as *igɨn 'ground possum > *igɨn*, *ibi 'name' > *ib*, *umai 'bean' > *ume*, and *upri 'dog' > *uvri*. A similar change, which affected only *u, took place in Kursav (§3.4.5.4).

3.3.4.2 *h-loss

PNS *h [ɣ] was lost between *ɨ and *i, creating the sequence /ɨi/ which exists in no other Sogeram language. Two Proto-Sogeram sequences of *ɨki show this change in Sirva: *-sɨki 'maternal grandfather' > -sii and *-pɨki 'maternal grandmother' > -vii 'parent's same-sex older sibling'. But this sound change can also be seen in the behavior of the different-subject paradigm. The *h from the Proto-North Sogeram DS suffix *-ɨha survives intact in some forms, like -hana '2SG.DS' (< PNS *-ɨha-na 'DS-2SG' < *-ɨka-na) and -har '1PL.DS' (< PNS *-ɨha-r 'DS-1PL' < *-ɨka-rɨŋ), but in others this sound change removed the *h: -iin '1SG.DS' (< PNS *-ɨh-in < *-ɨk-in) and -ii '3SG.DS' (< PNS *-ɨh-i < *-ɨk-i).

3.4 The East Sogeram languages

The East Sogeram (ES) branch consists of the two Aisian Languages—Magɨ and Aisi—as well as Kursav and Gants.

3.4.1 East Sogeram innovations

The Proto-East Sogeram phoneme inventory is presented in (24).

(24) *p   *t   *k   *kʷ <kw>   *i   *ɨ   *u
      *ᵐb <b>   *ⁿd <d>   (*ᶮɟ <j>)   *ᵑg <g>   *ᵑgʷ <gw>
      *ɸ <f>   *s   *a
      *m   *n   *ɲ <ñ>   *ŋ
                 *ɾ <r>

Like most languages in the family, Proto-East Sogeram voiced the Proto-Sogeram prenasalized stops (§3.4.1.1). It is unclear how this change affected *z [ⁿs], although one form (*mazɨn 'bowstring' > Gants majɨm) suggests a prenasalized palatal stop as the outcome. Otherwise, Proto-East Sogeram left the Proto-Sogeram phoneme inventory unaffected, although, as mentioned in the introduction, *kw and *gw may have not have been unit phonemes in Proto-East Sogeram, but rather clusters of *k and *w.

3.4.1.1 Voicing of prenasalized stops

As in other languages (§3.3.1.1), the voiceless prenasalized stops were voiced in Proto-East Sogeram. This took place with *b (*ibi [iᵐpi] 'name' > Aisi ib [iβ], Kursav -nibe [niᵐbe], Gants ibe [iᵐbe]), *d (*kɨdɨr [kɨⁿtɨr] 'root' > Aisi kɨrɨr, Kursav -kɨdɨr [kɨⁿdɨr], Gants kɨdi [kɨⁿdi]), *g (*miga [miⁿka] 'come down' > Magɨ miga [mɨɣa], Aisi mɨg- [mɨɣ], Gants mɨga [mɨᵑga]), and *gw (*tagwa [taⁿkʷa] 'step on' >

Aisi *togu-* [toɣu], Kursav *rago* [laᵑgo], Gants *tago* [taᵑgo]). It took place regardless of the nature of the surrounding vowels, and also when the prenasalized stop was part of a consonant cluster (*kugra [kuᵑkra] 'cook' > Aisi *kogr-* [koɣr], Kursav *kogra-* [koᵑgra]).

Unlike in Proto-North Sogeram, Manat, and Apalɨ, voiceless stops in non-homorganic nasal–stop clusters did not become voiced, but rather were simply lost: *tamkan 'eye' > PES *tama > Aisi *tamɨ*, Kursav *-tama*; *kwɨmka 'stomach' > PES *kuma > Aisi *kumu*.

The behavior of *z [ⁿs] in this change is unclear, since there is only one reflex of this phoneme in East Sogeram, and it is problematic: *mazɨn 'bow-string' > Gants *majɨm*. The final nasal calls into question whether this form is cognate, but if it is the form suggests *z became a prenasalized palatal stop or affricate in Proto-East Sogeram. This question will have to await further research.

3.4.1.2 Word-final nasal loss in Aisian and Kursav

Another change that Proto-East Sogeram shared with other languages is word-final nasal deletion (§3.3.1.3). This change appears to have originated in Proto-North Sogeram, where it was most regular, and from there to have spread west to Manat and east to Proto-East Sogeram, where it was only sporadic. Moreover, it only affected the Aisian languages and Kursav; Gants only underwent sporadic word-final *m-loss, which may or may not have been related (§3.4.6.1). For example, the correspondence set *uram 'house' > Magɨ *ur*, Aisi *uru*, Gants *wara* suggests a Proto-East Sogeram reconstruction *ura in which the loss of *m was shared by these languages. But *mɨrɨm 'sap' > Magɨ *mɨrɨm*, Aisi *mɨr*, Kursav *mɨrɨm*, Gants *mɨ* suggests a more complicated history. In general, nasal loss appears to have been most common in Aisi and Kursav, as illustrated by *iman 'louse' > Magɨ *iman*, Aisi *imu*, Kursav *ima*, Gants *iman*. Other forms illustrate the loss of word-final *n (*faŋan 'bag' > Aisi *waɲi*, Kursav *vaŋa*), *ñ (*sumiñ 'vine' > PES *sɨmiñ > Magɨ *simi*, Kursav *sime*), and *ŋ (*manɨŋ 'banana' > PES *man > Aisi *maŋ*).

3.4.1.3 *ɨ harmonization

In most East Sogeram languages, as well as Sirva, *ɨ changed to *i or *u when followed by either of those vowels. So for example *kɨmi 'bow' > Sirva *kimi*, Aisi *kim*; *-sɨki 'maternal grandfather' > Aisi *-siki*, Kursav *-sike*; and *sɨgi 'pot' > Sirva *sigi*, Aisi *sig*, and Kursav *sigi* illustrate the change *ɨ > *i, which appears to have been quite regular. And *kɨmu 'die' > Sirva *kumu-*, Aisi *kum-*, Kursav, Gants *kumo*; and *mɨgu 'go down' > Sirva *mugu-*, Magɨ *mugu-*, Aisi *mug-*, Kursav *moga-* illustrate the change *ɨ > *u, which appears to have been less regular. Gantɨ, in particular, usually did not participate in these changes. It sometimes harmonized *ɨ > *u, as in 'die,' but sometimes did not; cf. its form for 'go down,' *mɨgo*. And it appears not to have participated in *ɨ > *i at all. For example, *tɨki 'fill' > Gantɨ *tɨki*, but Magɨ *tɨk-* and Aisi *tiki-*.

While *ɨ > i may have been fully regular in the languages besides Gantɨ, *ɨ > u does not appear regular in these languages. For example, *tɨbu 'tie' > Magɨ *tɨb-*, Aisi *tɨb(ram)-*, Kursav *(ne)rɨbu-* 'swallow,' and Gantɨ *tɨbo*.

3.4.1.4 Lowering of *i and *u in Kursav and Gantɨ

Kursav and Gantɨ underwent two changes that lowered *i and *u to *e and *o. One took place word-finally, and the other took place before *a.

Word-final *i and *u lowering appears to have been quite regular. Thus *ibi 'name' > Kursav *-nibe*, Gantɨ *ibe*, *miti 'cough (n)' > Kursav *mite*, Gantɨ *mire*, *kamu 'fog, cloud' > Kursav *kamo* 'breath, wind', Gantɨ *kamo(ren)*, and *kɨmu 'die' > Kursav, Gantɨ *kumo*. One form did not undergo the change in either language: *mi 'thought' > Kursav, Gantɨ *mi*. Note, however, that this change does appear to have affected monosyllabic words, such as *su 'feces' > Kursav *so*. In Kursav, this change also appears to have preceded word-final nasal deletion (§3.4.1.2), as most tokens of these vowels that were followed by nasals did not lower, such as *takun 'moon' > *taku* and *nagum 'neck' > *-nagu* 'nape'. Final *i does not appear to have been lowered when it followed *a: *umai 'bean' > Kursav *wamai*, *kusai 'first' > Gantɨ *kusai*.

The other environment in which *i and *u were lowered to *e and *o is preceding an *a in the next syllable. Thus *kinakina 'crooked' > Gantɨ *kenakena*, *mirkwa 'cordyline' > Kursav *merkwa*, and *kukra 'grow' > Kursav *kokra*, Gantɨ *kokra* 'be born'. However, these vowels had to be preceded by a consonant to undergo this change. Word-initial *i remained *i*, as in *iman 'louse' > Kursav *ima*, Gantɨ *iman*, and *irka 'cry' > Kursav *irika-*, Gantɨ *ika*. And word-initial *u, rather than lowering to *o, appears to have been broken to *wa in the presence of an upcoming *a: *umai 'bean' > Kursav *wamai*, *ura 'call out' > Kursav *wara-*, *uram 'house' > Gantɨ *wara*.

3.4.2 Aisian innovations

The two Aisian languages, Magɨ and Aisi, are quite closely related and share several phonological innovations. The phoneme inventory of Proto-Aisian (PAɪs) is given in (25).

(25) *p   *t   *k   *kʷ \<kw\>   *i   *ɨ   *u
      *b   *d   *g   *gʷ \<gw\>   *e
      *β \<v\>   *s   *a
      *m   *n   *ŋ
            *ɾ \<r\>

The most significant change in Proto-Aisian is the loss of prenasalization in the Proto-East Sogeram voiced stops, creating a series of plain voiced stops (§3.4.2.2). This change also merged PES *b [ᵐb] with *β [ɸ] in non-initial position, leaving only the initial tokens of *β as contrastive phonemes, and it seems initial *β became voiced. Proto-Aisian also lost PES *ñ, merging it with *n (§3.4.2.6) and created *e from *ai (§3.4.2.5).

Proto-Aisian also underwent sporadic word-final nasal velarization with Apalɨ (§3.2.5.1). Recall that Aisian and Kursav sporadically lost many word-final nasals (§3.4.1.2). Of those that remained, *n and *ñ velarized to PAIS *ŋ. So *kuman 'arm, hand' > Aisi komaŋ 'branch,' *sɨkan 'completely' > Aisi sɨkaŋ, and *kɨbañ 'saliva' > Aisi kibiŋ (but Magɨ kibin). This change took place after the word-final nasal loss referred to above, as shown by *manɨŋ 'banana' > PES *man > Magɨ, Aisi maŋ. This form also suggests that word-final nasal velarization in Aisian may be a separate change from the similar Apalɨ innovation, since Apalɨ preserves man 'banana'. This change only happened with one token of word-final *m (*muyam 'cassowary' > muyaŋ 'cassowary's call'), while others remained at the bilabial place of articulation: *tadam 'foot, leg' > Magɨ, Aisi taram 'thigh,' *naŋram 'frog' > Magɨ, Aisi naŋam.

3.4.2.1 Word-final *i deletion
Word-final *i was consistently lost in Proto-Aisian. This sound change was partially shared with Proto-North Sogeram, where it was only sporadic (§3.3.2.4). Examples include *ibi 'name' > Magɨ, Aisi ib and *kɨmi 'bow' > PES *kimi > Magɨ, Aisi kim. When the preceding consonant was a voiceless plosive, *i became *ɨ, as in *kɨki 'new' > PES *kiki > Magɨ, Aisi kikɨ.[13] This ɨ may also have been created when final *i was in a monosyllabic word, although only one form suggests this: *mi 'thought' > PAIS *mɨ > Magɨ, Aisi mɨ(ndam)- 'think'. When the preceding

---

[13] The interaction of this change with East Sogeram *ɨ-harmony (§3.4.1.3) creates a pattern in which PSOG *CɨCi sequences often appear to metathesize to *CiCɨ in PAIS, an analysis that I tentatively proposed in previous work (Daniels 2010: 181). Further study has now revealed that this pattern is actually due to these two separate changes. First, East Sogeram *ɨ-harmony changed *CɨCi > *CiCi, and second, Aisi word-final *i loss changed some instances of *CiCi > *CiCɨ.

consonant was a voiced plosive, no *ɨ appears to have been created: *kadi 'sick' > Magɨ, Aisi *kar*. This change preceded word-final *a centering (§3.4.2.4), as illustrated by *kia 'speech,' which became Magɨ and Aisi *ki*, not †*kɨ*.

3.4.2.2 Stop denasalization

All the prenasalized stops lost their prenasalization and became plain voiced stops. In both varieties the bilabial and velar stops are realized as the stops [b g] word-initially and after nasals, and as the fricatives [β ɣ] elsewhere. The alveolar stop initially showed different allophony, being realized as [ɾ] word-finally and [d] elsewhere, as I discuss below. This distribution of reflexes of *d is preserved in Magɨ, but Aisi later lenited word-medial *d to *r* (§3.4.4.3). Examples of the change include *aba [aᵐpa] 'speak' > Magɨ, Aisi *ab-* [aβ]; *madɨŋ [maⁿtɨŋ] 'side' > Magɨ *madɨŋ* [madɨŋ]; *miga [mɨⁿka] 'come down' > Magɨ, Aisi *mɨg-* [mɨɣ]; and *igw- [iⁿkʷ] 'give' > Magɨ, Aisi *igw-* [iɣw].

This change probably followed word-final *i loss (§3.4.2.1), as illustrated by the two instances of word-final *di with Aisian reflexes, *kadi 'sick' and *naudi 'woman'. Both yield *r* in both Aisian varieties: *kadi 'sick' > Magɨ, Aisi *kar*, and *naudi 'woman' > PAɪs *nur 'daughter' > Magɨ *nur*, Aisi *nor*. If stop denasalization came first, we would expect these sequences to become *di with a voiced stop, and for that *d to be retained word-finally in Magɨ today (although it is of course possible that it was retained for a while and only later lenited to *r*). But it is simpler to propose that *i loss came first, and that it left no epenthetic *ɨ after a prenasalized stop. Thus *kadi > Pre-PAɪs *kad with a prenasalized *d. Then when stop denasalization took place, it affected word-final *d differently than other stops by not only removing the prenasalization, but also leniting it to *r.

Stop denasalization also had the effect of merging PES *b [ᵐb] and *v [β] in non-initial position. An example is PSᴏɢ *af 'fire'. When *b lost prenasalization and developed the non-initial allophone *[β], it merged with *f [ɸ], which was also pronounced *[β] in non-initial position: Magɨ, Aisi *ab* [aβ] 'fire'. Word-initially, though, the contrast was preserved, and subsequent developments have preserved the contrast in Aisi (§3.4.4.4), but it appears to have been neutralized in Magɨ. I only have two (related) reflexes of initial *f in my Magɨ data, but they suggest it underwent fortition to *b*: *fɨr 'ground, land' > *bi* and *fɨr kama 'dawn (v)' > *bikame* 'dawn (adv)'.

3.4.2.3 Word-internal *r loss

PSᴏɢ *r was lost word-internally when it preceded *k (*mirkwa 'cordyline' > Magɨ *miku*, Aisi *meko* and *irka 'cry' > Magɨ, Aisi *ik-*) or when it followed *ŋ (*naŋram 'frog' > Magɨ, Aisi *naŋam*). These three examples are the only Proto-Sogeram forms that contain such a sequence and have Aisian reflexes, so the change appears regular, although there is not a great deal of supporting data.

3.4.2.4 Word-final *a centering
Word-final *a was centered to *ɨ in Proto-Aisian. So *maka 'tooth' > Magɨ, Aisi *makɨ* and *sɨka 'piece' > Magɨ, Aisi *sɨkɨ*. When final *a followed another vowel, the resulting *ɨ was lost, as in *kia 'speech' > Magɨ, Aisi *ki*. This change followed word-final nasal loss (§3.4.1.2), as instances of *a that were rendered final by that change centered to *ɨ: *aman 'breast' > PES *ama > Magɨ, Aisi *amɨ*, *kinaŋ 'axe' > *kina > Magɨ, Aisi *kinɨ*.

3.4.2.5 Simplification of vowel sequences
Vowel sequences that were syllabified together tended to be simplified to one vowel in Aisian. There are not many examples of this change, but *ai became *e (*umai 'bean' > Magɨ, Aisi *ume*), *au became *u (*naudi 'daughter' > Magɨ *nur*, Aisi *nor*), and *ui became *i (*kui 'shoot, pierce' > Magɨ *ki-* 'shoot'). Two-vowel sequences that were in different syllables were apparently unaffected, although they appear to have been resyllabified into one syllable: *kuar 'garden' > Magɨ, Aisi *kwar*. There is one counter-example to this change: *nabai 'daughter-in-law (1.POSS)' > Magɨ *nabai*, although in Aisi it is *nabe*.

3.4.2.6 Merger of *ñ and *n
Proto-Aisian appears to have merged *ñ [ɲ] and *n as *n, as in *ña 'eat' > Magɨ, Aisi *n-* and *kɨñɨ- 'stay' > Magɨ, Aisi *kɨn-*. This often happened with raising of adjacent vowels, as in *kɨbañ 'saliva' > Magɨ *kɨbin*, Aisi *kɨbiŋ* and *añɨr 'two days away' > Magɨ *anɨr*, Aisi *anir* 'the day after tomorrow'. These examples illustrate that this change appears to have taken place fairly late in the history of Proto-Aisian, as it is sometimes inherited differently into the two languages.

After *ñ loss, Magɨ appears to have borrowed the phoneme back into its inventory. My data contains two words with ñ, one of which appears to be reconstructible to Proto-Sogeram: *kañaŋ 'bone'.

3.4.3 Magɨ innovations

The Magɨ phoneme inventory did not change much from Proto-Aisian, as shown in (26).

(26) p t   k   kʷ <kw>   i   ɨ   u
      b d   g   gʷ <gw>   e
         s   a
      m n   ɲ <ñ> ŋ
         ɾ <r>

The most significant change is the merger of *b and *v [β] (§3.4.2.2). Magɨ appears to have borrowed ñ [ɲ] back into its phoneme inventory (§3.4.2.6). Otherwise, Magɨ is like Proto-Aisian in every respect, including that it has *e* but lacks *o*. The status of *kw* and *gw*, as in most of East Sogeram, is ambiguous. While reflexes like *ikw-* 'go up' (< *yakw-) and *igw-* 'give' (< *igw-) appear to confirm that these phonemes were retained, reflexes of PSOG *ku are sometimes identical (*kuar 'garden' > *kwar*), which suggests that *kw has become two segments in Magɨ. I leave the question for future research.

3.4.3.1 *r vocalization

There are a couple examples of word-final syllabic *r vocalizing to *i*. These are *fɨr 'ground, land' > *bi* and *upri 'dog' > PAɪs *apɨr > *api*. The irregular development of *tar 'tree' > *te* is also suggestive of such a development, although consonantal *r did not behave this way in any other form. There is only one example of syllabic *r not vocalizing, and that is *añɨr 'two days away' > *anɨr*.

3.4.4 Aisi innovations

Aisi changed a few things about the phoneme inventory of Proto-Aisian, as shown in (27).

(27) p t k   i   ɨ   u
      b d g   e   o
         s   a
      m n ŋ

Aisi merged *d and *r, eliminating *r as a phoneme (§3.4.4.3). It also lost the labiovelar consonants (§3.4.4.2). The contrast between *b and *v [β] had become restricted to word-initial position in Proto-Aisian (§3.4.2.2), and in Aisi the remaining, word-initial tokens of *v merged with *u to become *u* and *w* (§3.4.4.4). Aisi also lowered many tokens of *i and *u, creating the phoneme *o* in the process (§3.4.4.1).

3.4.4.1 *i and *u lowering

After it separated from Magɨ, Aisi underwent several rounds of *i and *u lowering. This took place in several different environments, one of which was preceding *ɨ. This environment was somewhat rare, but the change is reflected in five forms in the data: *mukɨr 'white hair' > *mokɨr* 'white (of hair)'; *mu kɨm 'a certain thing' > *mokɨm* 'greed'; *kudɨ 'morning' > *kondɨ*; *sikɨñ 'three days away' > *sekɨr* 'the day after the day after tomorrow'; and *tidɨ 'star' > *tendɨ*. Two of these are problematic because they retain prenasalization, suggesting they were borrowed (*kondɨ* and *tendɨ*), and *mokɨm* 'greed' is semantically quite innovative. Nevertheless, this appears to be a consistent change.

Another environment in which *i and *u lowered to *e* and *o* is preceding or following an *a. Examples of lowering triggered by a preceding *a include *karif 'flying fox' > *kareb*, *amur 'tomorrow' > *amor*, and *kamu 'fog, cloud' > *kamo*. Examples of a following *a providing the lowering environment include *kiman 'firstborn' > *kemaŋ*, *kugra 'cook' > *kogr-*, and *kukra 'grow' > *kokr-*.

Occasionally, *i and *u lowered word-finally, although this was less common. This change took place much more regularly in Kursav and Gants (§3.4.1.4). Examples of this change include *kari 'betelnut' > *kare*, *sumɨñ 'vine' > PAIS *sɨmi > *sime*, and *mu 'SPEC' > *mo*.

All of these changes appear to have exceptions—whether because of subsequent borrowing or because they were only sporadic, it is unclear. So *nagum 'neck' > *nagum*, *ñagur 'mosquito' > *nagur*, *muyam 'cassowary' > *muyaŋ* 'cassowary's call,' *kia 'speech' > PAIS *ki > *ki*, and *isaŋ 'same-sex older sibling (1.POSS)' > *isam*.

3.4.4.2 Labiovelar loss and *a rounding

Not many word-internal tokens of *kw have reflexes in Aisi, but two that followed *a lost lip rounding and became plain velars, while the preceding *a rounded to *o*: *yakw- 'go up' > *yok-*, *tagw- 'step on' > *tog-*. Two labiovelars followed *i, and the one that came before *a also lost its lip rounding (*mirkwa 'cordyline' > *meko*), while the other did not (*igw- 'give' > *igw-*).

3.4.4.3 *d lenition

Aisi lenited all non-initial instances of *d to *r* after denasalization (§3.4.2.2). Because the contrast between PAIS *d and *r did not exist word-initially (*r did not occur there), this change had the effect of completely removing that contrast, as all tokens of *r now became non-initial allophones of /d/. Thus *kɨdɨr 'root' > *kɨrɨr*, *sɨdaŋ 'fat (n)' > *siri*, and *tadam 'leg, foot' > *taram* 'thigh'. (Note that I represent *r* orthographically in Aisi because it is now being reintroduced into the language from Tok Pisin.)

3.4.4.4 Glide formation

PAis *v [β] existed only word-initially; elsewhere the contrast between it and *b was neutralized, and all non-initial tokens of *v (< PSoG *f [ɸ]) have survived into modern Aisi as allophones of *b. Initial *v, on the other hand, changed to *u* or *w*. It changed to *u* when followed by *ɨ or a consonant, as can be seen in three examples: *frɨ- 'scratch' > PAis *vr- > *ur(i)-*; *fɨr 'land, ground' > *ur*; and *fɨka 'slice, cut' > PAis *vɨk- > *uk-*. When followed by another vowel, *v changed to *w*, as can be seen in *faŋan 'bag' > PAis *vaŋɨ > *waŋɨ* and *fai- 'come' > *way-*.

3.4.5 Kursav innovations

The Kursav phoneme inventory is given in (28). The inventory given here differs significantly from that given in Daniels (2010), which was based on poorer data and was inaccurate in several respects.

(28) p   t   k   (kʷ <kw>)   i   ɨ   u
      ᵐb <b>   ⁿd <d>   ᵑg <g>   (ᵑgʷ <gw>)   e   o
                s   a
      β <v>   ɣ <h>
      m   n   ŋ
                ɾ <r>

Kursav has preserved the Proto-Sogeram labiovelars (e.g., in *kwaka 'cut, chop' > *kwaka*), although it is unclear whether they should be considered one phoneme synchronically or a cluster of *k* or *g* with *w*. It has preserved the fricative *f [ɸ] as *v* [β] and added a voiced velar fricative *h* [ɣ]. This is reflected in only one form descended from Proto-Sogeram: *miŋra 'vomit' > *mehra*, where the *ŋ appears to have assimilated to the *r by losing nasality. But while *h* is a rare phoneme in Kursav, it does exist in contexts that do not include a following *r*, suggesting that more tokens of *h* have been borrowed into the language. Kursav lost the palatal nasal *ñ, merging it with *n and raising adjacent vowels (§3.4.5.3) in a process that may have been shared with Proto-Aisian (§3.4.2.6). It is unclear what happened to the possible Proto-East Sogeram phoneme *j [ⁿɟ] in Kursav, since there is no Kursav reflex of PSoG *z [ⁿs] in the data. Kursav also created mid vowels via some *i and *u lowering processes that it shared with Gants (§3.4.1.4).

3.4.5.1 Sporadic word-initial *t lenition

Word-initial *t was lenited to *r* in most cases. Thus *tama 'put' > *rama*, *tɨku 'look' > *ruko*, and *tɨgɨñ 'black' > *rigi* 'dirty'. There are three exceptions to this process, though: *takun 'moon' > *taku*, *tar 'tree' > *tar*, and *tɨm 'stick' > *tum*. This change seems to have followed the creation of inalienable possession prefixes for body parts, as shown by the forms for 'eye' (*tamkan > PES *tama > *-tama*) and 'tail' (*tam > *-tam*).

3.4.5.2 *e lowering
Some instances of *e that were created before *a (see §3.4.1.4) were lowered again in Kursav, this time to *a*. There are only two clear examples of this: *mira 'firelight' > *mera > *-mara* and *mita 'leave' > *meta > *mata*. Some other forms with phonologically similar environments did not undergo this change: *kiman 'firstborn' > *keman* 'lastborn' and *mirkwa 'cordyline' > *merkwa*. Uncovering the precise environment under which this change took place will have to await further research.

3.4.5.3 Merger of *ñ and *n
Kursav lost the palatal nasal, merging it with the alveolar one in all environments. Before being lost, *ñ fronted a preceding *ɨ to *i, as in *kɨña 'stay' > *in*, *kɨñam 'near' > *kinam*, and *tɨgiñ 'black' > *rigi* 'dirty'. The last of these suggests this *ɨ-fronting effect may have extended back to preceding syllables as well. The forms for 'near' and 'black' also illustrate that this change followed both *i-lowering changes described in §3.4.1.4. The form for 'near' illustrates that it followed *i-lowering triggered by a following *a, since the reflex is *kinam*, not ⁺*kenam*. And the form for 'black' illustrates that it followed word-final lowering, since the reflex is *rigi*, not ⁺*rige*. An additional form, *ña 'eat' > *ne*, suggests that *ñ may have also sometimes affected a following vowel, although *kañaŋ 'bone' > *-kana* makes it difficult to be sure how exactly this effect was realized.

3.4.5.4 Word-initial *u breaking
Initial *u appears to have sometimes become *wa* in Kursav. The two supporting examples are *umai 'bean' > *wamai* and *ura 'call out' > *wara*. One exception, *upri 'dog' > *ovɨra*, involves other unusual changes and exhibits an unusual, lowered reflex of *u. A more serious counterexample, which suggests the change may not have been fully regular, is *ufia 'morning star' > *uvia*. A similar change affected initial *i and *u in Sirva (§3.3.4.1).

3.4.6 Gants innovations

The Gants phoneme inventory is given in (29).

(29) p   t   c   k   i   ɨ   u
     ᵐb <b> ⁿd <d> ᶮɟ <j>   ᵑg <g>   e   o
            s   a
     m   n   ɲ <ñ>   ŋ

Gants added the palatal stops c [c] and j [ᶮɟ], although it is unclear how. The only token of c in my data that is inherited from Proto-Sogeram arose through an irregular assimilation process involving *k and *ñ: *kɨñɨ- 'stay' > cɨ-. The only two tokens of j inherited from Proto-Sogeram are in problematic cognate sets: *kugiŋ [kuⁿkiŋ] 'whistle' > kojɨŋ [koᶮɟɨŋ] and *mazɨn [maⁿsɨn] 'bowstring' > majɨm [maᶮɟɨm]. These appear to have arisen via the palatalization of PSog *g [ᵑk] and *z [ⁿs], but more research is needed to be sure. Gants also lost the bilabial fricative *f [ɸ], which it merged with *p (§3.4.6.3). It also lost *r, which it merged with *t (§3.4.6.2). Finally, it added the mid vowels e and o by lowering some tokens of *i and *u in a change it shared with Kursav (§3.4.1.4).

3.4.6.1 Sporadic word-final *m loss

Gants did not lose all word-final nasals, like the other East Sogeram languages (§3.4.1.2), although it did often lose final *m, as in *kuram 'man' > kura, *mumɨm 'earthquake' > mumi, and *uram 'house' > wara. But just as often, Gants retained final *m, as in *kɨñam 'near' > kɨñam, *pɨm 'weight' > pum, and *tadam 'foot, leg' > tadam 'thigh'. In two instances, it changed final *m > ŋ: *-mum 'husband' > -moŋ and *aŋam 'red brush turkey' > aŋaŋ.

3.4.6.2 Non-initial *t lenition

Gants lenited all non-initial tokens of *t to r, which eliminated the distinction between PES *t and *r. Recall that in Proto-Sogeram and Proto-East Sogeram the contrast only existed word-initially, so this change had the effect of turning all tokens of *r into allophones of /t/. The effect of this change can best be seen with a pair like *mita 'leave' and *mira 'firelight,' which became mera and meraŋ (with the irregular addition of final ŋ), respectively. But this change also affected other forms, such as *mɨti 'cough (n)' > mire.

3.4.6.3 Merger of *p and *f

Orthographically, *p and *f [ɸ] are now both represented in Gants as <p>, but conceiving of this change as *f fortition is not entirely accurate. Gants /p/ is most commonly pronounced [β] in connected speech, or [ɸ] at the beginning of an utterance. This is the allophonic variation that I reconstruct for PSog *f. In careful speech, though, Gants /p/ is usually pronounced [p], and this pronunciation is regarded as "basic" in some sense by speakers, in spite of its rarity. What seems to have happened, then, is that *p was lenited to initial [ɸ] and intervocalic [β], which merged it with *f. Because *p was much more common than *f, most instances of this new phoneme could be pronounced [p] in careful speech, and this pattern was then generalized to the reflexes of *f, which previously could not be pronounced that way. Thus *fɨka 'slice, cut' > *pɨka*, *ifra 'buy' > *epra*, and *fɨr kama 'dawn (v)' > *pi kam-*.

It may be the case that *f only merged with *p in onset position, and that in coda position it was vocalized instead. The two forms where *f appears in coda position are *af 'fire' > *au(r)* and *ifu 'hit, kill' > *yo*. The first is difficult because of the *r* that was added, while the second is difficult because the *f would sometimes have been in coda position and sometimes in onset position, and these different root forms probably interacted with each other analogically. But these two forms are the only examples of *f in coda position, so it is best to say that only onset *f merged with *p, while coda *f vocalized to *u* or *o*.

3.4.6.4 Syllable-final *r vocalization

In a development that resembles *r vocalization in Magɨ (§3.4.3.1), Gants changed syllable-final *r > *i*. In Magɨ this change only affected syllabic *r, and only occurred word-finally, but in Gants syllabic *r as well as consonantal *r were affected. This can be seen from syllabic forms like *kɨdɨr 'root' > *kɨdi* and *fɨr kama 'dawn (v)' > *pi kam-*, as well as consonantal forms like *kudar 'centipede' > *kodai* and *tar 'tree' > *tai*. Gants also seems to have changed word-internal *r > *i* when it came syllable-finally, as shown by *irka 'cry' > *ika*, where the new *i merged with the pre-existing one. (This change probably followed *i lowering [3.4.1.4], which was shared with Kursav, meaning that the history of Gants *ika* is probably actually *irka > *erka > *eika > *ika*.) The vocalization of *r followed word-final *m loss (§3.4.6.1), as illustrated by *mɨrɨm 'sap' > *mɨr > *mi*, not †*mɨr*. It also followed non-initial *t lenition (§3.4.6.2), as illustrated by *pat 'center' > Pre-Gants *par > *pai* 'side,' not †*par*.

This change was widespread, but it does not appear to have been fully regular. Forms that preserve final *r include *amur 'tomorrow' > *amor* and *añɨr 'two days away' > *añɨr*.

3.5 Orthographic conventions

The orthographies used for the various Sogeram languages, and for Proto-Sogeram, are not identical, and this can cause confusion. In the preceding chapter I used phonetic brackets in places where the relationship between an orthographic symbol and the sound it represented may have been unclear, but in the rest of this book I simply use each language's orthography. Below I provide a table that summarizes the orthographic conventions used for each language. Orthographic symbols are given in the top row, and the phonetic articulation represented by that symbol in the different languages is given below. A dash means the symbol is not used in the language—so, for example, there is no <f> used in the Nend orthography. If two phonetic symbols are given under one grapheme, this means they are allophones in complementary distribution. This is the case, for example, with Magɨ <b>, which represents [b] in certain contexts and [β] in others. The final column is formatted somewhat differently. All Sogeram languages have exactly one liquid phoneme, although it is not pronounced the same in every language. The final column simply gives the grapheme used to represent a language's liquid, however it is articulated.

Table 7: Orthographic conventions.

	<b>	<d>	<g>	<c>	<j>	<ñ>	<f>	<v>	<h>	<z>	liquid
Mand	ᵐb	ⁿd	ᵑg	tʃ	ⁿdʒ	ɲ	ɸ	β	ɣ	z, ʒ	<r>
Nend	–	–	–	tʃ	ⁿdʒ	ɲ	–	β	ɣ	z	<r>
Manat	ᵐb	ⁿd	ᵑg	tʃ	–	ɲ	–	β	ɣ	ⁿz	<r>
Apalɨ	ᵐb	ⁿd	ᵑg	tʃ	ⁿdʒ	–	ɸ	β	ɣ	–	<l>
Mum	ᵐb	ⁿd	ᵑg	–	ⁿdʒ	ɲ	–	β	ɣ	ⁿz	<r>
Sirva	ᵐb	ⁿd	ᵑg	–	–	ɲ	–	β	ɣ	ⁿz	<r>
Magɨ	b, β	d	g, ɣ	–	–	ɲ	–	–	–	–	<r>
Aisi	b, β	d	g, ɣ	–	–	–	–	–	–	–	<r>
Kursav	ᵐb	ⁿd	ᵑg	–	–	–	β, ɸ	ɣ	–	–	<r>
Gants	ᵐb	ⁿd	ᵑg	c	ɲɟ	ɲ	–	–	–	–	<r>
PSoG	ᵐp	ⁿt	ᵑk	–	–	ɲ	ɸ, β	–	–	ⁿs	<r>

One caveat about this table is in order. Nend is listed as not having the graphemes <b d g>, and while this is technically true, it does use those symbols in the digraphs <mb nd ŋg>. In other words, in Nend prenasalization is written out, and <b d g> are never used on their own as letters.

Chapter 4
Verbs and Verb Morphology

In the previous chapter I reconstructed the phonology of Proto-Sogeram (PSOG); in this chapter I reconstruct its verbal morphology. Readers may wonder why I devote so much space to these matters in a book that is ostensibly about reconstructing syntax. The answer is that it is necessary. Syntactic reconstruction is not possible without phonological and morphological reconstruction, so this chapter, along with the following chapter on nominal morphology, is a necessary prelude to the syntactic reconstruction in Chapter 6. Because fully schematic constructions cannot be directly reconstructed, as discussed in Chapter 2, it is necessary to reconstruct partially schematic ones—that is, constructions that contain grammatical morphology. And in order to reconstruct that morphology, an understanding of the comparative phonology is indispensable.

Verbs were the most complicated Proto-Sogeram word class, morphologically speaking, and their development in each of the daughter branches has been complex. However, this complexity also provides us with fertile ground for reconstruction, and the behavior of Proto-Sogeram verbs can be reconstructed in some detail: I reconstruct ten final verb categories, five medial categories (including one that functioned both medially and finally), three other verb suffixes, and several aspects of the Proto-Sogeram system of verb serialization.

But first there are several aspects of Proto-Sogeram verbs to introduce, which I do in §4.1. Then I present my reconstruction of verb serialization in §4.2, and verb morphology in the following three sections. Like many Papuan languages today, Proto-Sogeram distinguished medial and final morphology, so §4.3 is concerned with final morphology while §4.4 covers medial morphology. §4.3 also discusses the different sets of subject agreement suffixes that were used in various TAM categories, both medial and final. Then §4.5 covers verb morphology that is not easily categorized as medial or final. I forgo a discussion of the innovations that these reconstructions entail, since my focus here is on the methodology of reconstruction. However, readers interested in these innovations can consult Daniels (forthcoming) for a detailed analysis of changes to tense–aspect systems in the Sogeram languages and Daniels (2015) for a catalogue of other innovations.

4.1 The Proto-Sogeram verb

In this section I discuss several preliminary topics related to the Proto-Sogeram verb. I begin with what I call "root vowels" and the system of vowel elision in the next section. Then I address the issue of reconstructing a dual/plural distinction in §4.1.2, and the complicated way Proto-Sogeram marked 3PL in §4.1.3.

4.1.1 Root vowels and vowel elision

Proto-Sogeram verb roots had two forms: the uninflected form and the inflected form. The uninflected form is discussed in more detail in the section on verb serialization (§4.2); here I concern myself with the inflected form of the verb. When affixed, all Proto-Sogeram verbs ended in either *a, *u, *i, or a consonant. I call the first three classes *a*-roots, *u*-roots, and *i*-roots, and divide consonant-final roots into *kw*-roots—roots that ended in one of the labiovelar consonants *kw or *gw—and C-roots, which ended in any other consonant.[14] The verb classes behaved differently in the presence of certain kinds of suffixes, especially with respect to vowel elision.

When a vowel-final verb root was combined with a consonant-initial suffix, neither form was changed. But when a vowel-final root was combined with a vowel-initial suffix, one of the two vowels at the morpheme boundary was usually elided. Here the verb classes behave differently. The *a of the *a*-roots was elided in the presence of an *i, as in *-in '1SG.IPST' (§4.3.1), or an *ɨ, as in *-ɨt 'IRR' (§4.3.10). Only a few suffixes with initial *u can be reconstructed, such as *-u '2SG.IMP' (§4.3.7), but it seems that both vowels were retained in this circumstance. No suffixes have been reconstructed with an initial *a. Reflexes of each environment are given in Table 8 with the verbs *tama 'put,' *wa 'go,' and *mɨŋa 'get'.

Table 8: Vowel elision with *a*-roots.

Mand	Manat	Aisi	Gants	PSog	PSog Gloss
aba-n	rama-nad	tama-ŋ	tama-naŋ	*tama-na	put-2SG.IPST
ab-in	ram-in		tam-enɨŋ	*tam-in	put-1SG.IPST
wa-u		w-o		*wa-u	go-2SG.IMP
	mɨŋ-itɨŋ		mɨŋ-rɨŋ	*mɨŋ-ɨt-ɨn	get-IRR-1SG

The *u*-roots, like *a*-roots, lost their *u in the presence of an *i-initial suffix. It seems that the *u was also elided in the presence of *ɨ, but this is less clear. In

---

14 Verbs that ended in a consonant could also be said to end in *ɨ, since this vowel was often epenthetically inserted between the verb root and a following suffix. I choose not to call these *i*-roots, though, because the uninflected form of these verbs never contained the *ɨ; for example, *idarɨ- 'hear' had the uninflected form *idar.

Manat and Gants the reflex of a PSoG *u-ɨ morpheme boundary is ɨ, while in Apalɨ and Kursav the reflexes are somewhat more ambiguous, and a great deal depends on accidents of inheritance. (For example, only two Proto-Sogeram *u*-roots, *tɨbu 'tie' and *kapu 'carry,' survive into Apalɨ as *u*-roots, and even those are *a*-roots in some dialects.) But the forms in Table 9 suggest that the *u of *u*-roots was elided in the presence of both *i and *ɨ.

Table 9: Vowel elision with *u*-roots.

Manat	Gants	PSoG	PSoG Gloss
humu-nad	*kumo-naŋ*	*kɨmu-na	die-2SG.IPST
hɨm-in	*kum-enɨŋ*	*kɨm-in	die-1SG.IPST
	tub-ɨna	*tɨb-ɨt-na	tie-IRR-2SG
hɨm-ɨn		*kɨm-ɨt-na	die-IRR-2SG

Proto-Sogeram *i*-roots were quite rare, and their morphophonological properties are not well understood. When combined with *i-initial suffixes, the final *i of the root and the initial *i of the suffix probably became a single *i. In the presence of *ɨ-initial suffixes, it seems that the *i was not elided. For example, the Aisi reflexes of *tiki 'fill' and *-ɨbia-n 'FUT-1SG' are *tiki-* and *-ɨbyaŋ*, and when they combine the root vowel remains: *tiki-byaŋ*. Nothing is yet known about the interaction of *i*-roots with *u-initial suffixes.

This brings us to the consonant-final roots. Of these, the C-roots were quite simple. Before a vowel-initial suffix the root remained unchanged, and before a consonant-initial suffix an epenthetic *ɨ was inserted.

The *kw*-roots behaved like C-roots in the presence of *i-initial suffixes: their root shape did not change. This, incidentally, is often an important way to distinguish Proto-Sogeram *kw*-roots from *u*-roots in languages that no longer preserve the labiovelar consonant. For example, Table 10 shows several reflexes of PSoG *igw-in 'give-1SG.IPST,' and none of them exhibit the vowel elision that takes place in *u*-roots. In the presence of consonant-initial suffixes, like *-na '2SG.IPST' and *-ta 'SS.DELAY,' the final consonant of *kw*-roots became a sequence of *k or *g plus *u. This also appears to have been the case with *ɨ-initial suffixes, such as *-ɨka 'DS' and *-ɨt 'IRR'; it seems that the *ɨ was elided, and the *kw*-root behaved as if in the presence of a consonant-initial suffix. All of these environments are presented in Table 10.

In addition to the classes described above, three verbs ended in a diphthong: *fai- 'come,' *kui 'shoot, pierce,' and *tai 'go up'. The morphological behavior of these unusual verbs is not well understood, and remains a topic for future research.

Table 10: *Kw*-roots.

Mand	Apalɨ	Sirva	Aisi	Gants	PSog	PSog Gloss
ikw-in	igu-in	gw-in	igw-eŋ	go-inɨŋ	*igw-in	give-1SG.IPST
	igu-naŋ			go-naŋ	*igu-na	give-2SG.IPST
		gu-ra		go-da	*igu-ta	give-SS.DELAY
iku-c	igu-ci	gu-i		go-k-e	*igu-k-i	give-DS-3SG
		gw-in	igu-kiŋ		*igu-k-in	give-DS-1SG
ik-u		g-u			*ig-u	give-2SG.IMP
		igu-nda		gu-na	*igu-t-na	give-IRR-2SG

It should now be apparent that a verb's class was not always discernible in all morphological environments. For example, when suffixed with *-i '3SG.IPST,' *a*-roots, *u*-roots, *i*-roots, and C-roots all looked identical. This created a ripe environment for verbs to move between classes, and many did. A typical example is the *u*-root *kɨmu 'die,' which became an *a*-root in Proto-West Sogeram (PWS) and the Akɨ dialect of Apalɨ. It was most common for verbs to become *a*-roots, as this is by far the most numerous group in the reconstructed lexicon. Of 85 reconstructed verb roots in §7.1, 49 are *a*-roots. The rest consist of 12 *u*-roots, 9 C-roots, 6 *i*-roots, 6 *kw*-roots, and the three diphthong roots. But verbs also joined other classes, especially when phonological processes raised the proportion of roots that belonged to a particular class.

4.1.2 Dual and plural number

The issue of what number categories Proto-Sogeram marked—essentially, of whether it had a dual—is complicated. Certainly the predecessor to Proto-Sogeram had a dual. It has been reconstructed for Proto-Madang (Ross 2000) and has been inherited into the Josephstaal languages Moresada (Capell 1951) and Anamuxra (Ingram 2001). And traces of it can still be seen in some Sogeram languages: Mand and Manat have dual pronouns, and Sirva has a 1DU optative suffix. So it is likely that dual number played some role in Proto-Sogeram, but determining exactly what role that might have been is quite difficult.

It is clear that the Sogeram plural comes from the Proto-Madang and Proto-South Adelbert dual. This can be seen from a quick comparison of the Anamuxra near tense, shown in Table 11, and the reconstructed Proto-Sogeram immediate past tense in Table 12. The Proto-Sogeram 1PL suffix *-rɨŋ is plainly cognate with the Anamuxra 1DU suffix *-r*, and the Proto-Sogeram 2PL/3PL *-ra is cognate with the Anamuxra 2DU/3DU *-ra*. (Note that this table posits 2PL/3PL syncretism for the Proto-Sogeram suffix *-ra; I return to this point in §4.1.3 below.)

Table 11: Anamuxra near tense.

	SG	DU	PL
first person	-i-n	-r	-ŋ
second person	-na	-ra	-ŋa
third person	-ri		

Table 12: PSog immediate past tense.

	SG	PL
first person	*-in	*-riŋ
second person	*-na	*-ra
third person	*-i	

Because dual number is so rare in the Sogeram languages, I reconstruct that rarity to Proto-Sogeram. But the fact that it survives into some Sogeram languages suggests that it may still have been used infrequently at the Proto-Sogeram stage. However, I do not reconstruct a dual/plural distinction for Proto-Sogeram agreement suffixes for two reasons. First, the dual forms that survive into Mand and Manat are pronouns, not agreement suffixes. Second, those pronouns cannot be reconstructed, as I discuss in §5.2.1. And third, the only modern Sogeram verb agreement suffix I have found is the Sirva 1DU.OPT suffix *-idaŋ*. This suffix is formally very similar to the other first person optative suffixes (1SG *-ida* and 1PL *-idagra*), so it could easily have been innovated after the loss of the dual/plural distinction. Moreover, Sirva borders on three or four non-Sogeram Madang languages, which may have motivated this innovation.

So I reconstruct a Proto-Sogeram system in which neither verb agreement markers nor pronouns distinguish dual from plural. The Proto-Sogeram plural verb suffixes are descended from Proto-Madang and Proto-South Adelbert dual forms. As more is learned about Proto-Sogeram's sisters and parents, this picture may become more nuanced. In particular, it is possible that some Proto-Madang plural suffixes survived into Proto-Sogeram instead of the dual forms. But for now, since I see no compelling Sogeram-internal evidence for reconstructing a dual/plural distinction in verb morphology, I do not reconstruct one.

4.1.3 The third person plural

The Sogeram languages exhibit a bewildering array of strategies for marking 3PL subject agreement on their verbs. While agreement suffixes are often different in different TAM categories, each language does have a dominant strategy. These are shown in Table 13. For only four languages—Mum, Magɨ, Aisi, and Kursav—is this strategy a dedicated 3PL agreement suffix. The other Sogeram languages mark 3PL by combining the 3SG suffix with a separate plural suffix. This plural suffix is always to the left of the 3SG suffix; in some TAM categories the two are adjacent and in others they are not. Confusingly, the West Sogeram languages employ this strategy in the second person as well as the third person. Even more confusingly, none of the plural suffixes appear cognate with one another.

Table 13: Third person plural.

Language	Form
Mand	-e-3SG
Nend	-mgɨ-3SG
Manat	-(h)ura-3SG
Apalɨ	-havɨ-3SG
Mum	-yu
Sirva	-b/-rɨb/-rub-3SG
Magɨ	-uŋ
Aisi	-uŋ, -oŋ
Kursav	-o
Gants	-i-3SG
PSoG	*-?

What are we to make of this? If the strategy of marking the 3PL by combining the 3SG with a plural suffix were inherited into all of these languages from Proto-Sogeram that would help explain how common it is in the family—but none of the suffixes are cognate.

Some help comes from the system of verb serialization. Serial verb constructions (SVCs) are discussed in more detail in §4.2, but briefly, they consist of some uninflected verbs followed by a verb that carries all of the inflection. Sometimes this last verb would not have its normal lexical meaning, but rather contributed aspectual or other grammatical meaning to the predicate (§4.2.2). There are two pieces of evidence that the different plural suffixes originated as verbs in the final position of SVCs.

Verbs sometimes had a different root shape when they were the uninflected verb in an SVC; specifically, they often added a final *a to the normal shape of the root. Gants has retained this alternation with the verb 'stay,' for example, which is *ci-* when inflected but *ca* when uninflected. Interestingly, when the verb root is next to the plural suffix *-i*, it takes its *uninflected* form—suggesting that verbs in that position used to actually be uninflected. To illustrate with 'stay,' a typical 3SG form is *ci-k-e* 'stay-DS.SEQ-3SG,' and the corresponding 3PL is *ca-i-k-e* 'stay-PL-DS.SEQ-3'.

This brings us to the second piece of evidence: position in the template. Note that in the example just cited, *caike*, the plural suffix -*i* is to the left of the different-subject suffix -*k*. This is not always the case, and here the Manat verb template is particularly instructive. The Manat plural suffix is -*ura*, although it often triggers the appearance of an extra *h* in the morpheme that precedes it so one could argue that it is -*hura*. The Manat historic past habitual verb form is composed of the habitual suffix -*r(ha)*, the past suffix -*ma*, and an agreement suffix, the choice of which determines whether the verb is historic past habitual or middle past habitual. For example, *ñi-r-m-id* [stay-HAB-PST-3SG.HIS] 's/he used to stay (long ago)'. When the plural is added to this form, it comes between -*rha* and -*ma*: *ñi-rh-ura-m-id* [stay-HAB-PL-PST-3.HIS] 'they used to stay (long ago)'. In this case, -*ma* is a very old suffix, dating back at least to Proto-Sogeram (§4.3.4). The habitual suffix -*rha*, on the other hand, is newer; it was grammaticalized from the verb *riha-* 'do' (Daniels forthcoming) and has no cognates as a suffix outside of Manat.

When we examine the placement of plural suffixes more generally, this observation about the Manat historic past habitual becomes a generalization. The plural suffix always occurs to the left of old suffixes, and usually occurs to the right of new suffixes. And this is exactly what we expect if it originated as the last verb in an SVC. In this scenario, it started as a separate verb bearing Proto-Sogeram verb suffixes. Eventually, it grammaticalized and became a suffix on the verb that preceded it in the SVC. At this point it was the leftmost suffix in the template. But after it grammaticalized, other verb morphology continued to grammaticalize from the same serializing construction—that is, other verbs in the final position of an SVC followed the same grammaticalization path and became suffixes. These newer suffixes are now located to the left of the plural suffix. Occasionally, a newly grammaticalized TAM suffix is found to the right of the plural suffix. For example, the Sirva far past suffix -*s* was grammaticalized after the Proto-Sogeram stage (Daniels forthcoming), but it is found to the right of the plural suffix: *ki-rib-is-a* 'stay-PL-FPST-3'. This kind of situation can be explained either by positing that the TAM suffix was moved on analogy with other, older TAM suffixes, or by positing that the TAM suffix grammaticalized before the plural suffix did.

The evidence thus supports the conclusion that in Proto-Sogeram the 3PL was marked by placing a pluralizing verb in the last position of an SVC and marking it with 3SG agreement suffixes. Recall that Anamuxra sometimes does not distinguish between second and third person in non-singular number. This pattern is widespread in Madang languages (I encountered it in fieldwork on Panim, for example, from the distantly related Croisilles branch of the family), and likely dates back to Proto-Madang. Proto-Sogeram may thus have been filling a semantic gap by developing this strategy to differentiate between 2PL and 3PL. This means that in presenting reconstructed verb paradigms, there is no 3PL form to give, so I leave that cell blank. I remain agnostic as to whether the 2PL suffix could still be used with 3PL meaning in Proto-Sogeram, or whether this 3PL construction had completely replaced it when the subject was 3PL.

As regards the bewildering variety of plural suffixes now present in the family, I speculate that they arose in a manner similar to the French negative morpheme *pas*. In the Proto-Sogeram stage the 3PL construction was more productive, and the pluralizing verb was one that was semantically appropriate to the action that was being pluralized. As Proto-Sogeram split up the construction gradually lost productivity and the set of pluralizing verbs became more restricted. Eventually one verb became fixed, and at that point it grammaticalized into an affix. But the verb that became fixed was not the same in every language, giving rise to the modern situation. I should reiterate that this scenario is speculative, though; while it does explain the diversity of plural suffixes, there is no evidence that supports it.

4.2 Serial verb constructions

Serial verb constructions (SVCs) have been mentioned above, but I describe them here in more detail. Genuine SVCs, in which each verb is a separate phonological word, are found in only five of the Sogeram languages (Apalɨ, Sirva, Magɨ, Kursav, and Gants), but it is clear that verb serialization was common in Proto-Sogeram. Some languages that lack SVCs instead have verb–verb compounds (Nend, Manat, and Mum), which were created by a process of phonological attrition that turned adjacent verbs in an SVC into a single phonological word. And in Apalɨ and Sirva some SVCs have remained SVCs while others have become compounds.

The Proto-Sogeram system of verb serialization can be reconstructed in some detail. I begin in the next section by presenting the form of SVCs, and then discuss various types of SVC that can be reconstructed afterwards: aspectual SVCs (§4.2.2), orientation SVCs (§4.2.3), and causative and manner SVCs (§4.2.4).

4.2.1 The form of serialized verbs

SVCs were composed of a series of uninflected verb roots followed by a root that was inflected for person, number, TAM, and/or switch reference. With the exception of orientation SVCs (§4.2.3), no other words could intervene between the serialized verbs.[15] This structure has been inherited, in one form or another, into every Sogeram language; examples below are from Nend (30), Manat (31), Apalɨ (32), Sirva (33), Magɨ (34), Kursav (35), and Gants (36).

Nend
(30) Avɨ-z   ŋgw-am-e   **hɨr-ay-ma-r.**
     do.thus-3SG.DS go.inside-put-SS   **carry-come-HPST-3SG**
     'Then he put it and brought it.'   (K. Harris n.d.)

Manat
(31) **Aŋra-vata-n**   muhrit ka-b   inɨ-ba   aih-ura-ma-g=a.
     run-swim-2/3.SS some   MD-NOM   ND-LOC   come-PL-PST-3.FAR=EXCL
     'They fled (run-swim), and some came here.'

Apalɨ
(32) **Lagu-sɨjia-vɨla**   migɨla-vɨ-m-i.
     stand.on-close-SS watch-PL-HPST-3
     'They stood and blocked the trail and watched.'   (Wade n.d.b)

Sirva
(33) Ka-ma   ad-ɨi   beau   **miŋa-sɨisɨɨr-a** wa-ra   **miŋa-sɨkr-i-Ø.**
     MD-ADVZ   do-3SG.DS   DEF.ACC **get-itch-SS**   go-SS   **get-break-TPST-3SG**
     'So she scratched and scratched it (lit. 'scratched it and went') and broke it.'

Magɨ
(34) Ramu an=iŋ,   supe-s-uŋ.   **Supe   kapɨr-kɨtiŋ**   ga,   ya-s-uŋ.
     Ramu water=LOC   finish-FPST-3PL **finish throw-SS**   TOP   come-FPST-3PL
     'They finished (the road) at the Ramu River. They totally finished it, and came back.'

Kursav
(35) Om   **magra visa-da,**   ya-ba   ya-koma   bin   skra-da ...
     land **pull   get-SS**   1SG-EMPH   1SG.POSS-arm   LOC   put-SS
     'I'll get the land back, and put it in my own hands, and ...'

---

15 It is possible that the negative particle *ma could intervene between non-orientation SVCs, as it can today in Gants, but this is not certain.

Gants

(36) **Miga** ci-k-e miŋa yako-da ...
    come.down stay-DS.SEQ-3SG get go.up-SS
    'It had fallen down (come.down stay) and she picked it up (get go.up) and ...'

Note that this construction occurs in both medial and final clauses; the Sirva and Gants examples even include one of each. Reconstruction with only the data given above would be premature, but for the sake of discussion I present a formalization of the observed pattern. Further discussion will make it clear that this was the structure of Proto-Sogeram SVCs.

(37) *(NP$_{OBJ}$) V$_{UNINFLECTED}$ V-INFL

An additional feature of Proto-Sogeram SVCs can be reconstructed, namely the form of the uninflected verb roots. In Gants, where the uninflected roots remain separate words, some verbs have different root shapes when they are not inflected compared to when they are. For example, *maya* 'bring' becomes *mai-* when it is inflected (38). Note that this is not due to vowel elision, as the suffix here is *-da* 'SS,' which is inherited from PSog *-ta and which has never caused vowel elision.

Gants

(38) Sop **mai-da,** **maya** yo maka-da ...
    soap **bring-ss** **bring** clean clean-ss
    'She brought soap, brought it and cleaned and ...'

Similarly, when verbs are uninflected in Magɨ, they often add a final *ɨ*. For example, *ab-* 'speak' (< *aba) becomes *abɨ*, *tib-* 'close' (< *tɨbu 'tie') becomes *tɨbɨ*, and *miŋ-* 'get' (< *miŋa) becomes *miŋɨ*. Recall that word-final *a centered to *ɨ in Proto-Aisian (§3.4.2.4), suggesting that this final *ɨ* is cognate with Gants final *a*.

The Sirva far past tense gives another clue to the shape of Proto-Sogeram uninflected verbs. This tense was formed from an SVC in which an uninflected verb stem combined with the verb *sɨ- 'do' to form a past tense construction (Daniels forthcoming). This verb eventually grammaticalized into a new past tense suffix which was inherited into Proto-North Sogeram and Proto-Aisian. In Sirva, the SVC origin of this suffix can still be seen in the shape of the verb stems that combine with it. For example, *igwa 'give' is retained as *gwa-* in *gwa-s-a* (39), but as *gu-* in *gu-ra* (40). Other verbs exhibit similar allomorphy: *tua 'burn (intr.)' yields *tua-* and *tu-*.

Sirva

(39) Kwagɨ-a mir-a, kyumr-u nuru **gwa-s-a.**
cook-SS leave-SS distribute-SS 3PL.OBJ **give-FPST-3SG**
'She cooked it, distributed it, and gave it to them.'

Sirva

(40) Ma **gu-ra** wa-s-a.
NEG **give-SS** go-FPST-3SG
'He didn't give (it) and he left.' Elicited

Apalɨ verb forms give similar clues to the shape of Proto-Sogeram serialized verbs. Several modern Apalɨ verb suffixes have their origins in earlier SVCs, and some Apalɨ verbs can still be uninflected in a construction that is inherited from Proto-Sogeram orientation SVCs (§4.2.3). In both cases, verbs in these constructions often possess an extra final *a* that is not there in the presence of other suffixes. For example, the verb *lagua* 'step on,' from PSOG *tagwa, is *lagua* when uninflected (41) or when followed by the innovated suffix *-vɨla* 'SS' (42), but is *lagu-* when followed by the older suffix *-ma* 'HPST' (< PSOG *-ma; see §4.3.4), as in (43).

Apalɨ

(41) La avɨli aga-ŋ cɨhu **lagua** ve-mɨ-dɨ u-alɨ.
do water DEF-NOM again **stand.on** come-PROH-3SG say-3SG.FPST
'"It did (it) and the water again should not stand and come," he said.'

(Wade p.c.)

Apalɨ

(42) Ha-meŋ sadaŋ iŋam sabaŋ **lagua-vɨla** sɨbu lama-vɨ-la-lɨ.
MD-CPR because dog pig **stand.on-SS** spit put-PL-HAB-3.FPST
'Because of that when they step on a dog or pig they will spit on it.'

(Wade n.d.b)

Apalɨ

(43) Ve **lagu-m-i.**
come **stand.on-HPST-3SG**
'He came and stood.' (Wade n.d.b)

A final clue to the shape of Proto-Sogeram serialized verbs is the Kursav 1SG. NFUT, which is descended from serialized verbs (Daniels 2015). For many verbs, the shape of the 1SG.NFUT form is the same as the simple Proto-Sogeram root, with the relevant sound changes. For example, *tama 'put' gives *rama* and *aba 'speak' gives *aba* (44). But the reflex of *igwa 'give' is *ubua* (45) (with the irregular development of *gw > *b*). The irregular verb *ve* 'come' (< *fai) also has an irregular 1SG.NFUT form, *via* (46).

Kursav
(44) Ya   mi   **rama-Ø**   map ka   **aba-Ø**.
     1SG   thought   **put-1SG.NFUT**   like MD   **speak-1SG.NFUT**
     'I talked about what I thought about.'

Kursav
(45) Karia=si   sanav   **u-b-ua**.
     betelnut=BEN   money   **3SG.OBJ-give-1SG.NFUT**
     'I gave her money for (i.e., to buy) betelnut.'

Kursav
(46) Midim   skur   bin   i-da,   mata-da,   vuruva=ni   **v-ia**.
     before   school LOC   stay-SS   leave-SS   village=LOC   **come-1SG.NFUT**
     'Long ago, I was at school but I left and came home.'

The evidence from all these languages suggests strongly that we should reconstruct a serialized form of many verbs that adds an additional *a to the end of the root. However, deciding exactly which roots had this additional *a and which did not is quite difficult. Analogical leveling has been at play in every daughter language, removing allomorphy and changing the appearance of the lexicon so that determining the precise shape of Proto-Sogeram verb roots is often impossible. For example, the innovative *-s past tense suffix, derived from an SVC involving the verb *si 'do' (Daniels forthcoming), left evidence in Sirva of the shape of Proto-Sogeram serialized verbs. Presumably this evidence was also there at some point in Mum, Magɨ, and Aisi, since these languages all also inherited the *-s past. But the different root shapes, which presumably used to exist in these languages, have all been removed by analogy with the more common root shapes that occurred with older suffixes. For example, while in Sirva *igwa 'give' is retained as *gwa-* in the *-s past but *gu-* elsewhere, in Mum the *gu-* allomorph has been generalized to all contexts, including the *-s past (47).

Mum
(47) U-ta   tav   mu   **gu-sm-i**   harim ...
     go-SS   house   another   **give-FPST-3SG**   CAUS
     'He went and gave another house and because of this ...'   (Sweeney n.d.)

Similarly, after the -*ua* ending on many erstwhile serialized verbs had become reanalyzed in Kursav as a 1SG.NFUT suffix, it spread to several verbs that definitely did not end in *ua in Proto-Sogeram, such as *ne* 'eat,' which is descended from *ña (48).

(48) Kursav
Ya bua **n-ua.**
1SG enough eat-1SG.NFUT
'I've eaten enough.' Elicited

Unpacking the complicated processes that have created the modern diversity of verb endings, then, is a difficult task. To illustrate, Table 14 presents reflexes of Proto-Sogeram uninflected verbs in the four languages discussed above. Apalɨ reflexes are uninflected forms from the Akɨ dialect, except for *havu* 'carry,' *himu* 'die,' and *ifu* 'hit,' which are Acɨ forms. Sirva forms are from the *-s past. Kursav forms are either serialized, if uninflected, or 1SG.NFUT. Recall that Kursav retains a certain amount of verb serialization; serialized forms of verbs often differ from the 1SG.NFUT form. Gants forms are serialized, except for 'give' which is not attested in serialized form in my corpus, and which is given in its inflected form.

Table 14: Reflexes of PSOG uninflected verbs.

	Apalɨ	Sirva	Kursav	Gants	PSOG
'give'	igua	gwa-	-b-ua	go-	*igwa
'carry'	havu	kavu-	kap-ua		*kapu
'burn (intr.)'		tua-	ro	tua	*tua
'die'	himu	kumu-	kumo, kum-ua	kumo	*kɨmu
'go'	ua	wa-		wa	*wa
'go down'	migua	mugu-		migo	*mɨgwa
'go up'	iahua	yakiva-		yako	*yakwa
'step on'	lagua			tago	*tagwa
'hit'	ifu		ivo, iv-ua	yo	*ifu

As this table makes clear, not every Proto-Sogeram verb root ended in *a when serialized. For this reason, I prefer to analyze this extra *a as belonging to an alternate root shape, rather than as a linking suffix of some kind. Naturally it is possible that in a stage prior to Proto-Sogeram there was a linking suffix *-a which accreted onto many roots and created Proto-Sogeram SVCs, but this analysis does not seem best for the Proto-Sogeram stage.

4.2.2 Aspectual serial verbs

When Proto-Sogeram verbs were serialized, the last verb would often not contribute its normal lexical semantics to the SVC, but instead contributed aspectual semantics. Four such verbs can be reconstructed: *kɨda 'walk,' which contributed imperfective aspect; *kɨña 'stay,' which contributed stative aspect; *tama 'put,' which contributed completive aspect; and *tɨku 'see,' which contributed conative mood. I discuss each of these reconstructions in turn.

For *kɨda, I begin the discussion with Gants, where the reflex is *kɨda* 'walk'. When this verb is the last of an SVC, it can be interpreted as contributing habitual aspect: in (49) and (50), no literal walking is taking place. Note, though, that the habitual interpretation is not obligatory, and *kɨda* can also denote literal walking in this position.

Gants
(49) Krɨm mɨda, araka, dugep, kra nuduŋ rotu ada
night COM noon afternoon TOP 3SG.POSS worship do
kɨda-m-ek.
walk-FPST-3SG
'Night, day, and afternoon, she would always worship.'

Gants
(50) Node God kia miŋa **kɨd-ek.**
woman God speech get **walk-3SG.IPST**
'The woman holds (i.e., follows) God's talk.'

Manat does not have SVCs, but it does have verb–verb compounds. In these compounds the second verb root will sometimes contribute aspectual semantics instead of its normal lexical semantics; one such verb is *da-* 'walk,' which contributes progressive (51) or continuous (52) aspect.

Manat
(51) Trɨh-ura-s vihir ka-b **kubru-da-n=a ...**
pull-PL-3.DS bamboo MD-NOM **break-walk-2/3.SS=LNK**
'They pulled and the bamboo was breaking and ...'

Manat
(52) Pu **ara-da-n** bram ɨnɨ-n mɨgra-ma-g.
bang **say-walk-2/3.SS** arm ND-ACC cut-PST-3SG.FAR
'It made a big noise and cut their hands.'

Apalɨ possesses a suffix -*da* which Wade (1989: 165) labels 'continuous'. In combination with the historic past tense, this suffix "indicates historic habitual tense/aspect, i.e. something that was done regularly (repeatedly) in the historic past" (Wade 1989: 166), as in (53). With the immediate past, -*da* "indicates a kind of present continuous form, i.e. something going on at that time" (Wade 1989: 172), as in (54).

Apalɨ
(53) *Iauacaŋ   ia-dɨ   aga-ŋ   nibu   simiŋ **ma iga-da-m-i.***
      grandfather 1SG-OBL DEF-NOM 3SG.NOM food NEG see-CONT-HPST-3SG
      'My grandfather, he used to not see food.'   (Wade n.d.b)

Apalɨ
(54) *Viaŋ   simiŋ **na-d-in.***
      1SG.NOM food   eat-CONT-1SG.IPST
      'I am eating food.'   (Wade 1989: 172)

Unlike most TAM morphology, -*da* can occur on medial verbs, specifically those marked with different-subject suffixes. In this context, it signals "simultaneous or overlapping activities being done by different subjects" (Wade 1989: 165), as in (55).

Apalɨ
(55) *H-eŋ   **hɨni-da-mili**   hulaŋ   u-ava-lɨ.*
      MD-LOC stay-CONT-1PL.DS   man   go-PL-3.FPST
      'We were staying there while the men went.'   (Wade 1989: 173)

This Apalɨ suffix, then, has habitual meaning with the historic past, continuous meaning with the immediate past, and simultaneous meaning with different-subject forms. Its central meaning could probably be best described as 'imperfective,' although we should bear in mind that it appears to be developing slightly different functions in different contexts.[16]

---

[16] Indeed, in a 1997 paper, Wade opts to gloss the medial function 'SIM' and the other functions 'CONT,' although since -*da* was not the focus of that paper this decision should probably not be interpreted as a claim that they are different suffixes.

The description above pertains to the Akɨ dialect of Apalɨ. And while Wade devotes less discussion to the Acɨ dialect, she does provide a paradigm of Acɨ 'habitual' suffixes in one of her papers (Wade 1993: 92) in which the habitual suffix is -hɨda—no doubt a less-eroded reflex of PSOG *kɨda that is cognate with the Akɨ suffix -da described above.

Mum has a similar suffix -da, which marks habitual aspect (56).

Mum
(56) Arhad   kuyu-i   kuku   aru   **va-da-riŋ.**
     1PL.POSS speech-LOC   water   big   **say-HAB-1PL**
     'In our language, we usually say "big water".'   (Sweeney n.d.)

Finally, Kursav also has a habitual suffix -d (57).

Kursav
(57) Nin   ripa-da   **dai-d-o**   ma.
     3PL   fear-SS   **walk-HAB-3PL**   NEG
     'They were afraid and they didn't walk around (i.e., they stayed at home).'

Based on these reflexes, we can reconstruct an SVC to Proto-Sogeram in which the final verb was *kɨda 'walk' and that verb contributed habitual aspect instead of its normal lexical semantics. This function has been inherited into most modern languages, with the exception of Manat and Apalɨ, where it refers to different kinds of imperfective aspect.

The verb *kɨña 'stay' contributed stative aspect when it was in this position of an SVC. In Gants, its reflex ca 'stay' still has this function, as shown in (58).

Gants
(58) Ai-da   ada ga-k-e   ga, oŋai ma   mia   **cɨ-m-ek.**
     come-SS do   perceive-DS.SEQ-3SG   TOP possum NEG hold **stay-FPST-3SG**
     'He came back and when he looked, it wasn't holding a possum.'

This construction has also undergone grammaticalization, and the verb ca has become the present tense suffix -cɨ (59). Today both reflexes of stative *kɨña survive and they can be used together (60).

Gants
(59) Nɨ-komɨr   kaneŋ   kɨrmo aya   arpim **adɨ-c-ek.**
     3.POSS-brother   group   some   come   help   **do-PRS-3PL**
     'Now some of his brothers are coming to help him.'

Gants

(60) Oŋai   mia   **ci̱-ci̱-k**   aba   wa   ga-k-e   ma
    possum hold **stay-PRS-3SG**   speak go   perceive-DS.SEQ-3SG NEG
    ci̱-m-ek.
    stay-FPST-3SG
    'He thought it was holding (lit. 'said, "It's holding"') a possum and went and looked and there wasn't one.'

In Manat verb–verb compounds, ñi- 'stay' can contribute stative aspect when it is the second verb in a compound (61). Matters appear to be similar in Nend, where ñi- 'stay' seems to contribute stative or durative aspect in verb–verb compounds (62). However, while K. Harris (1990: 84) briefly discusses Nend verb–verb compounds, he does not go into detail about their semantic properties so this analysis remains conjectural.

Manat

(61) Migra-n   g-ura-s,   o   vaca tak   **agrama-ñi-ma-g.**
    cut-2/3.SS give-PL-3.DS oh   one   only **stand-stay-PST-3SG.FAR**
    'They cut them all up, and oh, just one was left standing.'

Nend

(62) Wiram   mba-na-mb   kirim **aŋkwa-ñi~ndiñ-i.**
    man   ND-CTR-NOM   just   **stand-stay~TPST-3SG**
    'This man just stood there.'   (K. Harris n.d.)

Similarly, in Apali̱ hi̱ni- 'stay' "realizes durative aspect in compound verb roots" (Wade 1989: 188), as in (63).

Apali̱

(63) Via   **migi̱la   hi̱ni-da-ci** ...
    get   **watch   stay-CONT-3SG.DS**
    'He got it and was watching while ...'   (Wade 1989: 188)

The verb *ti̱ku 'see, look' could contribute conative meaning ('try to V')[17] when it was the last verb of an SVC. This reconstruction is based on reflexes of this

---

[17] This "aspectual SVC" thus does not convey aspectual information, but modal. In addition, many forms that have grammaticalized via this construction, such as the many plural suffixes and the *-s past tense mentioned above are not really aspects. In spite of this, I prefer to call this

function in Manat and Kursav. In Manat, when the verb *riku-* 'see' is the second verb in a compound, it indicates that the first verb of the compound was (or should be) attempted (64). This function is quite gramamticalized, so that *riku-* can even mark itself conatively (65).

Manat
(64) **Huma   ini-n   migra-rik-itiŋd.**
coconut ND-ACC **cut-see-1SG.IMP**
'Let me try to cut this coconut.'   Elicited

Manat
(65) **Ruku-ruk-utiŋd.**
see-see-1SG.IMP
'Let me try to see.'   Elicited

In Kursav *ruko* 'see' also indicates that the action of the SVC was, or should be, attempted (66).

Kursav
(66) **Maski,   niga,   opim   du   ruko-ku.**
nevermind SPEC   open   do   **see-2SG.IMP**
'Nevermind, try to open another one.'

The similarity in form and function between these two constructions is striking. Given that Manat and Kursav are quite divergent languages and there is no evidence of their having been in contact in the past, this construction should be reconstructed to Proto-Sogeram.

The final aspectual SVC that can be reconstructed involves *tama 'put,' which contributed completive aspect. This function is still exhibited in Gants today, as illustrated in (67), where no literal putting is taking place. Rather, *tama* here indicates that the act of coming and standing was completed.

Gants
(67) **Kain   sirik   raŋa   adiko   pakai   aya   tagurama   tama-m-ek.**
dog   itch   CHAR   this   again   come   stand   **put-FPST-3SG**
'This mangy (lit. 'characterized by itching') dog came and stood up again.'

SVC construction "aspectual serial verbs" because a more appropriate label, such as "grammatical serial verbs," would be too broad.

This function also appears to be retained in Manat verb–verb compounds, although my corpus does not contain any examples as clear as (67). For example, in (68) *rama-* 'put' appears to contribute completive aspect, although it could also refer to literal putting.

Manat
(68) *Akei urum mu=k* **pravu-ram-ura-ma-g.**
 okay man SPEC=ACC **hide-put-PL-PST-3.FAR**
 'Okay, they hid one man.'

Another piece of evidence for this meaning in Manat, or rather Pre-Manat, comes from the innovative verb root *miŋatama-* 'hear'. This is the only Manat verb for hearing that I recorded; I found no reflex of PSoG *idar 'hear'. While *tama-* is not a verb root in Manat, the reflex of *tama being *rama-*, the behavior of *miŋatama-* in reduplication indicates that, etymologically at least, it was composed of two verbs. When the reduplicative nominalizing suffix is attached to it, only the *tama-* element is copied (69).

Manat
(69) *Hɨmñav vana* **miŋatama~dama=k** *Aminahu.*
 song speech **hear~NMLZ=ACC** Aminahu
 'The (place for) hearing about songs is Aminahu.'

The etymology of this verb is thus quite apparent: it comes from an older SVC or compound consisting of the verbs *miŋa 'get' and *tama 'put'. It is apparently quite old, since it fused before word-initial consonant lenition, which was shared with Apalɨ (§3.2.1.4), changed *tama to *rama-*. It only remains to posit a plausible path of semantic innovation that leads from 'get-put' to 'hear,' and here is where the completive meaning of 'put' comes to our aid. It is quite plausible to suppose that *miŋa 'get' came to mean 'understand' in some contexts, as it does in American English today. If *tama 'put' did not refer to literal putting, but rather contributed completive aspect, then this SVC would have meant 'understand completely'. It only takes a small semantic change to move from this meaning to 'hear'.

Finally, there is a Mum morpheme *-rama* which Sweeney glosses 'PL'. There are only three tokens of it in Sweeney's data, but all of them, like (70), occur between a verb root and its suffixes, and pluralize a motion event performed by many subjects. While this form is not well understood, the semantic link to the meaning of completion found in Gants and Manat is apparent: a shift from "they completely went" to "they all went" seems plausible.

	Mum						
(70)	Yad	kru	ha	kura-yɨ	mɨgu-i	ti-h-i	vahi
	1SG.POSS	man	MD	bush-LOC	go.down-3SG.IPST	do-DS-3SG	several
	sɨhanaga	kru	**yaha-rama-ta ...**
	everyone	man	**come.up-PL-SS**

"My boy went to the bush," he said and all the men came up ...'

(Sweeney n.d.)

To summarize, the four aspectual SVCs we have reconstructed to Proto-Sogeram are presented in Table 15, along with the languages in which reflexes can be found.

Table 15: Aspectual serial verb constructions.

Verb	Lexical sense	Grammatical meaning	Reflexes
*kɨda	walk	habitual	Manat, Apalɨ, Mum, Kursav, Gants
*kɨña	stay	stative	Nend, Manat, Apalɨ, Gants
*tɨku	see	conative	Manat, Kursav
*tama	put	completive	Manat, Mum, Gants

It should be noted that while these are the only aspectual SVCs that can be positively reconstructed to Proto-Sogeram, it is almost certain that more existed. This construction, as formalized in (71), has given rise to multiple new morphemes throughout the history of the family. In addition to the grammaticalization of the Apalɨ imperfective suffix, the Mum and Kursav habitual suffix, and the Gants present tense suffix described above, this construction gave rise to the *-s past tense forms in Proto-North Sogeram and Proto-Aisian (Daniels forthcoming) and to several plural suffixes (§4.1.3).

(71)   *(NP$_{OBJ}$) V$_{LEXICAL}$ V$_{ASPECTUAL}$-INFL

4.2.3 Orientation serial verbs

There is evidence for reconstructing a serialized verb position that was separate from the other serialized verbs, occurring to the left of the object in the Proto-Sogeram clause. Evidence for this reconstruction comes from SVCs in Gants, Sirva, Magɨ, and Apalɨ, as well as from a Manat quasi-verbal particle that appears to be descended from this construction.

In Gants SVCs, a serialized verb can occur to the left of the object, as illustrated in (72). Aside from their position away from the rest of the SVC, these verbs are identical to other serialized verbs: they are uninflected and they take the uninflected root shape, as (73) illustrates (the inflected root for 'come' is *ai-*).

Gants
(72) **Aŋa** asɨko mɨŋa-m-ek.
go ginger get-FPST-3SG
'He went and got ginger.'

Gants
(73) **Aya** maj taki kra ada ña tapr-ek.
come sweet.potato cold TOP do eat finish-3SG.IPST
'He came and ate up the cold sweet potatoes.'

Verbs in this position are necessarily intransitive, as the minimal pair in (74) and (75) illustrates. In (74) *aba* 'speak,' which is a labile verb that can take an object, is intransitive. In (75) it is difficult to say whether *aba*, *mɨŋa*, or both take the object *node*, but *aba* seems to have a transitivizing function in this clause; it often appears in this position when a verb takes a human object that normally would not, such as *mɨŋa* 'get'.

Gants
(74) Ya **aba** node mɨŋa-da …
1SG **speak** woman get-SS
'I talked and I got my wife and …' Elicited

Gants
(75) Ya node aba mɨŋa-da …
1SG woman speak get-SS
'I got my wife and …' Elicited

The rightmost verbs in Proto-Sogeram SVCs, which were all adjacent, fused in many languages and are reflected as compounds today. But in some languages where this took place, such as Sirva and Apalɨ, orientation SVCs are still retained as SVCs. In Sirva, uninflected verb roots can occur to the left of the object and other non-subject arguments, as in (76) and (77). All of the unambiguous examples of this construction involve motion verbs, although it is possible that other semantic classes of verbs can be used in this way. Nevertheless, it is fairly certain that verbs in this position must be intransitive. Even in ambiguous examples like (78), where the (potentially) serialized verb is adjacent to the inflected verb, the serialized verb is intransitive.

    Sirva
(76) *Be   kav   kid-a   **pi**   puza,   tik=iñ   hasa   gu-rub-ii ...*
     3SG just walk-SS **come** shaft piece=LI FOC give-PL-3.DS
     '(The fathers) used to just walk over and offer just a spear shaft, and ...'

    Sirva
(77) *Mir-a   **tiva**   od-on ki-rav-ri.*
     leave-SS **go.upstream** FD-LOC stay-HAB-3SG
     'He left and went upstream and lived there.'

    Sirva
(78) *Kiki   uhu   k-on   **yavru** ki-i~gii,   ni-si   be*
     drum hole MD-LOC **hide** stay-3SG.DS~SIM 3.POSS-older.sib 3SG
     pi~rapi   ga-s-a   ka-ga ...
     come~PTCP see-FPST-3SG MD-TOP
     'While he was hiding in the drum hole, his older brother came and looked, and ...'

It is unclear whether Sirva serialized verbs are descended from Proto-Sogeram uninflected verbs. Only three motion verbs are reconstructed with this pattern of root allomorphy: *wa/*u- 'go,' *yakwa/*yakw- 'go up,' and *migwa/*migw- 'go down'. Of these, the first two are not attested in the serialization construction, and the last has lost this pattern of allomorphy and is attested as *mugu* in every construction (79).

    Sirva
(79) *Wa-ra **mugu**   Buhati ada-ma mar wa-ra ...*
     go-SS **go.down** Bugati FD-ADVZ like go-SS
     'He went down and went like that to Bugati and ...'

Verb serialization in Magɨ is not well understood, but it consists primarily of intransitive verbs of motion (80) or posture (81) that can precede several kinds of non-subject argument, including the object (82). Serialized verbs sometimes possess an additional root-final *i*, as with *kipi* in (81) (compare the bound root shape *kip-*), but this alternation cannot be said to be cognate with the alternation between inflected and uninflected verb root shapes that has been reconstructed to Proto-Sogeram (§4.2.1). Rather, in Proto-Aisian, almost all verbs became *a*-roots, and because these verbs now ended in *a, all of these vowels, new as well as old, were reanalyzed as part of the suffix when they were present. Uninflected verbs, meanwhile, underwent a regular sound change in which word-final *a was centered to *ɨ (§3.4.2.4), as can be seen with *kɨpɨ* itself, which is descended from PSoG *kɨpa 'get up'. This sound change also had the effect of eliminating many word-final tokens of *a that *were* originally on uninflected verbs, such as the one on *mɨgwa 'go down,' in which the *ɨ that was presumably created from the *a by this sound change was merged into the preceding *u* and was lost, giving the form *mugu* seen in (80).

Magɨ
(80) Maban **mugu,** ka-niŋ kiti kiti ...
Mawan **go.down** MD-LOC stay.SS stay.SS
'I went down to Mawan and stayed and stayed there, and ...'

Magɨ
(81) Kundɨ **kɨpɨ** Sande ga, abi yaka=niŋ ab-is-iŋ.
morning **get.up** Sunday TOP woman 1SG.POSS=ACC speak-FPST-1SG
'I got up on Sunday morning and spoke to my wife.'

Magɨ
(82) Tewad taku sibi-kitiŋ **yakɨte,** tewad kapɨr-kitiŋ ...
leaf cut cover-SS **come.upstream** leaf throw-SS
'I cut a leaf and covered (myself) and came up and I threw the leaf away and ...'

Apalɨ possesses a construction which Wade labels the "immediate sequential same subject" construction. In this construction, verb roots are "juxtaposed to indicate that two activities follow each other immediately in time," and these roots "may have other arguments which occur between" them (Wade 1989: 70). While I have not conducted detailed counts, Apalɨ texts give the impression that verbs of motion are the most common kind in this construction (83). Additionally, verbs in this construction are almost always in the uninflected form with an additional final *a* (84).

Apalɨ
(83) Lihuŋ **iahua** sabɨ hɨvɨ hɨni-d-ɨ.
bird.type **go.up** top LI stay-CONT-3SG
'The *lihuŋ* bird is above on top.' (Wade n.d.b)

Apalɨ
(84) **Ua hɨnia** Anialɨci h-eŋ hɨlan-ava-lɨ.
    go stay Anialɨci MD-LOC cook-PL-3.FPST
    'They went and stayed and then they cooked there at Anialɨci.'

(Wade n.d.b)

Unlike in any of the languages described above, verbs in this Apalɨ construction do not have to be intransitive (85).

Apalɨ
(85) Kɨlɨ **iha** hulɨn **iha-laha** hulɨn hivɨ hah-avɨ-la-lɨ.
    tree **cut** plant.type **cut-tear** plant.type LI tie-PL-HAB-3.FPST
    'They cut a tree, break down hulɨn plants and tie it with them.'

(Wade n.d.b)

Finally, Manat possesses a quasi-verbal particle *hɨd*, which I gloss 'move' and which appears to be descended from PSOG *kɨda 'walk'. While this particle can head a clause on its own (86), it far more commonly functions as an adverb that adds motion semantics to a predicate headed by a proper verb. In this function it usually precedes the object (87) and other non-subject arguments (88). An additional piece of evidence that this particle is descended from a verb is the fact that it can take the reduplicative nominalizing suffix (§4.5.1), which derives nouns from verbs (89).

Manat
(86) Ara-n ta-n bɨ **hɨd.**
    say-2/3.SS leave-2/3.SS 3.NOM **move**
    'He said that, left, and went away.'

Manat
(87) **Hɨd** nadi añɨŋa kai inɨ-n gu-r-m-id.
    move woman two LOC ND-ACC give-HAB-PST-3SG.HIS
    'He used to go give it to the two women.'

Manat
(88) Akai **hɨd** mɨkɨñ kai mɨgu-ma-g.
    okay **move** fishing.net LOC go.down-PST-3SG.FAR
    'Okay, he went down into the fishing net.'

Manat
(89) Ini-ba **hid~ihid** rih-id ar-ura-ma-g.
ND-LOC **move~NMLZ** do-3SG.IPST say-PL-PST-3.FAR
'"She's wandering around here," they said.'

We have now examined constructions in Manat, Apalɨ, Sirva, Magɨ, and Gants. I have so far ignored the structural question: what is the relationship between the serialized intransitive verb and the other verbs? I present relevant facts from Apalɨ and Gants. In Apalɨ, these serialized verbs do not necessarily have the same value for negation (90) or illocutionary force (91) as the verbs that follow them; for this reason Wade considers them separate clauses.

Apalɨ
(90) Iga ma sihu-i.
see NEG defecate-3SG.IPST
'She saw it and did not defecate.' (Wade 1989: 72)

Apalɨ
(91) Iga sihu-minaŋ ...
see defecate-2SG.PROH
'You see it and don't you defecate ...' (Wade 1989: 71)

In Gants, while it is clear that serialized verbs can have different polarity and illocutionary force values, there are no clear examples of this for the intransitive SVC construction. Nevertheless, (92) demonstrates that serialized verbs can have different polarity values. And (93), where *sikasika tago miŋa* '(when you) get dirt on your feet' is not under the scope of the negative imperative marking of the clause, shows the same for illocutionary force.

Gants
(92) O **okra** ma ga-da bir kuyara-paŋ-dik.
oh **look.for** NEG perceive-SS TOP sit-FUT-3SG
'Oh, he'll look for it and won't find it and he'll sit down.'

Gants
(93) Sikasika **tago miŋa** kineb kenin yak ko ma ai-p-raŋ!
debris **step get** house inside 1SG.OBJ DEF NEG come-IMP-2PL
'Don't track dirt inside my house!'

The facts above suggest that orientation SVCs can be analyzed as coordinated verb phrases within a single clause. This accounts for the facts that the verbs do not share objects; they do share subjects; they are marked only once for inflectional categories; and they can have different values for polarity and illocutionary force.[18]

To review, the constructions presented above share several properties. Each is composed of an uninflected verb root situated to the left of other verb roots and their non-subject arguments. In Apalɨ and Gants, these verbs take their uninflected form; in Manat and Magɨ it is not possible, for phonological reasons, to discern whether the verbs are reflexes of the Proto-Sogeram uninflected forms; and in Sirva accidents of inheritance make the question difficult to settle. And in every language except Apalɨ the verbs are intransitive.

We thus have a valid correspondence set, although a rather tenuous one by the standards I have set. The form of the cognate constructions matches, as all are composed of an uninflected verb followed by a verb phrase. The meanings also match, as they all (with one exception) employ intransitive verbs. A reconstruction based on these considerations would look like (94): an intransitive verb followed by a verb phrase, itself composed of an optional object and the inflected verb.

(94) $*V_{INTR} [(NP_{OBJ}) \text{ V-INFL}]_{VP}$

But in this case there is precious little phonological material with which to ensure that syntactic borrowing has not taken place. The only piece of phonological material specific to this construction is the final *a that occurs on uninflected verb roots in Apalɨ and Gants—admittedly not much.

An additional problem with this reconstruction concerns the issue of arbitrariness. The construction in (94) is somewhat iconic: the intransitive verb, for which the subject is the only argument, is located immediately to the right of that subject; and the transitive verb is also located next to its object. It is thus possible that this construction did not exist in Proto-Sogeram but was rather formed independently in several daughter branches due to this iconic motivation. The

---

[18] Note that this last structural fact means that for many authors (e.g., Aikhenvald 2006: 1; Bohnemeyer et al. 2007: 501; Haspelmath 2016: 299), Sogeram orientation SVCs do not qualify as serial verbs. This is not a problem. I only use the term in the Sogeram context as a convenient label to distinguish these constructions from clause chains. I do not intend my use as a definitional challenge to the more widespread usage.

scenario I am alluding to would begin with all Proto-Sogeram serialized verbs, including orientation SVCs, being located at the right edge of the clause, after all the arguments. But intransitive verbs would then be moved leftwards in some daughter languages to be closer to the subject, for which they had a greater affinity. This would then also have created a contiguous verb phrase if the second verb had an overt object.

So we must ask ourselves which scenario is most likely. Did the construction in (94) exist in Proto-Sogeram, and was it inherited into the daughter languages as shown in the examples above? Or did this construction not exist in Proto-Sogeram but rather spread due to contact or iconicity after Proto-Sogeram had broken up? The former scenario seems more probable to me. The construction has reflexes in languages from every branch, Greater West Sogeram, North Sogeram, and East Sogeram. If it spread via contact it must have spread quite early in the history of the family to be inherited into both Manat and Gants—so early that even if it was a later innovation, it could at least be attributed to a late variety of Proto-Sogeram. As for the iconicity objection, while I have acknowledged that the construction in (94) is iconic to some degree, this iconicity does not strike me as so strong that it would be likely to motivate multiple instances of verb movement of the kind I have described above.

The result of applying my methodology for syntactic reconstruction to this data, then, is a somewhat tenuous reconstruction. The criterion of having cognate phonological material is met, but only just. Similarly, the criterion of avoiding iconic motivations for change has also been addressed, but not conclusively. In evaluating these criteria I have concluded that it is more likely than not that Proto-Sogeram had a construction like (94), which I refer to as the "orientation SVC". Note that this is a subjective conclusion, based on my assessment of the evidence. This is what the method requires. It does not provide "its own" answer to the question of whether a given construction existed in a given proto-language, but only provides the comparativist with a set of theoretical tools and a framework in which to apply them. Reconstructions are not sorted into two piles, those that are approved by the method and those that are not. Rather, the method structures the process of evaluating evidence, but still leaves it up to the practitioner to decide how well or how poorly a given reconstruction is supported. And this must be stated: in the present case, for example, we can say that the reconstruction of Proto-Sogeram orientation SVCs is less secure than many other reconstructions proposed in this book.

To summarize: uninflected verbs occurred to the left of the (other) verb phrase—that is, to the left of the other serialized verbs and of their arguments. These verbs were generally intransitive posture or motion verbs that oriented the subject with respect to the other events of the clause.

4.2.4 Causative and manner serial verbs

A further SVC position that can be reconstructed for Proto-Sogeram is what I call the causative position. The verb in the causative position of an SVC described the manner in which the action of the other verbs was caused. The causative verb could affect the valence of the SVC as a whole, although due to the limited number of manner SVCs that can be reconstructed the extent of this pattern is unclear. It is clear, though, that this construction involved a change of subject from the causative verb to the following verb: the causative verb described the causal action, which was performed by the subject of the clause, and the following verb described the result of that action. An example is the Mum verb *miŋahumu-* 'kill' in (95), which is descended from **miŋa kɨmu* 'get die,' which would have meant 'kill by hand'. The subject of *miŋa-* 'get,' as well as that of the clause as a whole (as shown by the 3PL agreement suffix *-u*), is the killers, but the notional subject of *humu-* 'die' is the victim.

Mum
(95) *Pa-ta   nin-ɨŋ   Aŋihuru   ñanɨŋ   amaz-ɨŋ   **miŋahumu-h-u** ...*
come-SS who-OBJ Angihuru his.son eighth.born-OBJ **kill-DS-3PL**
'They came and killed, uh, the son of Angihuru, the eighth born son ...'
(Sweeney n.d.)

Two verbs can be reconstructed for the causative position: **miŋa* 'get' meant 'cause to happen manually' and **igwa* 'give' meant 'cause to happen by giving'. A third verb, **aba* 'speak,' may have meant 'cause to happen verbally,' but it is not clear that this verb involved a change of subject in this position or had the same causative semantics. Rather, it may have simply had manner semantics and meant 'do by speaking'.

The causative use of **miŋa* 'get' can be reconstructed based on the Mum example above and the Gants example in (96). This latter example is somewhat curious, since it is the only Gants SVC in my corpus that contains a change of notional subject. Further reflexes of causative **miŋa* can be seen in the Sirva example in (97) and the Apalɨ example in (98). The Aisi lexeme *miŋimbr-* 'ruin' is also descended from this construction. This word is composed of reflexes of **miŋa* 'get' and **ibra* 'act badly, go bad,' which are retained in Aisi as *miŋ-* 'make' and *imbr-* 'spoil'.

Gants
(96) *Miga   cɨ-k-e   **miŋa   yako-da** ...*
come.down stay-DS.SEQ-3SG **get   go.up-SS**
'It fell down and she picked it up and ...'

Sirva
(97) *Ka-ma   ad-ii   beau   **miŋa-siisiir-a** wa-ra **miŋa-sikr-i-Ø**.*
     MD-ADVZ do-3SG.DS DEF.ACC **get-itch-ss** go-ss **get-break-TPST-3SG**
     'So she scratched and scratched it (lit. 'scratched it and went') and broke it.'

Apali
(98) *Nibu   nu-di   ibi   **miŋa-iaha-vi-hada-m-i**.*
     3SG.NOM 3SG-OBL name **hold-get.up-PL-CONT-HPST-3**
     'As for him, they were habitually lifting up his name.'   (Wade p.c.)

Finally, the Nend example in (99) may be cognate with the other examples if the verb *aka-*, glossed 'cut,' is labile and can mean 'become detached'. Such verbs are not uncommon among the Sogeram languages, but Harris's glossing suggests that this is not such a verb.

Nend
(99) *Avi-z   awar-oh-e   ahah   ha-n   **ŋ-ak-e** ...*
     do.thus-3SG.DS up.ridge-go-ss mature.betelnut MD-ACC **get-cut-ss**
     'Then he climbed up and picked the mature betelnut and ...'
                                                           (K. Harris n.d.)

The verb *igwa 'give' could also be used causatively, although only one SVC involving this verb can be reconstructed: *igwa ña 'give eat,' which meant 'feed'. The semantics match those of *miŋa in this construction, in that the action of *ña 'eat' is caused by the action of *igwa 'give' and there is a change of subject between the two verbs. The reconstruction of this SVC is secure based on reflexes in Nend (100), Manat (101), and Aisi (102), and it also occurs in Apali (Martha Wade p.c.). But it is unclear whether *igwa could occur with verbs besides *ña 'eat' or whether *igwa ña was a lexicalized pair that meant 'feed' or 'give to eat'.

Nend
(100) *Hirimbi-mb   kambir-ir   Aŋgimere   **eŋkwa-n-an-j**.*
      cook~NMLZ friend-kin Aŋgimere **give-eat-HPST-3SG**
      'Cooking (it), he used to give it to his friend Aŋgimere.' (K. Harris n.d.)

Manat
(101) *Ñaŋña   tak   ai-n=a,   mihra-n   **igu-ña-md=a**.*
      food only come-2/3.SS=LNK take.much-2/3.SS **give-eat-2SG.IMP=EXCL**
      'Please come take all this food and give it out.'

Aisi
(102) **Igon-ogi** na, kwi wa-s-uŋ.
feed-3PL.DS and back come-FPST-3PL
'They gave them (salt) and they came back.'

Finally, *aba 'speak' could occur in this position, although probably with manner semantics instead of causative semantics. The only example I can find in which the action of the following appears to be caused by speaking, and which involves a change of subject, is the Mum word *abahumu-* 'scold,' composed of reflexes of *aba 'speak' and *kɨmu 'die'—in other words, 'cause to die by speaking'. In every other language, though, *aba appears to simply mean 'do by speaking,' rather than 'cause by speaking'. For example, in the Gants examples below, the actions of the verbs following *aba* are performed verbally. In (103) the object is human and was 'gotten' via speech, since humans must in the main be reasoned with rather than picked up and moved. Similarly, in (104), *aba go* 'speak give' means 'tell'—that is, 'give (information) by speaking'.

Gants
(103) Ya nak **aba miŋa-da** aŋa-paŋ-nin wa-m-eniŋ.
1SG 2SG.OBJ **speak get-ss** go-FUT-1SG say-FPST-1SG
'I said, "I'm going to take you and we'll go".'

Gants
(104) Wisin mod ko migo-da aya **aba go-da** aŋa-m-ek.
sleep during DEF descend-ss come **speak give-ss** go-FPST-3SG
'He came and told me in a dream and left.'

The same SVC can be found in Kursav (105): *aba bu-* 'speak give' means 'tell, inform'. In Magɨ, *abɨ ir-* 'speak perceive' means 'ask' (106); in other words, 'investigate (or perceive) by speaking'.

Kursav
(105) Va-da ka-ka guro, midim **aba u-b-ua**.
say-ss MD-TOP speech before **speak 3SG.OBJ-give-1SG.NFUT**
'I said that and I told him this stuff before.'

Magɨ
(106) Ka-ŋga itɨ ga, yɨ **abɨ ir-is-iŋ**.
MD-ADJZ thus TOP 1SG **speak perceive-FPST-1SG**
'So I asked him.'

Finally, while Manat has lost its reflex of *aba, at least one SVC involving the verb survives. Example (107) shows the verb *abiva-* 'fight,' which is descended from *aba 'speak' and *ifu 'hit'.

(107) Manat
Bɨ **abiv-tara-n** agram-ur-id.
3.NOM **fight-PURP-2/3.SS** stand-PL-3.IPST
'They're standing up to fight.'

There are many examples of other verbs occurring in what appear to be reflexes of the causative/manner SVC position, and it is likely that some of these uses date to Proto-Sogeram. But in the absence of diverse reflexes, examples like these cannot confidently be reconstructed. For example, the Apalɨ compound *ifɨ-hima-* 'hit-die' means 'kill,' and appears to be descended from *ifu 'hit' in causative position, as the compound means 'cause to die by hitting'. Similarly, *kra* 'burn' in (108) has manner semantics very similar to those of *aba in the examples above—that is, the SVC means 'eat (or consume) by burning'. (Note that *kevɨ-* 'throw' here is contributing habitual semantics to the SVC.) But until further research uncovers similar examples in other Sogeram languages, these forms cannot be reconstructed to Proto-Sogeram.

(108) Kursav
Itu **kra ne kevɨ-d-o.**
tobacco **burn eat throw-HAB-3PL**
'They used to smoke tobacco.'

4.3 Final morphology

The verbal morphology of all the Sogeram languages, as well as that of Proto-Sogeram, can be divided into two types: medial and final. This is a common division among Papuan languages, particularly those of the Trans New Guinea family (Roberts 1997, Foley 2018). Medial morphology marks switch reference, that is, the identity or non-identity of a verb's subject with the subject of the following verb. Clauses with medial verbs are chained together and the last clause of each chain contains a final verb. Final verbs—verbs with final morphology—are marked for person and number, and also distinguish the full range of TAM categories. This information has scope over the preceding chain, as medial verbs are unmarked for tense. Medial verbs do, however, sometimes mark relative tense, that is, whether the events of the marked verb and the following verb are simultaneous or sequential. They also sometimes distinguish realis from irrealis.

In the following sections I present my reconstructions of the final verb categories: the immediate past tense, the today past tense, the recent and far past tenses, the historic past tense, the future tense, the habitual aspect, the imperative mood, the prohibitive mood, and the counterfactual mood. I also present one verb category, the irrealis, which could be used both medially and finally.

Before presenting the reconstructed paradigms, I present the general verb template that most TAM categories employed in (109).

(109) Root – TAM – Agreement

Proto-Sogeram verbs were composed of the root, followed by a TAM suffix, followed by a subject agreement suffix. The subject agreement suffix was taken from one of several sets of suffixes. These are often difficult to reconstruct, and there was often analogical replacement of suffixes from one set with suffixes from another set. The reconstructed sets are presented in Table 16. Recall that there was no dedicated 3PL agreement suffix. In the imperative paradigm a 3SG form cannot be reconstructed and it is unclear whether one existed.

Table 16: Agreement suffixes.

Name	1SG	2SG	3SG	1PL	2PL	TAM categories
Set I	*-in	*-na	*-i	*-rɨŋ	*-ra	Immediate past, historic past, DS realis
Set II	*-n	*-na	*-r, *-i	*-urɨŋ	*-ra	Today past, recent past, far past
Set III	*-n	*-na	*-ri	*-rɨŋ	*-ra	Future
Set IV	*-n	*-na	*-i	*-rɨŋ	*-ra	Habitual
Set V	*-ŋ	*-na	*-r, *-i	*-rɨŋ	*-ra	Counterfactual, Irrealis
Set VI	*-ŋ	*-u		*-ɨmɨri	*-mar	Imperative
Set VII	*-ñ	*-na	*-d	*-rɨŋ	*-ra	Prohibitive

Set II and Set IV could each be split into two sets based on the 3SG suffix that is used. For example, while three TAM categories use Set II, the today past uses 3SG *-i and the recent and far past use *-r. I have decided to present the suffix sets this way, though, because it is often quite difficult, for a given TAM paradigm, to reconstruct every subject agreement suffix with certainty. There is also often analogical change in suffix agreement paradigms: for example, reflexes of the today past are found with 3SG *-i in Mand and Apalɨ but with *-r in Nend.

Several aspects of these agreement suffixes pose problems. The 1PL suffix was probably not so consistently *-rɨŋ; Apalɨ and Gants both suggest it often had a round vowel *u, and may have lacked the final nasal in some agreement sets. I currently analyze these reflexes as generalizations of the Set II suffix *-urɨŋ with irregular phonological attrition yielding *-ru or *-ruŋ, but the issue remains cloudy.

There has been a great deal of analogical change to these sets. Often, suffixes from a lesser-used set will be replaced with suffixes from more common sets, most often Set I. Because of this, individual reconstructions in the less-common agreement sets sometimes rest on a single witness because all other languages have replaced the suffix with one from Set I. For example, in the counterfactual mood the Set V 1SG suffix *-ŋ is only retained in the Aisi form, while the only other reflex, Apalɨ, has *-in from Set I. I reconstruct *-ŋ because replacement of a Set V suffix with a Set I suffix is more likely than the reverse, but in cases like this the reconstruction is obviously suspect. I nevertheless propose these tentative reconstructions as the most likely explanation for the current diversity of reflexes, while acknowledging the uncertainty.

4.3.1 Immediate past

The immediate past tense has been reconstructed and discussed in previous work (Daniels 2010: 170; 2014: 387), and I present it again in Table 17. It was formed with no overt tense suffix (indicated by *-Ø in the table) and the Set I agreement suffixes.

Table 17: Immediate past.

	1SG	2SG	3SG	1PL	2PL	3PL
Mand	-in	-n	-i(d)	-inhw	-e-n	-e-d
Nend	-in	-n	-i	-rɨŋ	-mgɨ-n	-mg-i
Manat	-in	-nad	-id	-r	-rad	-ur-id
Apalɨ	-in	-naŋ	-i	-lu	-laŋ	-hav-i
Mum	-in	-na	-i	-rɨŋ	-ra	-yu
Sirva	-ri-n	-ri-na	-ri-Ø	-ri-r	-ri-ra	-b-ri
Magɨ	-iŋ	-aŋ	-i	-ar	-ar	-uŋ
Aisi	-iŋ, -eŋ	-aŋ	-i, -e	-aŋ	-ar	-uŋ, -oŋ
Kursav	-Ø	-na	-e	-r	-ra	-u
Gants	-enɨŋ	-naŋ	-ek	-ruŋ	-raŋ	-ik
PSoG	*-Ø-in	*-Ø-na	*-Ø-i	*-Ø-rɨŋ	*-Ø-ra	

A few observations are in order. Mand has added *d* to the 3SG (where it is optional) and 3PL suffixes, and has innovated a new 1PL suffix. Both it and Nend are innovative in forming the 2PL via a discrete plural suffix in combination with the 2SG suffix. Manat has added *d* to the vowel-final suffixes—that is, 2SG, 3SG, 2PL, and 3PL. Mum, Aisian, and Kursav have innovated new 3PL suffixes, and Sirva has innovated a separate IPST suffix. Aisian has merged almost all stem vowels to *a*, a process which has moved them, in the synchronic morphological analysis, onto those suffixes that began with consonants. Kursav innovated a new 1SG form. And Gants added velar consonants to each suffix: *ŋ* in first and second person, and *k* in third person.

In spite of these variations, the reconstruction is for the most part straightforward. 1SG *-in is reflected clearly in Mand, Nend, Manat, Apalɨ, Mum, and Aisian, and also in Sirva and Gants with little change.

2SG *-na is reflected as expected in Mand, Mum, Sirva, and Kursav. In Nend it lost final *a, but this is also expected. In Manat, Apalɨ, and Gants a consonant was added, and in Aisi final *a would have become *ɨ but this was then lost irregularly.

3SG *-i is retained in Mand, Nend, Apalɨ, Mum, Aisian, and Kursav. Manat and Gants again added consonants, and the process that created the Sirva IPST suffix -*ri* has obscured matters, but the *i* in this suffix is inherited from PSOG *-i.

In the 1PL things are more complicated. Nend, Manat, Mum, Sirva, Magɨ, and Kursav reflect *-rɨŋ (in some cases with regular loss of *ŋ and preceding *ɨ), which suggests that this suffix should be reconstructed. But Apalɨ and Gants both reflect a Proto-Sogeram 1PL suffix *-ru (with an *ŋ* in Gants). If these two suffixes did not appear cognate, they could perhaps be written off as innovations. But they do seem to be cognate, and because they are found in two disparate languages we must consider the possibility that they trace their ancestry to Proto-Sogeram. Several possible explanations present themselves. First, they could reflect dialect variation that existed in Proto-Sogeram but that has been lost in the other Sogeram languages. If this were the case, though, we would expect the geographical distribution of *-ru to be contiguous. Second, perhaps *-ru was actually *-ruŋ and *-rɨŋ was a fast-speech variant. This requires us to explain the unusual loss of final *ŋ in Apalɨ. Third, it is possible that one of the suffixes was 1DU (probably *-rɨŋ) while the other was 1PL (probably *-ru). On this analysis, we must explain why the Proto-Sogeram 1PL was generalized to plural in Apalɨ and Gants instead of the 1DU, as was usually the case. While this last account seems most plausible to me, at this stage we must condede that we do not know what explains the Apalɨ and Gants 1PL.IPST suffixes. And it is also possible that they are both unrelated irregular developments and do not date to Proto-Sogeram at all.

The 2PL suffix *-ra is again quite simple. It is reflected in Mum, Sirva, and Kursav. Manat, Apalɨ, and Gants have added consonants, and in Aisian final *a became *ɨ but was then lost irregularly.

The meaning of this tense is fairly homogeneous across the family. In most languages, it refers to events occurring in the present moment and extends some distance into the past. Only Nend and Gants have dedicated present tenses, and these are innovations. And even in these languages, the immediate past is used as a narrative present. In Mand, Nend, and Apalɨ this tense refers to events extending to a few hours before the speech act. In Manat it extends to the morning of the speech act, and in Sirva to the night before. In Aisi it covers past events on the day of the speech act as well as the day before it. And in Kursav it extends infinitely far back: it has become a non-future tense. In Gants the time reference of this tense is not as fixed as in other languages, and speakers have more latitude to construe events as "recent" or "remote" by the tense they choose. But of all the past tenses (Gants has four), it is the closest to the present.

So we reconstruct a tense that referred to the present moment and extended some distance into the past. It seems most likely that the time reference of this tense was restricted to the day of the speech act in Proto-Sogeram, as this meaning is found in every non-East Sogeram language. Because of the reconstruction of a separate today past tense (see below), this tense is reconstructed with a time reference that extended a few hours before the speech act.

4.3.2 Today past

Cognate past tenses that refer to recent events exist in Mand, Nend, and Apalɨ. The forms are presented in Table 18. In Mand this is a recent past tense, its time reference beginning the day before the speech act and extending an unknown distance into the past. In Nend it is a yesterday past, referring to "events that occurred between sunset last night and sunset the night before" (K. Harris 1990: 126). And in Apalɨ it is a today past, referring to events on the day of the speech act, but prior to the range referred to by the immediate past.

Table 18: Today past.

	1SG	2SG	3SG	1PL	2PL	3PL
Mand	-emɨ-n	-emɨ-n	-eb-i	-emɨ-nhw	-emɨ-n	-eb-i
Nend	-em-en	-em-an	-emɨ-r	-em-orɨŋ	-mg-em-an	-mg-emɨ-r
Apalɨ	-iem-in	-iemɨ-naŋ	-iem-i	-iemɨ-lu	-iemɨ-laŋ	-hav-iem-i
PSOG	*-iamɨ-n	*-iamɨ-na	*-iam-i	*-iam-urɨŋ	*-iamɨ-ra	

The reconstruction of the tense suffix *-iamɨ at first appears unwarranted, as every language has the vowel e. Recall, though, that Proto-Sogeram did not have the vowel *ᵗe*, and that raising **a* to *e* in this environment is a likely explanation for the presence of *e* in all three modern languages. This reconstruction is confirmed by Wade's observation that, although the Apalɨ form is usually *-iem*, "in the Uagalɨhu dialect the variant form *-iam* is used" (Wade 1989: 168). The reconstruction of **a* also reinforces the reconstruction of the suffix-initial **i*, as the presence of this vowel explains the West Sogeram reflex *e* for **ia*, whereas a reconstruction of simply **i* or simply **a* could not.

Reconstructing the agreement suffixes is somewhat more difficult. In the 2SG and 2PL every language reflects the usual **-na* and **-ra*, although Apalɨ adds its usual final *ŋ*. For the 1SG I reconstruct the Set II suffix **-n*, which is only retained in Mand, for two reasons. First, this reconstruction can account for the other forms: the Nend suffix *-en* can be explained via irregular harmony of **ɨ* to the preceding *e*, and the Apalɨ suffix *-in* is simply the more frequent Set I suffix replacing a less frequent form. Secondly, reconstructing another suffix would not explain the Mand form well. The suffix **-n* became homophonous in Mand with the reflex of the 2SG suffix **-na*, due to regular word-final loss of **a* (§3.2.2.4). Because of this, if the original 1SG suffix had been something other than **-n*, it is unlikely that Mand would have changed it to **-n* because that would have rendered it homophonous with the 2SG form. Rather, it is more likely that this homophony developed via the phonological change described above and has not been eliminated in Mand.

In the 3SG **-i* is reconstructed on the strength of the Mand and Apalɨ reflexes; Nend is taken to have replaced the agreement suffix with the other Set II suffix **-r*, as this suffix is generally associated with past tenses. The 1PL suffix is somewhat difficult. Mand and Apalɨ both have their usual 1PL agreement suffixes, which suggests this paradigm either had the common 1PL suffix **-rɨŋ* or Mand and Apalɨ replaced the original, less common agreement suffix with more common ones. I have decided to treat the Nend form as archaic for two reasons: (i) it is only reflected in two Nend paradigms—this one and the Nend far past—suggesting that it was not placed into this paradigm by analogy; and (ii) it is difficult to see how it could have been innovated.

Having reconstructed the tense suffix **-iamɨ* and its agreement suffixes, I now address the meaning of this paradigm. Here we must take into account both the semantic ranges of the modern reflexes and the Proto-Sogeram tense system into which this tense fit. The "median" meaning of this tense is a yesterday past, as reflected in Nend—in Mand its time reference is earlier than that, in Apalɨ more recent. This factor favors reconstructing a yesterday past for this paradigm, as it would involve only two innovations: one in Mand and another in Apalɨ. But there is another scenario that only involves positing two innovations, namely reconstructing the Apalɨ meaning of today past. In this scenario, the tense became a yesterday past in Proto-West Sogeram, and then its time reference was extended farther back in Mand.

So we are left with two possibilities—today past and yesterday past—and we turn to the reconstructed Proto-Sogeram tense system to help us decide. There is one past tense that has a more recent time reference (the immediate past, §4.3.1) and three that have more remote time references (the recent, far, and historic pasts; §4.3.3 and §4.3.4). As such, it seems likely that this tense had a more recent time reference rather than a more remote one, as temporal distinctions tend to be finer closer to the present. Thus we reconstruct a today past, as reflected in Apalɨ, and posit semantic innovations in Proto-West Sogeram and Mand.

Finally, we must address the question of the antiquity of this tense paradigm. It is reflected in Mand and Apalɨ. The genetic position of Apalɨ is ambiguous, as it has innovated with Greater West Sogeram, North Sogeram, and Aisian languages. The innovations Apalɨ shares with Greater West Sogeram languages raise the possibility that this paradigm only dates to an ancestor of Apalɨ and Proto-Greater West Sogeram, which might be called Late Proto-Sogeram, and not to Proto-Sogeram proper. An important factor to consider here is that there is no obvious path of innovation by which this paradigm could have been innovated. For that reason, I tentatively reconstruct it to Proto-Sogeram.

4.3.3 Recent and far past

These tenses are only attested in two languages, shown in Table 19 and Table 20, but the languages are disparate enough that reconstruction appears secure.

Table 19: Recent past.

	1SG	2SG	3SG	1PL	2PL	3PL
Manat	-ŋɨn	-ŋɨnad	-g	-gɨr	-grad	-ura-g
Gants	-gɨ-nɨŋ	-gɨ-naŋ	-g-rɨk	-g-ruŋ	-g-raŋ	-g-rek
PSog	*-gɨ-n	*-gɨ-na	*-gɨ-r	*-g-urɨŋ	*-g-ra	

The recent past was formed with the RPST suffix *-gɨ and the Set II agreement suffixes. In the Manat 1SG and 2SG, where prenasalized *g was followed by a nasal consonant, it lenited to ŋ. Both languages added consonants to many verbal suffixes—Manat usually d, Gants ŋ or k—and this paradigm is no exception. (These additions are most likely the vestige of an old subordination construction; see §6.4.2.) In the 1SG, Manat did not add anything while Gants added ŋ. In the

Table 20: Far past.

	1SG	2SG	3SG	1PL	2PL	3PL
Manat	-ma-ŋin	-ma-ŋinad	-ma-g	-ma-gɨr	-ma-grad	-ura-ma-g
Gants	-ma-gɨ-nɨŋ	-ma-gɨ-naŋ	-ma-g-rɨk	-ma-g-ruŋ	-ma-g-raŋ	-ma-g-rek
PSoG	*-ma-gɨ-n	*-ma-gɨ-na	*-ma-gɨ-r	*-ma-g-urɨŋ	*-ma-g-ra	

2SG, both languages added consonants. In the 3SG, Manat irregularly lost final *r, while Gants added *k*. The 1PL reflects the divergence between *ɨ and *u discussed for the immediate past above: Manat reflects the suffix *-rɨŋ while Gants reflects *-ru or *-urɨŋ. For the moment I reconstruct *-urɨŋ. In the 2PL both languages again added their respective consonants.

In both Manat and Gants, the recent past has a time reference that precedes the immediate past but follows the far past, so this order should be reconstructed for Proto-Sogeram. But we must also decide whether its time reference precedes or follows the today past (§4.3.2). In both Manat and Gants, the time reference of this tense can extend years into the past, as shown with the Manat statement in (110), which was uttered in 2010. Since the today past does not refer to events more than a few days before the speech act in any language, the recent past should be reconstructed with a time reference that precedes the today past.

(110) Manat
Vana ibid ini-n   tutausenfaif kai, **ara-ŋin.**
speech good ND-ACC   2005   LOC   **say-1SG.RPST**
'I said these good things in 2005.'

The far past was formed by adding the historic past suffix *-ma (which was also used in the historic past; see below) to the recent past forms. Note that *-ma preceded the other suffixes. Otherwise, the forms were identical to those used in the recent past. The time reference of this tense precedes the recent past in both languages, and should be reconstructed as such.

4.3.4 Historic past

The historic past was formed with the historic past suffix *-ma in combination with the Set I agreement suffixes, as shown in Table 21. The Manat forms here are from two paradigms. The 1SG, 3SG, and 3PL are from the historic past, which is directly inherited from the Proto-Sogeram historic past. This paradigm is defec-

4.3 Final morphology

Table 21: Historic past.

	1SG	2SG	3SG	1PL	2PL	3PL
Nend			-ma-r			-mgɨ-ma-r
Manat	-m-in	(-r)-ma-nad	-m-id	(-r)-ma-r	(-r)-ma-rad	-ura-m-id
Apalɨ	-m-in	-ma-naŋ	-m-i/-ma-lɨ	-mɨ-lu	-ma-laŋ	-havɨ-m-i
Mum	-m-in	-ma-na	-m-i	-ma-rɨŋ	-ma-ra	-m-u
Sirva	-ma-n	-ma-na	-m	-ma-r	-ma-ra	-bɨ-m
Gants	-m-eniŋ	-me-naŋ	-m-ek	-me-ruŋ	-me-raŋ	-m-aik
PSog	*-m-in	*-ma-na	*-m-i	*-ma-rɨŋ	*-ma-ra	

tive in Manat, though, and no longer hs 2SG, 1PL, or 2PL forms. So these cells are filled with far past habitual suffixes, which are formed with the Proto-Sogeram historic past in combination with the innovative habitual suffix *-rha* (Daniels forthcoming). The Apalɨ form *-m-i* is used in the Akɨ dialect, while *-ma-lɨ* is used in Acɨ. The Nend forms come from the Nend historic past paradigm, which is not cognate in the first and second person.

The first thing to notice is the variation in 3SG suffixes. Nend and Acɨ Apalɨ reflect *-r, which is the suffix used in the recent past and far past (§4.3.3), while other languages reflect *-i, the suffix used in the immediate past (§4.3.1). Note that Sirva reflects final *i, as it sporadically lost this vowel word-finally (§3.3.2.4), whereas the suffix *-r would yield *†-ma*, with loss of word-final *r (§3.3.2.3) and retention of *a.

We must therefore choose which change is more likely: from *-i to *-r, or vice versa. Both are plausible: *-i is from the immediate past paradigm, the most unmarked TAM category, and it could therefore be expected to become generalized to more positions. On the other hand, *-r was used in the other "true" past tenses (i.e., not the immediate past, which also had present time reference), and could therefore be extended to the historic past on the basis of this association with past-ness. Neither change appears significantly more likely than the other, so we must examine the distribution of witnesses. In this case, the distribution is decisive in favor of *-i. Positing PSog *-m-i requires two innovations: one in Nend and one in Acɨ Apalɨ. Positing *-ma-r, however, requires several. The presence of the Acɨ form means that the analogical replacement of *-r with *-i must be posited separately for Manat, Akɨ Apalɨ, and Proto-North Sogeram, in addition to Gants. This is clearly less likely than the former scenario, so the reconstruction of *-m-i in the 3SG should be preferred.

A few other innovations can be observed in this table. Mum changed the 3PL form with its innovative 3PL suffix; Sirva changed the vowel in the 1SG form; and Gants changed the vowel of *-ma to *e* on analogy with the 1SG and 3SG forms.

4.3.5 Future

Reconstructing the future tense is difficult because cognate paradigms are only found in Apalɨ and Aisian. These languages are adjacent and show evidence of contact, so this is not a broad enough attestation to reconstruct the paradigm to Proto-Sogeram. Luckily, two Josephstaal languages have a cognate future suffix: Moresada (Capell 1951) and Anamuxra (Ingram 2001). The relevant forms are presented in Table 22. The Aisi suffixes are identical in both Aisian languages with the exception of the 1PL suffix, which is *-iberar* in Magɨ. The reconstructed suffix *-ɨba was also used on its own in the irrealis infinitive verb form (§4.5.3).

Table 22: Future.

	1SG	2SG	3SG	1PL	2PL	3PL
Moresada	-mbam	-mbal	-mbat	-mbamaŋ	-mɔr	-mbiŋ
Anamuxra	-ba-m	-ba-ta	-ba-t	-ba-mŋ	-ba-taŋa	-ba-tŋ
Apalɨ	-ɨb-en	-ɨba-naŋ	-ɨba-li	-ɨba-lu	-ɨba-laŋ	-havɨ-ba-li
Aisi	-ɨbyaŋ	-ɨberaŋ	-ɨber	-ɨberaŋ	-ɨberar	-ɨberuŋ
PSOG	*-ɨbia-n	*-ɨba-na	*-ɨba-ri	*-ɨba-riŋ	*-ɨba-ra	

The Proto-Josephstaal future tense suffix was apparently *-ba. In Apalɨ the suffix is *-iba*, and in Aisi it seems to have been *-iber*, although the 1SG form is anomalous. Disregarding the 1SG for the moment, reconstructing the Proto-Sogeram suffix as *-ɨba seems the best solution. Both Sogeram languages have an initial *i*, so this vowel was probably part of the Proto-Sogeram suffix. The *b is clearly reflected in every language. The following vowel poses some difficulties, though, as Apalɨ has *a* while Aisi has *e*. It seems, though, that Aisi has combined PSOG *-ɨba with another element, possibly *-ira, which has resulted in the longer suffix. Indeed, the non-1SG Aisi forms may be built on the irrealis infinitive (§4.5.3) and not directly descended from this future paradigm. In any case, reconstructing the vowel as *a is warranted based on the Josephstaal and Apalɨ reflexes.

This brings us to the 1SG form, which is anomalous in both Apalɨ and Aisi. The Josephstaal forms are no longer any help, as they reflect a different subject agreement suffix, *-m. It is unclear how the Aisi form could have been innovated, as there are no known Proto-Sogeram processes that would have inserted an *i into a suffix in this way. Moreover, the *e* in the Apalɨ form could easily be a cognate with the Aisi *ya* sequence. Given that both Sogeram languages support this reconstruction, then, I have reconstructed an irregular form of the future tense suffix for the 1SG, *-ɨbia, which combined with the Set III agreement suffix *-n. This reconstruction seems somewhat odd, but it best fits the data available to us at present.

The other person–number forms are easier to reconstruct. The 2SG and 2PL forms show the usual reflexes, so *-na and *-ra are reconstructed. The usual 1PL suffix is innovative in both Apalɨ and Aisi so an exact reconstruction is impossible, but I have reconstructed the most common 1PL suffix *-rɨŋ. And the 3SG suffix -li in Apalɨ is attested in the Apalɨ future tenses only, and as such is taken to be archaic. The Aisi form could also be a reflex of this suffix, as word-final *i was regularly lost in Proto-Aisian (§3.4.2.1).

4.3.6 Habitual

There is good evidence that Proto-Sogeram had a set of suffixes that denoted habitual aspect. The reflexes of this paradigm and the Proto-Sogeram reconstruction are presented in Table 23.

Table 23: Habitual.

	1SG	2SG	3SG	1PL	2PL	3PL
Mand	-cɨ-n	-cɨ-n	-cɨ-n	-cɨ-nhw	-e-cɨ-n	-e-cɨ-n
Nend	-j-in	-rɨ-n	-j	-rɨ-rɨŋ	-mgɨ-rɨ-n	-mgɨ-j
Apalɨ	-ɨla-n	-ɨla-naŋ	-ɨla-li	-ɨla-lu	-ɨla-laŋ	-havɨ-la-li
Magɨ	-ite-ŋ	-ity-aŋ	-ite-i	-ite-r	-ite-r	-itya-uŋ
Aisi	-er-iŋ	-er-aŋ	-er-i	-er-aŋ	-er-ar	-er-uŋ
PSoG	*-ɨtia-n	*-ɨtia-na	*-ɨtia-i	*-ɨtia-rɨŋ	*-ɨtia-ra	

In Mand, Magɨ, and Aisi this form is the only habitual aspect and has no specific time reference. In Nend the paradigm given is the present and recent past habitual aspect, and it is distinguished from a historic past habitual paradigm. The Apalɨ paradigm is the (near) past habitual, which is distinguished from the present habitual and the historic past habitual.

The Mand forms are somewhat unusual in that a single agreement suffix appears to have been generalized to the whole paradigm, with the exception of the 1PL form. The form that was generalized appears to have been 1SG, which is somewhat unusual since in most TAM categories Mand has generalized the 3SG form to all person–number combinations.

Aside from Mand, the forms appear fairly straightforwardly cognate, although arriving at a precise reconstruction is somewhat challenging. I discuss several aspects of the reconstruction in turn: the reconstruction of the suffix-initial *ɨ, the reconstruction of the *t, the reconstruction of the vowel cluster *ia, and the reconstruction of the agreement suffixes.

Reconstructing the suffix-initial *ɨ is relatively unproblematic. The West Sogeram languages do not reflect it, but they often replace suffix-initial *ɨ with the root vowel of the verb; other examples of the same analogical process occur with the different-subject realis suffix *-ɨka (§4.4.2) and the irrealis suffix *-ɨt (§4.3.10). In Aisi it seems that the *ia sequence became *e, and that the *ɨ then harmonized to this upcoming *e. And indeed, *ɨ often harmonized to upcoming vowels in Aisi. Given, then, that the loss of suffix-initial *ɨ in Proto-West Sogeram appears to be a regular process, that *ɨ accounts for the suffix-initial *e in Aisi, and that no simple path of innovation presents itself to account for the suffix-initial ɨ in Apalɨ and Magɨ, we reconstruct *ɨ.

Turning to the reconstruction of *t, we see that this consonant is reflected unproblematically in Apalɨ and Magɨ, and in the Nend 1PL and second person. The innovation to j in the other Nend forms is plausibly the result of palatalization before *i; this would also explain the innovative Mand suffix, which, as mentioned above, appears to be a generalization of the 1SG form. This analysis requires positing several specific events. First, the *i was lost from the *ia sequence in *-ɨtia. Then the set of agreement suffixes was changed by analogy with other paradigms, and the 1SG and 3SG suffixes became *-in and *-i, respectively, in Proto-West Sogeram. Finally, the *t palatalized to *c and later voiced to j in Nend. The Aisi suffix is also divergent in reflecting r, which is never a reflex of *t in regular phonological change. But suffixes and other grammatical items are sometimes subject to irregular phonological attrition, and such a change could easily have produced this r.

We turn, then, to the vowel sequence *ia, which is a far less certain part of this reconstruction. It is reflected in its entirety only in one language, Magɨ, and even there only in two forms, the 2SG and the 3PL. In the West Sogeram languages it is reflected as ɨ and in Apalɨ and Aisi it is a. Nevertheless, reconstructing *ia provides explanations for several things, and appears to be the best analysis. The first benefit, of course, is an explanation of the Magɨ forms that retain it. These forms would be quite difficult to account for under any other analysis—and indeed, in reconstructing morphology, unless there is evidence to the contrary it is often correct to reconstruct the longest surviving reflex and to posit that in other languages it has undergone phonological attrition. Reconstructing *ia also explains the *e in the other Magɨ forms, as *e is rare in Magɨ and was probably created primarily through irregular processes, such as the monophthongization that appears to have happened here.

Another benefit is explaining the many differences in agreement suffixes, even between close neighbors. Mand has 1SG -n while Nend has -in; Magɨ has -ŋ while Aisi has -iŋ. While analogical changes to agreement suffixes are fairly common, one would still expect close relatives to exhibit less divergence.

By reconstructing *ia in the suffix, though, a partial explanation is reached. The 1SG form, as reconstructed, was *-ɨtia-n, with the Set IV agreement suffix. Simply dropping the *a, producing *-ɨtin, would render this form much more similar to 1SG verb forms that used the Set I agreement suffix *-in, which was much more common. Reconstructing *ia, along with the Set IV 1SG agreement suffix *-n, thus creates a simple path of innovation that would explain the parallel innovations that resulted in the peculiar distribution of -in suffixes today.

Reconstructing *ia also explains the Apalɨ reflex, a simple *a*, which cannot itself be reconstructed because it would plainly be inadequate to explain the variation seen in the other languages. And finally, reconstructing *ia offers an explanation for the suffix-initial *e* in Aisi, which was described above. Given that *ia appears superior to any alternative proposals, it should be reconstructed. Nevertheless, the diversity of reflexes casts doubt on this aspect of Proto-Sogeram verbal morphology.

I turn now to the subject agreement suffixes. The reconstruction of *-n for the 1SG has been discussed above. The reconstruction of 2SG *-na is straightforward, as every language exhibits its normal reflex of that suffix. The 3SG is more difficult: Mand has no reflex, Nend and the Aisian languages reflect *-i,[19] and Apalɨ reflects *-r. Moreover, Magɨ is unusual in that it reflects an *-i that did not elide the preceding vowel, as was normally the case in Proto-Sogeram (§4.1.1). This unusual form is thus probably archaic, for as Koch notes, "irregular or anomalous forms" are more likely to be archaic "since regular forms can easily result from regularising or simplifying processes" (1996: 219; see also Hetzron 1976). The analogy from the reconstructed form to the vowel-eliding -*i* reflected in Nend and Aisi is a simple process, as is the Apalɨ change to a reflex of the Set II 3SG agreement suffix *-r. In the 1PL, Nend and Magɨ show reflexes of *-rɨŋ, while Mand, Apalɨ, and Aisi each have their own innovative suffix. Given that Nend and Magɨ belong to divergent branches, and there is no evidence of contact between them, *-rɨŋ should be reconstructed. The 2PL is again straightforward, as every non-West Sogeram shows regular reflexes of *-ra.

Finally, we turn to the semantic reconstruction. Since this paradigm denotes simple habitual aspect in Mand and the Aisian languages, with no tense meaning, that reconstruction seems best. Add to that the fact that the other Nend and Apalɨ habitual paradigms are probably innovative, and the reconstruction of a simple habitual aspect with no special time reference seems quite secure.

---

19 The Nend evidence for *i is that *t palatalized to *j* before word-final *i was lost (§3.2.3.2).

4.3.7 Imperative

The Proto-Sogeram paradigm of imperative suffixes is difficult to reconstruct, although such a paradigm almost certainly existed. Table 24 presents the relevant forms and some reconstructed suffixes, although readers will note the paradigm is incomplete.

Table 24: Imperative.

	1SG	2SG	3SG	1PL	2PL	3PL
Mand	-ŋ	-u			-e-u	
Nend	-ŋ			-m		
Manat					-mar	
Apalɨ		-iha		-imili	-ihalaŋ	
Mum				-im	-mara	
Sirva		-u			-uhra	
Magɨ		-u	-ikur		-imai	-ikiruŋ
Aisi		-o(k)	-ikur		-imai(t)	-ikiruŋ
Kursav	-n	-ku	-koro		-kura	-konou
PSog	*-ŋ	*-u		*-imɨri	*-mar	

Most languages in this table have full paradigms of imperative suffixes, but many of those suffixes descend from another Proto-Sogeram TAM category, such as the irrealis (§4.3.10) or the participle (§4.5.2). The Sirva forms are synchronically analyzed as irrealis suffixes.

The reconstruction of *-u '2SG.IMP' is quite apparent, given the Mand, Sirva, and Aisian reflexes, and allowing for some semantic broadening in Sirva. Aisi occasionally adds final stops to some of its imperative forms, but a comparison with Magɨ and other Sogeram languages suggests they are innovative, perhaps the result of an utterance-final fortition process such as the one that created English *nope*. The 2PL reconstruction is also fairly straightforward, as Manat, Mum, and Magɨ reflect the sequence *-mar. Mum added final *a on analogy with other 2PL forms, most of which ended in *-ra. The Aisi form, which reflects word-final *r > *i*, looks like a borrowing from Magɨ. The only question to resolve is that of the suffix-initial *ɨ, which is present in Aisian but not in Manat or Mum. The prohibitive suffixes contain initial *-ɨm (§4.3.8), and given the semantic similarity between imperative and prohibitive that could have been an impetus for analogic change in Aisian. Moreover, Manat retains suffix-initial *ɨ in the prohibitive suffixes, and it would be peculiar for the imperative suffix to lose *ɨ when the prohibitive suffixes retain it. But this aspect of the reconstruction remains less secure.

For the 1PL we must make do with very little data. The Nend suffix is only possibly cognate; while Nend did lose word-final *i (§3.2.3.2) and suffix-initial *i, it did not usually lose final *r. This suffix may rather be a reflex of the Proto-Sogeram adjectival participle (§4.5.2). Mum *-im*, on the other hand, appears cognate with Apalɨ *-imili*. The suffix-initial *i* suggests this, as does the fact that Mum lost both final *i (§3.3.2.4) and final *r (§3.3.2.3). But reflexes in Apalɨ and Mum are not sufficient to date a form to Proto-Sogeram. Looking to Anamuxra, though, we find the cognate suffix *-mr-i* '1DU-NEG.IRR,' which marks the "negative irrealis/future" and signals that "an event will, would, or should not occur" (Ingram 2001).[20] This suffix, then, must date at least to Proto-South Adelbert with some kind of irrealis meaning. It has been retained in the Sogeram languages with imperative meaning, suggesting that this was the meaning it had developed by the Proto-Sogeram stage.

In the 1SG we have very little to go on: a single nasal consonant, found in the West Sogeram languages and Kursav. Unfortunately, the consonants are different and are probably not cognate. However, given that the West Sogeram languages generally retain Proto-Sogeram final nasals unchanged, and Kursav occasionally changes *ŋ to *n* irregularly, it is possible that all three suffixes trace their origin to a Proto-Sogeram suffix *-ŋ '1SG.IMP'.

Finally, we turn to the third person forms. Here we have only East Sogeram reflexes that begin with *k* or *ik*, which we can compare with two Apalɨ second person suffixes that begin with *ih*. While it is certainly possible that these forms are inherited from some Proto-Sogeram paradigm with a suffix that began with *-ik, it is far from certain. The Proto-East Sogeram (PES) 3SG.IMP suffix appears to have been *-ikur, but a reconstruction to Proto-Sogeram will have to await more data.

4.3.8 Prohibitive

The Proto-Sogeram prohibitive paradigm and its reflexes are presented in Table 25.

It seems likely that Proto-Sogeram had a prohibitive paradigm. The forms above suggest it and some Anamuxra forms seem to confirm it, such as the imperative suffixes *-mna* '1SG.IMP' and *-mra* '1DU.IMP'. But while these facts support reconstructing the existence of a prohibitive paradigm, reconstructing the details

---

[20] Interestingly, this suffix also marks the 1DU different-subject in Anamuxra, a function that Apalɨ *-imili* also fulfills. (In Anamuxra it functions only in irrealis chains, and in Apalɨ it functions in all chains.) This suggests that PSOG *-imɨri also had a different-subject function in some circumstances, but the details of this function remain unclear.

Table 25: Prohibitive.

	1SG	2SG	3SG	1PL	2PL	3PL
Mand		-mɨn			-e-mɨn	
Nend	-mɨ-ñ	-mɨ-n	-mɨ-nj	-mɨ-rɨŋ	-mgɨ-mɨ-n	-mgɨ-mɨ-nj
Manat		-ɨmɨn	-ɨnad		-ɨmɨr	-ɨnad-ur-id
Apalɨ	-ɨm-agaŋ	-ɨm-ɨnaŋ	-ɨm-ɨdɨ	-ɨm-agalu	-ɨm-ɨlaŋ	-avɨ-m-ɨdɨ
PSoG	*-ɨmɨ-ñ	*-ɨmɨ-na	*-ɨmɨ-d	*-ɨmɨ-rɨŋ	*-ɨmɨ-ra	

is almost impossible. In fact, most of the agreement suffixes in Table 25 are only speculative; I do not consider any besides the 2SG securely reconstructed. Moreover, the distribution, ranging from Mand to Apalɨ, does not give us full assurance that this paradigm existed in Proto-Sogeram. It may only have existed in a later variety, the last common ancestor of Proto-Greater West Sogeram and Apalɨ (see Figure 2 in Chapter 1).

Nevertheless, the prohibitive suffix *-ɨmɨ is attested in every one of these languages and can be reconstructed to Proto-Sogeram, although some Apalɨ forms suggest it might have sometimes been *-ɨma. And the 2SG form can be reconstructed since *-na is reflected in every language. But in the other person–number categories, agreement between Nend and Apalɨ is difficult to find—and even could it be found, it would not be sufficient for a secure reconstruction to Proto-Sogeram. The 1SG can perhaps be reconstructed as *-ñ if the Manat 2SG reflects changing the final *ñ > n, which may have been a regular process (cf. *añɨkwrɨñ 'day before yesterday > añihrin). The 1PL suffix *-rɨŋ is also reflected in Nend and Manat, and can tentatively be reconstructed. The Nend and Apalɨ 3SG suffixes may be cognate. If we posit that Nend added *-i on analogy with the Set I agreement suffixes, this vowel would have caused the *d to palatalize to *nj* before Nend word-final *i deletion (§3.2.3.2). For the 2PL the only reflex is Apalɨ -laŋ, so we must reconstruct *-ra and posit that ŋ accreted onto this form, which was fairly common in Apalɨ (§3.2.5.1). Thus we see that while the outlines of the paradigm are well reconstructed, many individual details depend for their reconstruction on a single reflex, and as such remain speculative.

4.3.9 Counterfactual

Two Sogeram languages, Apalɨ and Aisi, have counterfactual paradigms, and two others, Nend and Gants, appear to have cognate imperative suffixes. The forms are presented in Table 26 along with two Magɨ suffixes that are not well under-

4.3 Final morphology — 135

Table 26: Counterfactual.

	1SG	2SG	3SG	1PL	2PL	3PL
Nend (IMP)		-v			-var	
Apalɨ (CTRF)	-iv-in	-iva-naŋ	-iv-i	-ivɨ-lu	-iva-laŋ	-havɨ-v-i
Magɨ (CTRF?)		-ibaŋ			-ibas	
Aisi (CTRF)	-ibiŋ	-ibaŋ	-ibar	-ibir	-ibasɨri	-ibiruŋ
Gants (IMP)		-pɨ-naŋ			-p-raŋ	
PSOG	*-ifɨ-ŋ	*-ifɨ-na	*-ifa-r	*-if-riŋ	*-ifa-ra	

stood but that appear to be counterfactuals. In Gants these are the only imperative suffixes, suggesting what was previously an entire paradigm has become restricted to the second person. In Nend these are two forms from a complete imperative paradigm, but the other imperative suffixes are not descended from the Proto-Sogeram counterfactual.

There is considerable variety in the forms, although all of them involve reflexes of PSOG *f. The initial *ɨ should also be reconstructed, as both Apalɨ and the Aisian languages retain it, and Nend consistently removed initial *ɨ from verb suffixes. Beyond that, some forms suggest a suffix *-ifa while others suggest *-ifɨ, and the 2PL in the Aisian languages even suggests *-ifasɨ. The languages also disagree about the agreement suffixes used. Moreover, in the first and third persons we have only two poorly distributed witnesses, which are inadequate for a confident reconstruction. Given all this I tentatively offer the following reconstruction, while acknowledging that many of its details remain speculative.

Since both Apalɨ and Aisian retain forms with the *-ifa and *-ifɨ suffixes, this variation should be reconstructed to Proto-Sogeram. But deciding which form was marked with which suffix is difficult, and the issue is entwined with the issue of agreement suffixes since those often elide the final vowel of the counterfactual suffix. For the 1SG and 3SG, I consider the Aisian forms more archaic. The Apalɨ forms contain Set I agreement suffixes, and since languages often replace agreement suffixes with Set I forms I consider it more likely that Apalɨ is innovative here than Aisian. An issue remains, though: the Aisian form could be a reflex of either *-n or *-ŋ. I reconstruct *-ŋ since this suffix is also used in the irrealis paradigm (§4.3.10), which is most semantically similar to the counterfactual paradigm. But this may not be correct. For the 2SG, Nend and Gants reflect *-ifɨ while Apalɨ and Aisian reflect *-ifa. I reconstruct the form suggested by Nend and Gants, since they are more divergent witnesses and the Apalɨ and Aisian forms could be explained by a single shared innovation. In the 1PL we must simply decide between the Apalɨ and Aisian reflexes. Apalɨ has generalized the 1PL suffix -lu to almost every paradigm, suggesting that Aisian is archaic. In the 2PL every language supports reconstructing the usual 2PL agreement suffix *-ra. As for the mood suffix, Nend and Apalɨ support reconstructing *-ifa, Gants supports *-ifɨ, and Aisian supports *-ifasɨ. The anomalous Aisian form may well be archaic, as it is difficult to explain how it could have been innovated. But in the absence of more support for the reconstruction of *-ifasɨ, I tentatively reconstruct *-ifa.

Semantically, the Apalɨ paradigm refers to "something that would have or could have been done, but was not or will not be done" (Wade 1989: 170), as in (111). The Aisi paradigm also refers to things as they are not (112), but can also be used with an enclitic =de to form prohibitives (113).

Apalɨ
(111) Sibɨla apali li-ci   huaci **u-vɨ-lu.**
      work none do-3SG.DS good   **go-CTRF-1PL**
      '(If) there was no work, we easily could go.'   (Wade 1989: 170)

Aisi
(112) Ya   gi   ika   yaka   kɨn-i   akɨ   ga, ga-rɨb
      1SG FOC father.1.POSS 1SG.POSS stay-3SG.IPST maybe TOP MD-ADJZ
      kr-ibiŋ.
      walk-1SG.CTRF
      'If *my* father were alive, I'd walk around like that (too).'

Aisi
(113) W-i   kɨtiŋ gi, na   **lustiŋtiŋ** **am-ban=de.**
      go-SS and   FOC 2SG **forget**   **do-2SG.CTRF=PRAG**
      '(When) you go, don't forget.'

This meaning of the Proto-Sogeram paradigm was probably similar: it referred to hypothetical events and other events that did not happen. However, the fact that innovation to imperative meaning took place in both Nend and Gants suggests that this paradigm may also have been used to form directives. The existence of the negative imperative function in Aisi corroborates this hypothesis.

4.3.10 Irrealis

The verb category I reconstruct as irrealis has reflexes all across the family, in every Sogeram language except Sirva and Magɨ, in both medial and final contexts. When used finally, they usually have imperative meaning. When used medially, they have different-subject (DS) meaning. Since I also reconstruct a paradigm of realis DS suffixes (§4.4.2), I am positing that Proto-Sogeram DS medial verbs distinguished realis from irrealis mood. This distinction in DS suffixes is still preserved today in Kursav and Gants. The reflexes of this paradigm, which was formed with the IRR suffix *-ɨt, are shown in Table 27, along with the meaning of each row of suffixes. The Mum suffix -itiŋ is marked with an asterisk because it belongs to the irrealis paradigm, as the label indicates, but also to the imperative paradigm.

Table 27: Irrealis.

	1SG	2SG	3SG	1PL	2PL	3PL
Mand (IMP)				-r		
Nend (DS)	-ŋ	-n	-z	-riŋ	-mgɨ-n	-mgɨ-z
Nend (IMP)	-ŋ		-z			-mgɨ-z
Manat (DS)	-it	-in	-s	-r	-ir	-ura-s
Manat (IMP)	-itiŋ(d)		-s			-ura-s
Apalɨ (DS)	-ɨliŋ	-inaŋ		-imili	-ɨlaŋ	
Apalɨ (IMP)	-ɨliŋ			-imili		
Mum (IRR)	-itiŋ*	-ina	-iti	-itriŋ	-itra	-itu
Aisi (DS)		-inda				
Kursav (IRR)	-it	-ita	-ite	-itir	-itira	-ito
Gants (IRR)	-ɨriŋ	-ina	-ire	-ruŋ	-iraŋ	-i-re
PSoG	*-ɨt-ɨŋ	*-ɨt-na	*-ɨt-i	*-ɨt-riŋ	*-ɨt-ra	

In Kursav and Gants, this paradigm of suffixes can function both medially and finally. When it is medial, it marks different-subject in a clause chain that ends in an irrealis clause—that is, one that belongs to a TAM category such as imperative (114) or future (115). When this paradigm functions finally, it marks things like negative deontic modality (116) and imperative mood (117).

Kursav
(114) Nuaya kura niga, **rabɨra-t-a** ve-da ya soro inu-koro.
white man SPEC **send-IRR-2SG** come-SS 1SG COM stay-3SG.IMP
'Send a white man to come (lit. 'and he should come') stay with me.'

Gants
(115) **Ab-rɨŋ** ai-re ga-paŋ-nɨŋ wa-da ...
speak-1SG.IRR come-3SG.IRR perceive-FUT-1SG say-SS
'"I'll tell him to come (lit. 'talk and he will come') and I'll see him," she said, and ...'

Kursav
(116) I-ka   skur   bin, **in-it-o**   ma.
      ND-TOP school LOC   stay-IRR-3PL   NEG
      'They can't/shouldn't stay in this school.'

Gants
(117) Miñ   **wisik-ina**   wa-m-ek.
      vine   **untie-2SG.OPT**   say-FPST-3SG
      '"Untie the ropes," he said.'

This variation appears to be present in Mum, too, where these suffixes can serve as irrealis DS (118) or optatives (119). This paradigm is called a prohibitive paradigm by Wade (1993), but since a complete analysis of Mum verb morphology has yet to be done I provisionally gloss it 'IRR'.

Mum
(118) Turaha-ta   **miga-t-i**   ahutiv   ha   karha-irma-n
      burn.fall.down-SS   **come.down-IRR-3SG**   firewood   MD   sleep-FUT-1SG
      va-m-i.
      say-HPST-3SG
      '"When it is burned and has fallen down I will lie down," he said.'

(Sweeney n.d.)

Mum
(119) Mina   iduhu-ta   **g-it-in**   va-ta ...
      let.me enter.exit-SS   **look-IRR-1SG**   say-SS
      '"Let me go in and look," he said, and ...'

(Sweeney n.d.)

Based on these reflexes, the variation between medial and final functions should be reconstructed to Proto-Sogeram. Additionally, as can be seen from Table 27, the reflexes of this paradigm are inherited with both DS and imperative meaning, often within the same language. Matters are confused somewhat by the fact that often not the whole paradigm is inherited. For example, in Apalɨ the first and second person DS forms come from this paradigm, while the third person forms come from the realis DS paradigm (§4.4.2). Similarly, in Manat the 1SG and third person imperative suffixes come from this paradigm, while the 2SG comes from a participial form (§4.5.2) and the 2PL comes from the imperative paradigm (§4.3.7). Nevertheless, even though sometimes only a few irrealis suffixes are inherited into a paradigm, it is clear that the Proto-Sogeram irrealis is commonly inherited with both DS and imperative meaning.

A few reconstruction decisions must still be made, though. The first concerns the final nasal of the 1SG form. Manat and Gants suggest *ŋ, while Mum suggests *n. Apalɨ ŋ could be a reflex of either one. Nend also suggests *ŋ, although the Nend reflex has undergone a good deal of erosion, so that it is not entirely certain it is cognate. Still, in Manat and Gants two divergent witnesses support the reconstruction of the velar nasal, so it should be preferred. Moreover, the Mum form could have been formed by analogy with the Set III agreement suffixes, where the 1SG was also *-n. Supporting this conjecture is the fact that the Set III suffixes were also used with a semantically irrealis TAM category, the future (§4.3.5).

Another decision concerns the form of the 1PL suffix. Nend, Manat, Mum, and Kursav all support reconstructing *-ɨt-rɨŋ, and this fits well with the rest of the paradigm. But the Apalɨ suffix *-imɨli* was also present in Proto-Sogeram; this is assured because a cognate exists in the Josephstaal language Anamuxra (Ingram 2001): -mr-i '1DU.IRR-DS.SEQ'. Since Josephstaal is a sister to Sogeram, this suffix can be reconstructed to Proto-South Adelbert and was inherited into Proto-Sogeram and then Apalɨ. We must therefore decide what the respective functions of PSog *-ɨt-rɨŋ and *-mɨri were. A simple solution presents itself: *-mɨri may have been the dual form, and *-ɨt-rɨŋ the plural. This solution is less than ideal for a few reasons. First of all, it is simply an *ad hoc* stipulation to resolve the problem of having two suffixes. Second, the *-mɨri form lacks the reconstructed IRR suffix *-ɨt, which we would expect it to have. And third, the agreement suffix *-rɨŋ was probably dual in Proto-Sogeram, not plural; this is the meaning that has been reconstructed for it in §4.1.2. A better solution is to assign the *-mɨri suffix to the imperative paradigm, as I have done in that section (§4.3.7).

Finally, I briefly mention some of the irregular innovations that the forms in Table 27 contain. Mand lost final *ŋ in the 1PL form, for which the expected reflex is ᵗh. Nend and Manat both exhibit a great deal of erosion to the 2SG and third person form, and the third person suffix in particular may not be cognate. Because it performs the same functions as PSog *-ɨt-i, though—it markes DS and imperative—and because the affrication of *t to *s before *i is a plausible irregular change, I consider these forms cognate. Aisi retained only the 2SG suffix from this paradigm, preserving the *tn cluster as a (presumably metathesized) *nd*. Incidentally, the reconstructed *tn cluster has not, in general, fared well: only the *t is retained in Kursav, and only the *n in Nend, Manat, Apalɨ, Mum and Gants. No language preserves them both in their original order. Finally, Gants appears to have replaced the 1PL form with a form from a different paradigm.

4.4 Medial morphology

The medial morphology that can be reconstructed is presented here. Proto-Sogeram had two same-subject suffixes, *-i and *-ta, which were not marked for subject agreement. Different-subject verbs did agree with their subjects, and were marked either with a realis paradigm (§4.4.2) or with the irrealis paradigm (§4.3.10; this paradigm could be used both medially and finally). Different-subject verbs could also be reduplicated to indicate that the event of their clause occurred simultaneously with that of the following clause (§4.4.3).

4.4.1 Same-subject

The Sogeram languages exhibit reflexes of two same-subject suffixes, *-i and *-ta. Most languages only retain one of these two forms, as shown in Table 28, which makes reconstructing the semantic distinction between them difficult.

Table 28: Same-subject suffixes.

Mand	Nend	Apalɨ	Mum	Sirva	Magɨ	Aisi	Kursav	Gants	PSoɢ
-i	-e			(kiñ)i	-i	-i			*-i
		-(vi)la	-ta	-ra		(ki)ti, -ta	-da	-da	*-ta

First, it should be noted that reflexes of both suffixes are well-distributed and should be reconstructed to Proto-Sogeram. Mand, Nend, and Aisian reflect *-i, giving this suffix reflexes in West Sogeram and East Sogeram. The rest of the Sogeram languages reflect *-ta, giving it reflexes in Apalɨ, North Sogeram, and East Sogeram languages.

Adding to the diversity of reflexes is the fact that in some languages that only retain one suffix, the other is preserved in some irregular same-subject verb forms. For example, Sirva -ra is a regular reflex of *-ta, but the same-subject form of the verb kɨ- 'stay' (< *kɨñɨ-) is kiñi, reflecting PSoɢ *kiñ-i. Similarly, Aisi retains *-i unchanged as -i, but has an irregular form of kɨn- 'stay' (< *kɨñɨ-) which is kiti, reflecting *-ta with irregular loss of *ñ and regular centering of final *a > ɨ. At least two other Aisi verbs also have irregular same-subject forms that reflect *-ta: n- 'eat' (niti, from *ña-ta) and i- 'get' (iti, from *i-ta). Unfortunately, the distribution of these reflexes is not helpful for reconstruction: neither suffix seems to prefer certain semantic classes of verbs, for example.

Fortunately, Aisi appears to have retained *-ta as a productive verbal suffix -ta. The final *a did not center to ⁺ɨ as expected, but the meaning of the suffix is sufficiently similar to the reflexes of *-ta in Apalɨ, Mum, Sirva, Kursav, and Gants that it should be considered cognate with them. Aisi -ta is a same-subject delayed suffix; it indicates that a significant interval of time elapsed between the action of the marked verb and the action of the following verb, as illustrated by the minimal pair in (120) and (121).

(120)   Aisi
       Sikɨbyaŋ **krɨ-ta** n-ɨbyaŋ.
       food **cook-SS.DELAY** eat-1SG.FUT
       'I'll cook my food and eat it later.'   Elicited

(121)   Aisi
       Sikɨbyaŋ **kr-i** n-ɨbyaŋ.
       food **cook-SS** eat-1SG.FUT
       'I'll cook my food and eat it (afterwards).'   Elicited

Since Aisi is the only language to preserve a distinction between *-i and *-ta, the simplest analysis is that the same distinction existed in Proto-Sogeram. This analysis requires the fewest number of innovations to arrive at the modern situation, so we posit two Proto-Sogeram same-subject suffixes: *-i 'SS.SEQ' and *-ta 'SS.DELAY'. However, we must acknowledge that while the phonological forms *-i and *-ta are well distributed and securely reconstructed, and the more general meaning of 'SS' is also well distributed and securely reconstructed for both suffixes, the more specific meanings of 'SS.SEQ' and 'SS.DELAY' are not well distributed and therefore less securely reconstructed.

4.4.2 Different-subject realis

Proto-Sogeram had two paradigms of different-subject suffixes, one for realis chains and another for irrealis chains. Such modality distinctions are common in the switch reference systems of Trans New Guinea languages, especially of the Madang branch (Roberts 1990). Both paradigms denoted sequential action; simultaneous action was marked by reduplicating the appropriate different-subject verb (§4.4.3). The distinction between realis and irrealis different-subject suffixes is preserved in Kursav and Gants, and further reasons for reconstructing the distinction to Proto-Sogeram are presented in the section on the irrealis paradigm (§4.3.10). The different-subject realis suffixes are straightforward to reconstruct in some ways and challenging in others. The relevant synchronic forms are presented in Table 29. (Square brackets indicate that a form is not cognate.)

Table 29: Different-subject realis.

	1SG	2SG	3SG	1PL	2PL	3PL
Mand			-c			
Manat	-ih-in	-iha-nad	-ih-id	-iha-r	-iha-rad	-ih-ur-id
Apalɨ	[-ɨliŋ]	[-ɨnaŋ]	-ɨci	[-ɨmɨli]	[-ɨlaŋ]	-av-ɨci
Mum	-h-in	-ha-na	-h-i	-ha-rɨŋ	-ha-ra	-h-u
Sirva	-iin	-ha-na	-ii	-ha-r	-ha-ra	-b-ii
Magɨ	-ɨkɨŋ	-ɨkaŋ	[-ɨnɨŋ]	-ɨkar	-ɨkar	[-ɨnuŋ]
Aisi	-ɨkɨŋ	[-ɨnda]	-egi	-ɨkuŋ	-ogi	-ogi
Kursav	-ku	-kuna	-eke/-ike	-kuru	-kura	-oko/-uko
Gants	-k-enɨŋ	-ke-naŋ	-k-e	-ke-ruŋ	-ke-raŋ	-i-k-e
PSoG	*-ɨk-in	*-ɨka-na	*-ɨk-i	*-ɨka-rɨŋ	*-ɨka-ra	

In Mand the suffix *-c* is the only surviving member of this paradigm, and it refers to all person–number combinations. It is descended from the 3SG form.

The Manat forms in this table are not suffixes *per se*, but represent a pattern of verb root allomorphy. Some verb roots change their root shape in the presence of the immediate past suffixes and the plural suffix *-ura*. When these verbs precede a triggering suffix, they replace their final vowel with an *ɨha* sequence; the forms in Table 29 show the shape of these final sequences in the presence of the immediate past paradigm. An example of this kind of verb is given in (122), where the verb *ape-* 'thatch' becomes *apɨha-* in the presence of the 2SG immediate past suffix *-nad*.

Manat
(122) Am=avan   **apɨha-nad**   ara-ma-g.
      2.NOM=very   **thatch-2SG.IPST**   say-PST-3SG.FAR
      '"You yourself built it," she said.'

The other forms are all different-subject suffixes. In Mum and Sirva they contrast with a paradigm of different-subject simultaneous suffixes which is formed reduplicatively from the paradigm in Table 29. In Mand, Magɨ, and Aisi they are the only way to mark different-subject (although Magɨ has a suffix *-ɨsɨr* which is not well understood, but which may mark 2PL irrealis different-subject). And in Kursav and Gants this paradigm contrasts with both an irrealis paradigm and a simultaneous paradigm which is formed by reduplicating the irrealis forms.

A few aspects of the reconstruction fall into place immediately. The element *ka can be easily reconstructed. The agreement suffixes are clearly from Set I. And the meaning can be straightforwardly reconstructed, since 'different-subject

4.4 Medial morphology

realis sequential' is retained in every language but Manat (notwithstanding the fact that some languages have expanded the meaning to include irrealis clause chains).

Reconstructing the suffix-initial *ɨ is less clear, but becomes more apparent upon a closer examination of the data. The vowel is retained as ɨ in Manat, Apalɨ, Sirva (in the 1SG and third person), Magɨ, and Aisi (in the first person). It has been lost completely in Mand, Mum, and Gants, as well as from some forms in Sirva (1PL and second person) and Kursav (first and second person). The suffix-initial *e* or *i* in the Aisi and Kursav 3SG, and the initial *o* or *u* in the Kursav 3PL, should also be considered reflexes of *ɨ. Recall that *ɨ harmonized to *i and *u in these languages when followed by those vowels (§3.4.1.3), and that *i and *u were then sometimes lowered to *e* and *o* (§3.4.1.4, §3.4.4.1).

On distributional grounds, then, we could reconstruct either *ɨ or nothing—both reflexes are well distributed. So we must ask ourselves which innovation is the more likely, and here it becomes clear that *ɨ should be reconstructed. It is difficult to say how the preceding vowel, which would have been the last vowel of the verb root and could have been *a, *i, or *u, could have been consistently centered to *ɨ and reanalyzed as a part of the suffix. A sporadic vowel-centering change did take place in Mum (§3.3.3.3), but this is not nearly enough to account for all the reflexes of *ɨ. On the other hand, the change from *-ɨka to *-ka is easy to explain: languages simply removed the *ɨ by analogy with verb forms where the root-final vowel was retained, that is, verb forms with a consonant-initial suffix or no suffixes. For example, *tama 'put' would have been realized as *tama without a suffix, as *tama-na [put-2SG.IPST] with a consonant-initial suffix, and *tam-ɨk-i [put-DS.SEQ-3SG] with the suffix *-ɨka. The *ɨ in the last form could be changed to the root vowel on analogy with the other forms, creating, for example, Mand *aba-c* 'put-DS' and Mum *tama-h-i* 'put-DS-3SG'. Moreover, the West Sogeram languages consistently eliminate suffix-initial *ɨ (compare the habitual in §4.3.6 and the irrealis in §4.3.10).

Given the reconstruction of *-ɨka, we can now turn our attention to some innovations shown in Table 29. Some of these are easier to explain than others. Perhaps the most puzzling is the semantic innovation in Manat, where these suffixes have apparently become part of some verb roots and ceased to contribute any meaning at all. Many questions can be raised about this process (Why did *ɨha attach to certain verb roots and not others? Why was *k voiced when only word-initial *k usually voices in Manat? What was the syntactic environment in which this reanalysis took place?), none of which I have good anwers for.

I should note that Apalɨ has first and second person far past suffixes that resemble these forms: *-c-in* ('-FPST-1SG,' *-ha-naŋ* '-FPST-2SG,' *-hɨ-lu* '-FPST-1PL,' and *-ha-laŋ* '-FPST-2PL'. I do not consider these forms cognate and have four reasons for this. First, the semantic innovation from different-subject to far past seems unusual, although I do not know whether it is unattested. Second, the far past suffixes lack *i, while the reflex of the 3SG *-ik-i retains it in -ic-i. Third, the far past suffixes attach to reflexes of Proto-Sogeram uninflected verbs, suggesting they are inherited from SVCs (or later verb–verb compounds): *iahua-h-ilu* 'get up-FPST-1PL' is descended from *yakwa, not the bound form *yakw-, and *ua-c-in* 'go-FPST-1SG' is descended from *wa, not the bound form *u-. And fourth, a verb exists in the West Sogeram languages that is a plausible etymological source for this innovative Apali far past suffix: *ka-* 'do, say' (123).

Mand
(123) *Mac, dɨh=i ñac hr=i j-om* **ka-rd.**
enough DU=COM daughter 3SG.POSS=COM eat-AJTZ **do-FPST**
'Alright, she and her daughter ate.'

The Aisi suffix *-ogi* is unique in that it is both the 2PL and the 3PL form. It appears to be derived from the 3SG somehow—note that it ends in *i*—but it is unclear how, and it is unclear how this suffix came to refer to two person–number categories.

The *a in *-ika was changed to *u* in Kursav; I have no explanation for this.

Finally, in Gants the *a in *-ika was changed to *e*. This appears to have happened via analogy to the 1SG and 3SG forms. PSog *-ɨk-in and *-ɨk-i became -*k-en(iŋ)* and -*k-e* due to regular phonological changes, and then the -*ke* sequences from these suffixes spread to other person–number categories.

4.4.3 Different-subject simultaneous

Different-subject simultaneous markers are found in several Sogeram languages, and in all of them they are formed by reduplication. (Apali is an exception to this rule, but its strategy is innovative, being descended from the Proto-Sogeram imperfective SVC.) It seems, then, that a reduplicative morpheme of some sort marked simultaneous activities in Proto-Sogeram clause chains. Recall that Proto-Sogeram had two paradigms of DS suffixes: one for realis chains and another for irrealis chains. In many modern languages only one paradigm or the other is inherited, and in some languages a single DS paradigm is composed, etymologically, of suffixes from both the Proto-Sogeram paradigms. This is relevant because it is possible that in Proto-Sogeram only one of the two DS paradigms was reduplicated to add simultaneous meaning, and that this reduplication has then been analogically extended to the other paradigm in some languages. So we are faced with two questions about the reduplicative simultaneous suffix in Proto-Sogeram.

First, did it attach only to realis DS verbs, only to irrealis DS verbs, or to both? And second, how was it formed—what exactly did it copy from the DS verb? I address these questions below, beginning with the latter. But first, I present the reflexes of the Proto-Sogeram simultaneous suffix in Table 30, along with my proposed reconstruction. I have indicated the size of the reduplicant in square brackets: in Manat the whole word (ω) is copied; in Mum the preceding suffixes are copied (the μ here represents "morphemes," not moras); and in Sirva the suffix copies the preceding syllable (σ). The blank cells in the Mum rows indicate that a form is not attested in the data I have. I suspect that most of these forms are in fact possible.

Table 30: Different-subject simultaneous.

	1SG	2SG	3SG	1PL	2PL	3PL
Manat	-it~[ω]	-in~[ω]	-s~[ω]	-r~[ω]	-ir~[ω]	-ura-s~[ω]
Mum (R)	-h-in~[μ]		-h-i~[μ]	-ha-riŋ~[μ]		-h-u~[μ]
Mum (IRR)					-t-ra~[ω]	-t-u~[μ]
Sirva	-iin~[σ]	-ha-na~[σ]	-ii~[σ]	-ha-r~[σ]	-ha-ra~[σ]	-b-ii~[σ]
Kursav	-titi	-tata	-tete	-titir	-titira	-toto
Gants	-ire-riŋ	-ine-na	-ire-re	-ire-ruŋ	-ire-raŋ	-i-re-re
PSog	*~[ω]	*~[ω]	*~[ω]	*~[ω]	*~[ω]	*~[ω]

In Manat the suffix copies the preceding word, as illustrated in (124). This example also illustrates that the reduplicated morpheme is phonologically a separate word, as *sñ* is not a permissible consonant cluster in Manat. When the suffix attaches to a compound verb, only the last root is copied, as (125) illustrates. There are some exceptions to this, as shown in (126), but these are rare enough that they can be accounted for by positing that certain compound verbs are sometimes reanalyzed as single roots.

       Manat
(124) *Akai* **ñiŋ-ura-s~ñiŋuras=a,** *rum ini-b ini-ba da-ma-g.*
      okay **stay-PL-3.DS~SIM=LNK** man ND-NOM ND-LOC walk-PST-3SG.FAR
      'While they were there, this man was wandering around here.'

       Manat
(125) *Ñanik-ib*   **miga-ñi-s~ñis=a,**   *akai*
      son.3.POSS-NOM **come.down-stay-3SG.DS~SIM=LNK** COMP
      aih-ura-ma-g,   *ni-hav-ati-b.*
      come-PL-PST-3.FAR 3.POSS-uncle-PL-NOM
      'While her son was sleeping (lit. 'come down-stay'), his uncles came.'

Manat
(126) Nid   b=emtak,   **rapra-ñiŋ-ura-s~rapraniŋuras=a,** akai   ŋar
      2/3DU 3.NOM=alone **wait.for-stay-PL-3.DS~SIM=LNK**   COMP   sun
      ka-b   migu-n   viha=k   aku-ma-g.
      MD-NOM go.down-2/3.SS ripe=ACC   go.up-PST-3SG.FAR
      'As just the two of them were waiting for them, the sun went down and turned red.'

In Mum, DS simultaneous forms are usually formed by reduplicating the realis DS verb, which is formed with the -*ha* suffix. The reduplicant copies the -*ha* plus the agreement suffix; in the 1SG and third person this amounts to copying the last syllable (127), but in the 1PL it means copying two syllables (128).

Mum
(127) Karha-ta   **ma-ga-h-i~hi**   karagaravuz mizataya miŋa-m-i.
      sleep-SS   **NEG-look-DS-3SG~SIM**   rib   one   take-HPST-3SG
      'He slept and while he was not looking God took one of his ribs.'
                                                                (Sweeney n.d.)

Mum
(128) Blesim-ta   **u-ha-riŋ~hariŋ**   kutvu   kimu-m-i.
      bless-SS   **go-DS-1PL~SIM**   back   die-HPST-3SG
      'We blessed and while we were going he died at our backs.'
                                                                (Sweeney n.d.)

Additionally, in Mum this reduplicative suffix can apparently also be attached to irrealis verbs. There are only two tokens of this in the data I have, and they are presented below. In (129) the meaning appears to be similar to that of the examples above: DS simultaneous, only in an irrealis chain (imperative, specifically) instead of a realis one. The shape of the suffix is also the same, as it copies the preceding suffixes, but not the verb root. Example (130) is more confusing. Here the suffix copies the whole preceding word, including the verb root; the form is used at the end of a clause chain, not medially; and the meaning appears to be imperative. Without a more complete analysis of Mum verb morphology available it is difficult to interpret this example. But it appears from (129), at least, that in Mum this reduplicative suffix can attach to either kind of DS verb (realis or irrealis); that it copies the preceding DS suffix and the agreement suffix; and that it adds simultaneous meaning.

Mum
(129) **Yɨvu-t-u~tu**   navudi   yad   tav   ha   ñaŋra   tama-m-u.
hit-IRR-3PL~SIM   woman   1SG.POSS   house   MD   clean   put-IMP-3PL
'They must cut and the women must make my house clean.'

(Sweeney n.d.)

Mum
(130) *Migu-ta   dabu   wokman   da-ŋniŋ   naga   **kɨ-t-ra~gitra**,*
go.down-SS   FD.LOC   workman   FD-PL   with   **stay-IRR-2PL~SIM**
va-sm-u.
say-FPST-3PL
'"You go down over there with those workmen," they said.'

(Sweeney n.d.)

In Sirva the simultaneous suffix copies the preceding syllable. This usually only involves copying material from other suffixes, but in the 1SG and 3SG it involves copying some material from the verb root (131).

Sirva
(131) *Pev   **w-i~wi**   narah   be   hasa   wari*
forest   **go-3SG.DS~SIM**   younger.sib.3.POSS   3SG   FOC   village
kɨ-s-a.
stay-FPST-3SG
'While he went to the forest, his younger brother stayed in the village.'

In texts this suffix consistently copies only the preceding syllable. But when I conducted more extensive elicitation, my consultant would occasionally produce a longer reduplicant. For example, for *kumu-* 'die' he gave *kumu-in~gumuin* in the 1SG—although he said that *kumu-in~iin* was better. I believe this variation is a relic of the fact that the reduplicant used to be longer, as it still is in Manat and Mum.

In Kursav and Gants, the form of the suffix is no longer reduplicative, although its reduplicative origin is plain to see from the forms in Table 30. In Kursav it looks as though the reduplicant originally copied the irrealis suffix and the agreement suffix, and that the agreement suffix has been eroded since then. In Gants it seems that the same process took place, but the *-re* that was formed in the 3SG was then reanalyzed as a simultaneous suffix, which then spread to the rest of the paradigm. The only exception is 2SG, where the nasal that remains reveals the reduplicative origins of these forms.

Given all this, we must decide what length to reconstruct for the Proto-Sogeram reduplicative suffix. There are essentially two options. One is to reconstruct a shorter reduplicant, such as is found in most languages, and to posit some process that lengthened it in Manat and possibly Mum and Sirva. Another option is to reconstruct whole-word reduplication and to say that this reduplicant was eroded in every language except Manat. Normally this decision would be simple, as phonological reduction is typically not reversible so change could only have proceeded in one direction. But in the case of reduplication phonological reduction *is* reversible because the base on which the reduplicant is formed is still present, so there are two possible directions of change. Nevertheless, I still consider reduction more likely than lengthening because it can be motivated, namely on the grounds of ease of articulation, while a similar motivation for lengthening is more difficult to find. Ease of perception cannot account for it, since the forms in Kursav and Gants, though short, are still unambiguous. For this reason I reconstruct a Proto-Sogeram morpheme that copied a DS medial verb in its entirety to signal that the event of that verb occurred simultaneously with the event of the following verb. Given that modern reflexes copy both realis and irrealis DS medial verbs, I reconstruct a morpheme that functioned likewise, and could copy both realis and irrealis verbs.

4.5 Other morphology

A few pieces of morphology can be reconstructed that are not easily classified as medial or final. These include a reduplicative nominalization, discussed below, a participial suffix *-m (§4.5.2), and an irrealis infinitive suffix (§4.5.3).

4.5.1 Nominalization

Proto-Sogeram possessed a derivational suffix that formed nouns from verbs. This suffix was formed via reduplication, and reflexes are found across the family, in every language except Aisi and Kursav. The functions of these different reflexes show some variation, but largely correspond. In almost every daughter language this form can be used nominally as well as adverbially, much like English gerunds in *-ing*. They can often also be used adjectivally, but this can be understood as an example of the nominal function, since Sogeram nouns can function attributively.

In Mand this suffix derives nouns from verbs (132) and can also perform adverbial functions (133). The form of the reduplicant is not perfectly understood, but it is usually shortened and voiceless stops are lenited to fricatives.

Mand
(132) Pɨ aci w-e a, ya   **ka~h**   ka-p   aba-ŋarid.
       3   FOC go-SS ah speech **talk~NMPT** FD-LOC put-FUT
       'He'll go, uh, put it in that recorder (lit. 'speech talker').'

Mand
(133) **Ihra~hir**   ku-ŋari.
       watch~NMPT see-FUT
       'Watching, he'll see (it).'

The Nend form also derives "nominal forms from verbs" which "can function nominally and adjectivally as well as verbally" (K. Harris 1990: 86), as shown in (134) and (135). As in Mand, the reduplicant is shorter than the verb and stops are lenited to voiced fricatives. The phonological processes involved is described by Harris (1990: 81).

Nend
(134) Ya   **ka~h**   ohira   ha-n   eto-ma-r   wonjir-indiv.
       speech **talk~NMLZ** large   MD-ACC   leave-HPST-3SG fathers-BEN
       'They left the ones who could talk for the fathers.'   (K. Harris n.d.)

Nend
(135) Uyi-v   ŋaka-z   mira   **na-n**   **na-n**   ñi-mg-iz ...
       place-SBJ dawn-3SG.DS pig   **eat~NMLZ** **eat~NMLZ** stay-PL-3.DS
       'At dawn they stayed eating and eating the pig and ...'   (K. Harris n.d.)

The Manat form can function nominally (136) and adverbially (137). The reduplicant is usually a full reduplication of the last verb root (not the whole stem in compound verbs), but sometimes it is slightly abbreviated. Additionally, a velar nasal consonant will sometimes be inserted between the root and the reduplicative suffix, as in *ita~gita* 'leave~NMLZ' or *ña~ŋiñ* 'eat-NMLZ'. This intrusive nasal sometimes replaces the initial consonant of the root, as in *bata~gata* 'sit~NMLZ,' and sometimes combines with it to create a prenasalized stop, as in *rama~dama* 'put~NMLZ'.

Manat
(136) Na   bavad   pas   vaga   **vika~vika**   kai   v-itiha-nad=ik ...
       and   quickly banana   leaf   **write~NMLZ**   LOC   go-FFUT-2SG=ACC
       'And if you go to the missionaries (lit. 'paper-writers') quickly ...'

Manat

(137) Ñañña=k **miŋa~miŋ** gu-ñ-ura-ma-g.
food=ACC **get~NMLZ** give-eat-PL-PST-3.FAR
'Taking food, they fed them.'

Wade refers to the cognate Apalɨ construction as a gerund and observes that it can "fill nominal positions in postposition phrases and in non-verbal clauses" (Wade 1989: 119), as in (138), and also functions "verbally to indicate simultaneous same subject following" (Wade 1989: 189), as in (139). The reduplicant appears to usually be a full repetition of the last verb root. However, Wade observes that in "the Uagalɨhu dialect, which often retains final *ŋ*'s, the reduplicated forms of verbs take on a more complex form due to morphophonemics, i.e. *viŋ-viŋ* 'get-get' becomes *vi-biŋ*" (Wade 1989: 190). This passage suggests Apalɨ may have some vestiges of an *ŋ that was somehow involved in this construction. In addition, Wade (p.c.) reports that a small number of verbs have related nominal forms that contain an additional final *ŋ* or *iŋ*, such as *latɨhi* 'divide' and *latɨhiŋ* 'a division'. She says these forms "fill all the normal nominal positions, but are obviously formed from verb roots".

Apalɨ

(138) Libulɨbu **viha~viha** saŋ ab-in.
grass **cut.up~NMLZ** BEN talk-1SG.IPST
'I was talking about cutting the grass.' (Wade 1989: 189)

Apalɨ

(139) Hɨda hulaŋ mu aga-dɨ vaŋ **miŋa~miŋa** ab-i.
walk man another DEF-OBL string.bag **hold~NMLZ** talk-3SG.IPST
'He walked and was holding the other man's string bag while he talked.'
(Wade n.d.b)

The functions of the cognate Mum suffix have not been described, but Sweeney (n.d.) glosses it as a gerund, and examples can be found of what are apparently nominal (140) and adverbial (141) functions. The reduplicant copies the whole verb and lenites voiceless stops, sometimes to voiced fricatives as in (141), and sometimes to prenasalized stops. It appears that the same verb can take both forms: *kur-* 'shoot' is *kurhur* in (141) but the form *kurgur* is also present in the corpus.

Mum

(140) Musi kɨbadav **miŋa~miŋa** du sɨbra-rɨm abavara-ɨrma-n.
today house.on.posts **take~NMLZ** POSS work-BEN tell.story-FUT-1SG
'Today I will tell the story concerning the work building a house on posts.' (Sweeney n.d.)

Mum
(141) Kava kuñiv **kur~hur** nuɲuva **kɨs~hɨs** kakra-yɨ
bird bird.sp **shoot~NMLZ** his.father **smoke~NMLZ** limbum-LOC
tama-m-i.
put-HPST-3SG
'He was shooting birds of paradise and his father smoked them and put them on limbum.' (Sweeney n.d.)

In Sirva the reduplicative nominalization also creates forms that can be used as nouns (142) or adverbs (143). The form of the reduplicant is not well understood. It is sometimes a full reduplication as in *kwemgwem* and *miɲamiɲa* below, and sometimes partial, as in *adɨ~d* 'do~NMLZ'. Voiceless stops are sometimes left unchanged (*tai~tai* 'go.up~NMLZ'), sometimes prenasalized (*tama~dama* 'put~NMLZ'), and sometimes lenited to voiced fricatives (*kapara~vara* 'throw~NMLZ'). And two verbs, *kɨ-* 'stay' and *aku-* 'sleep,' have irregular nominalized forms that are made with the suffix *-ŋ* (144).

Sirva
(142) Uhu **kwem~gwem** be yakɨva-vanadi-Ø, n-i.
ground **unite~NMLZ** 3SG get.up-FUT-3SG ND-SET
'The land meeting will happen, here.'

Sirva
(143) Ivɨ siki beau, **miɲa~miɲa** kavar-a mir-a kusu k-i
grass.sp root DEF.ACC **get~NMLZ** throw-SS leave-SS food MD-SET
kur-ava-b-ri.
plant-HAB-PL-3
'Uprooting the *ivɨ* roots, they throw them away, and plant food there.'

Sirva
(144) Ka-ma ad-ɨi, asɨk=iñ **aku-ŋ** kɨd-i-Ø.
MD-ADVZ do-3SG.DS fire=LI **sleep-NMLZ** walk-TPST-3SG
'It would do that, and he would sleep by the fire.'

In Aisi and Kursav there is no cognate construction. However, I have found one form in Aisi that appears to be descended from a nominalization: *uror* 'shouting,' from a reduplication of PSOG *ura 'call out' (145), which itself survives into Aisi as *ur-*.[21]

---

[21] Interestingly, the cognate form in Sirva has also lexicalized. There the form *warwar* 'yelling' is the only reflex of PSOG *ura 'call out,' which is no longer a productive verb.

Aisi
(145) *Kaw-i   kitiŋ,   **uror=ɨra**   **uror=ɨra**,   ur=eŋ   w-e.*
carry-SS and   **shouting=COM shouting=COM** house-LOC go-3SG.IPST
'He carried them and went home hooting and hollering.'

Finally, verb reduplication in Gants is not very common and therefore not well understood. But it appears to form participles that function primarily as adverbs (146) or as verb adjuncts.

Gants
(146) *Tai mañ kra **tiga~tiga**   arip ko   arip ko   aŋ-ek.*
tree seed TOP **scatter~PTCP** right DEF right DEF go-3SG.IPST
'The fruit scattered and went all around.'

Given the geographic diversity of reflexes, the uniformity of functions presented in Table 31 is quite striking. In every Greater West Sogeram and North Sogeram language, reduplicated verbs can function as nouns and adverbs, which is sufficient evidence for reconstructing those functions to Proto-Sogeram. But the East Sogeram branch also supports this reconstruction, as there is evidence of the nominal function in Aisi and the adverbial function survives into Gants.

Table 31: Nominalizer properties.

	nominal function	adverbial function	formal properties
Mand	yes	yes	partial reduplication
Nend	yes	yes	partial reduplication
Manat	yes	yes	full reduplication; ŋ/g insertion
Apalɨ	yes	yes	full reduplication; irregular -ŋ
Mum	yes	yes	full reduplication
Sirva	yes	yes	full reduplication; irregular -ŋ
Aisi	yes?	no	
Gants	no	yes	full reduplication

Reconstructing the form of the reduplicant is more difficult. In resolving the difference between partial reduplication in West Sogeram and full reduplication elsewhere, we can reconstruct full reduplication to Proto-Sogeram for the same reason we reconstructed the longer reduplicant for the different-subject simultaneous (§4.4.3): a motivation can easily be proposed for shortening but not for lengthening. The shorter West Sogeram forms are thus considered innovative. But the velar nasals in Manat, Apalɨ, and Sirva are puzzling. Based on these witnesses we should also reconstruct an *ŋ that was involved in this construction. The irregular distribution of the velar pattern in Manat suggests a reconstruction similar to the modern Apalɨ and Sirva situation: most verbs were simply reduplicated, while a few irregular verbs were nominalized with *-ŋ. We can then posit that in Manat, some of the irregular *-ŋ verbs added reduplicants on analogy with the predominant pattern but also kept the *-ŋ. However, one problem with this reconstruction is the fact that I am unable to say which verbs took the irregular suffix because its inheritance into Manat, Apalɨ, and Sirva has been so inconsistent.

So I reconstruct a reduplicative nominalizer that copied bare verb roots in their entirety. Forms created with this nominalizer could be used as nouns or adverbs. And some irregular verbs were nominalized with a suffix *-ŋ instead.

4.5.2 Participle

Proto-Sogeram had a participial suffix *-m which derived adjectives from verbs. The primary evidence for this suffix comes from Mand and Kursav. In Kursav, this suffix derives adjectives from verbs. Kursav adjectives can either precede (147) or follow (148) their head noun. They have many nominal properties, and are actually best considered a subclass of nouns; they can head noun phrases on their own, although they are usually best understood as modifying an unexpressed head noun, as in (149).

Kursav
(147) Mɨda **kra-m** mɨnei, koɲe ne kevɨ-d-o.
grass.sp **burn-PTCP** time bandicoot eat throw-HAB-3PL
'At the time (we) burn the kunai grass, they eat bandicoots.'

Kursav
(148) Kura, ka-ka **dɨ-m** niga v-e.
man MD-TOP **do-PTCP** SPEC come-3SG.NFUT
'One such man (lit. 'a that-doing man') came.'

Kursav
(149) Kin **ragura-m,** v-e.
sore **care.for-PTCP** come-3SG.NFUT
'A doctor (lit. 'sore-caring-for (person)') comes.'

The function of this suffix in Mand is less well understood. Its primary function appears to be to derive verb adjuncts, verbal forms that occur with an inflected light verb to form a complex predicate. The most common light verb for Mand -*m* forms is *ga-* 'grab' (150), but they can also occur with others such as *ka-* 'do' (151).

Mand
(150) Ñɨ   ñac   zau   na-n   j-e   **uhra-m**   g-e-d.
      son daughter   fish ND-ACC   eat-SS   **grow-AJTZ**   grab-PL-3.IPST
      'The children eat this fish and grow big.'

Mand
(151) Arhw   **kre-m**   ka-cɨ-nhw.
      1PL   **make.so-AJTZ**   do-HAB-1PL
      'That's what we do.'

It is not clear, however, exactly what "verb adjuncts" are in Mand. For the moment I analyze them as a separate word class, semantically related to verbs but morphologically distinct. This is an attested feature of other languages in the area (notably Kalam; see Pawley and Bulmer 2011), but it has not yet been demonstrated that it is the correct analysis for Mand. It may turn out that there is no separate word class of adjuncts, but only a verb adjunct construction—and that the words I currently analyze as verb adjuncts are in fact nouns, adjectives, or other parts of speech that are simply used in this construction. This is a question for future research. For the moment it is enough to observe that Mand -*m* forms are deverbalized to some extent. There is even an example of an -*m* form occurring with a demonstrative, suggesting that these forms have some nominal or adjectival properties.

Mand
(152) **Awari-m**   ka-g,   ahw-ahw-ahw   ara.
      yell-AJTZ FD-NOM   boo-boo-boo   QUOT
      'As for the yelling, they said "Boo! Boo! Boo!"'

On the strength of the Mand and Kursav witnesses, then, we can reconstruct a Proto-Sogeram derivational suffix *-m that went on verbs. Reconstructing the grammatical function of words derived with *-m is a little trickier, but we can narrow the list of candidates down to nouns, adjectives, and verb adjuncts. Of these, nouns seem unlikely, both because the nominal function of -*m* appears to be marginal in both Mand and Kursav, and, less importantly, because other nominalizing morphology can be reconstructed (§4.5.1). Reconstructing a suffix that formed verb adjuncts is also not ideal, as it is not even clear that synchronic -*m* forms verb adjuncts in Mand, let alone that Proto-Sogeram had a word class of verb adjuncts. So we are left with the third option: reconstruct a suffix *-m that formed adjectives from verbs. This option accounts well for the data: Kursav -m currently forms adjectives, and adjectives are commonly employed as verb adjuncts in Mand. This can be seen in (153), where the adjective *urat* 'cold' is placed inside the two negative morphemes, indicating that it is functioning as a verb adjunct.

Mand
(153) *Yar   miz   mɨ   **urat** ka-m*.
      1SG.OBJ body   NEG   **cold** do-NEG
      'I'm not cold.'   Elicited

This reconstruction has been made based entirely on the Mand and Kursav witnesses. But *-m actually has reflexes in a number of other Sogeram languages, although *-m is retained as an imperative suffix in all of these languages. In Nend, it is a 1PL imperative suffix, in Manat and Aisi it is 2SG, and in Apalɨ and Mum it is 3SG and 3PL. The grammaticalization path from nonfinite verb form to imperative is well-trodden: for example, in her book on imperatives Aikhenvald (2010: 363) describes the common "pathway of desubordination," whereby imperatives are formed when the use of dependent verb forms as directives becomes routinized. The fact that -*m* marks several different person–number categories of imperative also suggests that these forms are innovative in the languages where -*m* is an imperative suffix, and the reconstructed participial meaning offers a very plausible etymology.

Finally, reflexes of *-m can also be seen in some grammaticalized periphrastic constructions. The Nend plural suffix -*mgɨ* is descended from a construction with an *-m participle plus a light verb, and the Kursav future tense is formed with an -*m* participle plus the verb *du* 'do' (Daniels forthcoming). This grammaticalization pattern suggests that PSog *-m participles were commonly used in conjunction with light verbs in a verb-adjunct-like construction—or at least, that they came to be in Nend and Kursav.

4.5.3 Irrealis infinitive

The Proto-Sogeram future tense suffix *-ɨba was used in combination with the Set III agreement suffixes to form the future tense (§4.3.5). But this suffix could also be used on its own in what was probably an irrealis infinitive construction. Reflexes of this survive into Apalɨ, Aisi, and Kursav. In Apalɨ the suffix -*ɨba* seems to function as a desiderative and is usually followed by the verb *lɨ-* 'do,' as in (154).

Apalɨ
(154) *Uleŋ* **u-ba** *lɨ-mili alu-dɨ ab-ava-lɨ.*
village **go-FUT** do-1PL.DS 1PL-OBL talk-PL-3.FPST
'We got ready to go to the village and they said to us.' (Wade 1989: 89)

In Aisi I analyze the suffix *-iba* as a form that derives participles; it usually functions adverbially to modify the action of the main verb of the clause (155). It can also be used on its own, in which case it appears to describe some typical or characteristic trait of its subject (156).

Aisi
(155) *Ga-rib* **ab-iba** *yok-e, pini garaŋ g-oŋ.*
MD-ADJZ **talk-PTCP** go.up-3SG.IPST palm.sp long MD-TOP
'Saying that, she went up a long *pini* palm.'

Aisi
(156) *Ameki ga-ku gyou pa* **n-iba.**
lastborn MD-NOM snake.sp only **eat-PTCP**
'The lastborn used to just eat *gyou* snakes.'

And in Kursav I analyze the suffix *-ba* as a negative nominalizer, which derives a noun (or verb adjunct) that refers to not performing the action of the verb. It is always followed by the verb *di-* 'do,' as in (157) and (158).

Kursav
(157) *Bua pa ma* **di-ba** *d-eke ...*
enough only NEG **do-NEG.NMLZ** do-3SG.DS
'It wasn't good, so ...'

Kursav
(158) *An ma* **na-bu-ba** *d-uar.*
1PL NEG **2SG.OBJ-give-NEG.NMLZ** do-1PL.NFUT
'We haven't given it to you yet.' Elicited

An apparently cognate Anamuxra suffix *-ba* is called the "negative realis/nonfuture" by Ingram (2001). This suffix also occurs without agreement suffixes, as in (159).

Anamuxra
(159) Aŋ-ma   yivŋanaz-ba.
       1PL-NEG   night.spear.fish-NEG
       'We didn't go night spear fishing.'   (Ingram 2001: 239)

These suffixes all exhibit obvious formal similarities, and their functions are also quite similar. Kursav has lost the suffix-initial *i, but otherwise the phonological reconstruction of *-iba is clear. Semantically, the suffixes are all deverbalizing to some extent, and in Apalɨ and Kursav they add irrealis meaning: future in Apalɨ and negative in Kursav. Only the Aisi form appears to have lost this meaning. For these reasons I reconstruct a suffix *-iba that created a deverbalized form with irrealis meaning. Its precise grammatical function remains unclear (i.e., it may have derived verb adjuncts or nouns, or been an infinitival form), as does its specific irrealis meaning. Clearly a future infinitive meaning is likely, given that the same suffix *-iba was used in the future tense paradigm, but for now I reconstruct an infinitive suffix with a more generalized irrealis meaning.

Chapter 5
Nominal Morphology

In this chapter I present reconstructions of three noun-related word classes and their attendant morphology. I begin with inalienably possessed nouns, which are a subclass of nouns, in the following section. I then cover pronouns in §5.2 and demonstratives in §5.3. The treatment of pronouns and demonstratives involves a lot of discussion of noun phrase-final enclitics, so some sections are actually devoted to those. There has also been a good deal of analogic change to these systems, which has been challenging to unravel. Consequently, the proportion of tentative reconstructions is somewhat higher in this section than in others, and I point out the more speculative lines of reasoning where appropriate.

5.1 Inalienably possessed nouns

Proto-Sogeram had a subclass of nouns, composed almost entirely of kin terms, that were inalienably possessed. Inalienably possessed nouns differed in a few respects from common nouns. First, as discussed in §5.2.2 below, they could host some enclitics that common nouns could not. Second, they took possessive prefixes that common nouns did not. And third, it is possible (although uncertain) that they took plural marking, which common nouns did not. The latter two features are discussed in the sections below.

5.1.1 Possessive prefixes

Inalienably possessed nouns took obligatory possessive prefixes that distinguished the person, but not the number, of the possessor. The prefixes were *a- '1.POSS,' *na- '2.POSS,' and *nɨ- '3.POSS'. Table 32 shows the reflexes that support these reconstructions.

Table 32: Possessive prefixes.

	Mand	Nend	Manat	Apalɨ	Mum	Sirva	Aisian	Kursav	Gants	PSoG
1.POSS	a-	a-	a-	a-	ya-	a-	a-	a-	a-	*a-
2.POSS	a-	a-	na-	na-	na-	na-	na-	na-	na-	*na-
3.POSS	Ø-	Ø-	nɨ-	nɨ-	niŋu-	nɨ-	nɨ-	nɨ-, no-	nɨ-, no-	*nɨ-

The loss of word-initial consonants in the West Sogeram (WS) languages (§3.2.1.1) resulted in the merger of the 1.POSS and 2.POSS prefixes into a speech-act-participant prefix. This now stands in opposition to a null 3.POSS prefix, which resulted from the same sound change deleting the Proto-Sogeram 3.POSS prefix *nɨ-. In Mum the 1.POSS prefix became *ya-* on analogy with the first person subject pronoun *ya. Also, the 3.POSS prefix added an element *ŋu* which I cannot explain. A rare variant of the Proto-Sogeram 3.POSS prefix was *nu-, which mimicked the third person subject pronoun *nu; Kursav and Gants have generalized this variant to more contexts. Otherwise, the reflexes of all three possessive prefixes are remarkably regular, and reconstruction is consequently unproblematic. The specific lexical histories of the nineteen reconstructed kin terms are discussed in §6.3.

5.1.2 Plural marking

It is possible that inalienably possessed nouns were marked for number, although the evidence is quite problematic. There are two suggestive correspondence sets, which I review in turn.

The first piece of evidence hinges on reflexes in Mand and Nend, on the one hand, and Sirva on the other. The Mand plural suffix for inalienably possessed nouns is usually *-oja*, although under certain circumstances, which are not fully understood, it can be *-oj* (160) or *-ja*. The Nend plural suffix is *-onj* (K. Harris 1990: 87), which appears to be cognate.

Mand
(160) *Agr-e   w-e   **v-oj**   hr=ɨr   ka-rd=a.*
      run-SS   go-SS **father.3.POSS-PL** 3SG.POSS=ACC   talk-FPST-LNK
      'She ran and told her fathers.'

Sirva has a wide variety of plural suffixes for kin terms, each of which is used with only one or two lexemes. The suffix for the words *mudu* 'male in-law' and *mudumɨge* 'mother-in-law' is *-ña*. (Other suffixes include *-zar*, *-har*, *-gar*, and *-nin*.)

If the only reflexes available to us were the Mand allomorph *-ja* and the Sirva allomorph *-ña*, we could easily reconstruct *-ña and each of these would be a regular reflex. But the suffix-initial *o* in Mand complicates matters; what happened to this vowel in Sirva? The Nend reflex *nj* also causes problems. Mand *j* is a regular reflex of *ñ because Mand underwent nasal fortition (§3.2.2.5). But Nend did not undergo nasal fortition, and would not be expected to borrow such a suffix from Mand, so we must question whether the West Sogeram and Sirva forms are even cognate. Unfortunately the question cannot be conclusively resolved with the available data. It may be that Proto-Sogeram had a plural suffix *-ña or *-uña for inalienably possessed nouns. It may also be that both these suffixes come from a construction involving the pronoun *uña 'who' (see §5.2.6). For example, an expression like *nɨ-van uña '3.POSS-father who' could have originally meant 'the father and whoever'. Such an expression could then have undergone grammaticalization so that the pronoun *uña 'who' eventually became a plural suffix. But the evidence for neither of these scenarios is conclusive, so for now this plural suffix, or plural construction, cannot be reconstructed.

The second possible plural morpheme, *kati, has reflexes that mean 'group' or 'people' in Manat and Mum, and 'head' in Apalɨ. Some plural suffixes, like Manat -ati (161) and Sirva -har (162) appear to be reflexes of *kati.

Manat
(161) *Igu-ma-g,*   **nɨ-hav-ati=k.**
give-PST-3SG.FAR   **3.POSS-uncle-PL=ACC**
'She gave it to his uncles.'

Sirva
(162) *Sue* **nu-husu-har** *bira añi pii-vana mugura-bi-s-a.*
SO   **3.POSS-son-PL**   3PL   water   bathe-DESID   go.down-PL-FPST-3
'So his sons went down to the water to bathe.'

These suffixes appear to have grammaticalized fairly recently, given that their likely source construction can still be found in Mum (163).

Mum
(163) *Arhina* **hati** *mɨgu-ta Josephstaal tavra-m-u.*
Arhina   **people**   go.down-SS   Josephstaal   wait-IMP-3PL
'The people of Arhina must go down to Josephstaal and wait.' (Sweeney n.d.)

Look-alike forms can be found in other languages, but they are divergent enough that it is unclear whether they should be considered cognate. These include Mand *ata* 'group,' Magɨ and Aisi *katam* 'head,' Kursav *-hata* 'plural kin term suffix,' and Gants *karaŋ* 'headwater'. Taken together these forms are all suggestive of a Proto-Sogeram form *kat(i/a)[m], for which the second vowel could have been *i or *a and which may or may not have had a final *m. This form, if it existed, would probably have meant 'head,' but the Mand and Kursav forms are semantically somewhat divergent. But the problems with the cognate set are numerous enough that reconstruction to Proto-Sogeram remains premature.

5.2 Pronouns and noun phrase enclitics

In this section I discuss the five sets of pronouns that can be reconstructed to Proto-Sogeram. Three of these were marked with an enclitic that could also mark other kinds of noun phrase, and I discuss the reconstruction of those enclitics as well. I begin in the next section with the subject pronouns and continue with the object pronouns and enclitic (§5.2.2), the oblique pronouns and enclitic (§5.2.3), the possessive pronouns (§5.2.4), and the emphatic focus pronouns and enclitic (§5.2.5). I also reconstruct the interrogative pronoun 'who' in §5.2.6.

5.2.1 Subject pronouns

The Proto-Sogeram subject pronouns have been reconstructed by Ross (2000: 9, under the label "pWanang") as well as in my previous work (Daniels 2010). The reconstruction presented in Table 33 below differs in some details from those reconstructions, but the general picture remains the same. Specifically, Ross proposes *ba '3SG' and *ba-ra '3PL' as variants of the third person pronouns, but I consider the data he cites in support of this reconstruction to be reflexes of the emphatic set (§5.2.5). Here and throughout this chapter I use [square brackets] to indicate that a form is functionally equivalent but that I do not consider it cognate. So for example, the Sirva 3SG and 3PL pronouns in this table are synchronically subject pronouns, but they are descended from the focus enclitic (§5.2.5), not from the Proto-Sogeram subject pronouns.

Table 33: Subject pronouns.

	1SG	2SG	3SG	1PL	2PL	3PL	1DU	2DU	3DU
Mand	[api]	[abi]	[pi]	[arhw]	[abi]	[pi]	[di]	[dih]	[dih]
Nend	[nzɨ]	[am]	[mbi]	ar	[am]	[mbi]			
Manat	[zɨ]	[am]	[bi]	ar	[am]	[bi]	[nad]	[nɨd]	[nɨd]
Apalɨ	[viaŋ]	[nama]	[nɨbu]	alan	[namɨlaŋ]	[nubɨlaŋ]			
Mum	yi	na	nu	ara	nar	nir			
Sirva	ya	na	[be]	ara	nara	[bira]			
Magɨ	yɨ	na	nɨ	arɨ	narɨ	nirɨ			
Aisi	ya	na	nu	anɨ	narɨ	nirɨ			
Kursav	ya	na	nɨ, nu	an	nan	nin			
Gants	ya	na	nu	ayu	nayu	niu			
PSog	*ya	*na	*nɨ, nu	*ara	*nara	*nɨra			

A few remarks about the data in this table are in order. First, Mand, Nend, Manat, and Apalɨ have innovated a new set of subject pronouns from the Proto-Sogeram emphatic pronouns, as I discuss in §5.2.5. The Apalɨ 3SG and 3PL forms exhibit variation between *i* and *u* in their first vowel, which has been left out of the table for space reasons. Thus the 3SG can be *nibu* and *nubu*, while the 3PL can be *nibilaŋ* and *nubilaŋ*. The Kursav 3SG is normally *ni* in connected speech, although speakers accept *nu* as a valid pronunciation and occasionally produce it themselves.

The 1SG and 2SG forms are fairly straightforward to reconstruct, especially since they date to Proto-Madang and cognates can be found in many languages outside the Sogeram group. Examples include Anamuxra *ya* '1SG' and *na* '2SG' (Ingram 2001), Kalam *yad* '1SG' and *nad* '2SG' (Pawley and Bulmer 2011: 41), Tauya *ya* '1SG' and *na* '2SG' (MacDonald 1990: 92), and Wasembo *ya-* '1SG.OBJ' and *na-* '2SG.OBJ' (McElhanon 1975: 900). Ross also reconstructs the same forms (2000: 9).

The 3SG forms are more difficult. We are faced with variation between *ni* forms and *nu* forms, sometimes as variants within a language (as in Kursav), sometimes as different reflexes in closely related languages (as in the Aisian languages). Finding the variation in both Apalɨ and Kursav is evidence that it dates to Proto-Sogeram. In addition, reflexes of both forms can be found throughout the family—if, that is, the Mand, Nend, and Manat third person pronouns are in fact reflexes of *nɨ, as I argue in §5.2.5 below. It remains to be discovered how, and whether, *nɨ and *nu differed in function.

The plural pronouns are all formed with an element *-ra. Previously I reconstructed this element as *-raN, with a final nasal reflected only by Apalɨ *ŋ* (Daniels 2010: 171). More careful comparative work has revealed that this segment is better accounted for as an Apalɨ addition. (Addition of final *ŋ* is not uncommon in Apalɨ.) In particular, the evidence from the Josephstaal branch of South Adelbert shows no evidence of a final nasal, suggesting a reconstruction of *-ra: Moresada *arɛ* '1DU,' *nara* '2DU' (Capell 1951: 144); Osum and Pondoma *arɨ* '1DU,' *narɨ* '2DU'; and Wadaginam *nara* '2DU,' *nɨra* '3DU' (Z'graggen 1980a: 86).

These forms make something else clear: the Proto-Sogeram plural pronouns are reflexes of Proto-South Adelbert duals. Proto-Sogeram generalized the dual to all non-singular numbers, losing the dual–plural distinction. Or so it would seem, but for two complicating factors: the presence of dual pronouns in Mand and Manat, and the nasal in the Aisi 1PL and the plural Kursav pronouns. The dual pronouns in Mand and Manat are difficult to explain; they do not appear cognate with any other Sogeram or Josephstaal pronouns. And the fact that the Sogeram plural pronouns are so plainly cognate with the Josephstaal dual pronouns makes it difficult to see where the Mand and Manat duals could have come from, since they did not originate as Proto-South Adelbert dual pronouns. One clue is the beginning of the non-first person dual pronoun, which is *di-* in Mand and *ni-* in Manat. Both of these are regular reflexes of *nɨ, the Proto-Sogeram 3SG pronoun, suggesting the Mand and Manat dual pronouns may have originated as members of some other, non-subject set of pronouns. But it is not even possible at this point to speculate about what set of pronouns that might have been. For now, then, their origin remains unresolved, although it does not appear to cast doubt on the reconstruction of the Proto-Sogeram pronoun system as contrasting only singular vs. plural number.

The Aisi form *anɨ* '1PL' and the Kursav plural pronouns *an* '1PL,' *nan* '2PL,' and *nin* '3PL' are a more serious problem. Previously I had accounted for these as an irregular innovation (Daniels 2010: 172), although it is difficult to see what might motivate the spontaneous nasalization of *r to *n*. This hypothesis also runs into subgrouping problems, as the nasal is not found in Magɨ, which shares a long history of common development with Aisi. Accounting for the presence of the nasal in Aisi and Kursav, and its absence in Magɨ, is difficult. An alternative hypothesis is that the Proto-South Adelbert plural pronouns were actually retained in Proto-Sogeram. This hypothesis faces the same subgrouping issues, and runs into other problems. First, there are no relics of the Proto-South Adelbert plural pronouns in any other Sogeram language. And second, the Josephstaal languages suggest that the Proto-South Adelbert plural pronominal formative was *-ŋa: Moresada has *-ŋa* (Capell 1951: 144) while every other language has *-ŋ* (Z'graggen 1980a: 86). Aisi and Kursav, though, reflect *-na, with regular centering to *-nɨ* in Aisi (§3.4.2.4) and irregular loss of final *a in Kursav. These forms are not wildly different, of course, but a change from velar to alveolar nasal, or vice versa, must have taken place at some point if we wish to maintain that these forms are related to the Josephstaal forms. And such a change would be somewhat difficult to motivate on phonological grounds.

These Aisi and Kursav pronouns thus remain a puzzle. Both possible explanations—that they are an irregular post-Proto-Sogeram development, or that they are reflexes of the Proto-South Adelbert plural pronouns—have problems. The data strike me as inconclusive so I remain essentially agnostic, although I lean towards the hypothesis that they are a post-Proto-Sogeram development. For this reason I do not reconstruct a dual–plural distinction in the Proto-Sogeram pronouns.

Having addressed those issues, we can now turn to the individual reconstructions of the three Proto-Sogeram plural pronouns. The 1PL is straightforward, as the initial element *a- is reflected in every language and is also reflected in the Josephstaal languages. The Mand form appears to be a reflex of a possessive pronoun (§5.2.4); Nend and Manat lost final *a (Daniels and Brooks forthcoming); and Gants appears to have irregularly lost final *a, then regularly changed final *r > *i* (§3.4.6.4), then irregularly added final *u*. Otherwise the forms behave as expected.

The 2PL forms exhibit the same regularity, with the exception of the innovative pronouns in the western area. Gants appears to have undergone the same process as in the 1PL.

The 3PL forms are less regular. The innovative western forms are present once again, and Sirva is also innovative. Gants appears to have undergone the same process as in the 1PL and 2PL, although in this instance loss of final *a resulted in *nɨr, in which the *r vocalization change resulted in a vocalic *i: *ni. This form then took the same final *u* found in the other plural pronouns. It is worth asking whether the same variation found in the 3SG might have also been present in the Proto-Sogeram 3PL: might the 3PL have varied between *nɨra and *nura? It does not seem so, as the evidence for *nura is quite weak. Reflexes of *ɨ are found in Apalɨ, Mum, Aisian, Kursav, Gants, and possibly the innovative western forms. The only possible reflex of *u is found in Apalɨ *nubɨlaŋ*, which varies with *nɨbɨlaŋ*. This form could easily have arisen on analogy with the 3SG pronoun *nubu*, and as such I consider it innovative. Thus I reconstruct only one form for the 3PL pronoun, *nɨra, to Proto-Sogeram.

5.2.2 Object pronouns and enclitic

The Proto-Sogeram object pronouns, as well as the oblique pronouns (discussed in the next section), were formed with case enclitics that were not restricted to use on pronouns but could also attach to the end of other noun phrases. In some languages these enclitics survive only as enclitics, in others they survive only on pronouns, and in still others both functions persist. The object enclitic is reconstructed as *=ŋ and the oblique enclitic as *=d. They sometimes occur together on pronouns, usually in the order *=d=ɨŋ but sometimes the reverse. The forms that reflect the object enclitic are given in Table 34. Note that when in the presence of a clitic, the plural pronouns lose their final *a. Thus, for example, the 1PL object pronoun is reconstructed as *ar=ɨŋ, not †ara=ŋ.

Manat does not have third person object pronouns; demonstratives are used instead. Some of these forms, notably the 1SG and 2SG with only *=ŋ, do not have a wide enough distribution on their own to be reconstructed to Proto-Sogeram. But when the paradigm is taken as a whole, the pattern in the 3SG and the plural forms, the reflex of *=ŋ in Gants, and the extant 1SG and 2SG reflexes in Mum, Sirva, and Aisi, make the reconstruction of *ya=ŋ '1SG=OBJ' and *na=ŋ '2SG=OBJ' quite likely.

The Mand 3SG form is a reflex of *nɨ=ŋ with the addition of an (apparently) innovative object enclitic =r; the changes of *n > d and word-final *ŋ > h are both regular (§3.2.2.5). The other Mand forms are more problematic. They also have

Table 34: Object pronouns.

	1SG	2SG	3SG	1PL	2PL	3PL
Mand (OBJ)	[yar]	[dar]	dɨhɨr	[arhur]	adɨhur	dɨhur
Nend (OBJ)	[yaŋ]	[nan]	[ndɨn]	ariŋ	andɨŋ	ndɨŋ
Manat (OBJ)	[zɨ]	nɨ		ar	nar	
Mum (OBJ)	yaŋ	naŋ	nɨŋ	ariŋ	nariŋ	nɨriŋ
Sirva (POSS)	yaŋ	naŋ	nɨŋ	ariŋ	nariŋ	nɨriŋ
Magɨ (OBJ)	yadɨŋ	nadɨŋ	nɨdɨŋ	adanɨŋ	nadanɨŋ	nɨdanɨŋ
Aisi (OBJ)	yaŋ	naŋ	nuŋ			
Gants (POSS)	yadɨŋ	nadɨŋ	nuduŋ	aiduŋ	naiduŋ	niduŋ
PSOG	*ya=ŋ	*na=ŋ	*nɨ=ŋ, nu=ŋ	*ar=ɨŋ	*nar=ɨŋ	*nɨr=ɨŋ

the object enclitic =r, along with a vowel u that is of unknown origin. The rest of the material in these pronouns can be explained as regular reflexes of hypothetical forms *nan=ɨŋ and *nɨn=ɨŋ, or as irregular reflexes of *nar=d=ɨŋ and *nɨr=d=ɨŋ in which the *r was lost and *d is retained as d instead of ⁺t. The latter scenario is more likely for three reasons. First, there is no evidence for *nan=ɨŋ or *nɨn=ɨŋ in any other language. Second, the loss of *r from the 2PL and 3PL forms before consonants is also seen in the possessive (§5.2.4) and emphatic (§5.2.5) pronouns. And third, the Nend forms andɨŋ '2PL.OBJ' and ndɨŋ '3PL.OBJ' are evidence that *nar=d=ɨŋ and *nɨr=d=ɨŋ were reflected in Proto-West Sogeram as *adɨŋ and *dɨŋ, which could easily have been retained in Mand with irregular reflexes of *d.

In addition to Nend andɨŋ and ndɨŋ, which reflect *=d=ɨŋ, the Nend 1PL form ariŋ reflects only *=ŋ and appears to be a fully regular reflex of *ar=ɨŋ.

Manat underwent word-final nasal loss (§3.3.1.3), and as such the Manat forms in Table 34 could be reflexes of forms with final *=ŋ or not. It is somewhat more likely that they are not, though, since word-final nasal loss also affected Mum, Sirva, and Aisian, and all of these languages have preserved reflexes of *=ŋ. The given Manat forms are therefore probably descended from the subject forms; in the first person Manat does not distinguish subject from object pronouns, while in the second and third person the subject forms are descended from Proto-Sogeram emphatic pronouns (§5.2.5).

The Mum and Sirva forms are straightforward reflexes of the reconstructed Proto-Sogeram forms, with the caveat that word-final nasal loss, which normally affected polysyllabic words quite regularly, did not affect the plural pronouns. It is possible that the nasals were initially lost but then added back to the plural pronouns on analogy with the singular pronouns, which, being monosyllabic, would have retained final nasals.

Additionally, these pronouns have possessive meaning in Sirva, as shown in (164). How this semantic shift happened is not clear, although it must have been recent since these pronouns still have object meaning in closely related Mum. Interestingly, the Proto-Sogeram possessive pronouns now have object meaning (see §5.2.4), meaning that these two paradigms have switched functions.

Sirva
(164) **Naŋ**   wari   wa-hana~na,   ara   ka-ma   ki-vadi-r.
      2SG.POSS   village   go-2SG.DS~SIM   1PL   MD-ADVZ   stay-FUT-1PL
      'When you go to your home, we'll stay like this.'

The Magɨ singular pronouns are the expected reflexes for forms with the enclitics *=d=iŋ. The plural forms, on the other hand, seem to have followed a more complicated path of development. The initial sequence, excluding the final -aniŋ that these pronouns share, appears to be a reflex of pronouns in *=d. The final -niŋ sequence appears to be a reflex of the 3SG object pronoun *nɨ=ŋ, which may have grammaticalized into an accusative postposition in Magɨ, as shown in (165). That leaves the *a* that is wedged in between these two forms, for which, unfortunately, I do not have an explanation.

Magɨ
(165) Abi   yaka   **niŋ**   ab-is-iŋ.
      woman   1SG.POSS   ACC   speak-FPST-1SG
      'I spoke to my wife.'

In examining the Aisi singular pronouns we once again find straightforward reflexes of the Proto-Sogeram pronouns in *=ŋ. The 3SG nuŋ is a clear reflex of a *nu form, meaning that both *nu=ŋ and *nɨ=ŋ should probably be reconstructed to Proto-Sogeram (the latter having reflexes in Mand, Mum, and Sirva). The plural forms are composed of the subject pronouns plus an element -gunuŋ, which probably grammaticalized from the genitive postposition *giniŋ*.

The Gants pronouns are reflexes of forms with the *=d=iŋ clitic complex. The plural forms have interposed a *u* between the two clitics, which is of uncertain origin. It may have spread from the 3SG, where *nu=d=iŋ apparently underwent irregular vowel harmony to become *nuduŋ*, but this is not certain. These pronouns are normally used as possessive forms (166), but they can also occur with subjects in a construction that is not well understood (167).

Gants
(166) *Tipa pi* **nuduŋ** *ai-m-ek.*
fear village **3SG.POSS** come-FPST-3SG
'He fled to his village.'

Gants
(167) *Kidik, pakai Don* **nuduŋ** *erkara ai-da=n ...*
later again Don **3SG.POSS** turn come-SS=LNK
'Later, Don will come back again and ...'

As mentioned above, the object clitic *=ŋ also survives in some languages as an enclitic on the noun phrase. Examples below are from Mum (168), Sirva (169), and Aisi (170). In Sirva the enclitic =ŋ has undergone the same meaning shift as the pronouns and is now a possessive form.

Mum
(168) **Niŋu-m=iŋ** *kur-ta irha-m-i.*
3.POSS-mother=OBJ shoot-SS cry-HPST-3SG
'He shot his mother and he cried.' (Sweeney n.d.)

Sirva
(169) **Nua=ŋ,** *kya beau, kapar-a mir-a ...*
father.3.POSS=POSS speech DEF.ACC throw-SS leave-SS
'He threw away (i.e., ignored) his father's speech and ...'

Aisi
(170) **Kris=iŋ** *ir-ibyaŋ aba yoku-s-iŋ.*
Chris=ACC perceive-1SG.FUT QUOT go.up-FPST-1SG
'I went up to see Chris (lit. 'I said, "I'll see Chris," and went up').'

These enclitics attach to the end of the noun phrase, but only under certain circumstances. The noun phrase must be headed by an inalienably possessed noun, as in (168) and (169), or a proper name, as in (170). Otherwise, a demonstrative must be present at the end of the noun phrase for the enclitic to attach to, as in (171) and (172).

Sirva
(171) *Uhu timu n-umu, amge* **n-udu=ŋ** *uhu va-bi-s-a.*
ground side ND-LOC woman **ND-PRAG=POSS** ground say-PL-FPST-3
'"On this side of the land, (it's) the woman's land," they said.'

Aisi
(172) Ya   kiti   kiti   ga,   ya,   ki   **ga-rib=iŋ**   aŋandam-s-iŋ.
     1SG   stay.SS   and   TOP   1SG   speech   **MD-ADJZ=ACC**   hear-FPST-1SG
     'I was staying, and I heard that kind of talk.'

While reflexes in Mum, Sirva, and Aisi are normally not enough for a reconstruction to Proto-Sogeram, this enclitic is quite plainly the same form that is found on the pronouns in Table 34, and as such can be reconstructed to Proto-Sogeram. The meaning should be reconstructed as accusative, and the distribution can be reconstructed as follows: the enclitic could attach to the end of a pronoun or any noun phrase headed by an inalienably possessed noun. It could also attach to the end of certain demonstrative forms.

Finally, it is worth briefly discussing the Nend enclitic =ŋ, which also attaches to the end of the noun phrase. This enclitic is almost certainly not a reflex of PSOG *=ŋ 'ACC,' in spite of its phonological and distributional similarities. It is semantically divergent, denoting 'LOCATIVE/INSTRUMENTAL' case; and it occurs most often on noun phrases headed by common nouns, as in (173).

Nend
(173) Nori-ri=v   oram   **inca=ŋ**   ñ-i.
      son-3.POSS=NOM   house   **inside=LI** stay-3SG.IPST
      'The son was in the house.'   (K. Harris 1990: 94)

5.2.3 Oblique pronouns and enclitic

The oblique pronouns were formed with the oblique enclitic *=d. This enclitic, and consequently the pronominal paradigm, are less securely reconstructed than the other paradigms. Reflexes of the enclitic are found in Mand, Nend, Apalɨ, and Mum, while reflexes of the pronouns are given in Table 35.

Several problems present themselves with this reconstruction. One is that only one of the modern pronoun sets has oblique meaning (although the enclitics in Mand, Nend, and Apalɨ also do), while possessive meaning is much more frequent. Another is the frequent co-occurrence of this enclitic with the object enclitic *=ŋ; this occurs in Nend, Magɨ, and Gants. Yet another is the Mand reflex d, which should be †t according to regular sound changes. But in spite of these difficulties, the frequent occurrence of d throughout the family, in pronouns and on noun phrase enclitics, calls for an explanation. The most likely explanation is that all of these d's date to a Proto-Sogeram enclitic *=d which had a distribution similar to the object enclitic *=ŋ, discussed above: it attached to pronouns and noun phrases.

Table 35: Oblique pronouns.

	1SG	2SG	3SG	1PL	2PL	3PL
Mand (POSS)	[adu]	[ahɨr]	[hɨr]	arhud	[akur]	[kur]
Nend (POSS)	ihind	[amakɨr]	[mbɨkɨr]	arɨŋind	amandiŋ	mbindiŋ
Manat (POSS)	[yak]	[amɨnak]	[banɨk]	arɨd	amarad	barad
Apalɨ (OBL)	iadɨ	nadɨ	nudɨ	aludɨ	naludɨ	nulɨdɨ
Mum (POSS)	yad	nad	nu(ŋ)ad	arhad	narhad	nuhurad
Magɨ (OBJ)	yadɨŋ	nadɨŋ	nɨdɨŋ	adanɨŋ	nadanɨŋ	nɨdanɨŋ
Gants (POSS)	yadɨŋ	nadɨŋ	nuduŋ	aiduŋ	naiduŋ	niduŋ
PSOG	*ya=d	*na=d	*nɨ=d, nu=d	*ar=d	*nar=d	*nɨr=d

Reconstructing the meaning of this enclitic is more difficult, but I make an attempt at semantic reconstruction after discussing the modern forms below.

The Mand, Nend, and Manat pronouns are simple possessive forms, with no apparent vestiges of other meaning. The Mand 1PL form *arhud* appears to consist of the enclitic *=d attached to a reflex of the 1PL possessive pronoun *arkw (§5.2.4). It is uncertain how the Nend 1SG was formed, but the 1PL appears to consist of both the object and oblique enclitics attached to the 1PL pronoun. The 2PL and 3PL likewise contain both enclitics, but in the reverse order. These forms are reflexes of *nar=d and *nɨr=d that have undergone the regular loss of initial consonants (§3.2.1.1), lost *r (which may have been a regular change to Nend pronouns; see §5.2.2 and §5.2.5), and then compounded with the second and third person subject pronouns *am* and *mbɨ*.

The Manat 2PL and 3PL forms followed a similar trajectory, except for the fact that they appear to be reflexes of pronouns with a final *a. (Recall that the Proto-Sogeram plural subject pronouns all had final *a, as in *nara '2PL,' but that cliticized forms lacked this vowel, e.g. *nar=ɨŋ.) How this happened is unclear. The 1PL form, on the other hand, appears to be a regular reflex of *ar=d.

The Apalɨ forms are mostly straightforward reflexes of the reconstructed Proto-Sogeram pronouns. The insertion of *u* in the 1PL and 2PL is the main inconsistency for which I have no explanation. The 3PL also contains *u* in the first syllable, which is a common change to Apalɨ 3PL pronouns. Wade (1989) glosses these pronouns as oblique markers, and their primary functions are to mark objects (174) and possessors (175).

Apalɨ
(174) **Nu-di**   iga-lɨ.
      3SG-OBL see-3SG.FPST
      'He saw **him**.'   (Wade 1989: 123)

Apalɨ
(175) **Nu-dɨ** iŋam hekɨlɨ aga-ŋ iava-m-i.
 3SG-OBL dog big DEF-NOM bite-HPST-3SG
 'His big dog bit (him).' (Wade 1989: 123)

The Mum 1SG and 2SG pronouns are clear reflexes of *ya=d and *na=d. Mum has innovated a new 3SG root, *nua-* or *nuŋa-*, for some pronominal categories, but otherwise the 3SG is also regular. In the 1PL and 2PL an element *ha* intervenes between the pronominal root and the enclitic; this element is difficult to explain. And the 3PL is problematic in several ways. This paradigm of pronouns marks possession.

In Magɨ and Gants, the singular pronouns are composed of reflexes of the reconstructed Proto-Sogeram oblique pronouns with the enclitic *=ŋ attached. In Gants the plurals are composed the same way, although an intrusive *u* has been inserted between the two clitics. The Magɨ plurals, as discussed above, are composed of Proto-Sogeram oblique pronouns, plus an intrusive *a*, plus the Magɨ accusative postposition *nɨŋ*.

The Gants forms illustrate that the Proto-Sogeram plural pronouns should not be reconstructed with an epenthetic *ɨ between the root and the enclitic. Syllable-final *r vocalized to *i* in Gants (§3.4.6.4), and since the tokens of *r in the plural pronouns vocalized, we can conclude that they were syllable-final. Thus, we reconstruct *ar=d, *nar=d, and *nɨr=d.

As the discussion above makes clear, this putative set of reconstructed pronouns is quite problematic. Matters improve somewhat when we discuss non-pronominal reflexes of the oblique enclitic *=d, found in Mand, Nend, Apalɨ, and Mum.

In Mand, the oblique enclitic *=d* attaches to the end of the noun phrase. Its primary function is to mark non-locative oblique arguments, as in (176). It can also occur within a larger noun phrase, in which case the item it marks functions attributively to modify the head noun (177). Finally, it can mark possession, as in (178); it is unclear whether the possessive function should be considered a subtype of the attributive function, or a separate function.

Mand
(176) Arhw **zau=d** ovra-cɨ-nhw.
 1PL **fish=OBL** barter-HAB-1PL
 'We used to barter with fish.'

Mand
(177) Kuram **taŋ=d** ka-g ai-d.
 man **yonder=OBL** FD-NOM come-IPST
 'A man from far away is coming.'

Mand
(178) ñac **adu=d** ñi
daughter **1SG.POSS=OBL** son
'my daughter's son'

The Nend oblique enclitic is =nd (K. Harris 1990: 96–97), and it most commonly marks possession (179), although it can also mark a noun as functioning attributively within a larger noun phrase (180). When functioning attributively, it often marks the place of origin of an unstated head noun (181). Finally, =nd can also mark goals (182).

Nend
(179) **Tɨhɨr=nd** ensa Arɨkɨm.
moon=OBL name Arɨkɨm
'The moon's name was Arɨkɨm.' (K. Harris 1990: 96)

Nend
(180) Ñaka aŋgwɨram-i, unsa **anta=nd**.
yam.type turn.into-3SG.IPST yam **jungle=OBL**
'He turned into a kind of yam, a wild yam.' (K. Harris 1990: 96)

Nend
(181) Mac **Norɨbu=nd** ha-mb ka-mg-ɨr ...
finish **Norɨbu=OBL** MD-NOM talk-PL-3.FPST
'Then (those ones from) Norɨbu said ...' (K. Harris 1990: 96)

Nend
(182) **Say=nd** oreŋ~eŋ r-in ar-em-en.
youth=OBL call~NMLZ do-1SG.IPST say-YPST-1SG
'"I was calling for the young people," I said.' (K. Harris 1990: 97)

In Apalɨ the oblique postposition dɨ "is an independent word when used with most words, but acts as a clitic with the unaffixed pronouns, definite markers and definite deictics" (Wade 1989: 92). It serves a variety of functions, which Wade characterizes as marking patients (183), addressees (184), and experiencers (185). It should be noted that all three of these functions can be construed as object-marking, but dɨ also appears to mark possessors (186).

Apalɨ
(183) Viaŋ **na-dɨ** miŋa-nikɨlɨ-lɨŋ.
1SG.NOM **2SG-OBL** hold-push-1SG.IMP
'I should shove (hold-push) you aside.' (Wade 1989: 93)

Apalɨ
(184) *Cakɨven **dɨ** abɨ-lɨŋ?*
Cakɨven **OBL** talk-1SG.IMP
'Should I tell Cakɨven?' (Wade 1989: 93)

Apalɨ
(185) ***Ia-dɨ*** *ihulu l-i.*
1SG-OBL tired do-3SG.IPST
'I am tired.' or 'I don't want to do it.' (Wade 1989: 93)

Apalɨ
(186) *Lɨ-ci dakɨta **dɨ** ninaŋ aga-ŋ iga aba-lɨ.*
do-3SG.DS doctor **OBL** son DEF-NOM see talk-3SG.FPST
'He did that and the doctor's son saw it and spoke.' (Wade n.d.b)

The Mum postposition *du* is glossed 'POSSESSIVE' by Sweeney (1994a), but it appears to serve a fairly wide array of functions. A more complete analysis of Mum grammar has yet to be done, but a brief examination of the Mum data I have available reveals that *du* marks possessors (187), origins (188), and possibly some locative oblique functions (189).

Mum
(187) *Yi muya **du** kuyu abavar-ɨrma-n.*
1SG cassowary **POSS** talk tell.story-FUT-1SG
'I will tell the story of the talk of the cassowary.' (Sweeney n.d.)

Mum
(188) *U-ta kura-ñ **du** miŋa-ta ña.*
go-SS bush-LOC **POSS** take-SS eat
'Go get some from the bush and eat it.' (Sweeney n.d.)

Mum
(189) *Kava suksɨrab sɨrab kiyɨ-m-i tiv ha-ñ **du** kur-ta*
bird small small stay-HPST-3SG beside MD-LOC **POSS** shoot-SS
kida-m-i.
walk-HPST-3SG
'The little birds were there nearby and he was shooting them and he walked.' (Sweeney n.d.)

Reviewing these reflexes of *=d, we see that in Mand, Nend, and Mum they can mark a noun phrase as functioning attributively to modify the head noun of a larger noun phrase; the Mand example (177) is typical. This construction can be expressed as in (190): a subordinate noun (phrase) with =d modifies the head noun of a larger noun phrase, with the semantic interpretation that the head noun is somehow characterized by the d-marked noun. The semantic leap from such a construction to a construction expressing possession is quite small—indeed, possession can be conceived of as a subtype of characterization. 'The son characterized by the doctor' can easily be interpreted as 'the doctor's son,' and that usage can then become routinized. Moreover, the semantic shift from a nominal oblique marker to a marker of attributive possession is common (Heine 1997: 144).

(190)   [N_i [N_j=d]]$_{NP}$ Semantics: "N_i is characterized by N_j in some way"

Reconstructing a construction like (190) and conceiving of possession as a subtype of characterization also explains why the pronouns with *=d so frequently have possessive meaning while the surviving enclitics have much more varied meanings. The range of meaning expressed by the Proto-Sogeram enclitic *=d probably included possession, since that is a natural way for one noun to be relevant to the interpretation of another. When this enclitic was used on pronouns, then, it probably had its possessive interpretation more often than usual, and this aspect of its meaning often became lexicalized on pronouns. On noun phrases, though, it was free to retain its broader range of meanings.

Then, to account for the fact that the Magɨ pronouns that reflect *=d mark objects, we simply observe that they reflect both pronominal enclitics, *=d=iŋ. Apparently the meaning of the accusative enclitic has predominated.

Two issues remain. One is the question of how *=d came to have object-marking meaning in some languages, notably Apalɨ. We lack the data to settle this issue at present, but it is possible that the non-attributive oblique function found in Mand and Nend dates to Proto-Sogeram. If this was so, this oblique case may have shifted its meaning to accusative, but for now this question remains unresolved.

Another issue is the question of placement: did the item bearing *=d precede or follow the head noun that it modified? I do not believe the available data are sufficient to answer this question. Modern reflexes vary, sometimes even within the same language (as in Mand and Nend). It is possible that the same variation was found in Proto-Sogeram, but it is also possible that word order in Proto-Sogeram was fixed and has changed for various reasons in certain languages. This question will have to await further research.

5.2.4 Possessive pronouns

The possessive pronouns were formed with a suffix *-kw, as shown in Table 36. The reflexes of these forms remain possessive pronouns in most languages, but in Sirva and Gants they have become object pronouns.

Table 36: Possessive pronouns.

	1SG	2SG	3SG	1PL	2PL	3PL
Mand (POSS)	[adu]	ahɨr	hɨr, kɨr	arhud	akur	kur
Manat (POSS)	yak	amɨnak	banɨk	[arɨd]	[amarad]	[barad]
Sirva (OBJ)	yau	nau	nu(hu)	aru	naru(hu)	nuru
Magɨ (POSS)	yaka	naka	nuku	arɨkuŋ	narɨkuŋ	nurukuŋ
Aisi (POSS)	yaka	naka	nɨku	andu	narɨkuŋ	nɨrukuŋ
Kursav (POSS)	yaku	naku	nuku	anuku	nanuku	nunuku
Gants (OBJ)	yak	nak	nuk	ayuk	nayuk	niuk
PSOG	*ya-kw	*na-kw	*nɨ-kw	*ar-kw	*nar-kw	*nɨr-kw

The reconstruction of the possessive pronominal suffix *-kw is also supported by Anamuxra, in which alienable possession is expressed with the help of a "possessor word" which can be either -ka or -xwu, the latter of which appears to be cognate with PSOG *-kw. This possessor word always takes a pronominal prefix and intervenes between the possessor and the possessed noun (191). The form of the possessive word -xwu with the Anamuxra singular and dual possessive prefixes is given in Table 37; note the similarities to the reconstructed Proto-Sogeram forms in Table 36.

(191) Anamuxra
Peter **n-xwu** mugu-pa
Peter **3SG.POSS-POSS** house-CLASSIFIER
'Peter's house' (Ingram 2001)

Table 37: Anamuxra possessive word -xwu.

	SG	DU
first person	ya-xwu	ar-xwu
second person	na-xwu	nar-xwu
third person	n-xwu	nr-xwu

Given the reflexes in Table 36 and in Anamuxra, the reconstruction of the possessive pronouns is secure, although we must still account for several innovative forms. In Mand the 1SG possessive pronoun, *adu*, is not cognate with this paradigm. Most of the other Mand forms have added a final *-r*, which is of unknown origin. The 1PL form has added *-d*, which may be a reflex of the oblique enclitic *=d. The singular pronouns lost the rounding from *kw and voiced it to *h*, while the 2PL and 3PL pronouns preserved the rounding as *u* and did not voice the stop. These two forms also seem to have lost the *r that was present in Proto-Sogeram, which offers a possible explanation for the innovative final *-r* in the second and third person pronouns: the 2PL and 3PL forms may have metathesized the *r and the *kw. This would have happened, in the 2PL for example, as follows: *narkw > PWS *arkw > *akwr > *akur*. This innovative final *r* may then have spread to the singular forms by analogy.

In Manat only the singular forms are reflexes of this Proto-Sogeram paradigm. Final *kw has become *k*, and otherwise these forms are straightforward. 1SG has remained unchanged, while 2SG has added *ami-* and 3SG *ba-*, both on analogy with the subject pronouns (*am* and *bi*, respectively).

In Sirva the normal reflex of *kw is *hu*. The velar fricative *h* has been irregularly elided in most possessive pronouns, although it occasionally surfaces in the 3SG and 2PL forms. Otherwise the reflexes show regular sound changes, including the assimilation of *i > *u* in the presence of an upcoming *u that is seen in the 3SG and 3PL (§3.4.1.3). Interestingly, the paradigm has undergone a semantic innovation to become the paradigm of object pronouns. How this happened is unclear, although a similar process took place in Gants.

In the Aisian languages things are less clear. The formative element in the 3SG, 2PL, 3PL, and the Magɨ 1PL is *-ku*, a normal reflex of PSog *-kw. But the *-ka* found in the 1SG and 2SG forms is difficult to account for, and I see two possibilities. First, it may simply be an irregular development, possibly a case of perseverative assimilation triggered by the *a in the first syllable. Alternatively, it may be a reflex of a different set of possessive pronouns. Recall that Anamuxra has two possessive words: *-xwu*, which is cognate with PSog *-kw, and *-ka*. It is possible that the Aisian 1SG and 2SG possessive pronouns are actually cognate with the latter possessive word. This hypothesis is not without its problems, though. Importantly, the expected reflex of Proto-Sogeram word-final *-ka would be Aisian †*-kɨ* (§3.4.2.4). This means that both scenarios involve positing unexpected phonological developments: the former *-akw > *-aka*, the latter *-ka > *-ka*. I thus see no internal reason to prefer one over the other. The former scenario, though, has the virtue of allowing us to reconstruct a simpler set of Proto-Sogeram possessive pronouns, and for this reason I prefer it.

A few other developments with the Aisian forms merit discussion. The 2PL and 3PL pronouns have added final *-ŋ*, which is probably a reflex of the accusative enclitic *=ŋ. The Aisi 1PL form *andu* is difficult to account for, and remains unexplained for now.

The Kursav forms are fairly straightforward reflexes of the Proto-Sogeram pronouns. The only difficulty is the nasals that are found in the plural pronouns; these are also found in the subject pronouns, and possible explanations for them are discussed in §5.2.1.

The Gants possessive pronouns are similarly straightforward. They exhibit the regular syllable-final change of *r > *i* (§3.4.6.4), followed by somewhat irregular changes of *kw > *uk* in the plural forms and *kw > *k* in the singulars. The Gants reflexes, like the Sirva reflexes, have become object pronouns. However, unlike in Sirva, they are still sometimes used to indicate possession (192). This construction is not well understood synchronically, but from a diachronic perspective it appears to be a relic of the possessive function of these pronouns in Proto-Sogeram.

Gants
(192) *Kineb* **yak** *kra aya ga-paŋ-dek wa-da ...*
house **1SG.OBJ** TOP come perceive-FUT-3PL say-SS
'"They'll come look at my house," she said, and ...'

Finally we must address the issue of third person variation between *ni forms and *nu forms. In the 3SG we have clear reflexes of *ni forms in Mand, Manat, and Aisi; in the 3PL clear reflexes of *ni are found in Mand, Aisi, and Gants. For these reasons the *ni forms must be reconstructed for both 3SG and 3PL. The other reflexes are all ambiguous; they could be reflexes of *nu forms, or of *ni forms that underwent regular harmony of *i > *u* before *u (§3.4.1.3). Additionally, Anamuxra exhibits only *n-* and *nr-*, never *nu-* or *nur-*. This means that all forms can be accounted for by the reconstructions of *nikw '3SG.POSS' and *nirkw '3PL.POSS,' and reconstructions of †nukw and †nurkw would be superfluous.

5.2.5 Emphatic pronouns and enclitic

I reconstruct a set of emphatic pronouns which marked contrastive and individuating focus. They were formed with an enclitic that had two allomorphs, *=ba and *=bi, and which is reconstructed in more detail in Daniels (2019). The forms to support this reconstruction are given in Table 38. In the Greater West Sogeram languages and Apali these forms have become the normal subject pronouns, replacing the forms reconstructed in §5.2.1, but they have retained their original meaning in the other languages. The question marks in the Magi row indicate a

Table 38: Emphatic pronouns.

	1SG	2SG	3SG	1PL	2PL	3PL
Mand (SBJ)	apɨ	abɨ	pɨ	[arhw]	abɨ	pɨ
Nend (SBJ)	[nzi]	am	mbɨ	[ar]	am	mbɨ
Manat (SBJ)	[zɨ]	am	bɨ	[ar]	am	bɨ
Apalɨ (SBJ)	[vian]	nama	nɨbu, nubu	[alaŋ]	namɨlaŋ	nɨbɨlaŋ, nubɨlaŋ
Mum (EMPH)	yabɨ	nabɨ	nu(ŋ)abɨ	arhabɨ	narhabɨ	nuhurabɨ
Sirva (EMPH)			bibi			
Magɨ (EMPH)	yabɨ	?	nɨbɨ	arɨb	?	?
Aisi (EMPH)	yabɨ	nabɨ	nɨbɨ	ambɨ	narɨb	nɨrɨb
Kursav (EMPH)	yaba	naba	nɨba	anɨba	nanɨba	nɨnɨba
Gants (EMPH)	yaba	naba	nɨba	aiba	naiba	niba
PSog	*ya=bi	*na=ba	*nɨ=ba	*ar=bV	*nar=ba	*nɨr=ba

lack of relevant data; Magɨ probably has 2SG, 2PL, and 3PL emphatic pronouns, but the forms were not recorded during fieldwork.

The emphatic enclitic is reconstructed as *=bi in the 1SG, as *=ba for the second and third persons, and with an indeterminate vowel in the 1PL. This is primarily because of the Mand witness. The Mand 1SG form *apɨ* reflects final PSoG *i, while the final ɨ in the second and third person pronouns reflects final *a. Since Mand is the only language to show this sort of internal diversity—the other languages all uniformly reflect either final *a or *i—this heterogeneity should be reconstructed to Proto-Sogeram. The reasoning is that either kind of homogeneous system could easily be created from the Mand-type system via a process of analogic levelling, but the reverse process is less plausible (Hetzron 1976: 92; Koch 1996: 219). However, since Mand lacks a 1PL reflex of this pronoun set, we cannot be sure which vowel, *a or *i, the 1PL emphatic pronoun took.

The developments in Mand, Nend, Manat, and Apalɨ have been complicated and somewhat irregular, masking the etymological origin of these pronouns to some extent. The first development was the loss of *r before *m in the plural forms. It is difficult to tell if this was a regular change because of the scarcity of *rC clusters in Proto-Sogeram, but it seems to have also happened to the object (§5.2.2) and possessive (§5.2.4) pronouns. This had the effect of merging the second and third person pronouns, although the distinction was subsequently recovered in Apalɨ via the addition of the plural pronominal formative *-laŋ* (< *-ra). After the loss of *r, the prenasalized stop in the second person pronoun irregularly became a simple nasal, yielding the form *nama. This development can only be explained as irregular phonological reduction in a high-frequency item. Following that, Mand, Nend, and Manat underwent word-initial consonant loss (§3.2.1.1), yielding the new forms *ama '2' and *ba '3'. These forms are then inherited with regular sound changes, including word-final loss of *a in Mand (§3.2.2.4) and prosodic-unit-final loss of *a in Nend and Manat (§3.2.1.2).

In Mum the 1SG emphatic suffix *-bi has been generalized to all pronouns. This appears to have happened at the Proto-North Sogeram stage, as traces of the process are inherited into Sirva. In Sirva the 3SG.EMPH pronoun *bibi* is descended from the layering of two separate reflexes of the emphatic enclitic (Craig 1991).

In the East Sogeram (ES) languages, the pronouns remain largely unchanged, although they do reflect each language's unique innovations to the subject pronouns. The Gants forms reflect syllable-final *r vocalization (§3.4.6.4), which suggests that the plural forms did not contain an epenthetic *i between the pronominal root and the clitic.

The emphatic pronouns serve to impart contrastive or individuating focus in the East Sogeram languages, and they seem to serve a similar function in Mum, although the data there is not extensive. They exhibit a clear preference for subject position: in order to occupy a different syntactic role they must be accompanied by additional case marking.

The enclitic *=bi/=ba could also mark non-pronominal noun phrases, but it is not clear which allomorph was used in this environment. Reflexes are found in Nend, Manat, and Sirva.

Nend has a nominative enclitic that is =*mb* after a nasal consonant and =*v* elsewhere (K. Harris 1990: 92). This clitic attaches to the end of the noun phrase. It appears to only occur on noun phrases with human referents, which means that usually it attaches to kin terms or proper names (193), although sometimes it attaches to a noun phrase with a common noun head (194).

    Nend
(193) **Dani=mb**   emga   ha-n   akwuh-e   hiray-em-ɨr.
    Danny=NOM   another   MD-ACC   go.up-SS   bring-YPST-3SG
    'Danny climbed another and brought (some).'   (K. Harris n.d.)

    Nend
(194) *Ha-n*   *ha-n*   **yupir**   **nimbir=iv**   *ka-mgɨ-j.*
    MD-ACC   MD-ACC   **skin**   **white=NOM**   talk-PL-3.HAB
    'That is what the white skin(ned people) say.'   (K. Harris n.d.)

This form also attaches as a suffix to demonstrative roots to form nominative demonstratives; in this context it is always -*mb*. These forms generally mark non-human noun phrases (195).

Nend
(195) *Nd-e-mi-ŋ* **nti** **ha-mb** *okaraw-emɨ-r.*
walk-SS-INDF-1SG.DS **blood** **MD-NOM** clot-YPST-3SG
'I walked and the blood clotted.' (K. Harris 1990: 120)

In Manat the nominative suffix -*b* only marks proper names and kin terms (196). It also attaches to demonstratives to create subject-marking forms (197).

Manat
(196) **Ni-min-ib** *mikiñ=ik* *miŋa-n* *aku-ma-g.*
3.POSS-mother-NOM fishing.net=ACC get-2/3.SS go.up-PST-3SG.FAR
'His mother got a fishing net and went up(river).'

Manat
(197) *O* **adar** **ka-b** *akunaih-id* *ara-ŋin.*
oh **spirit** **MD-NOM** bring-3SG.IPST say-1SG.RPST
'I said, "Oh, the spirit brought him".'

Interestingly, it also marks nonverbal predicates, if they are composed of a proper or inalienably possessed noun (198).

Manat
(198) *Akei yak,* *adavi=k* **Roda-b=a,** *avaŋ=k*
okay 1SG.POSS name=ACC **Rhoda-NOM=LNK** father.1.POSS=ACC
Barakam-b.
Barakam-NOM
'Okay my name is Rhoda, my father was Barakam.'

The Sirva third person subject pronouns *be* '3SG' and *bira* '3PL' have a number of interesting properties. They are frequently used as determiners to mark subject noun phrases, as in (199) and (200). Their use as determiners even extends to the subordinating function that Sirva determiners have (201).

Sirva
(199) *Sue udukib* **be,** *niriŋ* *tarma=ñ, sigudɨ-s-a.*
so road **3SG** 3PL.POSS eye=LI disappear-FPST-3SG
'Then the road disappeared from their eyes.'

Sirva

(200) Iru   mubu   **bira**   pi   kaha-b-ïi ...
      salt   fly   **3PL**   come   gather-PL-3.DS
      'Salt flies came and gathered and ...'

Sirva

(201) Oke   [uva   pigri   g-ri-n   ]   **be**   ni-ma   mar.
      okay   SPEC   custom   see-TPST-1SG   **3SG**   ND-ADVZ   like
      'Okay, another custom I see is like this.'

The construction found in Nend and Manat is composed of a reflex of *=ba, since word-final *i is consistently retained in Manat and final *a was lost from the right edges of prosodic units in these languages (§3.2.1.2). Like the pronominal emphatic paradigm in Greater West Sogeram, this construction now marks nominative case. A relic of its erstwhile function as a way of marking focus is seen in the fact that it marks nonverbal predicates, which tend to be conversationally focused, in Manat.

The Sirva pronoun *be* is a reflex of the *=bi allomorph, with irregular lowering of the vowel. This pronoun's origin as an enclitic to the noun phrase can be seen in the fact that, uniquely among Sogeram pronouns, *be* and its relatives can serve as determiners. The fact that it used to mark focus is also apparent from the existence of the new emphatic pronoun *bibi* '3SG.EMPH', which originated as a combination of Pre-Sirva *bi '3SG' and *=bi 'EMPH' (Daniels 2019). The semantic innovation from focus meaning to pronominal meaning is also a well-attested grammaticalization pathway (Heine and Song 2011).

These cognate constructions are summarized in (202), based on Daniels (2019).

(202) a. All languages   [PRON]-*bi/-ba*   Syntax: nominative noun phrase
                                               Semantics: contrastive or
                                               individuating focus
      b. Nend and Manat   [NP]=*b*   Syntax: nominative noun phrase
                                               Semantics: no non-compositional
                                               semantics
      c. Sirva   (NP) *be*   Syntax: nominative noun phrase
                                               Semantics: third person singular

These constructions are synchronically quite heterogeneous: a pronominal formative, a case marker that is an enclitic to the noun phrase, and a pronoun with determiner functions. But as the discussion above makes clear, they all share a common origin. This can be see in their formal and syntactic similarities, and also in the pathways of semantic change that derived the meanings in (202b) and (202c) from that in (202a). I thus reconstruct an enclitic with two allomorphs, *=bi and *=ba, which marked constrastive and individuating focus on subject noun phrases. The *=bi allomorph was used on the 1SG pronoun; the *=ba was used on the second and third person pronouns; and it is unclear which allomorph was used on the 1PL pronoun and on non-pronominal noun phrases. It also seems that this enclitic could not attach to demonstratives in Proto-Sogeram, as it is only found in that environment in Nend and Manat, suggesting those languages are innovative.

A final issue to address is how to relate the Gants topic pronoun *bɨr* to this reconstruction. This Gants morpheme refers to topical referents about whom something noteworthy is being said. It can occur alone, as in (203), in which case the referent must be understood from context, or following a pronoun, as in (204), in which case the referent is made clear by the pronoun.

Gants
(203) *Tama-da* **bɨr,** *miga-m-aik.*
 put-SS   TOP   sleep-FPST-3PL
 'They put (the food down) and slept.'

Gants
(204) *Ya   ai-k-enɨŋ,   ya* **bɨr,** *aba   tama-naŋ.*
 1SG come-DS.SEQ-1SG 1SG TOP speak put-2SG.IPST
 'I came and you threw me out.'

This form fits reasonably well semantically—it does not have focus meaning, but its meaning is related to information structure—but it is more problematic phonologically. There is no evidence for a change *i (or *a) > *ɨr* in Gants, although there is a change in the opposite direction, namely syllable-final *r > i (§3.4.6.4). It may be possible to invoke this sound change to relate *bɨr* to the *=bi allomorph of the enclitic, but the connection is quite speculative. For now I remain uncommitted as to the etymology of Gants *bɨr*.

5.2.6 Interrogative pronoun

The Proto-Sogeram interrogative pronoun was *ni or, in its reduplicated form, *nini. It is unclear how these two forms differed in Proto-Sogeram, but both appear with decent distribution in the family. The relevant forms are given in Table 39.

The three Greater West Sogeram languages reflect an innovative form *uña 'who'. The Mand reflex underwent expected nasal fortition (§3.2.2.5), and the Nend and Manat reflexes lost final *a, which is also expected.

Table 39: Forms for 'who'.

Mand	Nend	Manat	Apalɨ	Mum	Sirva	Magɨ	Aisi	Kursav	Gants
uja	uñɨ	uñɨ	ani	nin	ninɨ	niŋe	ninɨ	ne	nene

The other languages all reflect *ni, with reduplication in Mum, Sirva, Aisi, and Gants. In the former three it also underwent word-final *i-loss (§3.3.2.4, §3.4.2.1) to yield *nin* or *ninɨ*. In Kursav and Gants it also underwent regular lowering of *i > *e (§3.4.1.4). Only the Apalɨ and Magɨ forms are unusual reflexes, Apalɨ for adding initial *a and Magɨ for adding final *ŋe*.

There is a possibility, however, that *uña and *ni are related. Pawley reconstructs Proto-Trans New Guinea *wani 'who' (2005: 87), which, if correct, offers some suggestive links between the two form. The Apalɨ *a* may be archaic, and the initial *u* in the Greater West Sogeram forms may be the result of a *wa > *u sound change. Similarly the palatal nasal in *uña may be cognate with the *ni sequence in other languages. However, while these suggestions are intriguing, they remain speculative and do not sufficiently resemble regular sound changes. As such I prefer to reconstruct *ni(ni) 'who' for now.

5.3 Demonstratives

Proto-Sogeram demonstratives consisted of a root that distinguished deictic distance. This root could either stand on its own, or take a suffix (or enclitic) that marked the role of the demonstrative in the clause. It may also have been possible to reduplicate the root. The roots are fairly straightforward to reconstruct, but reconstructing the suffixes is much more difficult. Demonstratives in many Sogeram languages can take a large variety of suffixes: for example, Mand and Nend distinguish eleven demonstrative forms, Manat thirteen, Apalɨ fourteen, and Aisi ten. There has probably been a good deal of turnover and innovation, especially among the lower-frequency suffixes, so that now it is difficult to reconstruct more than four or five suffixes with confidence. It is also worth noting that the demonstrative system is quite different in Gants, and we should ask ourselves if this system might not be archaic.

Gants primarily makes do with a single definite demonstrative *ko*, which appears to be a reflex of the Proto-Sogeram middle demonstrative *ka with an irregular vowel change. Gants also has a specific form *koimo* and an indefinite form *kɨrmo*, both of which appear to be made with reflexes of the Proto-Sogeram specific marker *mu. Finally, Gants has two deictic demonstratives, *adɨko* 'this' and *kadiko* 'that'. There is no marking of case roles or information structure status, which are the categories most commonly marked by demonstratives in other Sogeram languages. There is also no system of deictic roots that combine with suffixes; the Gants system is not morphologically productive at all.

It is tempting to see such a different demonstrative system and frame the question of reconstruction as an either/or enterprise: either a Gants-like system changed into the system found in the other Sogeram languages, or the reverse happened. But the truth is probably more subtle. Recall that two of the demonstrative suffixes that I discuss below have already been reconstructed as enclitics on the noun phrase: *=ŋ 'ACC' and *=d 'OBL'. A third, *=ñ 'LOCATIVE/INSTRUMENTAL,' was also probably an enclitic. Furthermore, unaffixed demonstratives are reconstructed to Proto-Sogeram. These facts suggest a Proto-Sogeram system wherein demonstrative roots were free-standing forms that came at the end of the noun phrase and could host a noun-phrase-final enclitic. In Gants the free-standing form of the middle demonstrative became the definite article *ko*, while most other demonstrative forms fell out of use. In the other languages, the enclitics fused onto the root and became suffixes, giving us the systems we find today.

This reconstruction raises the question of how to reconstruct those suffixes for which we only find reflexes on demonstrative roots. Should they be reconstructed as enclitics, like *=d and the others, that could attach to the end of noun phrases? Or should they be reconstructed as suffixes that only attached to demonstrative roots? I prefer the latter analysis as it seems more conservative: it only reconstructs constructions for which we have direct empirical support.

In the following section I reconstruct the demonstrative roots, and then discuss their unaffixed use (§5.3.2) and the reduplication construction (§5.3.3). I then discuss their interaction with the accusative and oblique enclitics *=ŋ and *=d (§5.3.4). Finally, I discuss several other affixes that occurred on demonstratives: a topic/object suffix (§5.3.5), two locative suffixes (§5.3.6 and §5.3.7), and a focus suffix (§5.3.8).

5.3.1 Demonstrative roots

Proto-Sogeram demonstrative roots distinguished three distances: near, mid, and far. There was also a fourth root *aba- 'QD' that took the same suffixes and was used to form question words. The roots are given in Table 40. Mand has lost the three-way distinction, retaining only the near and mid forms; Nend has innovated new near, far, and interrogative forms; the Mum mid form varies between *ka-* and *ha-*, but it is unclear what conditions this variation; the Aisian mid forms are from Magɨ (*ka-*) and Aisi (*ga-*); and the Aisian interrogative form is from Aisi, as little is known about Magɨ question formation.

Table 40: Demonstrative roots.

	ND	MD	FD	QD
Mand	na-	ka-		
Nend	[mba-]	ha-	[ke-]	[nzɨ-]
Manat	inɨ-	ka-	itu-	ba-
Apalɨ	na-	ha-	ada-	aba-
Mum	nɨ-	ka-, ha-	da-	pa-
Sirva	nɨ-	ka-	ada-	aba-
Aisian	na-	ka-, ga-	ara-	nɨba-
Kursav	i-	ka-	do-	ba-
PSoG	*inɨ-	*ka-	*adu-	*aba-

A few things can be observed from this table. The first is that the middle demonstrative form *ka- has been remarkably stable throughout the history of the family. The middle serves as the unmarked deictic form in every daughter language, and *ka- was probably one of the highest-frequency morphemes in Proto-Sogeram, which goes some way in explaining its remarkable stability.

We can also observe that the other three forms were often reshaped on analogy with *ka. This analogy sometimes took the form of loss of the initial vowel, and other times change of the second vowel to *a*. So for example *inɨ- 'ND' lost *i in Apalɨ, Mum, Sirva, and Aisian, and changed *ɨ > *a* in Mand, Apalɨ, and Aisian. Similarly, *adu- lost *a in Mum and Kursav, and changed *u > *a* in Apalɨ, Mum, Sirva, and Aisian. And finally, *aba- lost initial *a in Manat, Mum, and Kursav. In each of these cases, the archaic form is still well-distributed throughout the family. Given that analogic change motivated by *ka explains the innovative forms, while the reverse changes would be difficult to explain, these reconstructions are reasonably secure.

The near demonstrative *inɨ- is retained completely only in Manat. And the initial vowel is only found in one other language, Kursav, where the rest of the Proto-Sogeram demonstrative has been lost. So the reconstruction of *inɨ- is not as secure as we might like, but it is still more plausible than a reconstruction without the initial vowel. If we reconstructed †nɨ-, we would have to posit two innovations of initial *i*, which, although not impossible, would be unlikely. But if we reconstruct *inɨ-, we have to posit two innovations in which *i was lost—one to explain the Mand form and another to explain Apalɨ, the North Sogeram languages, and Aisian. As discussed above, these changes can be easily explained as analogical change based on the middle demonstrative *ka, so the reconstruction of the initial vowel in *inɨ- is preferable.

The reasoning for the second vowel of the near demonstrative, for both vowels of the far demonstrative *adu-, and the first vowel of the interrogative demonstrative *aba-, is the same. In each case there are two reflexes, one of which can be explained as having been created on analogy with *ka-, the other of which cannot. In each case the reconstruction is thus fairly secure. The distribution of reflexes for each of these correspondence sets leads to a more secure reconstruction than the initial *i of *ini-, discussed above, so I do not individually discuss the reconstruction of each vowel.

Several innovations can be pointed out. Nend has reshaped the set of deictic roots quite drastically, leaving only the middle form unchanged. The near form may be derived from the interrogative form, although that would involve a peculiar semantic innovation. Nend demonstratives each come in two varieties: basic and expanded, the latter being used for "contrastive or specifying" functions (K. Harris 1990: 103). The expanded form of the near demonstrative is *mba-na-*; the second element may be a reflex of the Proto-Sogeram near demonstrative. The Nend far and interrogative forms are innovative, and I have no hypothesis as to their etymology.

In Manat, the far form is unusual in two respects. It has changed its initial vowel to *i*, presumably on analogy with the near form. And it has changed *d > t. It is interesting to note the voicing pattern for the mid form in Nend and Manat. In Nend, where medial *k sometimes lenites to *h* (§3.2.3.1), *k lenited. But in Manat, where initial *k sometimes lenites but medial *k does not (§3.2.1.4), *k remains unvoiced. This suggests that these demonstratives behaved, phonologically at least, more like bound forms than free forms.

The only difficulties in Mum are the variability in the middle form and the denasalization of *b > *p* in the interrogative form. I have no explanation for the latter.

The Aisi interrogative has added an initial *ni* which may be from the interrogative pronoun *ni 'who' (§5.2.6). This syllable does not appear to have changed the meaning of the root, and the fact that *niba-* still takes demonstrative suffixes to form question words suggests it is descended from *aba.

Kursav changed the near form considerably, retaining only the initial vowel and removing the second syllable.

5.3.2 Bare roots

Most languages allow the usage of bare demonstrative roots, without suffixes. Often it is a limited set of demonstratives that can be employed this way, although the middle demonstrative is always included in the set. The functions of these bare demonstratives frequently differ somewhat from the functions of suffixed demonstratives, as I discuss below. The relevant forms are given in Table 41.

5.3 Demonstratives

Table 41: Bare demonstratives.

	ND	MD	FD
Mand		kɨ?	
Manat		ka?	
Apalɨ	na	ha	
Mum	nɨ	ka, ha	da
Sirva	nu	ka	ada
Aisi		ga	
Kursav	i(ka)	ka	do
Gants		ko	
PSoG	*in?	*ka	*adu

The Mand and Manat forms are not well understood synchronically so I defer discussing them to the end of this section, where the parallels between their properties and the properties of the other forms will be easier to recognize.

Wade (1989: 131–133) refers to the Apalɨ forms as topic demonstratives and describes several functions that they perform. They can be used in topic position, either as a determiner for another noun (205) or on their own (206). Their topic-marking function extends to marking the subjects of nonverbal predicates (207). And it can also include the marking of non-nominal elements, such as the adverb *havɨ* in (208). In the topic-marking function, *na* is often used cataphorically to introduce what is about to be said, while *ha* is used anaphorically to recapitulate what was just mentioned.

Apalɨ
(205) Saba **ha,**   ua na-vɨla cɨhu   ala ve-vɨhe-m-i.
      pig **MD.TOP** go eat-ss again FOC come-do.quickly-HPST-3SG
      'As for that pig, it went and ate and again came back quickly.'
      (Wade 1989: 131)

Apalɨ
(206) **Na,**   viaŋ van   mɨŋ-in   kua   u-i.
      ND.TOP 1SG string.bag hold-1SG.IPST   uncertainty say-3SG.IPST
      '"As for this, I think I am holding a string bag," he said.'
      (Wade 1989: 132)

Apalɨ
(207) ... lali ibi   **ha**   sɨviaŋ.
      tree name **MD.TOP** tree.sp
      '... (it's) tree's name was *sɨviaŋ*.'
      (Wade 1989: 132)

Apali
(208) Havɨ **ha** hima u-m-i.
for.no.reason **MD.TOP** no say-HPST-3SG
'"If it was for no reason, then no (I wouldn't have done it)," he said.'
(Wade 1989: 132)

Like other demonstratives, *ha* can be used to subordinate clauses (209). But unlike other demonstratives, it can also be used to topicalize medial clauses (210). *Na* does not serve either of these functions.

Apali
(209) Avɨli sɨ-naŋ **ha** viaŋ avi mugua sɨ-b-eŋ u-i.
water wash-2SG.IPST **MD.TOP** 1SG also go.down wash-FUT-1SG say-3SG.IPST
'"Since you have already bathed, I also will go down and bathe," she said.'
(Wade 1989: 133)

Apali
(210) Nubu agalɨ-ci **ha** ataŋ hinia igahɨli-la-lu.
3SG call.out-3SG.DS **MD.TOP** far stay hear-HAB-1PL
'When he calls out, we are staying at a distance and habitually hear.'
(Wade 1989: 133)

In Mum all three demonstrative roots can occur without suffixes. Near *nɨ* and far *da* are realized as such, while the middle demonstrative varies between *ka* and *ha*; it is unclear whether this variation affects the meaning. These forms can mark nouns in topic position (211), as well as other topical items like *kɨvsuŋ* 'morning' in (212). They also appear to be able to subordinate clauses (213) and topicalize medial clauses (214).

Mum
(211) Kɨbɨ **ha** yahu-ta Usahri=ŋ naga Paharɨ=ŋ tara-h-u ...
response **MD** go.up-SS Usahri=OBJ with Paharɨ=OBJ shoot-DS-3PL
'For this revenge they went up and shot Usahri and Paharɨ ...'
(Sweeney n.d.)

Mum
(212) Kɨvsuŋ **da** u-ta ga-h-i saba **ha** yaha-ta ...
morning **FD** go-SS look-DS-3SG pig **MD** come.up-SS
'That morning he went and he looked and the pigs came up ...'
(Sweeney n.d.)

Mum
(213) U-m-i **ha,** mita-ta suwinda ...
go-HPST-3SG **MD** leave-SS again
'He went, leaving again ...' (Sweeney n.d.)

Mum
(214) Ña-ta mitu-ta **da,** abihañ, karha-m-i.
eat-SS finish-SS **FD** enough sleep-HPST-3SG
'He ate, and finished eating, alright, he lay down.' (Sweeney n.d.)

The Sirva bare demonstratives *nu*, *ka*, and *ada* have similar functions. They mark items in topic position (215), including the subjects of nonverbal predicates (216). They can also subordinate clauses (217), although they do not appear to topicalize medial clauses. Finally, they have a clause-initial function that seems to give focus to the upcoming predicate (218). This function appears to be related to the Apalɨ clause-initial function exemplified in (206).

Sirva
(215) Na uhusiv **ka,** be kava niriŋ wari.
and village **MD.TOP** 3SG bird 3PL.POSS village
'And the village, it was the birds' village.'

Sirva
(216) Kura **ada** zere mana.
man **FD.TOP** good no
'That man isn't good.' Elicited

Sirva
(217) U-rubɨ-s-a **ka,** kine k-i hasa kizidɨ-s-a.
go-PL-FPST-3 **MD.TOP** near MD-SET FOC evening-FPST-3SG
'They went, and very soon (lit. 'in a near place') it was evening.'

Sirva
(218) Ei, **ka** amge dua be pi~bi ad-i-Ø.
hey **MD.TOP** woman bad 3SG come~NMLZ do-TPST-3SG
'Hey, it's the bad woman coming doing (that).'

The data I have for Magɨ are insufficient to draw firm conclusions, so I focus on Aisi here. The only cognate form is the topic marker *ga*, which is related to the middle demonstratives; the near and far roots cannot be used without suffixes.

Ga marks topic fronted constituents (219), including the subjects of nonverbal predicates (220). It can also appear at the beginning of a clause to focus the main predicate (221). And it can subordinate final clauses (222) and topicalize medial clauses (223).

Aisi
(219) Mo **ga** mandɨ ga-niŋ, uk-ɨs-iŋ.
SPEC **TOP** COMPL MD-LOC cut-FPST-1SG
'One, I told a while ago.'

Aisi
(220) Yama yaka **ga,** Banam=iŋ gisiŋ.
mother.1.POSS 1SG.POSS **TOP** Banam=LOC from
'My mother is from Banam.'

Aisi
(221) Iskat-ɨber ma, **ga** n-ɨber.
leave-3SG.FUT NEG **TOP** eat-3SG.FUT
'He won't refuse (anything), he'll eat.'

Aisi
(222) Ya gi ika yaka kɨn-i akɨ **ga,** ga-rɨb
1SG FOC father.1.POSS 1SG.POSS stay-3SG.IPST maybe **TOP** MD-ADJZ

kr-ɨbiŋ.
walk-1SG.CTRF
'If *my* father were alive, I'd walk around like that (too).'

Aisi
(223) Ga-rɨb ar-i anɨgunuŋ mɨndam-i **ga,** kwi way-am.
MD-ADJZ do-SS 1PL.OBJ think-SS **TOP** back come-2SG.IMP
'So when you remember us, come back.'

As mentioned, Magɨ is poorly understood and the cognate morphemes cannot be confidently described. But it appears that the topicalizing morpheme *ga* is also found here, as in (224), where it topicalizes *Mande* 'Monday'. The clause-initial function may be served by a related morpheme *ka*, also illustrated in (224), although this morpheme is very infrequent and is hardly understood at all. Recall, though, that the Aisi middle root *ga-* is an irregular reflex of PSOG *ka in that the *k voiced to *g*. This irregular voicing did not affect Magɨ bound forms (the bound demonstrative root is still *ka-*), but it may have affected the unbound root in some contexts. But this topic requires further research.

Magɨ
(224) Mande **ga** s-iŋ, **ka** yɨ nu=ra sab tam-byaŋ
 Monday **TOP?** say-1SG.IPST ? 1SG 3SG=COM work put-1SG.FUT
 s-iŋ.
 say-1SG.IPST
 '"Monday," I said. "Then I'll work with him," I said.'

In Kursav the middle and far demonstratives can be used without affixes. The near root *i-* must be affixed with the topic suffix *-ka*, but when it is it appears to function very similarly to the unaffixed *ka* and *do*. It may be, then, that the unaffixed near demonstrative is simply not allowed due to a minimal word requirement or some similar length-related prohibition. The middle and far bare forms appear to function simply as unmarked demonstratives (225), marking deictic distance but not any particular information-structure status, such as topic.

Kursav
(225) Agɨdem **do** ruk-uana?
 good **FD** see-2SG.NFUT
 'Do you see that good one?'

The Gants definite article *ko* appears to be cognate with unaffixed middle forms in other languages, although the rounding of *a to *o* remains unexplained. This form can mark noun phrases as definite (226), can refer to definite referents on its own (227), and can nominalize clauses (228).

Gants
(226) Kura **ko,** miŋa gon tama-m-ek.
 man **DEF** get trap put-FPST-3SG
 'The man set a trap.'

Gants
(227) **Ko** pe maŋ.
 DEF pig no
 'That's not a pig.'

Gants
(228) Ped miŋi-da yig adi-m-ek **ko,** kada ci-m-ek.
paint take-ss festival do-FPST-3SG DEF thus stay-FPST-3SG
'The paint he taken and decorated himself with was right there.'

Gants also has a medial clause topicalizer *ga*, which follows a medial clause to render it topical in the discourse (229). There is also a form *ka* which is rare but which appears to be some kind of variant of *ga* (230).

Gants
(229) Miñ wisika-da adi-k-e **ga,** kura erkara-da ...
vine untie-ss do-DS.SEQ-3SG TOP man turn-ss
'When she untied the rope, it turned into a man and ...'

Gants
(230) Miŋa-da aŋa u-re-re **ka,** kura koimo, pe ko urod
get-ss go go-DS.SIM-3SG TOP man SPEC pig DEF path
koipoi miŋa-da ...
there get-ss
'When he took them, another man got a pig along the path and ...'

I now return to Mand and Manat, which have apparently cognate forms that are poorly understood due to their low frequency. The Mand form *ki* is a regular phonological reflex of *ka, but it appears only twice in my corpus, shown in (231) and (232). These uses both resemble the clause-initial function found in Apali, Sirva, and Aisi.

Mand
(231) Ida ka-n=ahw, ai-rd ka-n=ahw, misenare, **ki** naintintetiwan.
sun FD-ACC=FOC come-FPST FD-ACC=FOC missionary ? 1931
'The day they came, the missionaries, it was 1931.'

Mand
(232) **Ki** mad ar, ka-p watim ar.
? no QUOT FD-LOC after QUOT
'"No," she said, "He's behind (us)".'

The Manat form *ka* is more frequent than Mand *ki*, but still not well understood. It usually appears at the beginning of a clause and renders some understood referent topical, such as a picture that the speaker is holding in (233). More rarely it occurs with an overt noun, as in (234).

Manat
(233) **Ka** yaba ka-n ñ-id.
   MD.TOP water MD-ACC eat-3SG.IPST
   'This one, he's drinking beer (lit. 'water').'

Manat
(234) Pri **ka,** ŋara-rh-ura-m-id, arum hava ka-b. Ayaga=k
   dog **MD.TOP** speak-HAB-PL-PST-3.HIS big group MD-NOM sago=ACC
   ig-imir.
   give-2PL.PROH
   'As for dogs, the elders say, "Don't give them sago".'

The forms discussed above have many functions in common. To facilitate comparison, I summarize these in Table 42. Kursav is not included in the table because while its bare demonstratives are formally related to these forms, their functions have become so broad that comparison would not be meaningful. The functions referred to in the table are as follows: marking noun phrases in topic position, whether of verbal or nonverbal predicates; a bare demonstrative occurring clause initially without any accompanying noun phrase; subordinating a final clause; and topicalizing a medial clause.

Table 42: Bare demonstrative functions.

	Mand	Manat	Apalɨ	Mum	Sirva	Aisi	Gants	PSoG
topic position		x	x	x	x	x	x?	x
clause-initial	x	x	x		x	x		x
subordinating		x	x	x	x	x	x	x
medial clause			x	x		x	x	x

It is unclear whether the Gants definite article function should be considered cognate with the topic position function in other languages. Certainly it represents a plausible path of innovation: since topical discourse participants are almost always definite, the change from topic-marking in Proto-Sogeram to definite-marking in Gants could easily have happened. But as mentioned, the *o* in Gants *ko* casts some doubt on this etymology.

But even if the link between Gants *ko* and other reflexes of *ka is rejected, the distribution of reflexes in Table 42 allows for the reconstruction of two functions for PSoG *ka. The first is a topic-marking demonstrative function. On this analysis, the first two functions in Table 42 are understood as essentially the same function. The "topic position" label is given to reflexes that occur with an overt noun phrase, and the "clause-initial" label is given to reflexes that occur without one. This requires positing that the clause-initial function of *ka was initially always referential, as in (235), and that non-referential uses, like (236), arose later.

(235) Apalɨ
Na, viaŋ vaŋ miŋ-in kua u-i.
ND.TOP 1SG string.bag hold-1SG.IPST uncertainty say-3SG.IPST
'"As for this, I think I am holding a string bag," he said.' (Wade 1989: 132)

(236) Sirva
Ei, **ka** amge dua be pi~bi ad-i-Ø.
hey **MD.TOP** woman bad 3SG come~NMLZ do-TPST-3SG
'Hey, it's the bad woman coming doing (that).'

Reconstructing the subordinating function follows naturally from the reconstruction of a demonstrative function, as demonstratives were used to subordinate clauses in Proto-Sogeram (see §6).

The second function to reconstruct is the medial-clause topicalizing function. This function is well-distributed throughout the family, occurring from Gants to Mum and Apalɨ, so it can be reconstructed even though no other demonstrative serves such a function in any Sogeram language.

We must also decide how to reconstruct the demonstratives phonologically. The mid form *ka is simple, as there are plenty of reflexes. The far demonstrative *adu can also be reconstructed confidently; the extant reflexes support it widely enough, and comparison with the bound form *adu- confirms the reconstruction. But the near form is difficult to reconstruct. Apalɨ, Mum, and Sirva all lack the initial vowel, and Kursav does not retain a clear reflex of the unaffixed near demonstrative. I reason that the bound form *ini- probably corresponded to a bare form *in, but this reconstruction is not directly supported by the modern reflexes, so it remains somewhat speculative.

The last issue to resolve is what roots to reconstruct for what functions. Certainly *ka must be reconstructed for both reconstructed functions, since it serves every surviving function in every daughter language. But reflexes of the near and far demonstratives do not show up as consistently. For the medial clause topicalizing function, only reflexes of *ka are used in Apalɨ, Aisi, and Gants; Mum is the only language in which other demonstratives can serve this function. This suggests that Mum is innovative in this respect, and this function should only be reconstructed for the middle demonstrative *ka.

Near and far demonstratives are more widely distributed in the topicalizing function. The far demonstrative is found in Mum and Kursav, so it can be reconstructed to Proto-Sogeram. Unaffixed near demonstratives, however, are not found unambiguously in Kursav, but only in Apalɨ and Mum. (Sirva *nu* may be a reflex of the demonstrative **in* or of the 3SG subject pronoun **nu*.) This means that the topicalizing function cannot be directly reconstructed for the near demonstrative **in*. Rather, because we reconstruct a bare demonstrative construction in which **ka* and **adu* were used, we can reason that **in* was probably also used in this construction. But such a reconstruction is less secure, so bare **in* is only tentatively reconstructed.

5.3.3 Contrastive root reduplication

Proto-Sogeram may have had a reduplicated bare root form, although the evidence for this reconstruction is not wholly conclusive. The relevant forms are presented in Table 43, although I conclude below that the Sirva topic form *kaga* is not cognate with the rest.

Table 43: Reduplicated demonstratives.

	ND	MD	FD
Nend	*mba-na-*	*ha-na-*	*ke-ha-*
Apalɨ	*na-na*	*ha-na*	*ada-na*
Sirva (PRAG)	*n-udu*	*k-udu*	*ad-udu*
Sirva (TOP)		[*kaga*]	
Kursav	*i-ka(-)*	*ka-ka(-)*	*do-ka(-)*
PSOG	**in~in*	**ka~ka*	**adu~du*

Both Nend and Kursav possess expanded demonstrative roots that can be used in certain pragmatic circumstances. In Nend these forms must be followed by one of the regular demonstrative suffixes, although the expanded demonstratives do not take the full range of demonstrative suffixes, only a subset. In Apalɨ the expanded demonstratives must stand on their own. The Sirva PRAG forms can either stand on their own or take one of two enclitics, *=ŋ* 'POSS' and *=ñ* 'LOCATIVE/ INSTRUMENTAL'. The Sirva topic form *kaga* must stand on its own. And in Kursav the expanded demonstrative roots can either stand on their own or take one of the usual demonstrative suffixes.

The meaning of the Nend expanded demonstrative roots is centered around contrast. They function to "distinguish the referent from a larger group" or "clarify the identity of the referent" (K. Harris 1990: 104–105), as in (237) and (238).

Nend
(237) Ay-enta **ke-ha-n** mbikɨr mah.
tree-design **FD-CTR-ACC** 3PL.POSS NEG
'Those carvings are not theirs.' (K. Harris 1990: 105)

Nend
(238) Ke-n w-ɨn ha-n avɨ-z-ay-v, ntɨ **ke-ha-n**.
FD-ACC see-1SG.IPST MD-ACC throw-3SG.DS-come-2SG.IMP red **FD-CTR-ACC**
'Throw those that I see there, that is, the red (ones).' (K. Harris 1990: 104)

The Apalɨ forms are called "contrastive topic markers" by Wade, who describes them as being composed of the deictic roots "plus [the] near deictic functioning as the contrastive topic marker" (Wade 1989: 133). As the label implies, they serve to mark contrast. Her examples all involve the near deictic form *nana*, as in (239), suggesting that it may be the most common of the three.

Apalɨ
(239) Na na-dɨ. **Na-na** ia-dɨ.
ND.TOP 2SG.OBL **ND-CTR** 1SG-OBL
'This one is yours. This (other) one is mine.' (Wade 1989: 134)

The Sirva forms with *-udu* 'PRAG' have proven difficult to analyze semantically. They indicate that their referent is pragmatically salient in some way, but a simple label like 'topic' or 'focus' is problematic because *-udu* can mark both core arguments of a single clause (240).

Sirva
(240) Kwahe, yava mɨrada **n-udu,** uhu **n-udu** tam-ra ...
before father.1.POSS big **ND-PRAG** ground **ND-PRAG** put-SS
'Before, God (lit. 'our big Father') created the earth and ...'

As mentioned above, demonstratives in *-udu* can host the possessive enclitic =*ŋ* (241) and the locative/instrumental enclitic =*ñ* (242).

Sirva
(241) Uhu tɨmu n-umu, amge **n-udu=ŋ** uhu va-bɨ-s-a.
ground side ND-LOC woman **ND-PRAG=POSS** ground say-PL-FPST-3
'"On this side of the land, (it's) the woman's land," they said.'

Sirva
(242) Bira pigri ka-ŋa **k-udu=ñ** ma ki-rava-b-ri.
3PL custom MD-EXST **MD-PRAG=LI** NEG stay-HAB-PL-3
'They didn't live by such customs.'

The Sirva topic form *kaga* only marks subordinate clauses, as in (243). It usually signals that something important is about to happen, and marks a division between what came before (in the subordinate clause) and what happens next.

Sirva
(243) Ari=ñ kimam-daŋ v-ra ga-bi-s-a **ka-ga,** wara.
what=LI sleep-1DU.IRR say-SS see-PL-FPST-3 **MD-TOP** house
'They said, "What will we sleep in?" and looked, and (there was) a house.'

The Kursav expanded demonstratives add a suffix *-ka*. They can either stand on their own, as in (244), or take the other demonstrative suffixes, as in (245). Forms with *-ka* seem to perform a special contrastive topicalizing function. For example, (244) was uttered in a conversation about pictures of several troublemakers. *Kaka* here serves to contrast the virtuous subject of this clause (a policeman) with the miscreants being discussed beforehand.

Kursav
(244) Kura **ka-ka** agidem nitibu d-e.
man **MD-TOP** good custom do-3SG.NFUT
'That man is behaving well.'

Kursav
(245) **I-ka-n** skur idua d-e.
ND-TOP-LOC school bad do-3SG.NFUT
'The school here is bad.'

We can see, then, that the functions of the Nend, Apalɨ, and Kursav forms discussed here, and of the Sirva *-udu* forms, are quite similar. The function of Sirva *kaga*, however, does not seem to match the others. This consideration, combined with the unexpected prenasalization on the *g*, leads me to conclude that this form is not cognate with the other forms.

But it remains to be demonstrated that the four remaining forms are cognate with each other. Certainly they have a wide distribution through the Sogeram family, so that reconstruction to Proto-Sogeram would be assured if they were.

And, as mentioned, they match each other well semantically. But they do not match each other particularly well phonologically.

In spite of the phonological difficulties, though, I consider it likely that the explanation for the semantic similarities lies in a reduplicated demonstrative root that existed in Proto-Sogeram. It is noteworthy that, even though the contrastive suffixes in Table 43 do not all resemble each other, they do all take the shape of one of the three demonstrative roots. (Nend innovated a new near demonstrative root *mba-*, but the near expanded demonstrative retains the old Proto-West Sogeram form *na*.) This suggests that repeating bare demonstratives was a Proto-Sogeram strategy for communicating contrastive focus. The variety of focus markers found today can be explained as the outcome of different processes of analogical leveling. The near form gave the suffix *-na* in Apalɨ, the far form gave Sirva *-udu*, and the mid form gave Kursav *-ka*. Nend remains difficult to explain, but it does appear to have reflexes of both near and mid demonstratives in this construction.

Another feature that can tentatively be reconstructed is that this form could either occur on its own (as reflected in Apalɨ, Sirva, and Kursav) or could occur with the usual demonstrative suffixes (as reflected in Nend, Sirva, and Kursav).

So the outlines of this form can be reconstructed. But many details remain elusive. The exact form that the near demonstrative took when it was reduplicated cannot be directly reconstructed due to the amount of analogical change that has taken place. But *in~in, or *in~inɨ- when inflected, is probably the most likely shape. The middle form *ka~ka is more secure, given the Nend far reflex *ke-ha-* and the Kursav mid reflex *ka-ka*. But even this correspondence is not perfect, as the first Nend vowel is not expected to raise to *e*. And the far form must be reconstructed as *adu~du based solely on the Sirva witness *ad-udu*.

5.3.4 Object and oblique

The object enclitic *=ŋ and the oblique enclitic *=d were reconstructed in §5.2.2 and §5.2.3 above. In those sections I focused on the reflexes of these enclitics that mark pronouns and noun phrases; here I focus on the reflexes that occur on demonstratives. There are not many of these—in fact, there would not be enough to securely reconstruct these demonstrative forms if the enclitics had not already been reconstructed in other environments. This situation raises a methodological question. Given that *=ŋ and *=d are securely reconstructed, but only a few reflexes survive on demonstratives, should the demonstrative-marking function be reconstructed, or only the other functions? Reconstructing the demonstrative function entails positing that these demonstrative forms fell out of use in most languages. Not reconstructing the demonstrative function entails positing that it was innovated in the languages where it is found. Both scenarios are plausible. Reconstructing the demonstrative function creates a more symmetrical Proto-Sogeram system, in which all case-marking enclitics had roughly the same distribution. Not reconstructing the demonstrative function creates an asymmetrical system for Proto-Sogeram, but that very asymmetry explains the innovations that would have had to happen in the languages where these enclitics are found on demonstratives. I lean towards the view that the demonstrative-marking function should be reconstructed to Proto-Sogeram for *=d but not for *=ŋ, but recognize that the evidence could be interpreted otherwise.

The oblique enclitic *=d is found on demonstratives in Mand and Nend, and on a Manat postposition that used to be a demonstrative. In Mand its primary functions appear to be the marking of instrumental (246) and locative (247) obliques.

Mand
(246) Agem **ka-d** imi-rd.
knife **FD-OBL** shoot-FPST
'He stabbed it with a knife.' Elicited

Mand
(247) Abɨ **na-d** ac, akaj-u ar.
2 **ND-OBL** FOC wait-2SG.IMP QUOT
'"You wait here," she said.'

For Nend, K. Harris (1990: 107) only says that the oblique demonstrative form "is used in oblique noun phrases," and gives two examples, one possessive (248) and the other marking origin (249).

Nend
(248) Mor **ha-nd** ensa Mpahat.
crocodile **MD-OBL** name Mpahat
'The crocodile's name was Mpahat.' (K. Harris 1990: 107)

Nend
(249) Wiram ay-ampira **mba-na-nd=ɨv** ntiŋ ŋa-ndara-mg-i.
man tree-place **ND-CTR-OBL=NOM** work get-FUT-PL-3
'The men from this village will work.' (K. Harris 1990: 107)

In Manat the postposition *kad* marks benefactive case (250). This form appears to be quite plainly derived from *ka-d 'MD-OBL,' but the corresponding near and far forms have fallen out of use, and *kad* is no longer found without a preceding noun phrase. An interesting fact about *kad* is that it is in complementary distribution with another benefactive postposition *mad*. *Kad* marks noun phrases headed by common nouns, while *mad* marks other noun phrases. This may be a vestige of the distribution of the oblique enclitic. Recall that the accusative enclitic *=ŋ is reconstructed as occurring on its own on proper and inalienably possessed nouns, but requiring a demonstrative in order to mark common nouns. It may be that *=d had a similar distribution, which is why *kad* is only found marking common nouns in Manat today.

Manat
(250) *Mina* **kad** *ruku-ñi-rat-ur-id.*
pig **BEN** see-stay-HAB-PL-3
'They watch for pigs.'

Unlike *=d, which is found in three languages, the object enclitic *=ŋ is only found on demonstratives in Aisi. The Aisi nominative demonstrative suffix is -*ku*, and the accusative is -*kuŋ*. (The *ku* element is descended from a focus marker; see §5.3.8.) Aside from this, there are no demonstrative forms that have a reflex of *=ŋ.

As mentioned above, the support for reconstructing either *=d or *=ŋ with a demonstrative function is ambiguous. I tentatively reconstruct a demonstrative function for *=d because such a function is reflected in three languages and because its absence in the other languages can be explained by one or two innovations. I tentatively do not reconstruct a demonstrative function for *=ŋ because that function is only found in one language, and accounting for its absence in the other languages would require around four innovations. The decision not to reconstruct a demonstrative function for *=ŋ has one significant virtue: it results in a plausible complementary distribution between *=ŋ and demonstratives with the the topic/object suffix *-n (§5.3.5). The former would have marked proper names and inalienably possessed nouns, while the latter would have marked common nouns.

5.3.5 Topic/object

The demonstrative suffix *-n marked topics and objects. Topic position in Proto-Sogeram was a separate structural position in a sentence that preceded the subject and that was marked with its own case. A key assumption in this discussion is that nonverbal predicates in Sogeram languages have a topic–comment structure, not subject–predicate structure. What would be the subject in a subject–predicate language is structurally a topic in Sogeram languages, and is morphologically marked as such.

Reflexes of *-n are found in Mand, Nend, Manat, Apalɨ, and Aisi. In Mand, it marks objects (251) and the subjects of nonverbal predicates (252). It may also mark fronted topics as in (253), but there are no clear examples of this construction in which the fronted topic is not also the object.

Mand
(251) Kuram-iñ na-g, iwañ **ka-n** am kw-e aterɨ-rd.
man-DIM ND-NOM footprint **FD-ACC** just see-SS leave-FPST
'The boy just saw the footprints and left.'

Mand
(252) **Na-n** ikisopih.
ND-ACC head
'This is a head.'

Mand
(253) Asam far **ka-n,** dih=i k-ip ac ab-eu-rd.
breadfruit skin **FD-ACC** DU=COM FD-EXST FOC put-PL-3.FPST
'The breadfruit skin, the two of them put it there.'

In Nend this form usually marks objects (254), locations (255), or the subject of nonverbal predicates (256).

Nend
(254) Apa **ha-n** wa-rɨŋ, mamta.
bird **MD-ACC** see-1PL.DS dead
'We saw the bird and it was dead.' (K. Harris 1990: 106)

Nend
(255) Nzɨ **mba-n** ŋkañɨ-ndar-in.
1SG **ND-ACC** sit-FUT-1SG
'I will sit here.' (K. Harris 1990: 106)

Nend
(256) Yaŋ, **mba-n** uti?
mother **ND-ACC** what
'Mother, what is this?' (K. Harris 1990: 106)

Two of the Nend object pronouns, *yan* '1SG.OBJ' and *nan* '2SG.OBJ,' appear to contain reflexes of *-n. While these pronouns usually occur as objects, they can also occur as subjects of nonverbal predicates (257). Harris's translation of (258) suggests they may also function to mark fronted topics for verbal clauses as well.

Nend
(257) **Yan**   *Pasiŋkap=ind.*
     1SG.OBJ Pasiŋkap=OBL
     'I am from Pasinkap.'   (K. Harris n.d.)

Nend
(258) **Yan**   *aŋkwi=v*   *aha-z*   *mac*   *et-ay-em-en.*
     1SG.OBJ anger=NOM happen-3SG.DS finish depart-come-YPST-1SG
     'It made me angry so I came. (As for me, anger happened so then I left and came.)'   (K. Harris 1990: 93)

The Manat suffix *-n* also marks objects and topics. The object-marking function is seen with *kan* in (259), while the topic-marking function is seen with *inɨn*, which refers to a picture that the speaker is holding. Demonstratives with *-n* can also mark the subjects of nonverbal predicates (260) and some locative arguments in intransitive clauses (261). Note that *abim itun* in (261) is right-dislocated from the preceding clause; it is not the object of *rukusa*.

Manat
(259) **Inɨ-n** *añɨŋuta* *kai* *ka-b*   *pas*   *vaga* **ka-n**   *vuk-ur-id.*
     ND-ACC three   LOC MD-NOM banana leaf   **MD-ACC** write-PL-3.IPST
     '(In) this one, three men are writing a letter.'

Manat
(260) *Vɨhɨr*   **inɨ-n**   *ñi-bak?*
     bamboo **ND-ACC** who-POSS
     'Whose bamboo is this?'

Manat
(261) *As* *mɨgu-n=a,*   *abim*   **itu-n,**   *ruku-s=a ...*
     so go.down-2/3.SS=LNK boundary **FD-ACC** see-3SG.DS=LNK
     'So he went down to the edge and looked and ...'

In Apalɨ the cognate suffix *-n* is called the 'location of item' form and glossed 'ILOC' by Wade (1989: 129). This form marks locations (262) but seems to only mark objects when it is either in topic position or right-dislocated (263). It occurs frequently in topic position, either as the subject of a nonverbal clause (264) or as a topic-fronted item in a verbal clause (265).

(262) Apalɨ
Akoba akoba **na-n** hɨnɨ-d-i.
whatever whatever **ND-ILOC** stay-CONT-3SG
'The things are in this (box).' (Wade 1989: 130)

(263) Apalɨ
Lɨ-ci nu-dɨ hɨvɨ hugɨl-avɨ-m-i, sabaŋ **ha-n.**
do-3SG.DS 3SG-OBL LI cook-PL-HPST-3 pig **MD-ILOC**
'He did it and they cooked it at his (place) (or 'in his (pot)'), that pig that is.' (Wade 1989: 130)

(264) Apalɨ
Na-n sɨbɨlɨ u-i.
ND-ILOC bad say-3SG.IPST
'"This one here is bad," he said.' (Wade 1989: 129)

(265) Apalɨ
Ha-n analɨ abɨ-naŋ u-i.
MD-ILOC lie talk-2SG.IPST say-3SG.IPST
'"As for that, you lied," he said.' (Wade 1989: 130)

The final language with a reflex of *-n is Aisi, where the topic-marking demonstrative suffix is -oŋ. This form marks topic-fronted constituents (266) as well as objects (267). It does not mark the subjects of nonverbal predicates, as that function is performed by the nominative suffix -ku (268).

(266) Aisi
Kubro **g-oŋ** sab i-ba.
canoe **MD-TOP** work get-NMLZ
'They work on canoes (lit. 'the canoes, they work').'

(267) Aisi
Ga-nɨŋ kr-i kr-i kyaŋɨ **g-oŋ** iw-eŋ.
MD-LOC walk-SS walk-SS fish **MD-TOP** hit-1SG.IPST
'I walked around there and shot fish.'

Aisi
(268) *Yambar* **ga-ku,** *dibir* *yambar.*
story **MD-NOM** cucumber story
'This story is the cucumber story.'

The Aisi suffix *-oŋ* is somewhat problematic because of the vowel *o*, which is not an expected reflex. But Aisi *ŋ* is a common reflex of word-final *n, and the functions of *-oŋ* closely match the functions of *-n* in the other languages presented. I therefore consider the suffix cognate, and posit that *a raised to *o* irregularly in this form, perhaps in anticipation of the velar stop closure of the upcoming *ŋ*.

The demonstrative suffix *-n is thus reconstructed, but the question remains whether it should also be reconstructed as a clitic. The forms that raise this question are the Nend object pronouns *yan* '1SG.OBJ' and *nan* '2SG.OBJ'. These forms suggest that *-n may have attached, if not to all noun phrases, at least to pronouns. But there would be several problems with such a reconstruction. First, there is no evidence that *-n attached to noun phrases without demonstratives, so it could only be reconstructed as a pronominal suffix. But another set of object pronouns has been reconstructed (§5.2.2), rendering the reconstruction of object pronouns in *-n superfluous and unlikely. Second, there is no evidence for such a set of object pronouns in any language besides Nend. And third, even Nend does not have a full paradigm. It seems more likely that Nend *yan* and *nan* were innovated on analogy with the demonstrative forms. So we reconstruct a demonstrative suffix *-n which marked objects and fronted topics.

5.3.6 Locative 1

Proto-Sogeram may have had two locative demonstrative forms, which I discuss in this section and the following one. Here I present evidence for the more secure reconstruction: a locative enclitic which had two allomorphs, *=ñ and *=i, and which I refer to it by its *=ñ allomorph. The reflexes are presented in Table 44. The first line contains any reflexes that function as demonstrative suffixes and the second line contains reflexes that are enclitics to the noun phrase. The third line contains two apparent reflexes that have become postpositions. Before discussing the reconstruction, I first discuss the reflexes found in each language. In several languages a reflex has instrumental meaning in addition to locative meaning. I note this where it occurs, and discuss at the end of the section whether this enclitic should be reconstructed with instrumental meaning.

5.3 Demonstratives

Table 44: Locative enclitic.

	Manat	Apalɨ	Mum	Sirva	Magɨ	Aisi	Kursav	PSoG
Demonstrative	-i	-eŋ, -niŋ	-ñ	-i	-niŋ	-niŋ	-n	
Enclitic			=ñ, =i	=ñ	=iŋ	=iŋ, =eŋ	=(n)i	*=ñ/=i
Postposition	kai					katiŋ		

The Manat demonstrative suffix -i only has locative meaning. In this function it competes with another locative suffix -ba; the difference between the two is not well understood. Interestingly, -i does not elide the preceding vowel of the demonstrative, as we would normally expect of a vowel. This is suggestive of its consonantal origin as *ñ. The middle form of the demonstrative is ka-i 'MD-LOC,' and this form has grammaticalized into a postposition kai that can express instrumental meaning (269) in addition to the expected locative meaning.

Manat
(269) Akei amid **kai** avɨh-itiŋ ar-ura-ma-g.
okay axe **LOC** chop-1SG.IMP say-PL-PST-3.FAR
'Okay, they wanted to cut him with an axe.'

An additional Manat form that may be a reflex of *=ñ is the temporal demonstrative suffix -ñɨŋar, which is primarily used for question words (270). This form may be composed of *=ñ plus a reflex of *iŋar 'sun, day'.

Manat
(270) A-vɨ rudi-b, **ba-ñɨŋar** kai ai-tih-ur-id=a?
1.POSS-uncle PL-NOM **QD-TEMP** LOC come-FFUT-PL-3=EXCL
'When will my uncles come?'

In Apalɨ the demonstrative suffix -eŋ refers to definite locations (Wade 1989: 128), as in (271). It has no instrumental meaning. Apalɨ word-final eŋ is a regular reflex of final *añ, suggesting that Apalɨ changed the final vowels of the near and far demonstrative roots to *a before merging *ñ and *n (§3.2.5.2). The dialect variant -niŋ is somewhat rare and is probably related to the identical Aisi form.

Apalɨ
(271) Sabaŋ ha na-vɨla cɨhu ala ve-vɨhe-m-i,
pig MD.TOP eat-SS again FOC come-do.quickly-HPST-3SG

>
> *simin piŋ n-eŋ.*
> **tree.sp base ND-LOC**
> 'As for that pig, he ate and again came back quickly, to the base of the *simin* tree here that is.' (Wade 1989: 128)

Mum possesses a demonstrative suffix -*ñ* and a noun phrase enclitic that can be realized as =*ñ* or =*i*. No written grammar exists for Mum, so it is difficult to describe the functions of these morphemes, or what conditions the allomorphy in the enclitic. But an examination of the texts in Sweeney (n.d.) suggests that both forms have both locative and instrumental meaning, and that the enclitic is only =*ñ* after *a*, and is most frequently realized as =*i* after consonants and *u*. Examples below show the demonstrative with locative (272) and instrumental meaning (273), and the enclitic with locative (274) and instrumental (275) meaning.

Mum
(272) *Am   Godfried ahuvug yad   da-ñ   kuyu   nimata   tama-h-i...*
      yesterday Godfried **radio**   **1SG.POSS FD-LI** talk   this.kind put-DS-3SG
      'Yesterday Godfried put this talk on my radio ...' (Sweeney n.d.)

Mum
(273) *Muvata   timu   tama-da-riŋ,   ñaña ha-ñ.*
      sometimes party put-HAB-1PL   **food** **MD-LI**
      'Sometimes we have a party, with this food that is.' (Sweeney n.d.)

Mum
(274) **Puhu=i**   *ma-u-m-i.*
      village=LI NEG-go-HPST-3SG
      'He did not go to his village.' (Sweeney n.d.)

Mum
(275) **Yaŋ   kiu   sukir=i**   *aba-mara.*
      1SG.OBJ talk   vernacular=LI tell-2PL.IMP
      'You people must talk to me in the vernacular.' (Sweeney n.d.)

The Sirva suffix -*i* only has locative meaning. As with the Manat suffix, it contrasts in this function with another suffix, and the difference in meaning between the two is not well understood. Unlike Manat, Sirva -*i* does elide the preceding vowel of the demonstrative root. The Sirva enclitic =*ñ*, realized as =*iñ* after a consonant, has both locative and instrumental meaning.

The two Aisian languages have quite similar forms. The demonstrative suffix -niŋ is probably related to the identical Apalɨ suffix, and like the Apalɨ form it only has locative meaning. While -iŋ is a fairly regular reflex of final *Vñ, the origin of the siffix-initial n is unclear. The enclitic, =iŋ, also only expresses locative meaning. In Aisi this enclitic is realized as =eŋ when attaching to u, o, or ɨ. While neither the suffix nor the enclitic denotes instrumental meaning, both Aisian languages have a postposition *katiŋ* that marks locatives as well as instrumentals. While the origin of the *kat-* part of this postposition is obscure, the *-iŋ* may be the locative enclitic.

In Kursav the demonstrative suffix -n and the enclitic =(n)i both only have locative meaning. The enclitic is =ni after vowels and =i after consonants.

These forms show enough formal and semantic similarity that they can be confidently reconstructed. But we must resolve a few formal, distributional, and semantic questions before the reconstruction is complete. I begin with the formal question. Since allomorphs *=ñ and *=i can both be reconstructed, how did they pattern? The only languages in which this pattern of allomorphy can still be seen are Mum and Kursav, and both paint a similar picture. Reflexes of the nasal consonant are found after vowels—in the Mum case, only *a*—while reflexes of the vowel are found after consonants. Because these are two disparate witnesses, this variation can be reconstructed. The Proto-Sogeram locative enclitic was realized as *=ñ after vowels and *=i after consonants.

Recall, though, that the near deictic root was *in when unaffixed but *inɨ- when affixed. It would therefore be plausible for the near form to take either allomorph. Reflexes of the vocalic allomorph *=i are found in Manat (*in-i*) and Sirva (*n-i*), while reflexes of the nasal allomorph *=ñ are found in Apalɨ (*n-eŋ*), Mum (*nɨ-ñ*), and Kursav (*i-n*). The nasal allomorph should be reconstructed for three reasons. First, Manat and Sirva have generalized the *=i allomorph to all contexts, so their witnesses cannot be relied on as archaic. Second, Mum is the language that has best preserved the variation between *=ñ and *=i, and its reflex clearly supports a reconstruction of *=ñ. And third, the distribution of *=ñ reflexes is superior to that of *=i reflexes. We thus reconstruct the near form as *inɨ=ñ.

Reconstructing the distributional properties of this enclitic is fairly straightforward, since both the demonstrative and enclitic functions are widespread throughout the family. There is no reason to suspect that both functions did not coexist in Proto-Sogeram. So we reconstruct an enclitic that attached to noun phrases as well as to demonstratives.

Finally, we must resolve the semantic question: what did this form mean? Locative meaning is found for every reflex, so it must be reconstructed. A combination of locative and instrumental meanings is found in at least one reflex in Manat, Mum, Sirva, and Aisi. Although this is wide enough distribution to warrant reconstruction to Proto-Sogeram, I do not believe it should be reconstructed. This is because the conflation of locative and instrumental meanings is an areal phenomenon; for example, an unrelated locative/instrumental enclitic =ŋ is found in Nend (K. Harris 1990: 94). For this reason I consider it likely that the instrumental meaning spread via contact, rather than being inherited from Proto-Sogeram. This also explains its marginal place in Manat and Aisi, where it is found in only a single postposition.

5.3.7 Locative 2

While the evidence for the locative enclitic *=ñ is quite strong, the evidence for a second locative form is much weaker. The potential reflexes are given in Table 45.

Table 45: Reflexes of Locative 2.

Mand	Manat	Mum	PSoG
-p	-ba	-bu	*-bV

In all three languages the given form is a locative demonstrative suffix; none of these forms serve as enclitics to the noun phrase. Mand -p only attaches to the ka- root (276); the near root na- takes a different locative suffix -k.

    Mand
(276) Uram   kr=an   **ka-p**   aba-rd.
     house 3SG.POSS=very **FD-LOC** put-FPST
     'He put it in his own house.'

The Manat (277) and Mum (278) forms appear to be simple locatives. In both languages these forms coexist with reflexes of *=ñ, but in neither is it understood how exactly the two locative forms differ in meaning.

    Manat
(277) Asik   Soheram   **ka-ba**   vu-n ...
     again Sogeram   **MD-LOC** go-2/3.SS
     'They went back to the Sogeram (River) and ...'

    Mum
(278) Pa-ta   apar   **ni-bu**   kad   ñaŋura-ta   yahu-m-u.
     come-SS mountain **ND-LOC** true look.around-SS go.up-HPST-3PL
     'They came right to the mountain over there and looked around
     and went up.'   (Sweeney n.d.)

The Mand and Manat forms suggest a reconstruction of *-ba (although the normal Mand reflex of *-ba would be ⁺–pɨ), while Mum suggests a reconstruction of *-bu. One potentially cognate form comes from Moresada. Capell (1951: 146) gives the forms *uwaramba*, which he glosses 'village-in,' and *uwaːr* 'village'. These forms suggest a locative suffix *-amba*, but this cannot be interpreted as conclusive evidence given our present understanding of Moresada. Since, then, there is not yet enough data to reconcile these forms, for now I reconstruct the locative demonstrative suffix *-bV with an unspecified vowel.

5.3.8 Focus

There is some evidence for reconstructing a focus-marking demonstrative suffix *-kw to Proto-Sogeram. The case rests primarily on two reflexes, the Mand focus suffix *-hw* and the Aisian nominative suffix *-ku*, presented in Table 46.

Table 46: Focus suffix.

Mand	Magɨ	Aisi	Aisi	PSoG
FOC	NOM	NOM	ACC	
-hw	-ku	-ku	-kuŋ	*-kw

The Mand focus suffix is not well understood, but it appears to indicate that its referent is noteworthy and focused in some way (279). This suffix closely resembles the Mand focus enclitic =*ahw*, which seems to have similar meaning. Example (280) is a quote from someone trying to convince people that eating breadfruit with the skin is best, and =*ahw* here marks contrastive focus. The distributional properties of this enclitic are not well understood, but it frequently marks pronouns.

Mand
(279) *Arhw   kw-e   arhw   ŋɨrsɨc   ak-ebɨ.   **Ka-hw**   mɨz   ukam!*
      1PL   see-SS   1PL   earthquake chop-MPST   **FD-FOC** body   white
      'We looked and we were shocked (lit. 'chopped an earthquake'). That's a white man!'

Mand
(280) **Api=ahw**   *far   na-n   atad   j-in   ar.*
      1SG=FOC   skin   ND-ACC   INS   eat-1SG.IPST   QUOT
      '"I'm eating it with the skin," he said.'

The Aisian suffix -*ku* marks nominative case in both Aisian languages, as in (281).

Aisi
(281) Na   naŋ **ga-ku**   apɨr itɨ   kr-i   kr-i ...
      and son **MD-NOM** dog   get.SS   walk-SS   walk-SS
      'And this boy got his dog and walked and walked and ...'

The formal similarity between this suffix and the Mand focus suffix is apparent, but the semantic connection is more tenuous. Matters are helped somewhat by the presence of the Aisi accusative suffix -*kuŋ* (282), which appears to be composed of the nominative suffix -*ku* plus a reflex of the accusative enclitic *=ŋ (§5.2.2). This form is innovative, and it seems more likely for it to have developed from a form that did not have incompatible core argument meaning than from a form with nominative meaning. So although it would certainly be possible for *=ŋ to have been added to a nominative form, it is perhaps more plausible to suppose that it was added to -*ku* when -*ku* had non-nominative meaning, and that -*ku* developed nominative meaning afterwards.

Aisi
(282) **Na-kuŋ**   itɨ   we   na-nɨŋ   tam-o.
      ND-ACC   get.SS   come.SS   ND-LOC   put-2SG.IMP
      'Take this and come put it here.'

This hypothesis is supported by the fact that -*ku* indeed does serve non-nominative functions. In (283) it marks a topic-fronted constituent, albeit one that is coreferent with the subject of the clause, *nu* '3SG'. And in (284) it marks a noun phrase, *kuru Kris aba* 'the man they call Chris,' which is embedded in a postpositional phrase that modifies the head noun *ki* 'speech'. Interestingly, the referent Chris is being focused here. The speaker visited Chris's village and was asked by a resident why he had come, and this was his answer.

Aisi
(283) Gwandam   mo   **ga-ku,**   nu   wanɨ   aŋ   amug   tam-ɨs-i.
      old.man   SPEC   **MD-NOM**   3SG   bag   water   under   put-FPST-3SG
      'An old man, he was putting a bag in the river (to fish).'

Aisi
(284) Kuru   Kris   aba   **ga-ku**   ginɨŋ   ki   ir-i   kɨtɨŋ ...
      man   Chris   QUOT   **MD-NOM**   GEN   speech   perceive-SS   and
      'I heard the talk about a man they call Chris and ...'

So although Mand -*hw* 'FOC' and Aisian -*ku* 'NOM' no longer have the same meaning, there is evidence that Aisian -*ku* used to have non-nominative meaning. The semantic innovation from marking focus to marking nominative case is a plausible one, so I consider these forms cognate and reconstruct a suffix *-kw that occurred on Proto-Sogeram demonstratives and marked focus.

We must also consider whether this *-kw was an enclitic that marked focus on other constituents as well. The evidence for this reconstruction strikes me as insufficient. The Mand focus enclitic =*ahw* supports such a reconstruction, and the addition of *a* to the beginning of the enclitic could be the result of reanalysis after the loss of word-final *a from many words (§3.2.2.4). The Nend focus enclitic =*h*, which "serves to elevate the prominence of [non-subject arguments], marking them ... as being in focus" (K. Harris 1990: 100), also supports this reconstruction (285).

(285) Nend
Ar **Ompand=ih** onca ŋg-am-e hir-ay-riŋ,
1PL **Ompand=FOC** inside descend-put-SS carry-come-1PL.IPST
eŋka ziŋ-sind.
sago leaf-CHAR
'We put Ompand in the middle and brought (him), along with the sago leaves.' (K. Harris 1990: 101)

But this evidence is restricted to the West Sogeram branch, and as such is insufficient for reconstruction farther back than Proto-West Sogeram. Moreover, it is not the case that the other Sogeram languages lack focus markers. Morphological marking of focus is common in the family, but none of the other focus markers appear to be cognate with *-kw.

Chapter 6
Syntactic Constructions

Much of the material in the preceding chapters has been focused on phonological and morphological reconstruction, which may seem odd in a book that claims to be about reconstructing grammar. But let me reiterate that all this is necessary preparation for syntactic reconstruction. A solid grasp of the phonological and morphological history of a language family is a necessary foundation upon which to begin syntactic reconstruction, since it is impossible to reconstruct syntax without being able to tell which morphemes are cognate. Moreover, several of the reconstructions in the preceding chapters actually involved a fair amount of syntax, such as the reconstruction of verb serialization (§4.2), the dual function of the irrealis verb paradigm (§4.3.10), the disparate reflexes of the emphatic enclitic (§5.2.5), and the topicalizing role played by bare demonstrative roots (§5.3.2). All this is just to say that morphology and syntax are not really all that different from one another.

All the same, we now turn our attention to syntax, by which I mean constructions on the more abstract and schematic end of the lexicon–syntax continuum. I begin by reconstructing word class constructions for adjectives and adverbs (§6.1) and then reconstruct the order of certain elements within the noun phrase (§6.2). In §6.3 I discuss some clause-level syntactic constructions, and in §6.4 I discuss clause combining constructions.

6.1 Word classes

In previous chapters I have reconstructed nominal and verbal morphology, and as a result several word classes can already be established on morphological grounds. Proto-Sogeram had verbs and nouns, the latter of which contained a subclass of inalienably possessed nouns. It also had pronouns and demonstratives, and in the sections below I argue that Proto-Sogeram also had separate classes of adjectives and adverbs. Interestingly, no postpositions can yet be reconstructed for Proto-Sogeram, although every daughter language has at least a few.

6.1.1 Adjectives

Adjectives can be analyzed as a word class distinct from nouns in every language except Kursav, and as distinct from adverbs in every language but Sirva. They also occupy their own position in the noun phrase in every language except Kursav. All of this suggests that they formed a separate word class in Proto-Sogeram.

Fifteen adjectives can be reconstructed to Proto-Sogeram. These forms expressed the meanings 'good' (two reconstructed forms), 'bad,' 'long,' 'small,' 'new,' 'ripe,' 'unripe,' 'true,' 'crooked,' 'male,' 'wet,' 'black,' 'white,' and 'yellow'. Two of these forms also functioned, with slightly different meanings, as nouns, which raises the question of whether these forms should be treated as single lexemes or not at the Proto-Sogeram stage. The form *ñɨŋi 'small' also meant 'child,' and *mɨdɨ 'ripe' also meant 'blood'. Another adjective, *kada 'true,' also functioned as an adverb meaning 'very'. Two more adjective-like forms, *mu 'SPECIFIC' and *pam 'one,' are discussed below.

It seems that not all adjectival meanings—that is, meanings denoting properties rather than entities or events—were expressed with adjectives. At least one adjectival verb can be reconstructed: *mɨta 'be full'. And the form that meant 'red,' *yagum, was apparently not an adjective but a noun, with a primary meaning of 'blood'.

Two adjective-like words remain puzzling: the specific particle *mu and the numeral *pam 'one'. PSoG *mu indicated that the referent was identifiable to the speaker but not to the hearer. Like adjectives, it followed the noun which it modified, as can be seen in (286)–(289) below.

Manat
(286) *Akei urum **mu**=k pravu-ram-ura-ma-g, ni-ra=k.*
okay man **SPEC**=ACC hide-put-PL-PST-3.FAR 3.POSS-SS.young.sib=ACC
'Okay, they hid one man, the younger brother.'

Mum
(287) *Sia **mu** miɲarvu-ta miɲarvu-ta ...*
arrow **another** break-SS break-SS
'Other arrows he broke and broke and ...' (Sweeney n.d.)

Magɨ
(288) *Naŋgari, yɨ asad **mu** uku-byaŋ.*
now 1SG story **SPEC** tell-1SG.FUT
'Now I'm going to tell a story.'

Gants
(289) *Tai mañ **mo** miŋ-eniŋ.*
tree seed **some** get-1SG.IPST
'I took some fruit.' Elicited

But reflexes of *mu differ in subtle respects from other adjectives in some modern languages. For example, in Aisi, both adjectives and *mo* 'SPEC' follow the noun, but when they co-occur with a pronominal possessor, adjectives precede it while *mo* follows it. Similar observations in other languages cast doubt on the grammatical status of *mu. For now, it is enough to group it with the adjectives but observe that it may not have behaved in the same way as more prototypical members of that class.

The same is true of *pam 'one'. It appears to be an adjective in some languages, such as Mand, where it follows nouns to modify them (290).

     Mand
(290) *Igard   urim   ka-p,   bor-iñ   **vam**   im-i   pi-r.*
     noon   middle   FD-LOC   pig-DIM   **one**   shoot-SS   take-3SG.FPST
     'At midday he shot a little pig and took it.'

This analysis is complicated, though, by languages where numerals behave more like nouns, like Manat, or like a separate class of quantifiers, like Aisi. Furthermore, in some languages, like Aisi, reflexes of *pam serve as adverbs meaning 'only' (291).

     Aisi
(291) *Ameki   ga-ku   gyou   **pa**   n-iba.*
     lastborn   MD-NOM   snake.sp   **only**   eat-PTCP
     'The lastborn used to just eat *gyou* snakes.'

It is likely that *pam was an adjective like *mu in that it probably behaved somewhat differently from more prototypical adjectives. It also seems that it was like *kada 'true' in that it also had an adverbial function. The two functions are retained together in Apalɨ, as shown in (292) and (293), and Kursav, as shown in (294) and (295), and on the strength of these witnesses the variation in functions can be reconstructed.

     Apalɨ
(292) *Mugu   iak-ilu,   hibi   hadi   **pam**.*
     move.down.go   move.up-1PL   trail   big   **one**
     'We went down and went up, on the one big trail.'   (Wade n.d.b)

     Apalɨ
(293) *Hidili   **pam**   vala-lu.*
     root   **only**   leave-1PL.IPST
     'We left only the root.'   (Wade 1989: 148)

Kursav
(294) *Kavre ka **pa** in-e.*
there MD **one** stay-3SG.NFUT
'One is over there.' Elicited

Kursav
(295) *Nin-iba nuku vuruva bin **pa** in-o.*
3PL-EMPH POSS village LOC **only** stay-3PL.NFUT
'They only stayed in their own village.'

It is also unclear how other numerals behaved, since they cannot be reconstructed. Most of the Sogeram languages only have numerals 'one' through 'three,' and only 'one' can be securely reconstructed.

6.1.2 Adverbs

Nineteen adverbs can be reconstructed to Proto-Sogeram. As with adverbs in most languages, these forms possess a variety of meanings and perform a variety of grammatical functions, and a more fine-grained analysis may conclude that they constitute more than one part of speech. The largest group, semantically, is the temporal adverbs. These include words referring to times of day ('daytime,' 'morning,' and 'afternoon'), deictic terms centered on the present day ('yesterday,' 'tomorrow,' 'the day before yesterday,' 'two days away,' and 'three days away') and one other form ('later'). Adverbs of degree include two words meaning 'very' and one meaning 'completely'. The locative adverb 'near' and the modal 'maybe' can be reconstructed, as can five other adverbs: 'together,' 'just,' two related words for 'only', and an adverbial focus particle.

Two adverbs also belonged to other parts of speech: *iŋar 'day(time),' which was also a noun meaning 'sun,' and *kada 'very,' which was also an adjective meaning 'true'. Note also that not all potentially adverbial meanings were expressed with adverbs. The word for 'night' was *kifɨr, which was a noun.

Given that these adverbs can all be reconstructed, it is safe to also reconstruct the word class of adverbs to Proto-Sogeram, although no single diagnostic can be proposed to define them. To illustrate this reconstruction with one of the more securely reconstructed forms, examples (296)–(299) show reflexes of *sɨkan 'completely' (which could also be reduplicated as *sɨkansɨkan) modifying the predicate adverbially.

Apalɨ
(296) *Huligali-mɨdɨ* *ua-vɨla* **sɨkan** *la mɨhɨŋ*
 turn.back.towards-3SG.PROH say-SS **completely** do date
 lam-avɨ-la-lɨ.
 put-PL-HAB-3.FPST
 'Saying, "It should not reject us," they do it completely
 and put a date.' (Wade n.d.b)

Sirva
(297) *Wa-ra, wa-ra* **sɨhazɨha**   *ma* *u-rubɨ-s-a.*
 go-SS go-SS **completely** NEG go-PL-FPST-3
 'They went, but they didn't go all the way.'

Aisi
(298) *Nuŋ   itok-i*   **sɨkaŋ** *korɨm gunu amug suku, itok-s-i.*
 3SG.OBJ take.in-SS **totally** tree.sp dry under very take.in-FPST-3SG
 'It took him in, it took him all the way into the dry *korɨm* tree.'

Kursav
(299) *Nan gapɨra, sarigi na,* **sɨkasɨka** *so   iv   mo-kura-i*
 2PL all line.up do.SS **completely** feces house go-2PL.IMP-INT
 v-oko ...
 say-3PL.DS
 '"All of you, line up and go all the way to the toilet," they said, and ...'

6.2 The noun phrase

The grammar of the Proto-Sogeram noun phrase has proven very difficult to reconstruct. The main issue is that there is very little noun phrase-internal morphology, so that even in cases of complete or near complete identity among daughter languages, we cannot be sure that a construction existed in Proto-Sogeram. For example, every Sogeram language allows nouns to modify other nouns attributively, and in every language the attributive noun precedes the head noun. But because there is no morphology associated with this construction, it is difficult, according to the methodology we have set up, to reconstruct that word order to Proto-Sogeram.

A second issue is that when there is morphology that could assist us in reconstruction, sometimes there is no agreement between the daughter languages. This is the case with the order of possessors and head nouns.

In the following sections I discuss the placement of attributive nouns, attributive adjectives, and possessors with respect to the head noun. Although the data are often suggestive of a reconstruction, in no case am I able to propose a reconstruction that is fully sanctioned by my methodology.

A fourth item, the demonstrative, can be reconstructed more securely. Demonstratives exhibit cognate morphology across the family—both roots and suffixes—and they occur at the end of the noun phrase in every Sogeram language. There is no reason to suspect that it was otherwise in Proto-Sogeram.

6.2.1 Attributive noun

In every Sogeram language, a head noun can be modified by an attributive noun that precedes it in the noun phrase. A few examples of this construction are given in (300)–(302).

Nend
(300) O-e wa-z **mira** iñi ohɨr-on mb-ah.
go-SS see-3SG.DS **pig** track big-INT ND-EXST
'He went and looked and there were many pig tracks.' (K. Harris 1990: 134)

Sirva
(301) **Sibia** kina beau mi-ra ...
stone axe DEF.ACC get-SS
'They took the stone axe and ...'

Kursav
(302) **Tor** iv bin rubram-e.
court house LOC sit-3SG.NFUT
'He's sitting in a courthouse.'

The universal attestation of the [N$_{\text{ATTRIB}}$ N$_{\text{HEAD}}$] construction suggests that reconstruction to Proto-Sogeram would be justified. But because this construction is wholly schematic, we must be aware of the possibility that it has spread via contact and was not inherited from Proto-Sogeram. The construction specifies no phonological material, so confirming cognacy by checking for cognate phonemes is not possible. Finding cognate nouns in either position of the construction is also insufficient, since if the construction were borrowed into a language, it would presumably be possible to place any noun, native or borrowed, in either position.

One process of grammaticalization that has taken place in Mand also supports a reconstruction of [N$_{ATTRIB}$ N$_{HEAD}$] word order. The Mand diminutive suffix *-iñ* is descended from PSOG **ña* 'son,' showing regular loss of word-final **a* (§3.2.2.4) and non-fortition of the word-final nasal (§3.2.2.5). This suffix apparently grammaticalized from a construction in which **ña* occurred in head position of a noun phrase, modified by an attributive noun as in the Sirva example in (303). This construction underwent the semantic bleaching that is typical of grammaticalization and **ña* in this position stopped meaning 'son,' coming instead to contribute diminutive semantics to the noun phrase (304).

Sirva
(303) *Ka-ma   ad-ii,   ni-rima   be,   saba ña   mi-ra   mir-a ...*
      MD-ADVZ   do-3SG.DS   3.POSS-sister   3SG   **pig** **child** get-SS   leave-SS
      'He did that, and his sister got a baby pig and ...'

Mand
(304) *Mac   van   hir,   **bor-iñ**   ka-n   atihw-e   p-i ...*
      enough   father.3.POSS   3SG.POSS   **pig-DIM**   FD-ACC   take.out-SS take-SS
      'Okay, his father took the piglet out and ...'

While the existence of this suffix does not assure us that the head noun **ña* in Proto-Sogeram was preceded by its attributive noun, it does mean that this was the order in Pre-Mand. Thus we have established that the [N$_{ATTRIB}$ N$_{HEAD}$] construction occurred some distance into the past in Pre-Mand, which slightly increases the likelihood that the reconstruction also existed in Proto-Sogeram.

So there is suggestive evidence to support the reconstruction of *[N$_{ATTRIB}$ N$_{HEAD}$] to Proto-Sogeram. A reflex is attested in every daughter language, but the absence of cognate phonological material with which to test cognacy casts some doubt on the reconstruction.

6.2.2 Adjective

Adjectives consistently follow the head noun in every Sogeram language but Kursav, and Kursav exhibits approximately equal variation between noun–adjective (N–Adj) order and Adj–N order. Some languages, such as Sirva, possess a handful of aberrant adjectives that precede the head. The primary order exhibited in each language is shown in Table 47.

The overwhelming attestation of N–Adj word order places us in a similar position as with attributive nouns. The near identity between daughter language

Table 47: Word order of adjectives and nouns.

Mand	Nend	Manat	Apalɨ	Mum	Sirva	Magɨ	Aisi	Kursav	Gants
N–Adj	N–Adj	N–Adj	N–Adj	N–Adj	N–Adj	N–Adj	N–Adj	N–Adj, Adj–N	N–Adj

reflexes is suggestive that Proto-Sogeram also had N–Adj word order, but the lack of morphology associated with the attributive adjective construction makes this reconstruction suspect.

6.2.3 Possessor

Reconstructing the order of the possessor and the possessed noun is very difficult, and it is most likely the case that most Proto-Sogeram possessors could either precede or follow their heads. In this discussion I will treat nominal and pronominal possessors differently, and attempt to reconstruct a possessive construction for each.

Nominal possessors were marked with the oblique enclitic *=d (§5.2.3). This construction is found in Mand (305), Nend (306), Apalɨ (307), and Mum (308).

Mand
(305) Beten   ñi~ñ   werai-ri-n,   **Gau**   **Ohra=d**
      pray   stay~NMPT   go.and.come-FPST-1SG   **father.1/2.POSS** **big=OBL**
      ya   ka-n.
      speech   FD-ACC
      'I went around praying, God's (lit. 'the Big Father's') word.'

Nend
(306) **Rapael=nd** aniŋ   war   ohira
      Rapael=OBL   banana   garden   big
      'Rapael's big banana garden'   (K. Harris 1990: 133)

Apalɨ
(307) **sudɨ**   **dɨ**   iŋam   mɨka
      ghost **OBL** dog   tooth
      'ghost's dog tooth'   (Wade 1989: 76)

Mum
(308) Yi   **Avibri**   **du**   kru   va-m-i.
      1SG   **Avimbri** **POSS** man   say-HPST-3SG
      '"I am Avimbri's son," he said.'   (Sweeney n.d.)

In each of these languages an oblique-marked nominal possessor precedes the possessed noun, suggesting that this is the order that occurred in Proto-Sogeram as well. This is not entirely clear, though, since non-possessive oblique modifiers sometimes occur after the head noun, as in (309). For the moment, then, the order of nominal possessors with respect to the possessed noun can only tentatively be reconstructed as Poss–N.

(309)   Mand
       bor   **ata=d**
       pig   **forest=OBL**
       'a wild pig'

The issue of pronominal possession poses even greater difficulties. Recall from §5.2.4 that the possessive pronouns were formed with the suffix *-kw. Reflexes of these pronouns are found in Mand, Manat, Sirva (where they have become object pronouns), Aisi, Kursav, and Gants (where they have also become object pronouns). The Sirva reflexes cannot help us, since they no longer occur in a possessive construction; the Gants reflexes, although they are now object pronouns, are still sometimes used to mark possession. For these reflexes of the possessive pronouns in *-kw, then, the attested orders of possessive pronoun and possessed noun phrase are given in Table 48.

Table 48: Order of possessive pronouns and possessed noun phrases.

Mand	Manat	Magɨ	Aisi	Kursav	Gants
NP-Poss	Poss-NP	NP-Poss	NP-Poss, Poss-NP	NP-Poss, Poss-NP	NP-Poss

As this table and the examples below show, Mand has noun–possessor order (310) while Manat has the reverse (311). Magɨ also has noun–possessor order (312), but Aisi exhibits variation between noun–possessor (313) and possessor–noun (314) orders. Kursav exhibits the same variation, as shown in (315) and (316). Finally, when the Gants object pronouns are used possessively, they follow the head noun (317).

(310)   Mand
       Akac   **arhud**   vivi   c-id   ar.
       intestine   **1PL.POSS**   pain   be-IPST   QUOT
       '"Our stomachs hurt," she said.'

Manat
(311) **Yak** vana=k ka-b=avan.
1SG.POSS speech=ACC MD-NOM=very
'My story is just like that.'

Magɨ
(312) Asad **yaka** ka-nd pa.
story 1SG.POSS MD-EXST only
'That's my story.'

Aisi
(313) Katam **nɨku** pas am-egi na ...
head 3SG.POSS closed do-3SG.DS and
'His head was stuck and ...'

Aisi
(314) **Yaka** ib tuar-am. **Naka** lain ir-ɨberuŋ.
1SG.POSS name say-2SG.IMP 2SG.POSS group perceive-3PL.FUT
'(You can) say my name. Your people will hear it.'

Kursav
(315) Kursav guro **yaku** Makari pakwit ma.
Kursav speech 1SG.POSS Makari one NEG
'My Kursav language isn't (the language of) only Makari (clan).'

Kursav
(316) **Anuku** guro ka-ka kumo-mis d-e.
1PL.POSS speech MD-TOP die-DESID do-3SG.NFUT
'Our language is about to die.'

Gants
(317) pi **yak** ko
village 1SG.OBJ DEF
'my village'

We see that both N–Poss and Poss–N orders are widely distributed throughout the family, to such a degree that each of them could individually be reconstructed to Proto-Sogeram. It should be noted that N–Poss word order is more securely reconstructed, though, as it is the only allowable word order now in Mand, Magɨ, and Gants. The simplest explanation is that variation between these two orders existed in Proto-Sogeram and has been retained in Aisi and Kursav, but has been simplified to one order or the other in ever other language. But we must acknowledge that the lack of agreement between daughter reflexes is problematic and renders this reconstruction less secure.

6.3 Clause structure

In this section I examine a few topics relating to the structure of the clause in Proto-Sogeram. I focus on the negation of verbal clauses (§6.3.1), the formation of interrogative clauses (§6.3.2), and the structure of nonverbal clauses (§6.3.3).

As regards the basic word order of the clause, we can say this. All the Sogeram languages are SOV, as are all the known languages surrounding the Sogeram languages for many miles in every direction. Furthermore, all known Madang languages are SOV, and so are the vast majority of other languages belonging to the Trans New Guinea family, however its membership is formulated. Given all this, I feel safe in breaking from my stated methodological process and reconstructing SOV word order to Proto-Sogeram even though the word order construction [S O V] does not specify any phonological material. I recognize the methodological inconsistency, but feel that the overwhelming attestation of SOV word order in Sogeram and its relatives warrants an exception.

This illustrates the flexible nature of my methodology, which I also discussed in §4.2.3. The method I propose is not intended to be formulaic—that is, I do not intend to create a rigid procedure that must be followed for syntactic reconstruction to be successful. Rather, I have pointed out the sources of evidence and lines of reasoning that are most important to syntactic reconstruction, but scholars must still use their judgment in the application.

As for other constituents of verbal clauses, Sogeram languages place most oblique arguments between the object and the verb. But in this case there is enough variation for pragmatic reasons that reconstruction of any particular word order is probably not warranted.

6.3.1 Negation

Verbal negation was accomplished with the negative particle *ma. Reflexes of this particle are found in every Sogeram language, as Table 49 shows.

Mand and Nend are unique in employing reflexes of *ma on both sides of the verb. Manat combines *ma* with the contrastive verb suffix -*ip*. The other languages all simply use *ma*, although they still exhibit some variation. In Mum it

Table 49: Negators.

Mand	Nend	Manat	Apalɨ	Mum	Sirva	Magɨ	Aisi	Kursav	Gants	PSoG
mɨ=...-m	mɨ-...-m	ma ...-ip	ma (...-maŋ)	ma-	ma	ma	ma	ma	ma	*ma

has become a prefix; in Sirva, Magɨ, and Gants it comes before the verb; and in Aisi and Kursav it (usually) comes after it.

In the West Sogeram (WS) languages we find reflexes of *ma on both sides of the verb. In Mand the first element is a proclitic that attaches to the first element of the verb adjunct construction (see Donohue 2005: 202). This can be seen with the Tok Pisin loanword *kamap* 'appear,' which functions as an adjunct in (318). In Nend, by contrast, the negative construction is a true circumfix, being formed by "prefixing and suffixing" the negative morpheme to the verb (K. Harris 1990: 122).

Mand
(318) *Api yar na-g **mɨ**=kamap ji-**m.***
 1SG 1SG.OBJ ND-NOM **NEG**=appear stay-**NEG**
 'This (i.e., my beard) hadn't appeared on me (yet).'

Manat is similar in that verbs are negated with two morphemes. The first is the particle *ma*, which precedes the verb but is not phonologically bound to it. The second is the contrastive suffix *-ip*, which follows all other verb suffixes (319).

Manat
(319) *Vana=k **ma** vupar-itiha-nad-**ip.***
 speech=ACC **NEG** push-FFUT-2SG-**CTR**
 'You won't be disobedient (lit. 'push speech').'

In Apalɨ the negative marker is considered a separate word (Wade p.c.), although it sometimes undergoes phonological merging with an upcoming *i*. For example, when negating *iga-* 'see,' as in (320), the *a* in *ma* and the vowel from the verb are often merged to *e*. Thus *ma igadami* here can be pronounced *megadami*.

Apalɨ
(320) *Iauacaŋ ia-dɨ aga-ŋ nɨbu sɨmɨŋ **ma** iga-da-m-i.*
 grandfather 1SG-OBL DEF-NOM 3SG.NOM food **NEG** see-CONT-HPST-3SG
 'My grandfather, he used to not see food.' (Wade n.d.b)

Apalɨ is also interesting because a negative suffix *-maŋ* can optionally occur at the end of the verb, in lieu of any TAM or agreement suffixes (321). Because Apalɨ occasionally adds final ŋ to words that did not have it in Proto-Sogeram, this form may be a reflex of *ma, but that is not certain. This construction is less common than the alternative (Wade 1989: 171).

Apalɨ
(321) *Viaŋ   lamigaŋ hivi **ma**   igi-**maŋ**.*
       1SG.NOM eye   LI   **NEG** see-**NEG**
       'I didn't see it with (my) eyes.'   (Wade 1989: 159)

Sweeney (n.d.) glosses the Mum negative morpheme as a prefix. This choice may be due to the process of epenthetic ŋ-insertion that he describes in his paper on Mum phonology (Sweeney 1994a: 27). This epenthesis occurs when *ma-* is prefixed to an *a*-initial root like *aba-* 'tell' (322).

Mum
(322) *Nuŋad   pihu-yɨ   **maŋ**-aba-m-i.*
       3SG.POSS place-LOC **NEG**-tell-HPST-3SG
       'He did not tell his village.'   (Sweeney n.d.)

In Sirva only the negative particle *ma* is used in negation, and it is placed to the left of the verb.

The Aisian languages are an interesting case because they put the negative particle *ma* in different places: in Magɨ it precedes the verb (323) while in Aisi it follows it (324).

Magɨ
(323) *Nu   **ma**   ye-i,   yɨ   nɨdiŋ   **ma**   ir-iŋ.*
       3SG **NEG**   come-3SG.IPST   1SG   3SG.OBJ **NEG**   perceive-1SG.IPST
       'He didn't come, and I didn't see him.'   Elicited

Aisi
(324) *Yaŋ   ab-oŋ   **ma**.*
       1SG.OBJ talk-3PL.IPST **NEG**
       'They didn't tell me.'

It seems that the best explanation for this variation between closely related languages is to posit a recent innovation in Aisi. There is no evidence for postverbal *ma* in Magɨ, but there is evidence, from medial verb negation, that Aisi used to have preverbal *ma*. Medial verbs are rarely negated, especially in texts, but when they are *ma* comes before the verb it negates, as in (325). Note that in this example, *sab* 'work' is a noun and *ma* is negating *iti* 'get and'.

(325)   Aisi
*Nu sab **ma** iti   kitiŋ, nu sikibyaŋ n-iber   ma.*
3SG work **NEG** get.SS and 3SG food   eat-3SG.FUT NEG
'(If) s/he doesn't work (lit. 'get work'), s/he won't eat.'   Elicited

In Kursav, as in Aisi, the negative particle *ma* follows the verb (326), while in Gants, as in Sirva, it precedes it (327).

(326)   Kursav
*Nin ripa-da dai-d-o   **ma.***
3PL fear-SS walk-HAB-3PL **NEG**
'They were afraid and they wouldn't go (anywhere).'

(327)   Gants
*Nagi koimo **ma** ci-paŋ-dik.*
basket SPEC **NEG** stay-FUT-3SG
'One basket won't be there.'

The reconstruction of the Proto-Sogeram verbal negator *ma is thus quite secure both phonologically and semantically. But the reconstruction of the negative verb construction is somewhat more difficult, as reflexes of *ma are found on either side of the verb in modern languages. To review, the negative morpheme is found bracketing the verb in Mand, Nend, and optionally in Apalɨ. It is found on the left in Manat, Apalɨ, Mum, Sirva, Magɨ, Gants, and in Aisi medial clauses. And it is found on the right in Aisi final clauses and in Kursav.

Given this distribution, we clearly must reconstruct a *[ma V] construction, in which *ma preceded the verb. This order is found in every Sogeram language except Kursav. It is also found in many other Madang languages, for example with the Usan negator *me* (Reesink 1987: 275), the Waskia negator *me* (Ross and Paol 1978: 14), the Mauwake negator *me* (Berghäll 2006), the Kalam negator *ma=* (Pawley and Bulmer 2011: 50), and the Anamuxra negator *ma* (Ingram 2001).

The question remains, however, of what to do with the Sogeram reflexes that occur to the right of the verb. These are numerous enough—occurring in Mand, Nend, Apalɨ, Aisi, and Kursav—that we must at least consider reconstructing such a construction to Proto-Sogeram. However, the reflexes are not uniform. In Aisi and Kursav the reflex of *ma occurs after an inflected verb (328). But in Mand, Nend, and Apalɨ, it occurs in place of any verbal inflection (329).

Aisi
(328) *Sikɨbeŋ panda n-er-iŋ* **ma.**
food alone eat-HAB-1SG **NEG**
'I don't eat alone.'

Nend
(329) *Am ndɨn unsa* **m-**eŋkwana-**m**.
2 3SG.OBJ yam **NEG**-give.food-**NEG**
'You did not give him food.' (K. Harris 1990: 122)

This means that we really have at least two constructions on our hands: the western type, [*ma* V-*ma*], and the eastern type, [V-INFL *ma*]. One can try to relate the two constructions to each other in this way: the western type may be descended from the negation of uninflected serial verbs, the eastern type from the negation of inflected final verbs. But this is unlikely, as the Apalɨ negative suffix does not attach to a reflex of the uninflected verb stem. Rather, it often triggers reduction of the preceding vowel to *ɨ*, as with *aba-* 'talk' in (330).

Apalɨ
(330) *Li-ci ciaŋ* **ma** *abɨ-***maŋ**.
do-3SG.DS talk **NEG** talk-**NEG**
'He did it and she did not talk.' (Wade n.d.b)

It seems, then, that these two constructions are not related to each other—at least not closely. Given that, we cannot reconstruct postverbal *ma to Proto-Sogeram because neither the [*ma* V-*ma*] construction nor the [V-INFL *ma*] construction has a wide enough distribution on its own. The fact that postverbal *ma is found in every branch of the family, though, still calls for an explanation. The most likely account is that this is the outcome of parallel innovation. We know that negators often undergo cyclic renewal, with new negative constructions arising from erstwhile emphatic negative constructions (van der Auwera 2009). Postverbal *ma* thus probably originated as an emphatic variant of preverbal *ma. The patchy distribution of different kinds of postverbal *ma* throughout the family suggests several independent innovations, although of course it is also possible that *ma could be used postverbally at the Proto-Sogeram stage. But the syntactic facts and subgrouping distribution suggest separate innovations in Proto-Greater West Sogeram/Apalɨ, Aisi, and Kursav.

6.3.2 Interrogatives

Interrogative clauses can be divided into polar questions and content questions, which I discuss here in turn. Polar questions were formed with the interrogative enclitic *=bi. This morpheme, along with its question-marking function, can be reconstructed based on reflexes in Sirva (331), Magɨ (332), Aisi (333), and Kursav (334). Another reflex that is probably cognate is Gants *be* 'which'.

Sirva
(331) *Nu   kura suku=ñ   tagu-rama-bɨ-s-a   **bi?***
      ND.TOP man true=LI step-put-PL-FPST-3   Q
      'Did they come from real men?'

Magɨ
(332) *Narɨ   amur   ya-berar   **bi?***
      2PL   one.day.away   come-2PL.FUT   Q
      'Will you guys come tomorrow?'   Elicited

Aisi
(333) *Na   sab   si   way-aŋ   **be?***
      2SG   work BEN come-2SG.IPST   Q
      'Did you come for work?'

Kursav
(334) *Na-ra   soro   mo-marau   **be**   v-e.*
      2SG.POSS-k.o.sibling   COM   go-2PL.UFUT   Q   say-3SG.NFUT
      '"Will you and your younger brother go?" he asked.'

The phonological properties of this form are difficult to reconstruct. While the reconstruction of the initial *ᵇb (a voiceless prenasalized stop) is not in doubt, it is somewhat curious, since prenasalized stops did not occur word-initially in Proto-Sogeram. For this reason it is likely that *=bi was an enclitic that attached to the last element in the clause. This analysis would require positing that it debonded from its host and became an independent word, as it currently is in Sirva and the East Sogeram languages (335). This is not implausible, though; word-initial prenasalized stops now occur in all of these languages—in Sirva, for example, they were created by loss of initial *i (§3.3.2.4)—and once initial *ᵇb was allowed, it was much easier for *=bi to detach from its host.

Kursav
(335) Gwada mi rama-ra map, ka-ka sarua v-uar
slowly thought put-2PL.NFUT like MD-TOP work get-1PL.NFUT
be? Be?
Q Q
'Are we doing the work like you guys thought it out? Huh?'

Content questions were formed using specific question words. The word for 'who' was *ni (§5.2.6), and two other question words can also be reconstructed: the noun *ati 'what' and the demonstrative *aba=ñ [QD=LOC] 'where'. This form was composed of the interrogative demonstrative root *aba, which took regular demonstrative suffixes to form question words. Reflexes of *aba=ñ are found in Manat (336), Apalɨ (337), Sirva (338), Aisi (339), and Kursav (340), although it should be noted that the Aisi form *niba-niŋ* in (339) is somewhat problematic.

Manat
(336) Him-in **ba-i** añig-itih-in=a?
die-2SG.DS QD-SET dig-FFUT-1SG=EXCL
'(When) you die, where will I bury you?'

Apalɨ
(337) Ia-dɨ iamɨgali **ab-eŋ** ua-v-i ua-m-i.
1SG-OBL woman QD-LOC go-PL-3.IPST say-HPST-3SG
'"Where did my wives go?" he said.' (Wade 1989: 153)

Sirva
(338) Na **ab-i** ki-ri-na?
2SG QD-SET stay-TPST-2SG
'Where are you?' Elicited

Aisi
(339) Dɨbɨr ga-ku **nɨba-nɨŋ** w-i kɨn-i?
cucumber MD-NOM QD-LOC go-SS stay-3SG.IPST
'Where did that cucumber go?'

Kursav
(340) Anam **ba-n** n-o?
water QD-LOC eat-3PL.NFUT
'Where are they drinking beer (lit. 'water')?'

Unfortunately, while the root *aba can be securely reconstructed based on reflexes across the family, the only specific question word built on *aba that can be reconstructed is *aba=ñ 'where'. Presumably *aba could combine with other suffixes and enclitics, as it can in every language where it is retained. It is likely that it could also occur in an unaffixed form. But no single function, aside from locative *aba=ñ, is distributed widely enough throughout the family to warrant reconstruction. This is also true when we include Anamuxra in the analysis; the interrogative root there is *ab-*, but none of the suffixes it takes can be plausibly related to any Sogeram suffixes.

As regards the grammar of content questions, both *atɨ 'what' and *aba=ñ 'where' occur *in situ* in the clause in every daughter language. This is true of all Sogeram question words; they do not occur in any special focused position, but rather in the position that is appropriate to their part of speech and their role in the clause. This property can therefore be reconstructed for *atɨ and *aba=ñ.

6.3.3 Nonverbal predicates

No Sogeram language has a copula, so it is likely that Proto-Sogeram also lacked one. Nonverbal predicates were formed by simple juxtaposition. When the subject occurred with a demonstrative, that demonstrative took the topic/object suffix *-n (§5.3.5). This form marked sentence topics, in the sense described by Lambrecht (1994) and Chafe (1976), of verbal predicates. So nonverbal predicates are best understood as consisting of a topic constituent, marked by *-n, plus a predicate constituent. The topic was the notional subject, but nonverbal predicates did not contain syntactic subjects—that is, no constituent of a nonverbal predicate occupied the same structural position as the subject of an intransitive verbal predicate.

Reflexes of *-n marking the notional subjects of nonverbal predicates are found in Mand (341), Nend (342), Manat (343), and Apalɨ (344). In Aisi a nominative demonstrative suffix has been innovated and is normally used for the subjects of nonverbal predicates. But the reflex of *-n, the topic suffix -oŋ, is also occasionally used, particularly when the subject of a nonverbal predicate is a subordinate clause (345).

Mand
(341) Aca **na-n** uja aca ar.
woman **ND-ACC** who woman QUOT
'"What woman is this (lit. 'This woman is what woman')?" he said.'

Nend
(342) Anta **ha-n** mbikɨr.
jungle **MD-ACC** 3S.OBL
'That jungle is his.' (K. Harris n.d.)

Manat
(343) **Inɨ-n** mav.
ND-ACC loincloth
'This is a loincloth.'

Apalɨ
(344) **Na-n** sɨbɨlɨ u-i.
ND-ILOC bad say-3SG.IPST
'"This one here is bad," he said.' (Wade 1989: 129)

Aisi
(345) Ya ika=ra kr-ɨbɨŋ **g-oŋ** urunda.
1SG father.1.POSS=COM walk-1SG.CTRF **MD-TOP** good
'If I walked around with my father, it'd be good.' Elicited

As the examples above illustrate, the predicate constituent of nonverbal predicates was not normally marked for case. It seems that at least nouns, adjectives, and possessive pronouns could serve as nonverbal predicates. The examples above also illustrate that the predicates themselves were not marked for TAM. Occasionally, though, it would be desirable to specify verbal categories such as tense or switch reference, and in these situations speakers could use the verb *kiña 'stay' to carry verbal morphology. Reflexes of this construction can be found in Mand (346), Manat (347), Sirva (348), Aisi (349), and Kursav (350). (Note that in Sirva, this construction is only found when nonverbal clauses occur in medial position.)

Mand
(346) Mac abɨ dɨh mɨrɨmɨŋ **jɨ-n.**
enough 2 COMPL old.person **stay-2SG.IPST**
'That's it, you're an old person now.'

Manat
(347) Na vana inɨ-gɨm=ɨk mɨŋatam-ɨtɨha-nad=ɨk, a, nɨ
and speech ND-ADJZ=ACC hear-FFUT-2SG=ACC ah 2SG.ACC

urum ibɨd   **ñ-itiha-nad=a.**
man   good   stay-FFUT-2SG=EXCL
'And if you'll listen to this kind of talk, oh, you'll be a good man.'

Sirva
(348) Niŋ   uhuvar be   mur   **ki-i,**   o,   mi   tama-s-a.
      3SG.POSS door   3SG open stay-3SG.DS   oh   thought put-FPST-3SG
      'His door was open and he thought, "Oh".'

Aisi
(349) Ya   mandɨ   ga-niŋ   animini   **kin-ikiŋ,**   ika   yama
      1SG COMPL   MD-LOC   small   stay-1SG.DS   father.1.POSS   mother.1.POSS
      yaka   yaŋ   ab-er-uŋ.
      1SG.POSS   1SG.OBJ   talk-HAB-3PL
      'Long ago when I was small, my parents used to talk to me.'

Kursav
(350) Ka-ka   gapɨra pakwit na   i-ka   pakwit nuai   **in-e.**
      MD-TOP   all   one   and   ND-TOP one   different stay-3SG.NFUT
      'All those are one (kind) and this one is different.'

It is possible that the verb *ada 'do' could also carry verbal morphology in this construction. This is only found in Sirva (351) and Kursav (352), but that distribution is wide enough to warrant reconstruction. In both languages the sense of this verb is inceptive as opposed to stative, so those semantics are also reconstructible: *ada 'do' meant 'become' while *kiña 'stay' meant 'be'.

Sirva
(351) Wa-ra~ra~ra~ra~ra   ña   be   mirada   **ad-a,**   kazɨr-a ...
      go-SS~CONT~CONT~CONT~CONT   child 3SG   big   do-SS   crawl-SS
      'That will continue and continue and the child will become big and crawl and ...'

Kursav
(352) Tar   nisikɨr   nuaya   **d-e.**
      tree   fruit   ripe   do-3SG.NFUT
      'The fruit is ripe now.'   Elicited

The negation of nonverbal predicates is accomplished in the same way in every daughter language: a negative word is placed at the end of the predicate. This construction can therefore be reconstructed to Proto-Sogeram, provided that the negative morpheme can be reconstructed. This task proves difficult, though. In order to begin we must be more precise about our subject matter, for in fact there are at least three ways nonverbal clauses are negated in Sogeram languages. The first is composed of a subject, a nonverbal predicate, and a negative word, as in (353); in this construction the predicate is negated.

Nend
(353) *Oram ha-n* **imbir mah.**
house MD-ACC **good none**
'The house is not good.' (K. Harris 1990: 113)

The second construction is composed of a subject and a negative word (354). In this construction the negative word *is* the nonverbal predicate, and it has an existential interpretation: the subject is asserted not to exist. This construction is often used with a preceding topic to assert that the topic does not have any of the subject (355).

Kursav
(354) *Guro* **kwe.**
speech **none**
'There's nothing to say (lit. 'there's no speech').'

Mand
(355) *Arhw miros* **mah.**
1PL food **none**
'We don't have food (lit. 'As for us, there is no food').'

The last construction is composed of a negative word by itself. In this construction the negative word replaces an entire clause, thus serving as a nonverbal clause on its own. This construction is used to negate the expected result of a preceding clause (356) or when one of a set of options is negated (357).

Manat
(356) *Miŋa-n=a, ŋagar-ura-s* **manat.**
get-2/3.SS=LNK shake-PL-3.DS **no**
'They took him and shook him, but no (i.e., he was dead).'

Aisi
(357) *Kwar=iŋ ab kram-beruŋ be* **mabiŋ?**
garden=LOC fire burn-3PL.FUT Q **no**
'Will they make a fire in the garden or not?'

Throughout the family, two primary negative words can be found. Both begin with *ma*, one following it with a velar consonant and the other with an alveolar one. I refer to them as the K-negative and the T-negative, respectively. Unfortunately, in neither case are the expected phonological correspondences found, so reconstruction is difficult for both words. The correspondence sets are given in Table 50; Aisi is not included because its single negative word, *mabiŋ*, does not appear to be descended from either the K-negative or the T-negative.

Table 50: Negative words.

	Mand	**Nend**	**Manat**	**Apalɨ**	**Mum**	**Sirva**	**Magɨ**	**Kursav**	**Gants**	**PSoG**
K-negative	mah	mah	makat	hɨma	manga		magɨ	kwe	maŋ	*maka
T-negative	mad	nend	manat			mana				*manat

The reconstructions offered in this table are very tentative, particularly *maka. Both forms are obviously related to the verbal negator *ma (§6.3.1), but it is unclear how since the material that follows *ma does not appear obviously verbal. In the case of the K-negative the velar element may be related to the verb *kɨña 'stay,' but there is little evidence for this. If it were related to *kɨña the reconstruction would probably have to be changed to *makɨ or even *ma kɨña, with two words. The latter possibility could potentially explain the Apalɨ form *hɨma*, which has apparently undergone metathesis.

When we evaluate the correspondences of the K-negative, we see several problems. The loss of final *a in the West Sogeram languages is expected (§3.2.1.2), but its retention in Manat is not. The West Sogeram languages also voiced *k irregularly. Manat has added final *t (or possibly final *at, if it did in fact lose final *a), presumably on analogy with the T-negative. Apalɨ has metathesized. Mum has added non-homorganic alveolar nasal. Magɨ shows regular final *a > ɨ, but has irregularly voiced *k > g (which is [ɣ] word-medially). Kursav is probably not cognate, and Gants has irregularly nasalized *k > ŋ.

Turning to the T-negative, Mand has lost the second *a and merged the nasal *n and the stop *t into a prenasalized stop *d*. Nend may have lost the initial syllable, raised *a > e, and nasalized *t > nd, or it may not be cognate. Manat is unchanged, and Sirva lost final *t. Based on the Mand, Manat, and Sirva reflexes, this is a more secure reconstruction than the K-negative.

Now that we have tentatively reconstructed these negative words, we can ask which of the three nonverbal negation functions each one fulfilled. In answering this question, though, we are presented with a difficulty. Although both the K-negative and the T-negative are well-distributed through the family, and can therefore be reconstructed, the variation between them is only retained in the three Greater West Sogeram (GWS) languages Mand, Nend, and Manat. In every other language one of the two negative words has taken over all functions. This means that we are on methodologically shaky ground. Whatever function we find for a negative word in the three western languages, we can also find in languages in the east, and might therefore reconstruct. But the fact that we find that function in the east is trivial, because any language which exhibits a given function for a given word exhibits *all* functions for that word. This means that eastern witnesses cannot offer data that bears meaningfully on the question. We are thus restricted to the three Greater West Sogeram languages, and our reconstructions do not therefore have a broad enough attestation to be secure. Nevertheless, I present those reconstructions here, for what they are worth.

The pro-clausal negation function is fulfilled by the T-negative in all three languages. This can be seen when negating the expected result of a previous clause, as in (358)–(360), and when negating an alternative, as in (361)–(363). Note that in (358) and (360) a reflex of *kiña 'stay' is hosting verbal morphology, as discussed above. Note also that when the T-negative negates the expected result of a previous clause, the previous clause bears different-subject morphology in all three languages. This is also true in the rest of the family, so the use of different-subject morphology in this construction probably dates to Proto-Sogeram.

Mand
(358) Ku-c **mad** ji-c api sag uram=in ai-ri-n.
see-DS **no** stay-DS 1SG again house=LOC come-FPST-1SG
'I looked and no (i.e., it wasn't there), and I came back home.'

Nend
(359) Ng-am-e Raphael oreŋgi-ŋ oreŋgi-ŋ oreŋgi-ŋ, **nend.**
descend-put-SS Raphael call-1SG.DS call-1SG.DS call-1SG.DS **no**
'I put (it there) and called and called and called Raphael, but no.'
(K. Harris 1990: 113)

Manat
(360) O tri-s **manat** ñi-ma-g.
oh pull-3SG.DS **no** stay-PST-3SG.FAR
'Oh, they pulled but they couldn't (pull it down).'

Mand
(361) Borbed na-n abi ja-ŋara-n oh **mad** ar.
possum ND-ACC 2 eat-FUT-2SG Q **no** QUOT
'"Will you eat this possum or not?" she asked.'

Nend
(362) *Mbɨ marivay eka-ndara-mg-i=oh* **nend**=*oh?*
   3   dance   slice-FUT-PL-3=Q **no**=Q
   'Are they going to dance or not?' (K. Harris 1990: 113)

Manat
(363) *Mina ka-b   prihar-itrak-id o   **manat** akad   ara-rat-ur-id.*
   pig   MD-NOM flee-IFUT-3SG   or   **no**   maybe   say-HAB-PL-3
   '"Will a pig run out or not?" they say.'

The negative existential function is performed by the K-negative in Mand (364), Nend (365), and Manat (366), suggesting that it was also performed by the K-negative in Proto-Sogeram.

Mand
(364) *Pai   ota   **mah.***
   fire branch **none**
   'There's no firewood.'

Nend
(365) *Nzɨ   cokay   **mah.***
   1SG   tobacco **none**
   'I don't have any tobacco.' (K. Harris 1990: 113)

Manat
(366) *Nɨ   map   asi   **makat.***
   2SG.ACC   head   knowledge   **none**
   'You don't have any head knowledge (i.e., you're dumb).'

When it comes to the negation of nonverbal predicates, though, Mand, Nend, and Manat diverge. In Mand (367) and Nend (368) this is done by the K-negative; in Manat it is the T-negative (369).

Mand
(367) *Ya   adu   **ohra mah,** k-ip   ac.*
   speech   1SG.POSS   **big   none** FD-EXST   FOC
   'My talk isn't big, it's just like that.'

Nend
(368) *Oram ha-n* **imbir mah.**
house MD-ACC **good none**
'The house is not good.' (K. Harris 1990: 113)

Manat
(369) *Maŋa=k* **arumad manat** *tak=a.*
ground=ACC **big.PRED no** only=EXCL
'There just isn't much land (lit. 'the ground just isn't big').'

When the three witnesses in the west disagree and we have no meaningful witnesses in the east, reconstruction is all but impossible. Nevertheless, I very tentatively reconstruct the K-negative for this function, because of some speculation involving Aisi and Kursav. These two languages have dedicated nonverbal negators for the two functions described above. But for the negation of nonverbal predicates, both languages employ the verbal negator *ma*, as illustrated in (370) and (371).

Aisi
(370) *Ya* **mokim kuru ma.**
1SG **greed man NEG**
'I'm not a greedy man.'

Kursav
(371) *Ya* **kura agidem ma.**
1SG **man good NEG**
'I'm not a good man.'

Recall that the Gants nonverbal negator is *maŋ* (372), which may be descended from the K-negative.

Gants
(372) *Ko pe maŋ.*
DEF **pig no**
'That's not a pig.'

Recall also that Aisian and Kursav commonly lost word-final nasals (§3.4.1.2). If the negator *maŋ* dates to Proto-East Sogeram, Aisian and Kursav *ma* may actually be reflexes of the Proto-East Sogeram nonverbal negator *maŋ, not the verbal negator *ma. And *maŋ may itself have been a reflex of the Proto-Sogeram K-negative

*maka. This scenario has the virtue of accounting for the fact that the verbal negator is negating nonverbal predicates in Aisian and Kursav, which is unexpected, and the fact that it occurs after the predicate, which is also unexpected. But it remains quite a speculative explanation, and it is probably better to say that we do not know how nonverbal predicates were negated in Proto-Sogeram.

6.4 Clause combining

Three complex constructions can be reconstructed for Proto-Sogeram. The first of these is switch reference, which is widespread in Trans New Guinea languages (Roberts 1997; Foley 2000, 2018, Pawley and Hammarström 2018) and which is securely reconstructed to Proto-Sogeram by the fact that the associated morphology can be reconstructed. The second is a kind of subordination in which a clause, or clause chain, was subordinated by a following demonstrative and functioned as a noun phrase in a matrix clause. The last is quoted speech, which can also be considered complex. I discuss these constructions in the three following sections.

6.4.1 Switch reference

A switch reference system can be securely reconstructed to Proto-Sogeram by virtue of the fact that switch reference morphology can be reconstructed. In §4.4.2 and §4.3.10 I argue for the reconstruction of a realis and an irrealis paradigm of different-subject suffixes, and in §4.4.1 I argue for the reconstruction of two same-subject suffixes. The different-subject paradigms are presented in Table 51 and Table 52. The same-subject suffixes were *-i 'same-subject sequential,' which indicated that the action of the marked verb and the following verb were sequential, and *-ta 'same-subject delayed,' which indicated that an interval of time elapsed between the event of the marked verb and the event of the following verb.

Table 51: PSog different-subject irrealis.

	SG	PL
first person	*-it-iŋ	*-it-riŋ
second person	*-it-na	*-it-ra
third person	*-it-i	

Switch reference marking works the same way in every Sogeram language, and we can therefore infer that it was the same in Proto-Sogeram. Clause chains were

Table 52: PSOG different-subject realis.

	SG	PL
first person	*-ɨk-in	*-ɨka-rɨŋ
second person	*-ɨka-na	*-ɨka-ra
third person	*-ɨk-i	

formed consisting of medial clauses—that is, clauses headed by verbs bearing medial switch reference suffixes—and these chains ended in a final clause, one with a verb that was marked for TAM. The TAM information from the final clause had scope over the whole chain.

Switch reference marking functioned as follows. The suffix on each medial verb indicated whether the subject of that verb was the same as, or different from, the subject of the verb of the following clause. When the subject of the following verb was the same, the same-subject suffix did not mark person information. Same-subject marking did, however, distinguish between chains of events that were close together temporally (with the sequential marker *-i) and chains of events that were broken up by longer periods of time (with the delayed marker *-ta). When the subject of the following verb was different, the switch-reference marker indexed the person and number of its own subject. It also indicated the realis status of the clause chain it was in: chains that ended in a realis TAM category used the realis switch-reference suffixes, while chains that ended in an irrealis TAM category used the irrealis set. It is not possible to reconstruct exactly which TAM categories were considered realis or irrealis for this purpose in Proto-Sogeram, but it is likely that the immediate past, the other past tenses, and the habitual aspect were realis, while the imperative, prohibitive, counterfactual, and irrealis moods were irrealis. How the future tense was treated is unknown. In addition, different-subject markers distinguished sequential events, which were unmarked, from simultaneous events, which were marked by reduplicating the verb bearing the different-subject marker.

These conclusions about the Proto-Sogeram switch reference system can be reached via simple morphological reconstruction. In other words, all that is necessary is to reconstruct the different pieces of switch reference morphology and their meanings. More abstract questions are more difficult to answer. Two questions that are commonly asked about Papuan switch reference systems are, How do they handle situations of partial subject overlap? And, what exactly does the system track? The first question cannot yet be answered for Proto-Sogeram, as I have not conducted targeted elicitation on this question and the data available from texts is insufficient.

The second question is more answerable, but the answer is unfortunately rather vague. Papuan switch reference systems vary considerably in terms of what they track. Some track a very syntactically defined category of subject; others track more semantic notions like agent or discourse-oriented notions like topic. This range of variation can be conceived of as a continuum, with wholly syntactic systems on one end and wholly pragmatic systems on the other. (This is something of an oversimplification, since in reality there is more than one dimension of variation among switch reference systems.) All that can be said about Proto-Sogeram is that it probably existed closer to the syntactic end of that continuum. The grammatical subject plays a prominent role in the switch reference system of every Sogeram language, and it is possible to find examples in every language where the system tracks the subject even when subject, topic, and agent diverge. But every language also allows exceptions, including the most exclusively subject-tracking language, Manat. Unfortunately, these exceptions are not consistent. For example, topic plays an important role in Aisi switch reference, while in Sirva the notion of control is more relevant. For this reason the exceptions cannot be reconstructed to Proto-Sogeram, and we must content ourselves with the vague conclusion that Proto-Sogeram was probably a relatively strict, but not completely strict, subject-tracking language.

6.4.2 Clause chain nominalization

The Sogeram languages possess a subordination construction in which a clause, or clause chain, is nominalized by placing a demonstrative or some other piece of nominal morphology after it. This subordinate clause chain then serves as a noun phrase in the matrix clause. While the details of this construction vary somewhat from language to language, the general properties just outlined are found throughout the family. In this section I argue that such a subordination construction should be reconstructed for Proto-Sogeram (I also discuss this reconstruction in Daniels 2017a).

I begin by reconstructing the form of this construction that involved the topic/object suffix *-n (§5.3.5). Recall that this case suffix occurred on demonstratives and indicated that their noun phrase occurred either in topic position or object position of the clause. The topic-marking function of subordinators in *-n can be seen in the Mand (373), Nend (374), Manat (375), and Aisi (376) examples below.

      Mand
(373) [P=ahw p-id   ] na-n,   p=ahw uci   pi-ŋarid?
      3=FOC   write-IPST ND-ACC 3=FOC what take-FUT
      'What's he going to do with what he wrote?'

Nend

(374) [Ar ha-n ereri-mandɨ-rɨŋ] ha-n, ohɨra ka mah ñ-i.
1PL MD-ACC leave-HPST-1PL MD-ACC large big NEG stay-3SG.IPST
'Because we abandoned this, it is not very big.' (K. Harris n.d.)

Manat

(375) [Azɨ=k ini-n ram-in] ini-n, arum hava ka-barad.
decoration=ACC ND-ACC put-1SG.IPST ND-ACC big group MD-POSS.PL
'This decoration that I'm wearing here is our ancestors'.'

Aisi

(376) [Ya iti w-ir-iŋ] g-oŋ, maket tam-er-iŋ ma.
1SG get.SS come-HAB-1SG MD-TOP market put-HAB-1SG NEG
'I bring them, but I don't put them in the market (i.e., sell them).'

Similarly, the object-marking function of these subordinators is found in the same languages: Mand (377), Nend (378), Manat (379), and Aisi (380).

Mand

(377) [Ukɨ iveri-ŋ=an] ka-n ku-n?
drum hit-PURP=very FD-ACC see-2SG.IPST
'Do you see me beating the drum?' Elicited

Nend

(378) [Awaz ŋg-amɨ~ndam-in] ha-n kɨr-in.
betelnut descend-put~TPST-1SG MD-ACC look.for-1SG.IPST
'I am looking for the betelnut I put (here).' (K. Harris 1990: 148)

Manat

(379) [Ɲar-in] ka-n mɨɲatama-nad ag?
speak-1SG.IPST MD-ACC hear-2SG.IPST FOC
'Did you hear what I said?'

Aisi

(380) [Kwar na-niŋ ayak=ra kon-eŋ] g-oŋ, mandɨ n-eŋ.
garden ND-LOC what=COM plant-1SG.IPST MD-TOP COMPL eat-1SG.IPST
'However many gardens I've planted here, I've eaten.'

Based on these witnesses, we can reconstruct the construction *[S DEM-n], which functioned syntactically as a topic/object noun phrase. Semantically, the construction referred to some salient aspect of the subordinate clause, such as its object (378) or the event it describes (374).

Demonstratives with the locative enclitic *=ñ (§5.3.6) can also serve as subordinators. This construction is found in Apalɨ (381), Mum (382), Sirva (383), and Kursav (384).

Apalɨ
(381) Viaŋ   [haca mav-av-i] n-eŋ   ala   ve-iem-in.
      1SG.NOM hole dig-PL-3.IPST ND-LOC FOC come-TPST-1SG
      'It was here where they dug a hole that I came.'   (Wade 1989: 21)

Mum
(382) Yahu-m-i   da-ñ [pina   mu   kaha-m-i   ] da-ñ.
      go.up-HPST-3SG FD-LI platform another fasten-HPST-3SG FD-LI
      'He went up over there to where he had fastened the platform.'

Sirva
(383) [Nɨ-mɨ   kɨ-s-a   ] k-i   tama-s-a.
      3.POSS-mother stay-FPST-3SG   MD-SET put-FPST-3SG
      'He put it where his mother was.'

Kursav
(384) [Nan vuruva in-uara   ] i-ka-n,   ya   ramɨra-da ve-md-ua.
      2PL   village stay-2PL.NFUT   ND-TOP-LOC 1SG return-SS come-FUT-1SG
      'I'll come back to the village you guys live in.'   Elicited

Additionally, the Aisian locative demonstrative suffix -niŋ, which may be composed of topic/object *-n plus the locative enclitic *=ñ, can also occur in this construction (385). (Note that *=ñ was an enclitic that attached to noun phrases—either to the demonstrative at the end, or to something else if the noun phrase lacked a demonstrative. But only the *DEM=ñ combination functioned as a subordinator, not *=ñ by itself.)

Magɨ
(385) Naŋgari, yɨ   asad   mu   uku-byaŋ,   [mandɨ yabɨ
      now   1SG   story SPEC tell-1SG.FUT   before 1SG.EMPH
      kɨ-t-eŋ   ] ka-niŋ.
      stay-HAB-1SG   MD-LOC
      'Now, I'll tell a story, about where I used to live.'

These reflexes support reconstructing a construction *[S DEM=ñ], which functioned syntactically as a locative noun phrase and which referred to a salient aspect of its subordinate clause.

Finally, reflexes of the unaffixed middle demonstrative *ka (§5.3.2) also appear in this construction in Apalɨ (386), Sirva (387), Aisi (388), Kursav (389), and Gants (390). It seems that the Mum bare middle demonstrative can also fulfill this function, although (391) is not perfectly understood.

Apalɨ
(386) [Na   nubu   magɨ mugu-la-lɨ   ] ha
      ND.TOP   3SG.NOM   egg   move.down.go-HAB-3SG.FPST   MD.TOP
      lamakɨŋ   haca   hɨvɨ mugu-la-lɨ.
      palm.sp   hole   LI   move.down.go-HAB-3SG.FPST
      'Now, as for when (or 'Now given that') he habitually lays eggs,
      he habitually lays eggs in the hole of the *lamakɨŋ* palm.'   (Wade 1989: 22)

Sirva
(387) [U-rubɨ-s-a] ka,   kine   k-i   hasa   kɨzɨdɨ-s-a.
      go-PL-FPST-3   MD.TOP near   MD-SET   FOC   evening-FPST-3SG
      'They went, and very soon (lit. 'in a near place') it was evening.'

Aisi
(388) [Ya   gi   ika   yaka   kɨn-i   akɨ] ga,
      1SG   FOC   father.1.POSS 1SG.POSS   stay-3SG.IPST maybe TOP
      ga-rɨb   kr-ɨbɨŋ.
      MD-ADJZ   walk-1SG.CTRF
      'If *my* father were alive, I'd walk around like that (too).'

Kursav
(389) [Rainim   d-ua   ] ka   ruk-uana?
      line.up do-1SG.NFUT   MD   see-2SG.NFUT
      'Do you see the ones I've lined up?'

Gants
(390) [Ped   mɨŋɨ-da yig   adɨ-m-ek   ] ko,   kada   cɨ-m-ek
      paint   take-SS festival   do-FPST-3SG   DEF   thus   stay-FPST-3SG
      'The paint he had taken and decorated himself with was right there.'

Mum
(391) [Nu   mubu   sih   mɨŋa-h-u~hu   yɨvuraha-ta
      3SG   tanget.leaf   design take-DS-3PL~SIM   arrive-SS

> *nagwinagwi-ti-m-i*] *ka va-ta-ti-h-u* *miŋamiŋarama-ta* ...
> motion.with.head-do-HPST-3SG MD say-SS-do-DS-3PL follow-SS
> 'They thought back to when they were working with the tanget
> leaves and the men motioned to them. They were following
> this line of talk and ...' (Sweeney n.d.)

Again we can reconstruct a subordination construction based on these witnesses: *[S *ka*]. And again it had the syntactic property that it served as a typical noun phrase marked by *ka—that is, as a topic-fronted noun phrase—and the semantic property that it referred to a salient aspect of the subordinate clause.

So we have reconstructed three subordination constructions, which are represented schematically in (392).

(392) a. *[S DEM-*n*] Syntax: noun phrase in topic or object position
    Semantics: pragmatically salient aspect of S
  b. *[S DEM=*ñ*] Syntax: locative noun phrase
    Semantics: pragmatically salient aspect of S
  c. *[S *ka*] Syntax: left-peripheral topic noun phrase
    Semantics: pragmatically salient aspect of S

All of these constructions, like their modern reflexes, referred to some aspect of the subordinate clause. This could be a participant in the action of the clause, the setting of the clause, or the event of the clause. The referent was determined pragmatically; it was not marked in any way. This is a general property of these subordination constructions that is nicely illustrated by the pair of Sirva subordinate clauses given below.

> Sirva
> (393) [*Ni-mɨ*   *kɨ-s-a*   ] *k-i*   *tama-s-a.*
> 3.POSS-mother stay-FPST-3SG MD-SET put-FPST-3SG
> 'He put it where his mother was.'

> Sirva
> (394) [*Aba-s-a*] *k-i*   *tagu-rama-s-a.*
> talk-FPST-3SG MD-SET step-put-FPST-3SG
> 'She stood in the place he had talked about.'

Example (393) contains a clause subordinated by a setting demonstrative which serves a locative function in the matrix clause. The subordinate clause refers to the location of its event. Example (394) is structurally identical, but it does not refer to the location of its event—it doesn't mean 'she stood in the place where he spoke'. Rather, in the context of the story that it is found in, a pragmatically more sensible interpretation is 'she stood in the place he had talked about', and that is what it meant.

These three reconstructed constructions thus share several formal, syntactic, and semantic properties and were clearly related to each other in the grammar of Proto-Sogeram. Because we know that constructions are organized in default inheritance hierarchies in speakers' memories, we can generalize over these commonalities and propose a parent construction that accounts for all three:

(395) *[S DEM=CASE] Syntax: noun phrase with function CASE
                    Semantics: pragmatically salient aspect of S

This construction, like its daughters, was composed of a subordinate clause, a demonstrative, and some case suffix. It had the syntactic property that it formed a noun phrase of case CASE, and functioned as such in a matrix clause. Semantically, it had the property of referring to a salient aspect of S.

A natural question to ask about this reconstructed construction is how productive it was. Could any demonstrative category function as a subordinator? Could case enclitics subordinate clauses without demonstrative roots? In attempting to answer these questions we run into methodological issues. To illustrate, consider the case of the focus demonstrative suffix *-kw. This form has reflexes in Mand and Aisian. In Mand, it does not function as a subordinator (at least not in my data; I have not conducted elicitation on this question). In Aisian it does, as (396) shows.

Aisi
(396) [Na   tam-aŋ   ] ga-ku   mugram-e.
      2SG   put-2SG.IPST   MD-NOM   fit-3SG.IPST
      'What you put on fits.'

The data can be interpreted in two ways: either *-kw could subordinate in Proto-Sogeram, and this function has been lost in Mand; or *-kw did not subordinate in Proto-Sogeram, and this function was innovated in Proto-Aisian. Either scenario is plausible, so based on our current data we cannot propose a reconstruction.

We are faced with a similar situation when we attempt to decide whether case enclitics could subordinate clauses on their own, without demonstratives. The accusative enclitic *=ŋ and the oblique enclitic *=d both occurred on pronouns and some noun phrases, so it is reasonable to suppose they may have also functioned as subordinators. And there is evidence for this in Manat and Gants. In both of these languages, several Proto-Sogeram verbal paradigms are found with an additional consonant at the end. In Manat, this consonant is *d*, while in Gants it is often *ŋ*. Examples (397) and (398) illustrate how these consonants have accreted onto the Proto-Sogeram 2SG immediate past suffix *-na.

Manat
(397) Mina=k=a,   **ruku-nad**   ag?
pig=ACC=LNK   **see-2SG.IPST**   FOC
"Have you seen any pigs?"

Gants
(398) Tworp   okrok   stret   ai-niŋ   ko   **ga-naŋ?**
twelve o'clock exactly come-1SG.IPST   DEF   **perceive-2SG.IPST**
'Did you see that I came right at noon?'

There is no trace of oblique meaning in Manat -*nad*, nor any trace of accusative meaning in Gants -*naŋ*. Yet these consonants must have come from somewhere, and a likely explanation is that they come from an old subordinating construction that has undergone insubordination and lost its matrix clause (per Evans 2007; Evans and Watanabe 2016). On the other hand, there is no trace of such a construction in any other Sogeram language, even where the enclitics survive. That is, the enclitic =*ŋ* cannot subordinate clauses in Mum or Aisi, and the enclitic =*d* cannot subordinate clauses in Mand or Apalɨ. We are thus faced with the same problem as with *-kw. Either *=d and *=ŋ could not subordinate clauses in Proto-Sogeram and we are seeing an increase in productivity in Manat and Gants, or they could subordinate and we are seeing a loss of productivity in the other Sogeram languages. As before, there is no clear way to decide which scenario is the more plausible. In this case, though, we can invoke the "majority rules" principle. Reflexes of *=d and *=ŋ are found with (vestiges of) subordinating functions in only one language each, while they are found without those functions in multiple languages. It is therefore preferable to say that these enclitics could not serve as subordinators on their own, but rather that these functions developed later in Manat and Gants, and then those constructions underwent insubordination.

We can thus reconstruct the subordination construction *[S DEM=CASE] (in which case was sometimes marked by a demonstrative suffix and sometimes by a case enclitic) which referred to some aspect of S and which served as a noun phrase in a matrix clause. We can also reconstruct at least three demonstratives that could instantiate the construction. It remains beyond our capacity, though, to demarcate precisely the construction's productivity—what demonstratives and other nominal morphology it could contain—but its general properties remain secure nevertheless.

6.4.3 Quoted speech

Quoted speech does not contain special morphological marking in any Sogeram language to distinguish the quotation from the surrounding material. Rather, the quotation is usually marked on the edges. The beginning of a quotation is marked by a pre-quote verb, like the Manat verb *ŋara-* in (399). The end of a quotation is marked either by a post-quote verb like Sirva *va-* in (400), or a quotative particle like Aisi *kwe* in (401).

Manat
(399) *Ni-min-ib*   *ŋara-ma-g.*   *Mina=k=a,*   *ruku-nad*   *ag?*
3.POSS-mother-NOM **speak-PST-3SG.FAR** pig=ACC=LNK see-2SG.IPST FOC
'His mother spoke. "Have you seen any pigs?"'

Sirva
(400) *Aku-dagra*   *v-ii,*   *aku-dagra*   *va-bi-s-a.*
sleep-1PL.IRR **say-3SG.DS** sleep-1PL.IRR **say-PL-FPST-3**
'"Let's sleep," she said, and they said, "Let's sleep".'

Aisi
(401) *Ga-rib*   *ar-i*   *ga,*   *ni-sim*   *ab-e.*   *Mai*   **kwe.**
MD-ADJZ do-SS TOP 3.POSS-brother talk-3SG.IPST friend **QUOT**
'It was like that, and the older brother said, "Friend," he said.'

Neither the pre-quote verb nor the post-quote material is required if it is clear that the quotation is a quotation, but both are common. The typical pattern is to begin a quotation with a single pre-quote verb and then to tag each quoted intonational unit with a post-quote marker, but stylistic variation is common.

Both a pre-quote verb and a post-quote verb can be reconstructed. The pre-quote verb was *aba 'speak,' and the post-quote verb was *wa- 'say,' which may have been a special sense of *wa 'go' (this polysemy is reminiscent of the way English *go* is colloquially used as a verb of speech). Reflexes of the two verbs in these functions can be seen in Apalɨ (402), Sirva (403), Kursav (404), and Gants (405).

Apali
(402) Li-ci **ab-in.** Ia-di iamigali sivi ahila
do-3SG.DS **talk-1SG.IPST** 1SG-OBL woman after on.own
ve-d-i **u-in.**
come-3SG.FUT **say-1SG.IPST**
'He did it and I talked. "My wife will come afterwords on her own,"
I said.   (Wade n.d.b)

Sirva
(403) G-ra **aba-s-a.** Mina **va-s-a.**
see-SS **talk-FPST-3SG** wait **say-FPST-3SG**
'He saw (that) and spoke. "Wait!" he said.'

Kursav
(404) **Ab-e,** ve-da ya sarim d-it-Ø ma **v-e.**
speak-3SG.NFUT come-SS 1SG sell do-IRR-1SG NEG **say-3SG.NFUT**
'He talks. "I'll come and I won't sell them," he says.'

Gants
(405) Jisas **aba-m-ek,** ya ai-paŋ-niŋ **wa-m-ek**
Jesus **speak-FPST-3SG** 1SG come-FUT-1SG **say-FPST-3SG**
'Jesus said, "I'll come".'

The grammatical machinery of quotation is also used in many Sogeram languages in what I call a desiderative construction. In these constructions, the desires or intentions of an agent are expressed as a quote in which those desires are stated in the first person. Each language uses a particular TAM category for this construction: for example, Manat uses the imperative (406), Sirva the irrealis (407), Aisi the future (408), and Kursav the imperative (409).

Manat
(406) Amid kai avih-itiŋ ar-ura-ma-g.
axe LI chop-1SG.IMP say-PL-PST-3.FAR
'They wanted to chop (him) with an axe'

Sirva
(407) Itu wi-ra, yakiv-ra u-dagra va-bi-s-a ka-ga mana.
tobacco smoke-SS get.up-SS go-1PL.IRR say-PL-FPST-3 MD-TOP no
'He smoked a cigarette, and they wanted to get up and go (lit. 'said, "let's get up and go"'), but alas.'

Aisi
(408) *Kris=iŋ   ir-ibyaŋ   aba   yoku-s-iŋ.*
       Chris=ACC perceive-1SG.FUT QUOT   go.up-FPST-1SG
       'I went up to see Chris (lit. 'I said, "I'll see Chris," and went up').'

Kursav
(409) *Sake   bin   ini-n   va-da   v-e.*
       three   LOC   stay-1SG.IMP   say-SS   come-3SG.NFUT
       'She wanted to be in (grade) three (lit. 'said, "Let me be in three"')
       and she came.'

The desiderative construction is instructive because even though it is widespread throughout the family, it *cannot* be reconstructed to Proto-Sogeram (Daniels 2017a). The examples above are from Manat, Sirva, Aisi, and Kursav—languages with a broad enough distribution that one would think the desiderative construction would be a secure reconstruction. This reconstruction might be proposed as †[[V-INFL$_{1.IRR}$] wa-INFL]. That is, a verb inflected for a first person irrealis verb category was followed by an inflected post-quote *wa 'say'. The meaning of this construction could be expressed as "the subject of *wa intends to perform the action of the other verb".

But in this case the morphology, crucially, is not cognate. In the examples above, Manat uses the imperative to mark the quoted verb, Sirva uses the irrealis, Aisi the future, and Kursav the imperative. Importantly, the Manat imperative suffixes are etymologically descended from the Proto-Sogeram irrealis (§4.3.10) while the Kursav forms are descended from the imperative (§4.3.7). And this is what we find throughout the family; every language uses a different verb category to mark the quoted material that expresses the desires or intentions of the agent. The categories are all semantically irrealis—future, imperative, irrealis, etc.—but this is quite natural given the semantic properties of the construction.

This, then, is exactly the sort of situation we would expect to find in cases of widespread syntactic borrowing. Many languages possess essentially the same construction, but they all fill it with different morphology. In this case the locus of difference is the suffix slot on the first verb. And because this morphology is not cognate, there is no convincing evidence that this construction occurred in Proto-Sogeram. It seems eminently possible that this construction was borrowed from language to language and that each borrowing language copied the donor language pattern but did so with its own morphology. Consequently, we simply cannot say whether the original construction existed in Proto-Sogeram or was created later.

Chapter 7
Lexical Reconstructions

In this chapter I present the 324 lexical forms that I have reconstructed for Proto-Sogeram (PSOG). Each entry is organized as follows:

*[reconstructed form] *[word class]* '[meaning]'
   GWS MND *[reflex]*
           NEN *[reflex]* (S)
           MNT *[reflex]*
           APA *[reflex]* (C), *[reflex]* (K)
   NS   MUM *[reflex]*
           SIR *[reflex]* '[innovative meaning]'
   ES   MAG *[reflex]*
           AIS *[reflex]*
           KUR *[reflex]* (PAIS)
           GAJ *[reflex]*
[Comments].

The language abbreviations are: MND – Mand, NEN – Nend, MNT – Manat, APA – Apalɨ, MUM – Mum, SIR – Sirva, MAG – Magɨ, AIS – Aisi, KUR – Kursav, and GAJ – Gants. Although Apalɨ's subgrouping position is ambiguous, it is grouped with the Greater West Sogeram (GWS) languages here. Where a language lacks a reflex, that language is omitted. For two languages, Nend and Apalɨ, dialect differences are occasionally relevant: Northern (N) and Southern (S) for Nend, and Akɨ (K) and Acɨ (C) for Apalɨ. Most of the reflexes given come from the Northern and Akɨ dialects, respectively, so reflexes from those dialects are not marked. When a reflex from the other dialect is given, that fact is indicated next to the form, as with Nend above. When reflexes from both dialects are given, both are marked, as with Apalɨ. Semantic innovations are indicated next to a given reflex, as illustrated with Sirva. Semantic retentions are not indicated. Suspected loanwords are indicated by giving the donor language in parentheses next to the reflex: in the example above, the Kursav reflex is marked as a suspected loan from Proto-Aisian (PAIS).

Due to the nature of the sound changes the Sogeram languages have undergone, it is occasionally possible to reconstruct a final nasal consonant but not its place of articulation. This is indicated by reconstructing a capital *N: *sabaN 'pig'. The word class can be reconstructed for most, but not all, Proto-Sogeram roots. When it can, it is given next to the form, using the following abbreviations: *adj.* adjective; *adv.* adverb; *n.* noun; *n.inal.* inalienably possessed noun; *phrs.*

phrase; *pro.* pronoun; *svc.* serial verb construction; *v.* verb; *vac.* verb adjunct construction. Some Proto-Sogeram verbs exhibited variation between an uninflected form and an inflected form, such as the verb for 'open,' which was *idua when uninflected and *idu- when inflected. In such cases I present the uninflected root first and the inflected root after a comma: *idua, idu-. Many verbs, such as *miga 'come down,' did not exhibit this variation and took the same shape whether inflected or not. These are presented with no hyphen on the right edge.

Unexpected phonological developments are mentioned in the comments. For space reasons, I do not explicitly state that they are unexpected; the presence of a comment such as "Mum changed *ŋ > n" indicates that this development is unexpected. Naturally, the reconstructions are not of uniform quality or reliability, but in general I have not attempted to provide my own evaluation of the reliability of each entry. Occasionally I do indicate that a form is particularly problematic, but in the main I allow readers to form their own judgments. The comments may also provide cross-references to other Proto-Sogeram forms that are related, either semantically or formally, to other Madang words that appear to be cognate, or to Proto-Trans New Guinea reconstructions. The sources for these cross-references are Ingram (2001, 2003) for Anamuxra, MacDonald (1990, 2013) for Tauya, Pawley (p. c.) and Pawley and Bulmer (2011) for Kalam, Pawley (1995, 2005, 2006b, 2012) for Proto-Trans New Guinea, and Reesink (1987) for Usan. I have made no attempt to make these cross-references systematic or exhaustive in any way.

When a reflex contains some non-cognate material, that material is placed in parentheses. For example, *ak(imin)* would indicate that *ak* is a reflex of the posited proto-form, but *imin* is not. When I can speculate as to the etymology of the non-cognate material, I do so in the comments; e.g., "Sirva compounded with *si* 'place'". The non-cognate material may be a synchronic form in that language, or it may be a reconstructed Proto-Sogeram proto-form.

In order to be considered a minimally reliable Proto-Sogeram reconstruction, I have required that a given etymon have reflexes in two of the three primary branches: Greater West Sogeram (composed of Mand, Nend, and Manat), North Sogeram (Mum and Sirva) and East Sogeram (Magɨ, Aisi, Kursav, and Gants). Because of the unusual subgrouping position of Apalɨ, I have decided that Apalɨ reflexes can only be paired with reflexes from Mand, Kursav, or Gants in order to warrant reconstruction. In applying the "two branches" criterion I have also excluded the following pairs of languages that have probably been in contact: Manat and Mum; Sirva and Magɨ; and Sirva and Aisi. This procedure is not foolproof; the least secure reconstructions that it endorses are probably those supported by witnesses in Mand and Apalɨ, which may only date to a late variety of Proto-Sogeram. But I hope that I have excluded most of the post-Proto-Sogeram borrowings from the cognate sets, and that the list will prove useful for future comparativists who attempt to delve deeper into the prehistory of Madang and Trans New Guinea. Only one form is included solely based on one Sogeram witness and one external witness: *yau 'fish'.

I have included a few lexicalized expressions that can be reconstructed to Proto-Sogeram. These include serial verb constructions (such as *ipa mɨga 'appear'), adjunct–verb constructions (*fɨr kama 'to dawn'), and one pair of an adjectival form and a noun (*mu kɨm 'a certain thing'). This employs the approach to lexicography modeled by, among others, Pawley and Bulmer (2011), which considers certain multi-word units lexemes in their own right. The reasoning that if these multi-word units were lexemes in the Proto-Sogeram speech community, then they were passed from generation to generation in the usual way and can therefore be reconstructed, follows naturally from this position (albeit with the caveat that forces such as analogy may interact differently with complex lexemes than with simplex ones).

I have excluded grammatical morphemes from the list, as they are presented more systematically in the Proto-Sogeram grammar sketch. The distinction between grammatical morphemes and lexical ones is, of course, fuzzy, and I have had to draw the line somewhat arbitrarily.

Finally, inalienably possessed nouns present unique challenges to reconstruction, and often require more discussion. For this reason I only give their phonological form in this section, and discuss them more fully in §7.2 below. Some inalienably possessed nouns had multiple suppletive roots, such as 'same-sex younger sibling,' which was *ñama for first person and *-ra for second and third person possessors. In such cases both roots are given in the list below, unless they are so similar that they would occur next to each other (like first person *midaŋ and non-first person *-mida 'cross cousin'). An English–Proto-Sogeram finderlist is provided in §7.3.

7.1 Proto-Sogeram lexemes

*aba v. 'speak'

	Apa	aba-
NS	Mum	aba-, ba-
	Sir	aba-
ES	Mag	ab-, aba 'QUOT'
	Ais	ab-, aba 'QUOT'
	Kur	aba
	Gaj	aba

The Aisian quotative particles descend from uninflected serialized forms.

*abi n.inal. 'wife'

NS	Mum	inaburi
ES	Mag	abi
	Ais	abi

See *-nabɨr 'wife'.

*abiŋ n. 'wing'

GWS	Mnd	apɨh
	Nen	mpiŋ
	Mnt	(v)ab
	Apa	abɨŋ

	NS	Mum	*abɨ*
		Sir	*abɨ*
	ES	Mag	*ambiŋ*
		Ais	*ambiŋ*

Proto-Aisian retained prenasalization in *mb.

*abɨta *n.* 'sleep'

| | GWS | Nen | *ampɨta* 'sleep dust' |
| | ES | Mag | *ambɨt* (ajt) |

Magɨ kept prenasalization in *mb. See *aku 'sleep'.

*abra *n.* 'place, area'

	GWS	Mnd	*apɨr* 'flatland'
		Nen	*ampɨra*
		Mnt	*abra*
		Apa	*abɨla*
	NS	Sir	*(s)abrɨ*
	ES	Mag	*ambra(kɨm)* 'village'
		Ais	*ambɨr* 'bed, area'
		Kur	*abre* 'below'

Sirva compounded with *si* 'place' and changed final *a > ɨ. Kursav raised final *a > e, possibly due to locative *=ñ. See *kayabra 'village' and *si 'place'.

*ada, adɨ- *v.* 'do'

	GWS	Mnd	*(ipañ) at-* 'spit'
		Mnt	*adɨ-* 'process (sago)'
	NS	Mum	*adɨ-*
		Sir	*adɨ-*
	ES	Mag	*ada, ar-*
		Ais	*ar-*
		Kur	*du, dɨ-*
		Gaj	*ada, adɨ-*

Mand combined with *ipañ* 'water'. Magɨ lenited *d > r in the inflected form. Kursav lost initial *a and changed the verb class of the uninflected form.

*af *n.* 'fire'

		Apa	*avɨŋ*
	NS	Mum	*awu* 'tree'
		Sir	*au*
	ES	Mag	*ab*
		Ais	*ab*
		Kur	*av*
		Gaj	*au(r)*

Apalɨ added *iŋ.

*afɨr *n.* 'air, wind'

	GWS	Mnt	*avɨr*
	NS	Mum	*avɨr* 'winded'
		Sir	*avrɨ*

May also have been *awɨr.

*agi *adv.* 'focus particle'

	GWS	Nen	*ag* 'also'
		Mnt	*ag*
		Apa	*ci* 'completive'
	NS	Sir	*agi* 'completive'
	ES	Mag	*gi*
		Ais	*gi*; *agi* 'alright'

Manat lost final *i. Apalɨ is problematic. Proto-Aisian lost initial *a.

*agu *n.* 'throat'

	GWS	Mnd	*aku(tɨr)*
		Apa	*agu(nigi)*
	NS	Sir	*ugu(pap)*
	ES	Mag	*ug(am)*
		Ais	*ug(am)*

7.1 Proto-Sogeram lexemes

  Kur *agu*
  Gaj *og*
Sirva and Proto-Aisian changed initial *a > *u*. Gants is problematic.

*agwa *v.* 'cry out'
 GWS Nen *aŋkwa-* 'call out'
 NS Sir *agwa-* 'yell (involuntarily)'
This referred to more involuntary yelling (e.g., in pain or laughter) than *ura 'call out'.

*akar *n.* 'chin'
 GWS Nen *kar* 'face'
 ES Mag *akar*
  Ais *akar* 'beard'
  Gaj *akar*

*akɨru *n.* 'sugar (*Saccharum officinarum*)'
  Apa *ahɨlu*
 ES Kur *akuru*

*aku *n.* 'sleep'
 GWS Mnt *ak(ɨmɨn)* 'dream (n.)'
 NS Mum *akw*
  Sir *au*; cf. *aku-* 'sleep (v.)'
 ES Kur *aku(sa)-* 'sleep (v.)'
Sirva lost *h. See *abɨta 'sleep'.

*akwra *v.* 'carry away'
 GWS Mnd *ahwro-* 'take away'
  Mnt *akɨru-* 'carry on shoulder'
  Apa *ahɨla-* 'gather'
 ES Gaj *akro* 'carry'
Apalɨ changed verb class and is semantically divergent.

*aman *n.* 'breast'
 GWS Mnd *aman*
  Apa *amaŋ*
 NS Mum *ama*
  Sir *ama*
 ES Mag *amɨ*
  Ais *amɨ*
  Kur *amɨna* (Tauya)
  Gaj *aman*
The expected Kursav reflex is †*ama* or †*aman*; the attested form may be borrowed from Tauya *amena*.

*amɨr *adv.* 'yesterday'
 GWS Mnd *abɨr* 'one day away'
  Nen *mɨr* 'one day away'
  Mnt *amɨ(ñ)*
  Apa *amɨli* 'one day away'
 NS Mum *am*
  Sir *amɨn*
Manat added locative *=ñ.
Sirva added final *n*. See *amur 'tomorrow'.

*amur *adv.* 'tomorrow'
 GWS Mnt *abr(us)*
 NS Mum *amu*
  Sir *amu, amu(s)*
 ES Mag *amur*
  Ais *amor*
  Kur *amar* 'yesterday,' *amar(te)* 'tomorrow'
  Gaj *amor* 'one day away'
See *amɨr 'yesterday'.

*añɨr *adv.* 'two days away'
 GWS Mnd *ajɨr*
  Nen *ñɨr*
  Mnt *añɨr(i)* 'day after tomorrow'

	NS	SIR	*añɨr*
	ES	MAG	*anɨr*
		AIS	*anɨr* 'day after tomorrow'
	GAJ		*añɨr*

Manat added locative *=ñ. Sirva fronted *ɨ > i.

*añɨkwriñ adv. 'day before yesterday'
GWS	MNT	*añɨhrin*
	APA	*anihuliŋ*
NS	MUM	*aikuriŋ*
ES	AIS	*aniriŋ*

This set is problematic in many ways, but suggestive of a form derived from *añɨr 'two days away' that referred specifically to the past.

*aŋam n. 'collared brush-turkey (*Talegalla jobiensis*)'
NS	SIR	*aŋam*
ES	GAJ	*aŋaŋ*

Gants changed final *m > ŋ.

*apapara n. 'butterfly'
GWS	MND	*apipar*
	MNT	*apapara* 'grasshopper'
	APA	*afafaŋ*
NS	MUM	*apapura*
	SIR	*apapara*
ES	MAG	*apapar*
	AIS	*apapara*
	KUR	*apapɨre*
	GAJ	*aporor*

The onomatopoetic nature of this word makes reconstruction difficult.

*apar n. 'mountain'
GWS	MND	*apar*
	NEN	*apar*
	MNT	*apar*
NS	MUM	*apar*

*arɨka n. 'middle'
GWS	NEN	*arɨha*
	APA	*alihaŋ*
NS	SIR	*arha*
ES	MAG	*akɨr*
	AIS	*akɨr*
	KUR	*arik*

Apalɨ added final ŋ. Aisian metathesized *rk. Kursav lost final *a.

*arɨN 'laugh'
GWS	NEN	*ariŋ* (S)
ES	KUR	*arim*

The final nasals are difficult to reconcile.

*arum adj. 'good'
GWS	MND	*arom*
	MNT	*arum* 'big, old'
NS	MUM	*aru* 'big'
ES	AIS	*uruŋ*

Mand lowered *u > o. Aisi changed initial *a > u.

*asɨŋ n. 'leaf'
GWS	MND	*asɨh*
	NEN	*zɨŋ* (N)
	APA	*asɨŋ*

Nend voiced *s > z. See *faga 'leaf'.

*ataŋ 'far'
GWS MND (ur)ataŋ
    NEN taŋ(opɨr)
    APA ataŋ
ES MAG ataŋ

*atɨ *pro.* 'what'
GWS MND ucɨ
    NEN utɨ
    APA atɨ, akɨ, acɨ
NS SIR arɨ
ES MAG ai
    AIS ai (Magɨ)
    KUR atɨ

Proto-Greater West Sogeram changed *a > u, possibly on analogy with PGWS *uña 'who'. The Mand and Apalɨ consonants are difficult.

*aya *v.* 'come.IMP'
GWS MND aya
    MNT aya
    APA aia
NS SIR aya
ES GAJ aya, ai- 'come'

This was an irregular suppletive root for the imperative of 'come'. It may also have been the uninflected form. See *fai- 'come'.

*-b *n.inal.* 'daughter-in-law'
NS MUM -b(as)
    SIR -b(as)
ES KUR -b(isim)

See *-nab 'daughter-in-law'.

*-f, -fɨ *n.inal.* 'mother's brother'
GWS MND -v(ar)
    MNT -vɨ
NS MUM -vɨ

ES KUR -v
    GAJ -pu

See *-kaf 'mother's brother'.

*-fa *n.inal.* 'sister-in-law of female ego'
    APA ava
NS SIR -vah
ES GAJ apa

See *-kun 'co-wife'.

*faga *n.* 'leaf'
GWS MNT vaga
NS SIR paga
ES KUR vaga

See *asɨn 'leaf'.

*-fai *n.inal.* 'maternal grandmother'
GWS MNT -vay(ag)
            'grandfather'
    APA -ve
ES MAG -be(b)
    AIS -boi
    KUR -vi(s)

See *-pɨkɨ 'paternal grandmother'.

*fai- *v.* 'come'
GWS MND ai-
    NEN ay-
    MNT ai-
    APA ve-
NS MUM pai-
    SIR pi-
ES AIS way-
    KUR ve
    GAJ ai-

Sirva simplified *ai > i. Gants lost *f on analogy with the suppletive imperative root *aya 'come.IMP'; that root may also have been the uninflected form of 'come'.

*-fan *n.inal.* 'father'
- GWS MND van 'father.3.POSS'
- NEN wan(ɨr) 'father.3.POSS'
- MNT -vaŋ, -va
- APA (ia)vaŋ
- NS MUM -va
- SIR (ya)va
- ES MAG (wa)ba
- KUR awi

See *-ŋti 'father'.

*faŋan *n.* 'bag'
- GWS MND aŋan
- NEN aŋan
- APA vaŋaŋ (C)
- NS MUM paŋa
- SIR paŋa
- ES MAG waŋɨ
- AIS waŋɨ
- KUR vaŋa
- GAJ waŋa (Kursav)

Gants changed *f > w and lost final *n.

*figau *n.* 'mist'
- GWS MND iku 'cloud'
- ES KUR vigau 'mist'

See *kamu 'fog'.

*fim *n.* 'sore'
- APA fim
- NS SIR we
- ES GAJ poim

Sirva did not change initial *w > p and lowered *i > e. Gants added o.

*fika *v.* 'slice, cut'
- GWS NEN ka-
- MNT (i)vika-
- APA vih- (K), vika- (C)
- NS MUM piha-
- SIR piha-
- ES MAG uk- 'tell (a story)'
- AIS uk- 'cut, tell (a story)'
- GAJ pika

*fikara *v.* 'finish'
- GWS MND karɨ-
- APA fihala-

*fiku *v.* 'burst'
- APA viku-
- NS MUM pihu-
- SIR puhu- 'appear, break out'
- ES KUR vuko 'slap'

Kursav is semantically divergent.

*fir *n.* 'ground, land'
- APA fili
- NS MUM pɨr 'dry land'
- ES MAG bi
- AIS ur
- GAJ (ka)pɨr

See *fɨr kama 'dawn'.

*fɨr kama *vac.* 'dawn'
- GWS MND vr(ah)-
- APA fili (miŋalah-)
- NS SIR ukama- (PAIS)
- ES MAG bikame (adv.)
- AIS urkame (adv.)
- GAJ pi kam-

Mand and Apalɨ changed the verb. See *fɨr 'ground'; the meaning of *kama is unclear.

*fɨr, fri- *v.* 'scratch'
- APA (lɨ)vil-
- NS MUM pri-

| ES | Ais | ur(i)- |

Aisi compounded with i- 'get'.

*fumra v. 'fly'

| NS | Mum | pɨmra- |
| ES | Kur | vumra |

*fVkra v. 'look for'

GWS	Nen	kira-
	Mnt	kr(iva)-
NS	Mum	puhra-
	Sir	puhra-
ES	Mag	wakr-
	Ais	wakr-
	Gaj	okra

The first vowel is difficult to reconstruct: Nend and Manat reflect *ɨ, North Sogeram reflects *u, Proto-Aisian suggests *a, and Gants is unclear. Manat compounded with iva- 'hit'.

*i v. 'hold, carry'

GWS	Mnd	(kahɨ)zɨ- 'carry on head'
	Nen	i- 'bathe'
	Mnt	yɨ- 'carry on head'
NS	Sir	i-, ya- 'distribute, hit'
ES	Mag	y- 'do'
	Ais	i- 'get'
	Kur	i(ta)- 'hold'
	Gaj	(miŋ)ia 'take'

Kursav added *-ta 'ss'. Gants compounded with *miŋa 'get'.

*ibi n. 'name'

GWS	Mnd	ipi(a)
	Apa	ibi
NS	Mum	ñibi
	Sir	ib
ES	Mag	ib
	Ais	ib
	Kur	-(n)ibe
	Gaj	ibe

Kursav n- may have been epenthetically inserted when the form became inalienably possessed. Compare Kalam yb, PTNG *ibi.

*ibɨd adj. 'good'

GWS	Nen	imbɨr
	Mnt	ibɨd
ES	Ais	imbɨr (PNS?) 'bad'

Aisi kept prenasalization in mb and did not lower *i > ᵗe before ɨ.

*ibra v. 'act badly, (of food) go bad'

GWS	Mnt	ibra- 'do mischief, be happy'
	Apa	ibɨl- 'be hungry'
NS	Mum	ibra- 'play'
ES	Ais	imbr- 'spoil'
	Kur	ibra 'stink, rot'

Aisi kept prenasalization in mb.

*idar, idari- v. 'hear, perceive'

NS	Mum	idar-
	Sir	dari-
ES	Mag	ir- 'perceive'
	Ais	ir- 'hear, see'

The expected Aisian reflex is ᵗirar-, making this correspondence set uncertain. See *iga 'see, perceive'.

*idua adj. 'bad'

| NS | Sir | dua |
| ES | Kur | idua |

*idua, idu- v. 'open'

| GWS | Nen | endɨwa- |
| NS | Sir | idu- |

*-ifi *n.inal.* 'father's younger brother'
    GWS MND *-ivi*
              APA *ivɨ*
    ES   MAG *(a)yib*
              AIS   *(a)yeb*
              GAJ *-ipi*

*ifra *v.* 'barter, exchange'
    GWS MND *uvra-* 'barter'
              MNT *vra-* 'buy'
    ES   GAJ   *epra* 'buy'
Mand changed *i > u. (Or Gants changed *u > *i.)

*ifu *v.* 'hit'
    GWS MND *iv(eri)-*
              MNT *iva-*
              APA *ifa-*
    NS   MUM *yɨvu-*
    ES   MAG *iw-*
              AIS   *iw-, yo-*
              KUR *ivo*
              GAJ *yo*
Manat and Apalɨ changed verb class.

*iga *v.* 'see, perceive'
    GWS NEN *ŋgɨ-* 'touch'
              MNT *g(ipu)-* 'peer'
              APA *iga-*
    NS   MUM *ga-*
            SIR   *ga-*
    ES   MAG *ŋg-*
              GAJ *ga* 'perceive'
Initial *i was lost in Nend and Proto-East Sogeram. Manat compounded with *ipu-* 'go in'. Magɨ retained prenasalization in *ŋg*. See *idar 'hear, perceive' and *tɨku 'see'. Compare Usan *ig* 'hear'.

*igif *n.* 'anger'
    GWS MND *ikɨv(ɨr)* 'noise'
              NEN *ihɨrɨv* 'noise'
              MNT *igɨv*
              APA *igivɨ*
    NS   SIR   *igɨv* 'angry'
Nend is problematic, and may be a Mand loan.

*igin *n.* 'ground possum'
    GWS MND *(bor)ikɨn*
              NEN *iŋkɨr*
    NS   MUM *(pr)igin*
            SIR   *igin*
Mand compounded with *bor* 'pig'. Mum compounded with *pɨr* 'ground'. Proto-North Sogeram did not lose final *n.

*igwa, igw- *v.* 'give'
    GWS MND *ikw-*
              NEN *eŋgwa-* (N),
                      iŋgwa- (S)
              MNT *igu-*
              APA *igu-*
    NS   MUM *gu-*
            SIR   *gwa-, gu-*
    ES   MAG *igw-*
              AIS   *igw-*
              KUR *-bu-*
              GAJ *go, gw-*
Kursav and Gants lost initial *i. Kursav also changed *gw > b.

*ika *v.* 'cut, chop'
    GWS MND *ika-*
              NEN *eka-*
              APA *iha-*
    NS   SIR   *yaha-*
    ES   MAG *ik-*

7.1 Proto-Sogeram lexemes

	Ais	ik-
	Kur	ika
	Gaj	eka

*ikakara n. 'chicken (*Gallus gallus*)'

GWS	Mnd	ikɨkar
	Mnt	akakara
	Apa	akakala
NS	Mum	akakara
ES	Mag	kyarɨ
	Ais	kyarɨ

Manat, Apalɨ and Mum changed *i > *a. Proto-Aisian removed one *ka syllable and metathesized *ik.

*ikudɨ adv. 'morning'

GWS	Mnd	ikud
ES	Mag	kundɨ
	Ais	kondɨ

Mand changed *dɨ > d. Proto-Aisian lost initial *i and kept prenasalization in nd.

*iman n. 'louse'

GWS	Mnd	iman
	Nen	eman (S)
	Mnt	ma(g)
	Apa	iman
NS	Mum	ñima
	Sir	ima
ES	Mag	imaŋ
	Ais	imu
	Kur	ima
	Gaj	iman

Aisi shows u for expected †i.

*imu v. 'put in pot'

GWS	Mnd	iba- 'boil'
	Nen	ema- (S) 'cook'
	Mnt	imu- 'cook'
ES	Mag	im- 'put in'
	Ais	im- 'put in'
	Kur	imo 'put in'

West Sogeram changed the verb class.

*ina n. 'sun'

GWS	Mnd	ida
NS	Mum	ina
	Sir	ina

See *iŋar 'sun, day'.

*iŋar n. 'sun,' adv. 'day'

GWS	Mnd	igar(ɨd) 'noon'
	Mnt	iŋar 'sun'
NS	Mum	ñaŋari 'moon' (Sirva)
	Sir	yaŋari 'sun'
ES	Ais	aŋar 'sunshine'
	Gaj	aŋai 'day'

Mum changed initial *i > *ya. Sirva added locative *=ñ. Proto-East Sogeram lowered initial *e > a. See *ina 'sun'.

*irɨka v. 'cry'

GWS	Mnd	irɨka- 'talk to'
	Mnt	irha-
	Apa	ilɨha-
NS	Mum	irha-
	Sir	irɨha-
ES	Mag	ik-
	Ais	ik-
	Kur	irɨka-
	Gaj	ika-

Mand is semantically innovative.

*ipa v. 'come out, across'

GWS	Mnd	ipa(hɨ)- 'come across'

	NEN	*(ah)evay-*
	MNT	*ipa-*
	APA	*iva-* 'move across'
ES	GAJ	*ipa* 'get up, fly'

Nend added final *y* on analogy with *ay-* 'come'. See *ipa miga 'appear (at)'.

*ipa miga *svc.* 'appear (at)'
| | GWS | MNT | *ipamiga-* 'arrive' |
| | ES | GAJ | *ipa miga* 'get up' |

See *ipa 'come out, across' and *miga 'come down'.

*ipra *v.* 'hide (intr.)'
	GWS	MNT	*pra(vu)-* 'h. (ambitr.)'
		APA	*(si)vila-*
NS		MUM	*(s)ipru-*
		SIR	*yavru-*
ES		AIS	*ipr-, ipra(m)-* 'h. (tr.)'
		GAJ	*epria, epri-*

Manat compounded with *vu-* 'go'. Apalɨ changed initial *i > ɨ. Mum, Sirva, and Gants changed the verb class.

*ipu *v.* 'go in'
	GWS	NEN	*(ah)evo-*
		MNT	*ipu-*
		APA	*ivo-*
	ES	GAJ	*ipo*

Apalɨ lowered final *u > *o*.

*ir, iri- *v.* 'turn, spin'
	GWS	MNT	*(arar)iri-* 'weave'
NS		SIR	*iru-* 'spin (twine)'
ES		GAJ	*er(kara)* 'turn, become'

Sirva changed verb class. See *ir wara 'exceed'.

*ir wara *vac.* 'exceed'
| NS | SIR | *irvara-* |
| ES | GAJ | *erwara* |

See *ir 'turn'. The meaning of *wara is unclear.

*iran *n.* 'parrot species'
| GWS | MNT | *iran* 'red parrot' |
| ES | KUR | *era* 'green parrot' |

*irañ *n.* 'sharpness, edge'
	GWS	MND	*irañ* 'sharp (adj.)'
		NEN	*irañ* (S) 'sharp (adj.)'
NS		MUM	*(k)ira-* 'peel (v.)'
		SIR	*(k)ira-* 'peel (v.)'
ES		AIS	*irar* 'edge'

Proto-North Sogeram added *k and may not be cognate. Aisi changed final *ñ > *r*.

*isa *v.* 'bite'
	GWS	MND	*isa(kri)-* 'tear'
NS		MUM	*sa-*
		SIR	*isa-*
ES		MAG	*is-*
		AIS	*is-*
		KUR	*isa-*

Mand is questionable.

*isaŋ *n.inal.* 'same-sex older sibling'
	GWS	MND	*asaŋ*
		NEN	*aziŋ* (N)
		MNT	*(ta)saŋ*
		APA	*isaŋ*
ES		MAG	*isaŋ*
		AIS	*isam*

See *-si and *pafa 'same-sex older sibling'.

*isi *v.* 'fetch water'
    GWS   MND   *isi-*
                NEN   *ici-* (S)
                MNT   *isɨ-*
    NS   SIR   *sɨi-*
    ES   MAG   *is-*
          AIS   *isi-*
Sirva changed final *i > *ɨi*. Nend and Manat changed the verb class. See *tɨki 'fill'.

*iwi *n.inal.* 'nephew, niece'
          APA   *iui*
    ES   GAJ   *(ne)yue*
See *-mku 'nibling'.

*kaba *adv.* 'together'
    GWS   APA   *haba*
    NS   MUM   *kaba*
    ES   KUR   *kaba* 'fight'
Kursav is a verb adjunct that occurs with *ivo-* 'hit'.

*kaban *n.* 'jaw'
    GWS   NEN   *amban* (S)
    NS   MUM   *kaba(gina)* 'beard'

*kada *adj.* 'true,' *adv.* 'very'
    NS   MUM   *kad*
          SIR   *hada* 'also'
    ES   KUR   *(nɨ)kada*
Mum lost final *a.

*kadi *n.* 'sickness'
    NS   MUM   *kadi*
    ES   MAG   *kar*
          AIS   *kar*
          KUR   *kada*
See *kadi 'body'.

*kadi *n.* 'body'
          APA   *hadi*
    NS   SIR   *kad*
    ES   GAJ   *kade*
Sirva lost final *i. See *kadi 'sick'; these two were probably one word, which was used in an expression like '(my) body does me' to mean 'I'm sick'.

*-kaf *n.inal.* 'mother's brother'
    GWS   MNT   *-hav*
    NS₁   MUM   *-hav*
See *-f 'mother's brother'.

*kag *n.* 'hook'
    GWS   MNT   *hag*
    NS   SIR   *kag*

*kaka *v.* 'tie, fasten'
    GWS   APA   *haha-*
    NS   MUM   *kaha-*
          SIR   *kaha-*
    ES   MAG   *kak-*
          AIS   *kak-*
          GAJ   *kaka* 'bury, encircle'

*kakri *n.* 'axe'
    GWS   NEN   *ahɨr* (S)
    NS   MUM   *kahri*
    ES   GAJ   *kakɨr*
Gants lost final *i.

*kamɨŋawa *n.* 'millipede'
    GWS   MND   *amɨŋau*
               APA   *hamɨŋauaŋ*
Apalɨ added final *ŋ*.

*kamu *n.* 'fog, cloud'
- GWS APA *hamu*
- NS SIR *kamu(hu)*
- ES MAG *kamɨ*
- AIS *kamo*
- KUR *kamo* 'breath, wind'
- GAJ *kamo(ren)*

Magɨ changed **u > ɨ*. See **figau* 'mist'.

*kamura *n.* 'betel pepper (*Piper betle*)'
- GWS MNT *hamura*
- APA *hamulaŋ*
- NS MUM *kamura*
- SIR *kamura*
- ES MAG *kamur*
- AIS *kamor*

Apalɨ added *ŋ*. Proto-Aisian lost final **ɨ*.

*kañaŋ *n.* 'bone'
- APA *henaŋ*
- ES MAG *kañaŋ*
- KUR *-kana*

*kaŋra *v.* 'run'
- GWS MND *agra-*
- NEN *aŋra-*
- MNT *aŋra-*
- APA *haŋɨla-*
- ES GAJ *aŋra-* 'go'

Gants lost **k*.

*kap *adv.* 'just'
- GWS MND *av(ɨr)*
- MNT *av(an)* 'very'
- APA *havɨ* 'j., for no reason'
- NS SIR *kav*
- ES KUR *(u)kap*
- GAJ *kap(i)*

The frequent augmentation of this form is suspicious.

*kapa *n.* 'bird'
- GWS NEN *apa*
- MNT *havagava* 'bird sp.'
- APA *havaŋ*
- NS MUM *kava*
- SIR *kava*
- ES MAG *kapɨ*
- AIS *kapɨ*
- KUR *kapa*

Manat is reduplicated. Apalɨ added final *ŋ*.

*kapra *v.* 'throw'
- GWS MND *aprɨ-*
- MNT *apara-*
- APA *havala-*
- NS MUM *kavara-*
- SIR *kapara-*
- ES MAG *kapr-*
- AIS *kapr-*

Mand changed the verb class.

*kapu *v.* 'carry'
- APA *havu-* 'c. on shoulder' (C)
- NS MUM *kavu-*
- SIR *kavu-* 'c. on head'
- ES MAG *kaw-*
- AIS *kaw-*
- KUR *kapo-*

Proto-Aisian changed **p > *w*.

*kari *n.* 'betelnut (*Areca catechu*)'
- NS MUM *kari*
- SIR *kari*

7.1 Proto-Sogeram lexemes

ES AIS *kare*
    KUR *karia*
Kursav added final *a*.

*karif *n.* 'flying fox'
    APA *halav(iŋ)* (C)
NS MUM *karev*
    SIR *karev*
ES MAG *karib*
    AIS *kareb*
    KUR *karap*
Apalɨ changed **i* > *a* and added -*iŋ*.

*kasam *n.* 'breadfruit (*Artocarpus altilis*)'
GWS MND *asam*
    NEN *asam*
    APA *hasam*

*kasɨñ *n.* 'sand'
GWS MND *(z)akɨñ*
    NEN *kɨñ* (S)
    MNT *has*
    APA *hacɨŋ*
NS MUM *kas*
    SIR *kas*
Proto-West Sogeram metathesized **k* and **s*. See **mia* 'sand'. Compare PTNG **sa(g,k)asiŋ*.

*kaur *adj.* 'unripe'
GWS MND *kor*
    NEN *kor* (S)
    MNT *har*
NS SIR *kor* 'young'

*kaura *n.* 'loincloth'
NS SIR *kavɨr*
ES KUR *kaura*
Sirva lost final **a*.

*kayabra *n.* 'village'
GWS MND *azapɨr*
    NEN *ayampɨra*
    APA *haiabɨla*
See **abra* 'place'.

*kayagi *n.* 'sulphur-crested cockatoo (*Cacatua galerita*)'
    APA *haiaji*
NS SIR *kayagi*
ES AIS *kayaŋgi*
    KUR *kayag*
Aisi kept prenasalization in *ŋg*. Kursav lost final **i*.

*kazɨŋ *n.* 'festival decoration'
GWS MND *asɨh(ɨd)*
    NEN *ansɨŋ* 'flower'
    MNT *azɨ*
    APA *hajɨŋ*
NS MUM *kaz*
Referred to flowers, etc., with which people decorated themselves at festivals.

*kia *n.* 'speech'
GWS MND *ya*
    NEN *ya*
    MNT *ya(dama-)* 'mock'
    APA *ciaŋ*
NS SIR *kya*
ES MAG *kɨ*; cf. *ke* 'song'
    AIS *kɨ*
    KUR *(ni)kia* 'celebration'
    GAJ *kia*; cf. *kiaŋ* 'noise'
Manat compounded with **tama* 'put'. Apalɨ added *ŋ*. Compare Anamuxra *xya* 'idea, talk'.

*kibañ n. 'saliva'
- GWS MND ipañ
- ES   MAG kibin
-      AIS kibiŋ

*kikra v. 'watch'
- GWS MND ihra-
-      NEN ihra- (S)
- NS   MUM kihra-

Mand lenited *k to h. Compare Anamuxra kixr- 'see'.

*kiman n. 'firstborn male'
-      APA cime(geŋ)
- NS   MUM kimagima 'first'
-      SIR kima 'first'
- ES   MAG kema, kimeŋge
-      AIS kemaŋ
-      KUR keman 'lastborn'

*kɨmri 'cold'
- GWS NEN imɨr (S)
-      MNT hɨmri
-      APA (vu)mɨli
- NS   MUM kɨmri
-      SIR (ti)hɨm

Nend changed *ɨ > i.

*kina, kinakina adj. 'crooked'
- GWS MNT hinahina
-      APA cina 'crook (n.)'
- NS   MUM kinakina
- ES   MAG giŋ(gunda)
-      AIS geŋ(goŋ)
-      GAJ kenakena

Aisian is divergent.

*kinaŋ n. 'axe'
- GWS MND idaŋ 'bamboo'
-      APA cinaŋ
- NS   SIR kina
- ES   MAG kinɨ
-      AIS kinɨ

Bamboo was used as a blade, but Mand is semantically problematic. It also changed *n > d before a nasal.

*kira n. 'fight'
- GWS NEN era
- ES   GAJ kera

Gants is a verb adjunct.

*kiwañ n. 'footprint'
- GWS MND iwañ
-      MNT hiva
- NS   SIR kiva

*kɨbar, kɨbari- v. 'carry on shoulder'
- GWS MNT bari-
- NS   MUM kɨbar-
-      SIR kɨbara-
- ES   AIS kɨbar-

Sirva changed verb class.

*kɨbaram n. 'eel'
- GWS NEN mbaram
-      MNT hɨbra(gam)
-      APA hɨbalam
- NS   SIR kɨbra
- ES   AIS kɨbar

Nend voiced *b. Manat and Sirva elided the first *a. Aisi lacks final †i.

*kɨda v. 'walk'
- GWS MND ta-
-      NEN nda-
-      MNT da-
-      APA hɨda-

NS	Mum	kida-
	Sir	kida-
ES	Mag	kr-
	Ais	kr-
	Kur	da(ini)-
	Gaj	kida

Nend voiced *d. Proto-Aisian deleted *i from expected †kir-. Kursav is probably not cognate.

*kidir n. 'root'

GWS	Mnd	tir
	Nen	ntir (S)
	Apa	hidili
NS	Mum	kidi
ES	Ais	kirir
	Kur	(ni)kidir
	Gaj	kidi

Compare Anamuxra xd-, Kalam kdl.

*kifir n. 'night'

GWS	Mnd	vi(himd)
	Mnt	vi
	Apa	hifili
NS	Mum	kivi
ES	Kur	kivir

Manat lost final *r. See *kiftiti 'afternoon'.

*kiftiti adv. 'afternoon'

NS	Mum	kivtiti
ES	Kur	kiutete

Kursav changed *f > u. See *kifir 'night'.

*kiki adj. 'new'

	Apa	hihi
NS	Mum	kihi
ES	Mag	kiki
	Ais	kiki

*kimi n. 'bow'

	Apa	himi
NS	Mum	kim
	Sir	kimi
ES	Mag	kim
	Ais	kim
	Kur	kim (PAis)

Kursav lost final *e. Compare Anamuxra xm-.

*kimu v. 'die'

GWS	Mnd	bi-
	Nen	ma-
	Mnt	himu-
	Apa	hima-
NS	Mum	kimu-
	Sir	kumu-
ES	Mag	kum-
	Ais	kum-
	Kur	kumo
	Gaj	kumo

Mand, Nend, and Apali changed verb class to -a (cf. Mand irregular adjunct form ma-) before Mand again changed to -i. Compare PTNG *kumV-.

*kiña, kiñi- v. 'stay'

GWS	Mnd	ji-
	Nen	ñi-
	Mnt	ñi-
	Apa	hinia, hini-
NS	Mum	ki-, kiñ
	Sir	ki-, kiñ(i) 'stay.ss'
ES	Mag	kin-, ki(ti) 'stay.ss'
	Ais	kin-, ki(ti) 'stay.ss'

    Kur *in*
    Gaj *ca, ci-*
Kursav lost initial *k. Gants merged *k and *ñ into *c*. Compare Anamuxra, Kalam *kn-* 'sleep' and PTNG *kin(i,u) 'sleep'.

***kiñakuŋ** n.* 'wattled brush-turkey (*Aepypodius arfakianus*)'
    Apa *hiniahuŋ* (PNS)
NS Mum *kiñaku*
  Sir *kiñaku*
ES Mag *kiŋyoŋ*
  Ais *kiŋakuŋ*
  Kur *kwinaku*
Magɨ is unusual. Kursav added *w*.

***kiñakw** n.* 'paint tree'
GWS Mnd *joku*
ES Gaj *kiñak*
Mand changed *a > *o* and final *kw > *ku*. Gants changed final *kw > *k*.

***kiñam** adv.* 'near'
NS Sir *kine, kina(mana)* 'far'
ES Kur *kinam*
  Gaj *kiñam*
Sirva changed final *a > *e* in 'near' and compounded with *mana* 'NEG' in 'far'.

***kiŋaN** n.* 'kind of arrow'
    Apa *hiŋaŋ*
NS Mum *kina*
  Sir *kiŋa*
ES Mag *kiŋi*
  Ais *kiŋi*
Mum changed *ŋ > *n*.

***kɨpa** v.* 'get up'
NS Sir *kɨva-* 'wake'
ES Mag *kipɨ*
  Ais *kɨp-*
  Kur *kɨva-*
  Gaj *kɨp* 'up'
Kursav voiced *p > *v*. Gants is questionable.

***kisar** n.* 'spear'
    Apa *hisali*
NS Sir *kisar* 's., stick'
ES Mag *kisar*
  Kur *kisar*

***kra** v.* 'blow'
GWS Mnd *kr(ezi)-* 'start fire'
  Nen *kr(esi)-* (S)
  Mnt *hra-*
  Apa *(ma)kɨla-* (C), *(ma)hɨla-* (K)
NS Mum *kra-*
ES Mag *(ma)kr-*
  Ais *(u)kr-*
Frequent compounding may have been motivated by homophony with *kra 'roast'.

***kra** v.* 'roast'
GWS Mnd *kra-*
  Nen *hɨra-* (N), *kra-* (S)
  Mnt *hra-*
  Apa *hɨla-*
NS Mum *kra-*
ES Mag *kr-*
  Ais *kr-*
  Kur *kra-*
  Gaj *kra*
Northern Nend lenited *k. Compare Anamuxra *xr-*.

7.1 Proto-Sogeram lexemes — 269

*kuar *n.* 'garden'
	GWS	MND	var
		NEN	war
		MNT	var
		APA	huali
NS		MUM	kiva
		SIR	kiva
ES		MAG	kwar
		AIS	kwar

Z'graggen has Mand *uari*, suggesting PGWS *w > Mand *v* was recent.

*kubin *n.* 'Victoria crowned pigeon (*Goura victoria*)'
		APA	hubin
NS		SIR	kubi
ES		KUR	kobe

Kursav lowered *u > *o*.

*kubɨ *n.* 'path'
		APA	hibɨ
NS		MUM	kubɨ
		SIR	(udu)kib
ES		MAG	kib
		AIS	kib
		KUR	kubu

Apalɨ, Sirva, and Proto-Aisian centered *u > *ɨ*.

*kubra *v.* 'take off, remove'
		APA	hubila-
NS		MUM	(ara)hubra- 'pluck'
		SIR	kubra-
ES		GAJ	(ma)kubra

*kubru *v.* 'break (intr.)'
	GWS	MNT	(a)kubru-
ES		AIS	(muŋ)gubr- 'b. (tr.)'

		KUR	kobra-
		GAJ	kobr-

Aisi compounded with *miŋa 'get'. Kursav changed the verb class.

*kudar *n.* 'centipede'
	GWS	MND	utar
NS		SIR	kuda(gau) 'snake sp.'
ES		GAJ	kodai

*kuga *adj.* 'yellow'
		APA	huga
NS		MUM	kuga
		SIR	kuga
ES		AIS	kogɨ

*kugiŋ *n.* 'whistle'
		APA	hujiŋ
NS		MUM	kugi
ES		GAJ	kojiŋ

Gants lowered *u > *o* and changed *gi > *ji*.

*kugɨ *n.* 'knot'
	GWS	MND	ucɨ(ri)- 'tie up'
		NEN	uŋkɨ(mpa)- (S) 'fasten'
		MNT	uzɨ(miŋa)- 'fasten'
		APA	hugɨ

Mand and Manat palatalized *k. Mand compounded with *ra-* 'do'. Manat compounded with *miŋa-* 'get'.

*kugra *v.* 'cook, boil'
		APA	hugila- 'cook'
NS		MUM	kugra- 'c. in pot'
		SIR	kwagra-

ES	Mag	kugur-
	Ais	kogr-
	Kur	kogra- 'boil'

Magɨ inserted u between gr. May be related to *kra 'roast'.

*kui v. 'shoot, pierce'

GWS	Mnd	uz- 'stab, pierce'
	Nen	uyɨ- 'stab, pierce'
	Apa	hui- (C)
ES	Mag	ki
	Gaj	kuya, kwi-

Gants has merged with *kur 'plant, shoot'.

*kuimaŋ n. 'coconut (Cocos nucifera)'

GWS	Mnd	koim
	Mnt	huma
	Apa	himaŋ
NS	Mum	kwima
	Sir	kwima
ES	Gaj	koimaŋ

Mand lost final *ŋ. Compare Kalam koymaŋ.

*kukasa n. 'frog'

GWS	Mnd	ukis
	Nen	ohaz (N), ohas (S)
	Mnt	kwasa
NS	Mum	kukasa

See *naŋram 'frog'.

*kukɨ n. 'sago grub (Rhynchophorus ferrugineus)'

GWS	Mnd	ukɨ 'caterpillar, slug, grub'; cf. awaŋ ukɨ 'sago grub'
	Apa	huhɨ (K), hukɨ (C)

Mand combined with awaŋ 'sago' in 'sago grub'.

*kukra v. 'grow, swell'

GWS	Mnd	uhra-; cf. uhra 'big'
	Nen	ohɨra (S) 'big'
	Mnt	ukra-
	Apa	huhɨla- 'g., give birth'
NS	Mum	kuhra- 'g., give birth'
ES	Mag	kukr-
	Ais	kokr-
	Kur	kokra-
	Gaj	kokra- 'g., be born'

A meaning associated with birth may go back to Proto-Sogeram, as suggested by Apalɨ, Mum, and Gants.

*kuman n. 'arm, hand'

GWS	Nen	oman
	Mnt	ubr(am)
	Apa	human
NS	Mum	kuma
	Sir	kuma
ES	Ais	komaŋ 'branch'
	Kur	-koma

Manat -am may be on analogy with tadam 'leg'.

*-kun n.inal. 'co-wife'

GWS	Mnd	(ai)hun
	Mnt	-kɨna
	Apa	(a)hun
ES	Gaj	-kun

See *-fa 'sister-in-law'.

*kunaŋ n. 'plate'

	Apa	hunaŋ
NS	Sir	kuna
ES	Gaj	kinaŋ

Gants centered *u > ɨ.

*kupra v. 'jump'
- NS SIR kuvra-
- ES MAG kupra(t)-
- AIS kopra(t)-; cf. kopr- 'run'
- KUR kopra- 'run'
- GAJ kopara

Gants inserted *a* between *pr*.

*kur, kuri- v. 'plant, shoot'
- GWS NEN uri- (S)
- MNT (i)kuru- 'copulate'
- APA hulia-, huli-
- NS MUM kur-
- SIR kuru-
- ES GAJ kuya, kwi-

Manat may have compounded with *i 'hold, carry'. Gants has merged with *kui 'shoot, pierce'.

*kuram n. 'man'
- GWS MND kuram
- NEN wiram (N), kuram (S)
- MNT urum
- APA hulaŋ
- NS MUM kru
- SIR kura
- ES MAG kuri
- AIS kuru
- KUR kura
- GAJ kura

Mand and Southern Nend retained initial *k. Manat changed *a > u. Mum is irregular. Aisi changed final *i to u. Compare Anamuxra -kura 'male classifier' and wuraN- 'person'. Kursav and Gants did not lower *u > ᵗo.

*kusai 'first, before'
- APA huse
- NS MUM husa
- SIR kusi 'after'
- ES GAJ kusai

*kut n. 'back'
- GWS MNT (ipa)kut 'back of house'
- APA huli
- NS MUM kut
- SIR kur
- ES MAG kud
- GAJ kor 'spine'

Compare Kalam *kud*.

*kutaŋ adj. 'long'
- APA hutaŋ
- NS MUM kuta
- SIR kuta
- ES GAJ oraŋ

Apali is archaic. Gants lost initial *k.

*kuyif n. 'bird of paradise'
- GWS MND wajeu
- APA huiavi
- NS MUM kuñiv
- SIR kwiv
- ES MAG koyeb

This was phonemically *kuiif, and the form has several problems. Mand changed *u > wa and strengthened *y > *ñ before nasal fortition. Apali changed *i > a and added final i. Mum nasalized *y > ñ in a non-nasal environment. Magi lowered *u and *i to o and e.

*kuza n. 'yam (*Dioscorea* sp.)'
    GWS   MND   usa 'taro'
              NEN   unsa
              MNT   huza 'thornless yam'
              APA   huja
    NS   MUM   kuja

*kwaka v. 'cut, chop'
    GWS   MND   aka-
              NEN   aka-
    NS   SIR   kwaha-
    ES   KUR   kwaka
              GAJ   aka
Gants lost initial *kw.

*kwɨgɨs n. 'armpit'
    GWS   NEN   ŋkɨs(impɨŋ) (S)
              MNT   gisɨ
              APA   huji
    NS   MUM   kugɨs
              SIR   kugus
    ES   KUR   -kwegɨ
Nend compounded with *mpɨŋ* 'wing'. Apalɨ changed final *ɨs > i. Kursav lost final *s.

*kwɨmka n. 'stomach'
    GWS   MND   pɨ
              NEN   mpɨ
              APA   humɨgaŋ
    ES   AIS   kumu
Greater West Sogeram changed final *a > i. See *tamkan 'eye'.

*kwɨñaŋ n. 'palm cockatoo (*Probosciger aterrimus*)'
    GWS   MND   ukɨñah
              MNT   kuña(k); cf. *kuña* 'p.c.'s call'

    NS   SIR   kuña(m)
Mand changed initial *kw > uk.

*madɨŋ n. 'side (of body)'
    GWS   NEN   antɨŋ
              MNT   mad 'back'
              APA   madɨŋ 's., rib'
    ES   MAG   madɨŋ 'nape, shoulderblade'
              AIS   mar 'half'
Aisi may not be cognate.

*maga n. 'egg'
    GWS   MND   akɨ
              NEN   aŋkɨ
              APA   magɨ
    NS   SIR   miga (Mum)
Apalɨ changed final *a > i.
Compare Kalam *magi*.

*magra v. 'pull'
    GWS   MND   akra- 'net fish'
              APA   magɨla-
    ES   MAG   magr(i)-
              KUR   magra
              GAJ   (ma)magra
Magɨ compounded with *i*- 'get'.

*maka n. 'tooth'
    GWS   MND   aka(mgam) 'jaw'
              MNT   mɨka 'tusk'
              APA   mɨka
    NS   MUM   mɨka 'mouth'
              SIR   mɨka
    ES   MAG   makɨ
              AIS   makɨ
              KUR   maka
              GAJ   maka 'mouth'
Manat, Apalɨ, and North Sogeram changed the first *a > i.

*maka *adj.* 'male'
GWS MNT *mika* (Mum)
ES   MAG *maki*
     KUR *maka* 'husband'
Manat changed initial *a > ɨ.

*maka *v.* 'pick (from plant)'
GWS NEN *(ŋ)aka-*
ES   AIS *mak-*
Nend compounded with
ŋ- 'get'.

*makaN *n.* 'branch'
GWS MNT *maka*
     APA *makaŋ*
NS   MUM *(kuku)maka*
          'tributary'
     SIR *maka*
ES   GAJ *maka* 'b., log'
Mum compounded with *kuku*
'water'. The form may also have
been *maka with addition of *ŋ* in
Apalɨ.

*makin *n.* 'sago (*Metroxylon* sp.)'
     APA *maci*
NS   MUM *maki* 'plate'
ES   MAG *maki* (Apalɨ)
     GAJ *maken*
Apalɨ lost final *n. Magɨ retained
final *i.

*maniŋ *n.* 'banana (*Musa* sp.)'
GWS NEN *aniŋ*
     APA *man*
NS   MUM *man*
     SIR *man*
ES   MAG *maŋ*
     AIS *maŋ*

*mapa *v.* 'dig'
     APA *mava-*
ES   MAG *map-*
     GAJ *mapa*

*mapin *n.* 'liver'
GWS MNT *map* 'head'
     APA *mavin*
NS   MUM *mav* 'heart,
          innards'
     SIR *mav* 'belly'
ES   AIS *mapin* 'sorrow'
     KUR *-map*
     GAJ *mapin*
This was (and remains) the
metaphorical seat of emotion,
similar to English *heart*.

*mara *v.* 'call to (an animal)'
GWS MND *ara-* 'say'
     NEN *ari-* 'say'
     MNT *ara-* 'say'
     APA *mal-*
ES   AIS *mar-*
Nend changed the verb class.

*marik *n.* 'sorcerer'
GWS NEN *marih*
     MNT *marik*
NS   MUM *mark*

*maru *v.* 'handle'
NS   SIR *maru* 'break'
ES   MAG *mar-* 'build'
     AIS *mar-* 'make'
     GAJ *mar(epa)* 'tear, take
          off'
Gants compounded with *ipa
'come out'.

*mata *v.* 'paddle'
        APA   *mata*
ES   AIS   *mat-*
        GAJ   *mar(wara)* 'push'
Gants compounded with *wara* 'move'.

*mafra *n.* 'crocodile'
GWS NEN   *mor*
        MNT   *mavra*
        APA   *mavɨlaŋ*
NS   MUM   *mavra*
Nend kept initial *m. Apalɨ added *ŋ*.

*mazɨn *n.* 'bowstring'
GWS MND   *asɨn*
NS   SIR   *maz*
        GAJ   *majɨm*
Gants palatalized *z > *j* and changed *n > *m*.

*mi *n.* 'thought'
        APA   *mi* 'soft spot on baby's head'
NS   SIR   *mi*
ES   MAG   *mi(ndam)-* 'think'
        AIS   *mi(ndam)-* 'think'
        KUR   *mi*
        GAJ   *mi*
Aisian compounded with *tama 'put'. Kursav and Gants did not lower final *i > ⁺*e*. See *mi tama 'think'. Compare Usan *misir* 'thought'.

*mi tama *vac.* 'think'
NS   SIR   *mi tama-*
ES   MAG   *mindam-*
        AIS   *mindam-*
        KUR   *mi rama*
        GAJ   *mi tama*
Proto-Aisian nasalized *t > *nd*. See *mi 'thought' and *tama 'put'.

*mia *n.* 'sand'
        APA   *mia(savɨ)* 'sandbar'
ES   MAG   *mi(sab), mi(sakam)*
        GAJ   *(ku)mia*
See *kasɨñ 'sand'.

*midaŋ, -mida *n.inal.* 'cross-cousin'
GWS MNT   *-mida*
        APA   *midaŋ*
NS   MUM   *-mida*
        SIR   *-mida*
ES   MAG   *-mari*
        AIS   *-mari*
        GAJ   *-mdaŋ*
Compare Kalam *-md/-mud*.

*mikuŋ *n.* 'brain'
NS   MUM   *miku* 'head'
        SIR   *miku*
ES   MAG   *mekuŋ*
        AIS   *mekoŋ*
Proto-Aisian lowered *i > *e. See *mi 'thought'. Compare PTNG *muk.

*miŋra *v.* 'vomit'
GWS MND   *igra-*
        NEN   *eŋa-* (N), *iŋa-* (S)
        APA   *miŋɨla-*
NS   MUM   *mɨhra-*
ES   KUR   *mehra*
        GAJ   *meŋra*
Nend lost *r. Mum and Kursav changed *ŋ > *h*.

*mir *n.* 'tongue'
- GWS MND *ir(ihwabiñ)*
- MNT *mir(vab)*
- APA *mel(ivik-)* 'lick'
- NS MUM *mir*
- SIR *mir*
- ES MAG *mi(gin)*

Mand lost initial *m from a monosyllable. Manat compounded with *vab* 'wing'. Apali lowered *i > e. Compare PTNG *me(l,n)e.

*mira *n.* 'firelight'
- GWS NEN *era* (S)
- MNT *mira* 'light'
- APA *mila* 'white'
- NS MUM *mira* 'flame'
- SIR *mira* 'flame'
- ES KUR *(ni)mara*
- GAJ *meraŋ*

Gants added final *ŋ*. Compare PTNG *(m,b)elak.

*mirkwa *n.* 'cordyline (*Cordyline fruticosa*)'
- GWS NEN *ekwa(nz)* (S)
- APA *milihu*
- ES MAG *miku*
- AIS *meko*
- KUR *merkwa*

Nend lost *r.

*mita *v.* 'leave'
- GWS NEN *et(o)-*; cf. *era-* 'allow'
- MNT *ita-*
- NS MUM *mita-*
- SIR *mira-*
- ES MAG *mit-*
- AIS *mit-*
- KUR *mata*
- GAJ *mera*

Nend compounded with *o-* 'go'. Proto-Aisian centered *i > i.

*mida *n.* 'sword grass (*Imperata cylindrica*)'
- GWS MND *ta*
- NEN *nta*
- APA *mida*
- ES MAG *minde*
- KUR *mida*

Magi changed final *a > e.

*midi *n.* 'blood,' *adj.* 'ripe'
- GWS MND *ti* 'b.'
- APA *midi*
- NS MUM *midi* 'r.'
- ES MAG *mindi* 'r.'

Magi kept prenasalization in *nd*. See *yagum 'blood, red'.

*miga *v.* 'come down'
- GWS MND *ka(ji)-* 'sit'
- NEN *ŋka-* 'descend'
- MNT *miga-*
- APA *miga-*
- NS MUM *miga-*
- SIR *miga-*
- ES MAG *miga, mig-*
- AIS *mig-*
- GAJ *miga* 'c. d., sleep'

Mand compounded with *ji-* 'stay'.

*migin *n.* 'penis'
- GWS NEN *ŋgir* (S)
- MNT *migin*

	NS	Mum	mig
	ES	Ais	miŋir

Nend voiced *g > ŋg. Z'graggen has *muŋgun* for Apali, which could reflect expected *migin*. Aisi lost *k and rhotacized *n > r, although this may be inherited from an alternate Proto-Sogeram form *miŋri; cf. the alternate Mum form *mihri*. Compare Kalam *mgn* 'vulva'.

*migra v. 'cut'

GWS	Nen	ŋkira- 'split'
	Mnt	migra-
	Apa	migil- 'c. into pieces'
NS	Sir	migra-

*migu, migw- v. 'go down'

GWS	Nen	ŋkw-
	Mnt	migu-
	Apa	migu-
NS	Mum	migu-
	Sir	mugu-
ES	Mag	mugu
	Ais	mug-
	Kur	moga- (PAis)
	Gaj	migo

Aisi changed the verb class, losing *w. Kursav changed *i > o and changed the verb class.

*mikum n. 'cheek'

GWS	Mnd	kum 'neck'
	Mnt	miku(g); cf.
		miku(visa) 'mouth'
	Apa	mihum
NS	Sir	muhu(pa)

Mand is semantically divergent. Manat compounded with *visa* 'skin' for 'mouth'. Compare PTNG *mVkVm.

*mini adv. 'later'

	Apa	mini
ES	Mag	mini(ŋ)
	Ais	mine(g)
	Kur	mine(i) 'a while'
	Gaj	mine 'morning'

Kursav and Magɨ added locative *=ñ.

*minɨ n. 'hair'

GWS	Mnd	di(d)
	Apa	mini
NS	Mum	min
	Sir	mini
ES	Ais	mini 'back of head'

Mand may be reduplicated. Mum lost final *ɨ.

*-miŋ n.inal. 'mother'

GWS	Mnd	miŋ 'mother.3.poss'
	Nen	miŋ(ir) 'mother.3.poss'
	Mnt	(a)miŋ
NS	Mum	-m
	Sir	-m
ES	Mag	(ya)ma
	Ais	(ya)ma
	Gaj	-miŋ

See *-mkam 'mother'.

*miŋa v. 'get, hold'

GWS	Mnd	ga- 'grab'
	Nen	ŋa-
	Mnt	miŋa-
	Apa	miŋa-
NS	Mum	miŋa-
	Sir	miŋa-
ES	Mag	miŋ-
	Ais	miŋ- 'make'
	Gaj	miŋa

7.1 Proto-Sogeram lexemes

*mir *n.* 'sister of male ego'
- GWS MND *mir(iñ)* 'male's s.'s child'
- MNT *mit*
- NS MUM *yarma*
- SIR *-rima*
- ES GAJ *(-ka)mir* 'brother of m.e.'

This form was not inalienably possessed. Proto-North Sogeram metathesized *m and *r and added inalienable possession prefixes. Gants compounded with possessive pronouns to create an inalienably possessed form.

*miraŋ *n.* 'mushroom'
- GWS MNT *(hi)mra*
- APA *milaŋ*
- ES AIS *miri*
- GAJ *miraŋ*

*mirim *n.* 'sap'
- GWS NEN *rim* (S)
- MNT *mirmir*
- APA *milim*
- NS MUM *miri*
- ES MAG *mirim* (Apali)
- AIS *mir*
- KUR *mirim*
- GAJ *mi*

Manat reduplicated. Magɨ fronted the second *ɨ > *i* and did not lose the final nasal as Aisi did, which suggests borrowing.

*mita *v.* 'be full'
- GWS MND *t(or)-*
- NEN *t(or)-* (S)
- APA *mil-*
- ES MAG *mitate* 'full (adj.)'
- KUR *mite* 'full (adj.)'

Both East Sogeram forms appear to have the 3SG.IPST suffix *-i.

*miti *n.* 'cough'
- APA *miti*
- NS MUM *miti*
- SIR *muti*
- ES KUR *mite*
- GAJ *mire*

Sirva changed *ɨ > *u*.

*-mkam *n.inal.* 'mother'
- APA *(nu)migaŋ*
- NS MUM *-maka*
- ES MAG *-ŋgi*
- AIS *-ŋgi*
- KUR *-mige*
- GAJ *ami*

See *-miŋ 'mother'.

*-mku *n.inal.* 'nibling'
- GWS MND *(ña)mku*
- MNT *-muhu*
- NS MUM *-migw*
- SIR *-mugu*

See *iwi 'nephew, niece' and *-saŋu 'different-sex nibling'.

*mu *n.* 'nose'
- APA *mu(gaŋ)*
- NS MUM *mu(duhu)*
- SIR *mi(dima)*
- ES MAG *mu(ŋgaŋ), mumu(katam)*
- AIS *mumu*
- KUR *-mo(ta)*
- GAJ *mo(demej)*

Sirva centered *u > i. Aisi reduplicated. The fact that every language has augmented the word is suspicious.

*mu 'SPEC'
	GWS	MND	b(ih)
		MNT	mu
		APA	mu 'another'
NS		MUM	mu 'another'
ES		MAG	mu
		AIS	mo
		GAJ	mo 'some'; cf. (koi)mo 'SPEC,' (kir)mo 'INDF'

Mand may not be cognate.

*(mu) kim *phrs.* '(a certain) thing'
NS	MUM	muhim 'another thing'
ES	AIS	mokim 'greed'
	GAJ	kim(na) 'thing'

This may have been a fixed expression in Proto-Sogeram. See *mu 'SPEC'.

*-muk *n.inal.* 'brother'
	GWS	MND	-(i)moh
		MNT	(a)muh
		APA	(a)mu
NS		SIR	-muv
ES		MAG	(a)muk
		AIS	-mok
		KUR	-mog

Compare Kalam -mok 'male in-law'.

*mukir *n.* 'white hair'
	GWS	MND	ukir
		NEN	ukir
		MNT	kur(umin)
		APA	muhili
ES		AIS	mokir 'white (of hair)'

Manat may have compounded with a reflex of *mini 'hair'.

*muku *n.* 'ball, round thing'
	GWS	MNT	muku 'egg'
NS		SIR	muku 'bump'
ES		AIS	muku 'ball'

*-mum *n.inal.* 'husband'
	GWS	MND	mam 'husband.3.POSS'
		NEN	mam(ir) 'husband.3.POSS'
		MNT	-mam
		APA	muŋ(aŋ)
NS		MUM	-muŋ(a)
		SIR	-muŋ
ES		MAG	-mum
		AIS	-mom
		KUR	-mo
		GAJ	-moŋ

See *kuram 'man'.

*mumim *n.* 'earthquake'
	APA	mumim
NS	SIR	mimi(nugus)
ES	GAJ	mumi

Sirva changed initial *u > i.

*muŋmi *n.* 'bee'
	GWS	MND	muŋbi 'bee sp.'
ES		AIS	mome 'bee, fly'

This Proto-Sogeram form is unusual.

*mut *n.* 'period of time'
- GWS MNT *mut* 'week'
- ES KUR *mot* 'day'
- GAJ *mod* 'during'

Proto-East Sogeram lowered *u > o. Gants nasalized *t > d.

*muyam *n.* 'cassowary (*Casuarius unappendiculatus*)'
- GWS MND *uyam*
- NEN *oyam*
- APA *muiaŋ*
- NS MUM *muya*
- SIR *muya*
- ES AIS *muyaŋ* 'c.'s call'

*-nab *n.inal.* 'daughter-in-law'
- GWS MND *-nab*
- MNT *-nab(u)*
- APA *nabe*
- NS MUM *-nab(as)*
- SIR *-nab(as)*
- ES MAG *nabai*
- AIS *nabe*

See *-b 'daughter-in-law'.

*-nabɨr *n.inal.* 'wife'
- NS MUM *(i)nabur(i)*
- SIR *-nabrɨ*
- ES MAG *abi*
- AIS *abi*
- KUR *-naba*

*nagum *n.* 'neck'
- GWS MND *akunahun* 'chin, area under jaw'
- NEN *ŋgu(rɨmb)* (S)
- MNT *ag(inɨb)* 'nape'
- NS MUM *nagw*
- SIR *nagu* 'n., nape'
- ES AIS *nagum*
- KUR *-nagu* 'nape'

Mand changed *m > n and reduplicated.

*naŋram *n.* 'frog'
- GWS MND *agram(am)* 'frog sp.'
- ES MAG *naŋam*
- AIS *naŋam*

See *kukasa 'frog'.

*naudi *n.* 'woman'
- GWS MND *aca*
- NEN *ancɨ*
- MNT *nadi*
- APA *nadi* 'daughter'
- NS MUM *navudi*
- SIR *nawad* 'daughter'
- ES MAG *nur* 'daughter'
- AIS *nor* 'daughter'
- KUR *navɨda* 'girl, daughter'
- GAJ *node*

Mand changed final *ɨ > a.

*ni, nini *pro.* 'who'
- GWS MND *ja-*
- NEN *na-*
- APA *(a)ni*
- NS MUM *nin*
- SIR *ninɨ*
- ES MAG *ni(ŋe)*
- AIS *ninɨ*
- KUR *ne*
- GAJ *nene*

Compare PTNG *wani.

*ña *v.* 'eat'
- GWS MND *ja-*
- NEN *na-*

	MNT	ña-
	APA	na-
NS	MUM	ña-
	SIR	ña-
ES	MAG	n-
	AIS	n-
	KUR	ne
	GAJ	ña

See *ñaŋña 'food'.

*ña *n.* 'son'

	GWS	MND	ñɨ
		MNT	ña
NS		SIR	ña
ES		MAG	naŋ
		AIS	naŋ
		GAJ	ne

This form was not inalienably possessed. Proto-Aisian added *ŋ*. Compare Kalam *ñ*.

*ñagur *n.* 'mosquito'

	APA	*iagui* (Mum)
NS	MUM	*ñaguri* 'bee'
	SIR	nagru
ES	MAG	nagi
	AIS	nagur

Apalɨ is difficult. Sirva changed *ñ > n and metathesized *u* and *r*. Magɨ changed *u > *ɨ before *r vocalization.

*ñama *n.inal.* 'same-sex younger sibling'

	GWS	MND	ñam
		NEN	nam
		MNT	ñama(ŋ)
		APA	ima
ES		AIS	i(rak)

See *-ra 'same-sex younger sibling'.

*ñaŋña *n.* 'food'

	GWS	MND	ñañ
		MNT	ñaŋña
NS		MUM	ñaña

An irregular nominalization of *ña 'eat'. Mand and Mum lost *ŋ.

*ñɨŋi *adj.* 'small,' *n.* 'child'

	GWS	MNT	ñiŋi
NS		MUM	ñiŋi 'child'
ES		GAJ	ñɨŋe

Manat fronted *ɨ > i.

*-ñki *n.inal.* 'paternal grandfather'

	GWS	MND	-ca(ñ)
		NEN	nca
		APA	(iau)acaŋ (PAIS)
NS		MUM	-ñigi
ES		MAG	-ky(am)
		GAJ	-ñike

See *-sɨki 'maternal grandfather'.

*-ŋti *n.inal.* 'father'

NS	SIR	(na)ŋidi
ES	MAG	-gi
	AIS	-gi
	GAJ	-ŋdoi

See *-fan 'father'.

*pafa *n.inal.* 'same-sex older sibling'

NS	SIR	pava
ES	KUR	apava

See *isaŋ and *-si 'same-sex older sibling'.

*paka *adv.* 'only'

	GWS	MNT	vaca 'one'
NS		SIR	paka 'empty'

7.1 Proto-Sogeram lexemes — 281

ES GAJ *paka* 'only,'
paka(raŋ) 'one'
Manat changed *k > c. Gants probably added =*raŋa* 'CHAR' to 'one'. See *pam 'one, only'.

*pam *adj.* 'one,' *adv.* 'only'
GWS MND *vam* 'one'
NEN *pam* 'one'
APA *pam* (C), *vam* (K)
NS MUM =*va(t)* 'one'
ES MAG *pan(da)* 'one';
pa 'only'
AIS *pan(da)* 'alone';
pa 'only'
KUR *pa*
Mand lenited *p > v. Akɨ Apalɨ is archaic. Proto-Aisian added =*ra* 'COM'. Kursav lost *m. See *paka 'only'.

*pat *n.* 'center'
GWS NEN *pa* (S) 'spine, trunk'
MNT *vat*
APA *valɨ* '(dead) body'
NS MUM *pat* 'body'
SIR *pat*
ES MAG *pad* 'log'
AIS *pɨr* 'trunk'
GAJ *pai* 'side'
Aisi changed *a > ɨ.

*pia, pi- *v.* 'take'
GWS MND *pi-*
APA *vi-, via-*
ES KUR *vu-*
Kursav changed the verb class and lenited *p > v.

*pɨdum *n.* 'stump'
GWS NEN *ntum* (S)
NS MUM *pɨdɨ*
Mum changed final *u > ɨ.

*-pɨki *n.inal.* 'paternal grandmother'
GWS MND *pic*
NEN *(a)vij*
MNT *-pas*
APA *(a)vaci*
NS MUM *-pi*
SIR *(a)vɨi*
ES GAJ *-pike*
See *-fai 'maternal grandmother'.

*pɨm *n.* 'weight'
GWS MND *ubɨ* 'heavy'
MNT *hɨm*
NS MUM *pɨm* 'heavy'
ES MAG *pum*
AIS *pum*
GAJ *pum*
Mand changed initial *ɨ > u and added final ɨ. Manat changed initial *v > h.

*pɨŋ *n.* 'buttress root'
GWS MND *pɨh*
NEN *pɨŋ*
APA *pɨŋ*
NS SIR *pɨ(gɨ)*
ES KUR *(nɨ)p*

*pɨsa *n.* 'skin'
GWS MND *sa* 'rind'
MNT *vɨsa*
APA *vɨsaŋ*

*pɨta *adj.* 'wet'
GWS NEN *(yambɨ)ta* (S)

	MNT	vita
	APA	pita
NS	SIR	pra(v)
ES	MAG	piti
	AIS	piti

Nend compounded with *yamb* 'water'.

*pubiŋ *n.* 'sweat'
GWS	MND	upɨh
	APA	vubiŋ
NS	MUM	pibi
	SIR	pubu

*puziŋ *n.* 'bone'
GWS	NEN	unsɨŋ
NS	MUM	puj
	SIR	puzu

Sirva added final *u*.

*-ra *n.inal.* 'same-sex younger sibling'
GWS	MND	(a)ri(n)
	NEN	ra(nɨr)
	MNT	-ra
	APA	-la
NS	MUM	-ra
	SIR	-ra(h)
ES	AIS	-ra(k)
	KUR	-ra
	GAJ	-ra

See **ñama* 'same-sex younger sibling'.

*=rɨ- *v.* 'be'
GWS	MND	ra- 'do'
	NEN	ra- 'do'
	MNT	rɨ- 'do'
	APA	li-, la- 'do'
NS	SIR	=rɨ-
ES	AIS	=r-

Proto-West Sogeram changed the verb class. Initial **r*, clearly reflected in West Sogeram and Aisi, strongly suggests that this form was an enclitic, which in turn suggests that the Sirva and Aisi forms, which cliticize to adjectives, are archaic.

*saban *n.* 'shore'
GWS	MND	apa(k)
	NEN	ampa
	APA	caba
ES	MAG	siban
	AIS	siban 'plain'
	GAJ	aban

Apalɨ affricated **s > c*. Proto-Aisian centered the first **a > ɨ*. Gants lost initial **s*.

*sabaN *n.* 'pig'
	APA	sabaŋ
NS	MUM	saba
	SIR	saba
ES	AIS	sabɨ

*sagam *n.* 'fight'
GWS	MNT	agam
	APA	sagaŋ
NS	MUM	saga
	SIR	saga
ES	AIS	sagɨ

*sakai *n.* 'bamboo'
GWS	NEN	ahai
	APA	sihai (Mum)
ES	GAJ	aki

Apalɨ centered the first **a > ɨ* and is archaic. Gants lost initial **s* and simplified **ai > i*.

*-saŋu *n.inal.* 'different-sex nibling'
   GWS   MND   *asagu*
   NS   SIR   *-saŋ(am)*
   See *-mku 'nibling'.

*sar *n.* 'snake'
        APA   *sa(naguŋ)*
   NS   SIR   *sa(nagu)*
   ES   KUR   *sar*
        GAJ   *sora*
   Apalɨ and Sirva compounded with the latter element from *unagu 'lizard'. Gants is problematic.

*si *n.* 'place'
   GWS   NEN   *s(am)*
        APA   *s(abɨlɨm)* 'p. of activity'
   NS   SIR   *si*
   ES   GAJ   *se*
   The forms besides Sirva and Gants are questionable. See *abra 'place'.

*-si *n.inal.* 'same-sex older sibling'
   GWS   MND   *-ze(n)*
        MNT   *-i*
        APA   *-si*
   NS   MUM   *-si*
        SIR   *-s*
   ES   MAG   *-sɨ(m)*
        AIS   *-sɨ(m)*
        KUR   *-s*
   See *isaŋ and *pafa 'same-sex older sibling'.

*siar *n.* 'starling (*Aplonis* sp.)'
   GWS   MND   *zar(hriñ)* 'red-eyed bird'
   NS   SIR   *siar*
   ES   KUR   *siai* (Gants)
   Probably referred to both *A. cantoroides* and *A. metallica*. Kursav changed final *r > *i*.

*sibirim *n.* 'navel'
   GWS   MND   *ipiriŋ*
        APA   *sibilim* (C), *cibilim* (K)
   NS   MUM   *sibirip*
        SIR   *sibir*
   ES   MAG   *sibin*
        KUR   *sibur*
   Mand changed final *m > *ŋ*. Mum changed final *m > *p*. Magɨ changed *r > *n*. Kursav changed the second *i > *u*. Compare Kalam *sblŋ*, PTNG *sibil[VC].

*sikiñ *adv.* 'three days away'
   GWS   MND   *ikij*
        APA   *ciheŋ* '3 d.a.', *cikɨli* '4 d.a.'
   ES   MAG   *sikɨr*
        AIS   *sekir* 'day after day after tomorrow'
   This set is difficult. Mand changed final *ñ > *j* and Proto-Aisian rhotacized it to *r*.

*sɨ *n.* 'smoke'
   GWS   NEN   *(piri)z*
        MNT   *(hi)s*
        APA   *(mɨ)si*
   NS   SIR   *(amuhu)s*
   ES   MAG   *sɨ*
        AIS   *(pi)sɨ*
        GAJ   *su(kum)*
   Frequent compounding makes this form questionable.

*sɨ- v. 'do'
- GWS MND sɨ- 'work'
-     NEN sɨ-
- NS MUM -s 'YPST,' -s(ma) 'FPST'
-     SIR -s 'FPST'
- ES MAG -s 'FPST'
-     AIS s- 'say,' -s 'FPST'
-     KUR (so)s- 'defecate'

The Mum FPST includes the suffix -ma 'HPST'. Kursav combined with so 'feces'.

*sɨbɨ n. 'mouth'
-     APA sɨbɨ(saŋ) 'lips'
- ES MAG simbɨ(katam)
-     KUR sɨbɨ(ka)

Magɨ kept prenasalization in mb and compounded with katam 'head'.

*sɨdaŋ n. 'fat'
-     APA sɨdaŋ
- NS MUM sija
-     SIR sɨda
- ES MAG siraŋ
-     AIS siri

Mum palatalized *d > j.

*sɨdia, sɨdi- v. 'close'
-     APA sijia- 'c., block'
- ES MAG sid-
-     KUR sidi 'closed (adj.)'

*sɨf n. 'family'
- GWS MND siv
- NS SIR (uhu)siv 'village'
- ES AIS sɨb 'village'

Sirva fronted *ɨ > i and compounded with uhu 'ground'.

*sɨgɨ n. 'pot'
- GWS NEN ncɨ
-     APA siji
- NS MUM sɨg
-     SIR sigi
- ES AIS sig
-     KUR sigi

Compare Kalam sgi.

*sɨka n. 'piece'
-     APA sɨha 'leftovers'
- NS SIR sɨha(v)
- ES MAG sikɨ
-     AIS sikɨ 'p. of wood'
-     KUR (nɨ)sika
-     GAJ sika

Kursav fronted *ɨ > i. See *tɨm 'piece'.

*sɨkan, sɨkansɨkan adv. 'completely'
-     APA sɨkan, sɨkasɨkan
- NS MUM sɨha(naga) 'everyone'
-     SIR sɨhazɨha 'c., all'
- ES AIS sɨkan, sɨkansɨkaŋ
-     KUR sikasika
-     GAJ sikasika 'debris (n.)'

Mum compounded with naga 'with'.

*-sɨki n.inal. 'maternal grandfather'
- GWS MNT -sɨh(at)
- NS MUM -sɨhi
-     SIR -sɨi
- ES MAG -siki
-     AIS -siki
-     KUR -sike

See *-ñki 'paternal grandfather'.

*sikif *n.* 'dove species'
  GWS   MNT   *(pi)hiv(ra)* 'long-tailed black and brown dove'
         APA   *sici* 'bird type'
  NS   SIR   *siiv*
  ES   AIS   *sikɨb*
  Aisi changed *i > ɨ. The Manat meaning, and the fact that I recorded this as the "basic" form for 'dove' in Sirva and Aisi, suggest the great cuckoo-dove, *Reinwardtoena reinwardti*.

*sikra *v.* 'break (intr.)'
  GWS   MND   *(esa)kri-* 'b. down the middle,'
                (uzi)kri- 'b. apart'
         APA   *sihil-* 'b., lay egg'
  NS   MUM   *sihra-*
         SIR   *sikra-*
  Mand changed the verb class.

*siku *adv.* 'very'
  NS   MUM   *sɨkw*
         SIR   *suku*
  ES   MAG   *suku*
         AIS   *suku*

*sirifir 'straight'
  GWS   MND   *irivir*
         NEN   *irivir* (Mand)
         APA   *silivɨ*
  NS   SIR   *sarawara-* 'heal'
  ES   KUR   *sururu*
  Mand changed initial *sɨ > i. Apalɨ lost final *r. Sirva and Kursav are divergent.

*sis *n.* 'grass, hair'
  GWS   MND   *sis(an)* 'grass'
         MNT   *sis* 'grass'
  ES   MAG   *sisi* 'hair'
  Magɨ fronted *ɨ > i.

*su *n.* 'feces'
         APA   *su*
  NS   MUM   *su*
  ES   MAG   *su*
         AIS   *su*
         KUR   *so*
         GAJ   *po*
  Gants changed initial *s > p.

*sudɨ *n.* 'spirit'
  GWS   MND   *itɨ*
         MNT   *sud*
         APA   *sudɨ*
  NS   MUM   *sud*
  Mand changed initial *su > i.

*sukan *n.* 'reed sp.'
  GWS   MND   *ukan*
         APA   *suhan* (K), *sukan* (C)
  Tok Pisin *tiktik*.

*sumiñ *n.* 'vine'
         APA   *sumiŋ*
  NS   SIR   *sumu*
  ES   MAG   *simi*
         AIS   *sɨme* (Kursav)
         KUR   *sime*
         GAJ   *miñ*
  Proto-East Sogeram changed initial *u > *ɨ. Gants lost initial *s.

*sura *n.* 'forest'
- GWS MNT *ura*
- APA *suli*
- ES MAG *suri*

Apalɨ and Magɨ added locative *=ñ.

*taba *n.* 'stone'
- GWS NEN *(oman)ampɨ* (S) '(finger)nail'
- APA *liba*
- NS MUM *tɨba*

Nend compounded with *oman* 'arm, hand'.

*tabra *v.* 'distribute'
- GWS MNT *rabra-* 'abound'
- APA *labɨla-*
- ES KUR *rabɨra-* 'send'

*tadam *n.* 'leg, foot'
- GWS NEN *andam*
- MNT *adam*
- NS MUM *tada*
- SIR *tada*
- ES MAG *taram* 'thigh'
- AIS *taram* 'thigh'
- GAJ *tadam* 'thigh'

*tagwa, tagw- *v.* 'sharpen'
- GWS NEN *aŋkwa-*
- MNT *agɨva-* 'scratch' (Nend)
- APA *lagu-*
- ES AIS *tuk-*

Manat changed *gw > gɨv. Aisi raised *o > u and lost *ŋ.

*tagwa, tagw- *v.* 'step on'
- GWS MND *akw-*
- NEN *aŋkwa-*
- MNT *ragu-*
- APA *lagu-*
- NS SIR *tagu-*
- ES MAG *dugwa*
- AIS *tog-*
- KUR *rago*
- GAJ *tago*

Magɨ is a verb adjunct and is difficult phonologically. See *tagwa tama 'stand'.

*tagwa tama- *svc.* 'stand'
- GWS MNT *agrama-*
- APA *lagulama-*
- NS MUM *tagurama-*
- SIR *tagurama-*
- ES KUR *ragota-*
- GAJ *tagurama, tagroma*

Kursav deleted the last syllable. See *tagwa 'step on' and *tama 'put'.

*tai *v.* 'go up'
- GWS MND *ai(nag)-* 'jump'
- NS SIR *tai-* 'go up'
- ES KUR *rai(wa)-* 'follow'

Kursav compounded with *wa 'go'. See *yaku 'go up'.

*taka *v.* 'tear'
- APA *laha*
- ES GAJ *taka* 'remove, open'

*takam *n.* 'vulva'
- GWS MND *akam*
- NEN *aham* (S)
- MNT *akam*
- NS MUM *taha*
- ES AIS *takɨ*

*takun *n.* 'moon'
	APA	*lakun*
NS	MUM	*takw*
ES	KUR	*taku*
	GAJ	*takun*

Apalɨ is archaic. Compare PTNG *takVn[V].

*takwɨ *n.* 'snake'
GWS	NEN	*akwɨ*
	APA	*lahu*
NS	MUM	*tau*

Mum deleted *h.

*tam *n.* 'tail'
GWS	MND	*tam*
NS	SIR	*tam*
ES	KUR	*-tam*

*tama *v.* 'put'
GWS	MND	*aba-*
	NEN	*ama-*
	MNT	*rama-*
	APA	*lama-*
NS	MUM	*tama-*
	SIR	*tama-*
ES	MAG	*tam-*
	AIS	*tam-*
	KUR	*rama*
	GAJ	*tama*

See *tagwa tama 'stand'.

*tamkan *n.* 'eye'
GWS	NEN	*ampin*
	MNT	*amiga*
	APA	*lamigaŋ*
NS	MUM	*tamga*
	SIR	*tarma*

ES	MAG	*tamɨ*
	AIS	*tamɨ*
	KUR	*-tama*

Nend changed the second *a > ɨ. Sirva is divergent. See *kwɨmka 'stomach'.

*tar *n.* 'tree'
GWS	NEN	*arɨ* (S)
	MNT	*tat* 'wood, fire'
	APA	*lali*
NS	SIR	*tar*
ES	MAG	*te*
	AIS	*tar*
	KUR	*tar*
	GAJ	*tai*

Nend added final *ɨ*.

*tauka *v.* 'buy'
	APA	*lava-*
NS	MUM	*tavha-*
	SIR	*taviha-*
ES	MAG	*taku, takw-*
	AIS	*takw-*

Apalɨ lost *k. Proto-Aisian metathesized *u and *k.

*ti *v.* 'become'
NS	MUM	*tɨ-* 'be, do'
	SIR	*tii-*
ES	GAJ	*ti*

Mum changed the verb class. Sirva changed *i > ii.

*tidɨ *n.* 'star'
GWS	MND	*tɨ(bah)*
	NEN	*ndɨ(vah)* (S)
	APA	*lidɨ*

	NS	Mum	tidɨ
		Sir	kidɨ (Mum)
	ES	Mag	tindɨ
		Ais	tendɨ

Proto-Greater West Sogeram lost the first *ɨ and Nend voiced *d. Sirva changed *t > k. Proto-Aisian kept prenasalization in nd.

*tɨbu v. 'tie'
	GWS	Nen	mpo(ri)-
		Mnt	rɨbu-
		Apa	lɨbu- (C)
	NS	Sir	tub(rama)-
	ES	Mag	tib- 'close'
		Ais	tib(ram)-
		Kur	(ne)rɨbu 'swallow'
		Gaj	tibo

Nend lowered *u > o. Sirva and Aisi compounded with *tama 'put'. Kursav compounded with ne 'eat'.

*tigiñ adj. 'black'
	GWS	Mnd	kiñ
		Nen	ŋkiñ
		Apa	ligiŋ 'scraps in pot'
	ES	Kur	rigi 'dirty'
		Gaj	tigin

*tɨka v. 'peel, detach'
	NS	Sir	tɨha- 'peel'
	ES	Mag	tɨka(w)- 'take,'
			tɨka(y)- 'bring'
		Ais	tik- 'take'
		Gaj	tɨko 'scrape'

Magɨ compounded with w- 'go' and y- 'come'. Gants changed verb class.

*tiki v. 'fill'
		Apa	lici- 'fetch water'
	NS	Mum	tih- (Sirva)
	ES	Mag	tik- 'fetch water'
		Ais	tiki-
		Gaj	tiki-

Apalɨ and Mum fronted *ɨ > i. See *isi 'fetch water'.

*tiku, tikw- v. 'look, see'
	GWS	Mnd	kw-
		Mnt	rɨku-
	ES	Kur	ruko

See *iga 'see, perceive'.

*tikwɨ n. 'area under'
	GWS	Nen	kwɨ
		Mnt	rɨk
		Apa	lɨhu
	NS	Mum	tuhwɨ
		Sir	tuhu
	ES	Kur	tuki

Manat lost final *u. Mum changed the first *ɨ > u. Kursav added locative *=ñ.

*tɨm n. 'piece'
	GWS	Mnd	tɨm
		Nen	tɨm (S) 'short'
		Mnt	rib
		Apa	tɨbɨ 'short'
	NS	Mum	tɨm
		Sir	timi 'stick'
	ES	Mag	tum 'stick'
		Ais	tum 'stick'
		Kur	tum 'stick'

Manat and Apalɨ changed final *m > b. Sirva added final i. See *sɨka 'piece'.

*tɨpa *v.* 'fear, be afraid'
- NS MUM *tiva-* 'run'
- ES KUR *ripa*
-    GAJ *tipa*

*tua, tu- *v.* 'burn (intr.)'
- GWS MND *va-*
-    NEN *o(ŋgi)-*
-    MNT *riva-*
- NS MUM *tu-* 'be cooked'
-    SIR *tua-*
- ES MAG *tuw-*
-    AIS *tu-*
-    KUR *ro*
-    GAJ *tua, tu-*

*tutɨm *n.* 'salt'
- GWS MND *utɨm*
-    NEN *utɨm* (S)
-    MNT *utɨm*
-    APA *lulɨm*

*ubaŋ *n.* 'heart'
- NS MUM *uba* 'lung'
-    SIR *uba*
- ES MAG *umbaŋ* 'chest'
-    AIS *umbaŋ* 'liver, chest'

Proto-Aisian kept prenasalization in *mb. Compare PTNG *mapVn.

*ufia *n.* 'morning star'
-    APA *uvia*
- NS MUM *uvia*
-    SIR *uvia*
- ES MAG *ube*
-    AIS *ubia*
-    KUR *uvia*

*ugam *adj.* 'white'
- GWS MND *ukam*
-    NEN *okam* (Mand)
- NS SIR *waga(ra)*

Nend deleted *ŋ.

*umai *n.* 'bean'
- GWS MNT *mai*
-    APA *ume*
- NS MUM *umai*
-    SIR *ume*
- ES MAG *ume*
-    AIS *ume*
-    KUR *wamai*

*upri *n.* 'dog'
- GWS NEN *uvi* (N), *ovɨr* (S)
-    MNT *upri*
- NS MUM *upri*
-    SIR *uvri*
- ES MAG *api*
-    AIS *apɨr*
-    KUR *ovɨra*
-    GAJ *opre*

Proto-Aisian changed initial *u > *a*. Kursav and Gants lowered initial *u > *o*.

*ura *v.* 'call out'
- GWS MND *ura-*
-    NEN *ora-* 'crow'
-    MNT *ura-*
-    APA *ula-*
- NS MUM *ura-*
-    SIR *warwar* 'yelling'
- ES MAG *ur-*
-    AIS *ur-*
-    KUR *wara*

Sirva is a reduplicated nominalization. See *agwa 'cry out'.

*uram *n.* 'house'
  GWS MND uram
      NEN oram
      APA ulaŋ
  NS SIR wara
  ES MAG ur
      AIS uru
      GAJ wara (Kursav)
The Aisian forms deviate from expected ⁺uri. Gants diphthongized *u > wa.

*urir *n.* 'parrot species'
  GWS MND urir
      MNT urir
      APA ulilɨ
  ES AIS wiwi
Aisi is problematic.

*wa, u- *v.* 'go, say'
  GWS MND wa- 'go'
      NEN w-, o- 'go'
      MNT vu- 'go'
      APA u-, ua-
  NS MUM u- 'go,' va- 'say'
      SIR wa- 'go,' va- 'say'
  ES MAG u- 'go'
      AIS u- 'go'
      KUR va- 'say'
      GAJ wa
This may have been two words—a motion verb and a post-quote verb—or one. The North Sogeram reflexes suggest the latter, but the polysemy in Apalɨ and Gants suggests the Proto-North Sogeram split could have been conditioned by phonological environment. Manat changed *a > u. Kursav changed *u > v.

*waka *adv.* 'maybe'
  GWS MNT aka(d)
      APA uaku (C), akua (K)
  NS MUM vaha
      SIR vaha 'when'
  ES KUR waka
      GAJ waka 'Q'
Apalɨ changed final *a > u in Acɨ and moved *w to the second syllable in Akɨ.

*yaka *v.* 'come up'
  GWS MND akai-
      NEN akay-
      MNT aka-
      APA iaha-
  NS MUM yaha-
      SIR yaha(vi-)
  ES MAG yak-
      AIS yak-
      GAJ (a)yaka
West Sogeram added final *i on analogy with *ai- 'come'. Sirva compounded with *pi-* 'come'. Gants added initial *a* by compounding with *aya* 'come,' followed by reduction.

*yaku, yakw- *v.* 'go up'
  GWS MND ako-, akw-
      NEN akwɨ-
      MNT aku-
      APA iahua-
  NS MUM yahu-
      SIR yak(ɨva)-
  ES MAG ikw-
      AIS yok-
      GAJ yako, yakw-
Sirva *-kɨv-* may be an irregular reflex of *kw. See *tai 'go up'.

*yagum *n.* 'blood, red'
    APA   *niaguŋ* (Mum) 'b., sap'
NS   MUM   *ñagw*
ES   MAG   *yaŋgum* 'b.'
    KUR   *yagum(ura)* 'r.,'
                  -*gum* 'b.'

Magɨ kept prenasalization in *ŋg*. Kursav reanalyzed the first syllable as the possessive prefix *ya-* in 'blood'. See *mɨdɨ 'blood, ripe'.

*yau *n.* 'fish'
    GWS   MND   *zau*
Compare Tauya *yau*.

7.2 Inalienably possessed nouns

Proto-Sogeram inalienably possessed nouns present a unique challenge to reconstruction because of their morphology and the pervasiveness of analogical change. Each individual etymon usually requires more discussion than a typical member of another word class, so I present the reconstructed inalienably possessed nouns here, with discussion about the semantic and morphological changes that have taken place in each form.

Recall that the class of inalienably possessed nouns is primarily composed of kin terms. In fact, all reconstructed inalienably possessed nouns are kin terms, although terms for concepts like 'friend,' 'caretaker,' or 'widow' are inalienably possessed in some modern languages and similar words may have existed in Proto-Sogeram.

Each kin term distinguished, via a possessive prefix, between first person, second person, and third person possessor. The prefixes were *a- '1.POSS,' *na- '2.POSS,' and *nɨ- '3.POSS,' although the variants *ya- '1.POSS' and *nu- '3.POSS,' which imitated the form of the singular subject pronouns, also existed. Note that the number of the possessor was not indicated by the prefix. A typical root in this regard was *-sɨki 'maternal grandfather, grandchild (through daughter) of male ego,' which could be realized as *a-sɨki 'my/our grandfather,' *na-sɨki 'your grandfather,' or *nɨ-sɨki 'his/her/their grandfather'. (Incidentally, this term and two of the other terms for grandparents end in *ki; the others are *-ñiki 'paternal grandfather' and *-pɨki 'paternal grandmother'. This is probably not a coincidence, but the significance of this *ki is still unknown.)

The form of the entries below is as follows. The primary root is given on the left, followed by the reconstructed 1.POSS, 2.POSS, and 3.POSS forms, given with any prefixes. The meaning of the form is given following these on the first line. Subsequent lines contain the cognate words from the various languages, also arranged into 1.POSS, 2.POSS, and 3.POSS columns. Sometimes I only have one form available for a language (usually 1.POSS), in which case the 2.POSS and 3.POSS columns are left blank. But blank columns may also indicate that a language has innovated a new form for a particular meaning. (This means that I do not distinguish notationally between the absence, in my data, of a form for a given meaning, and the presence of non-cognate material to refer to that meaning.) When a single form can be used with any possessor, it repeated in each column. Comments are given below the correspondence sets. The Apalɨ and Mum kin charts in Wade (1991) and Sweeney (1994b), respectively, have been particularly helpful. A few terms are used that are specific to kinship studies. 'Nibling' covers both 'nephew' and 'niece'. 'Motherling' and 'fatherling' refer to a child of a woman or a man, respectively, irrespective of the sex of the referent. Children of same-sex siblings are 'parallel cousins'; children of different-sex siblings are 'cross-cousins'.

*-f		*a-fɨ	*na-f, na-kaf	*nu-f	'mother's brother'
GWS	Mnd	a-v(ar)	a-v(ar)	Ø-v(ar)	'same-sex cross-cousin'
	Mnt	avɨ	na-hav	nɨ-hav	
NS	Mum	avav	na-hav, na-vɨ(tak)	nɨŋu-vɨ(tak)	
ES	Kur	a-v	na-v	no-v	'm.'s b., man's sister's child'
	Gaj	a-pu	na-pu	nu-pu	

The Greater West Sogeram forms reflect a change of the 3.POSS prefix to *nɨ- (> PGWS *Ø-) by analogy with the predominant pattern. Manat changed the 3.POSS root on analogy with the 2.POSS form. Mum reduplicated the 1.POSS form. Gants changed final *ɨ > u in 1.POSS and generalized that form.

*-fa		*a-fa	*na-fa	*nɨ-fa	'sister-in-law of female ego'
GWS	Apa	ava			'female ego's brother's wife'
	Sir	a-vah	na-vah	nɨ-vah	
ES	Gaj	apa			

Referred to a female ego's brother's wife or her husband's sister. The Apalɨ term is also used by the husband of ego to refer to his wife's brother's wife. Sirva added h.

*-fai	*a-fai	*na-fai	*nɨ-fai	'mother's mother, motherling's motherling, wife's mother'

GWS	Mnt	a-vay(aŋ)	na-vay(aŋ)	nɨ-vay(aŋ)	'grandfather, wife's father'
	Apa	a-ve			'grandfather'
ES	Mag	-be(b)			'grandmother, woman's grand-child, mother's older sister'
	Ais	a-boi	na-boi	nɨ-boi	'grandmother, mother's older sister'
	Kur	a-vi(s) 'voc'	na-vi(s)		'grandmother'

'Grandparent/grandchild' meanings are found in every language. An affinal meaning is only found in Manat, but I reconstruct affinal meaning based on patterns of meaning in other grandparent terms (similar patterns of polysemy between grandkin and parents-in-law are also found in some Australian languages; Koch forthcoming). I also reconstruct 'maternal grandmother' for external reasons: given that two 'grandmother' terms can be reconstructed, and the other means 'paternal grandmother' in Mum, this one is most likely to have referred to maternal grandmothers even though it only means 'grandmother, grandchild of female ego' today—if it even means 'grandmother' at all. Aisi changed *a > o.

*-fan, *-ŋti		*ya-faŋ	*na-ŋti	*nɨ-fan	'father, father's brother'
GWS	Mnd			van	
	Nen		on(ar)	wan(ɨr)	
	Mnt	a-vaŋ	na-va	nɨva	
	Apa	iavaŋ			
NS	Mum	yava, yavad(ak)	nava, navad(ak)	niŋuva, niŋuvad(ak)	
	Sir	yava	naŋidi	nua	
ES	Mag	waba	na-gi	nu-gi	
	Ais		na-gi	no-gi	
	Kur	awi 'voc'			
	Gaj	yaŋ, yaŋdoi	naŋ, naŋdoi	noŋ, noŋdoi	

This form probably referred to father's older and younger brothers, but is restricted to younger brothers in Sirva and Magɨ, and to older brothers in Gants. Compare *-ifi 'father's younger brother'. The 2.POSS and 3.POSS reconstructions may have been coexisting variants that were each used in both 2.POSS and 3.POSS functions; only in Sirva are the reflexes restricted to 2.POSS and 3.POSS, respectively. Proto-Greater West Sogeram and Mum generalized the 3.POSS root to 2.POSS. Nend changed PWS *a-wan to on. In Mum the suffix -tak, frequently found on kin terms, is -*dak*, showing evidence of the root-final *n. Proto-East Sogeram generalized the 2.POSS root to 3.POSS, and Gants generalized it to 1.POSS as well. Proto-Aisian merged *ŋt > *ŋg > *g*. Magɨ changed *[j] > *w* in 1.POSS. Kursav changed 1.POSS final *aŋ > *ɨ* by analogy with the other forms. Gants inserted *o* and made the last syllable (-*doi*) optional (although this may have been the pattern in Proto-Sogeram).

*-ifi		*a-ifi	*na-ifi	*n-ifi	'father's younger brother'
GWS	MND	a-ivi	a-ivi	Ø-ivi	
	APA	ivɨ			
ES	MAG	a-yib			
	AIS	a-yeb			
	GAJ	a-ipi	na-ipi	n-ipi	

Apalɨ lost initial *a and changed final *i > *ɨ*. Gants did not lower final *i > ⁺*e*.

*-kun		*a-kun	*na-kun	*nɨ-kun	'co-wife'
GWS	MND	aihun	aihun	aihun	'woman's sister-in-law'
	MNT		na-kɨna	nɨ-kɨna	'man's sister'
	APA	ahun			'co-wife'
ES	GAJ	a-kun	na-kun	no-kun	'co-wife, woman's sister'

This term referred to a woman's husband's other wife, or his brother's wife. Mand refers to a woman's brother's wife or her husband's sister. The form adds *i, which may be cognate with the Proto-Kainantu prefix *i-, which specified "maleness of ego in affinal linkage" (Kerr 1973: 786), although there is little internal Sogeram data to support that hypothesis. Manat changed *u > *ɨ* and added *a.

*-mida		*midaŋ	*na-mida	*nɨ-mida	'cross-cousin'
GWS	MNT	midaŋ	na-mida	nɨ-mida	
	APA	midaŋ			
NS	MUM	ya-mida	na-mida	nɨ-mida	
	SIR	mida	na-mida	nɨ-mida	
ES	MAG	ya-mari	na-mari	nɨ-mari	(Aisi)
	AIS	ya-mari	na-mari	nɨ-mari	
	GAJ	ya-mdaŋ	na-mdaŋ	nɨ-mdaŋ	'same-sex cross-cousin'

Mum and Proto-East Sogeram added the prefix *ya- by analogy with the 1SG pronoun. Proto-Aisian metathesized the vowels, and Magɨ changed *d > *r*, suggesting the form is an Aisi loan. Gants lost *i and generalized the final nasal from the 1.POSS form to the other forms.

7.2 Inalienably possessed nouns

		*-miŋ,	*-mkam	*ya-miŋ	*na-miŋ, na-mkam	*ni-miŋ, ni-mkam	'mother, m.'s sister, man's older brother's wife'
GWS	MND					miŋ	
	NEN			yaŋ	yaŋ(ar)	miŋ(ɨr)	
	MNT			a-mɨŋ	na-m	nɨ-m	
	APA			iamɨga	iam(ɨna)	iam(ɨnu), numɨgaŋ	
NS	MUM			yam, yamaka	nam, namaka	nɨŋum, nɨŋumaka	
	SIR			yam(da)	nam	nɨmɨ	
ES	MAG			yama	naŋgi	nɨŋgi	
	AIS			yama	naŋgi	nɨŋgi	
	KUR				namɨge	nɨmɨge	
	GAJ			ami, yamɨŋ	nam(doi), namɨŋ	no-m(doi), no-mɨŋ	

The meaning 'mother' is found in all languages; 'mother's sister' in all but Mand. 'Older brother's wife' is in Mand, Apalɨ, Sirva, Magɨ, Aisi, and Kursav, and in the non-East Sogeram languages the term is restricted to male egos. The Proto-Sogeram final element *-kam is also found in other terms for female kin (e.g. Manat *nadɨgam* 'daughter'). Nend changed final *mɨŋ > ŋ in 1.POSS and generalized that root to 2.POSS. Manat and Gants changed the 1.POSS prefix to *a-* by analogy with the predominant pattern. Apalɨ extended the *-mkam root to 1.POSS, with loss of the final nasal. Mum inserted *a* between *mk. Proto-East Sogeram changed the 2.POSS and 3.POSS root *-mkam > *-mgi by analogy with PES *-gi 'father'. Proto-Aisian changed final *ɨ > a in 1.POSS and merged *mg to ŋg in 2.POSS and 3.POSS. Gants added *-doi* to 2.POSS and 3.POSS by analogy with *-ŋdoi* 'father'.

		*-mku	*iwi	*na-mku	*ni-mku	'nibling'
GWS	MND		ñamku	ñamku	ñamku	'female ego's brother's child'
	MNT		a-muhu	na-muhu	ni-muhu	'female ego's brother's child'
	APA		iui			'male ego's sister's child'
NS	MUM		ya-mɨgw	na-mɨgw	ni-mɨgw	
	SIR			na-mugu	ni-mugu	'male ego's sister's child'
ES	GAJ		(ne) yue			

This term probably referred to the child of any different-sex sibling. Mand changed *n in the 2.POSS form > ñ (possibly on analogy with *ñama 'same-sex younger sibling') and generalized that form. Manat and Mum formed 1.POSS forms by analogy with other forms. Gants *yue* is no longer inalienably possessed, but occurs with *ne* 'child'.

*-muk		*a-muk	*na-muk	*ni-muk	'brother of female ego'
GWS	Mnd	*a-imoh*	*a-imoh*	Ø-*imoh*	'wife's brother'
	Mnt	*amuh*	*amuh*	*amuh*	'woman's b., woman's b.'s son'
	Apa	*amu*		*nu-mɨ*	
NS	Sir	*a-muv*	*na-muv*	*ni-muv*	
ES	Mag	*amuk*			
	Ais	*a-mok*	*na-mok*	*ni-mok*	
	Kur	*a-mog*	*na-mog*	*nu-mog*	'nibling, cross-cousin'

This term also referred to parallel cousins. Mand added *i, which may be cognate with the Proto-Kainantu prefix *i-, which specified "maleness of ego in affinal linkage" (Kerr 1973: 786), although there is little internal Sogeram data to support that hypothesis; cf. *-kun 'sister-in-law'. The Manat 1.POSS form was generalized to all persons. Apalɨ lost final *k and changed final *u > ɨ in 3.POSS. Sirva changed final PNS *h > v. Kursav changed final *k > g.

*-mum		*kuram	*na-mum	*ni-mum	'husband'
GWS	Mnd			*mam*	
	Nen			*mam(ɨr)*	
	Mnt		*na-mam*	*ni-mam*	
	Apa	*muŋ(aŋ)*			'h., h.'s younger brother'
NS	Mum	*ya-muɲa*	*na-muɲa*	*ni-muɲa*	
	Sir	*kura*	*na-muŋ*	*nu-muŋ*	
ES	Mag	*kur*	*na-mum*	*ni-mum*	
	Ais	*kuru*	*na-mom*	*ni-mom*	
	Kur		*na-mo*	*nu-mo*	
	Gaj	*kura*	*na-moŋ*	*ni-moŋ*	cf. -*mam* 'brother of female ego'

Proto-Greater West Sogeram changed *u > a, although the Gants term for brother of female ego suggests there may have been two Proto-Sogeram terms, *-mum and *-mam, which differed somehow. The 1.POSS term is not an inalienable noun but just the word for 'man'; this was replaced by analogy with forms based on the 2.POSS and 3.POSS root in Apalɨ and Mum.

*-nab		*nabai	*na-nab	*ni-b	'daughter-in-law'
GWS	Mnd	*a-nab*	*a-nab*	Ø-*nab*	
	Mnt	*nab(u)*	*na-nab(u)*	*ni-nab(u)*	'daughter- or sister-in-law'

7.2 Inalienably possessed nouns — 297

	APA	*nabe*			
NS	MUM	*inab(as)*	*na-nab(as)*	*nɨ-b(as)*	'd.i.l., woman's brother's wife'
	SIR	*inab(as)*	*na-nab(as)*	*nɨ-b(as)*	
ES	MAG	*nabai*			
	AIS	*nabe*			'man's daughter-in-law'
	KUR	*ya-b(isim)*	*na-b(isim)*	*nɨ-b(isim)*	

Mand generalized the pattern in 2.POSS and 3.POSS to 1.POSS. Manat added final *u* and generalized the 2.POSS root to 3.POSS. Proto-North Sogeram added initial *ɨ in 1.POSS and generalized the 2.POSS root to 1.POSS. Kursav generalized the 3.POSS root to 1.POSS and 2.POSS, and added a 1.POSS prefix by analogy with the 1SG pronoun.

*-nabɨr			***abi**	***na-nabɨr**	***nɨ-nabɨr**	'wife'
	NS	MUM	*inaburi*			'wife, woman's son-in-law'
		SIR		*na-nabri*	*nabri*	
	ES	MAG	*abi*	*na-kabi*	*nɨ-kabi*	
		AIS	*abi*	*na-kabi*	*nɨ-kabi*	
		KUR		*na-naba*	*ni-naba*	

Mum seems to be an analogic combination of the *abi* root and the *-nabɨr* root. AIS combined *abi with possessive pronouns to form the 2.POSS and 3.POSS forms. Kursav changed final *ɨr > *a*, but the reconstruction of 2.POSS and 3.POSS forms, at least, seems secure based on Sirva and Kursav.

*-ñki			***a-ñki**	***na-ñki**	***nɨ-ñki**	'father's father, fatherling's fatherling, husband's father'
	GWS	MND	*a-ca(ñ)*	*a-ca(ñ)*	*Ø-ca(ñ)*	
		NEN	*nca*			
		APA	*aji* 'grandchild'			cf. *(iau)acaŋ* 'grandfather' (PAIS?)
	NS	MUM	*a-ñigi*	*na-ñigi*	*nɨ-ñigi*	cf. *-igi* 'ancestor'
		SIR	*aji(da)*			'father's older brother'
	ES	MAG	*a-ky(am)*	*na-ky(am)*	*nɨ-ky(am)*	
		GAJ	*a-ñɨke*	*na-ñɨke*	*nɨ-ñɨke*	

'Grandfather/grandchild' meanings are found in every language but Sirva. 'Father-in-law' meanings are in Manat and Gants, where it also means 'son-in-law'. This was one of two 'grandfather' terms, the other being *-sɨki. For discussion of the semantic reconstruction and innovations, see that entry. Proto-Greater West Sogeram changed final *ɨ > *a. Apalɨ and Sirva merged *ñk to *j*. Aisi lost *ñ but palatalized *k > *ky*, and added final *am*; its cognacy is doubtful. This form also seems to have been borrowed into Apalɨ as *iauacaŋ* 'grandfather'.

*-pɨki		***a-pɨki**	***na-pɨki**	***nɨ-pɨki**	'father's mother, motherling's fatherling, husband's mother'
GWS	Mnd	a-pɨc	a-pɨc	Ø-pɨc	
	Nen	avɨj	avɨjar	pajɨr	
	Mnt	a-pas	na-pas	nɨ-pas	
	Apa	avaci			'parent's mother's brother'
NS	Mum	a-pi	na-pi	nɨ-pi	
	Sir	a-vɨi			'parent's same-sex older sibling'
ES	Gaj	a-pɨke	na-pɨke	no-pɨke	

'Grandmother/grandchild' meanings are found in every language but Apalɨ and Sirva. 'Mother-in-law' meanings are in Manat and Gants, where it also means 'daughter-in-law'. This was one of two 'grandmother' terms, the other being *-fai. It means 'paternal grandmother' only in Mum, but other meanings specify a male linking relative in Manat ('husband's mother') and Gants ('son's wife'), suggesting that the Mum meaning is archaic. Nend voiced *p > v and changed PGWS *c > j. Manat changed final *ki > s. It also changed *ɨ > a, along with Apalɨ. Mum lost PNS *ɨh; this may have been a borrowing from Sirva.

*-ra		***ñama**	***na-ra**	***nɨ-ra**	'same-sex younger sibling (ssys), spouse's ssys, ssys's spouse'
GWS	Mnd	ñam	a-rɨ(n)	ɨran	
	Nen	nam		ra(nɨr)	
	Mnt	ñama(ŋ)	na-ra	nɨ-ra	
	Apa	ima		nu-la	
NS	Mum	ya-ra	na-ra	niŋu-ra	
	Sir		na-ra(h)	nara(h)	
ES	Ais	i-ra(k)	na-ra(k)	nɨ-ra(k)	
	Kur		na-ra	no-ra	
	Gaj	a-ra	na-ra	no-ra	'different-sex sibling-in-law'

This term also referred to parallel cousins. In Mand, Apalɨ, Aisi, and Kursav, the term can be extended to different-sex younger siblings as well, suggesting the extension was possible in Proto-Sogeram. Meanings referring to spouse's sibling are found in Mand, Manat, Apalɨ, Mum, and Gants; meanings referring a sibling's spouse are in Mand, Apalɨ, Mum, and Gants. The Mand 3.POSS form is difficult. Manat added final *ŋ* to the 1.POSS form by analogy with *tasaŋ* 'same-sex older sibling'. Apalɨ and Aisi changed initial *ña > i in 1.POSS by analogy with *isaŋ 'same-sex older sibling'. Mum, Aisi and Gants changed the 1.POSS form by analogy with other forms. Apalɨ, Kursav, and Gants changed the 3.POSS prefix by analogy with the 3SG pronoun.

*-saɲu			***a-saɲu**	***na-saɲu**	***nɨ-saɲu**	'different-sex nibling?'
GWS	MND		*asagu*			'woman's brother's son'
NS	SIR		*a-saŋam*	*na-saŋam*	*nɨ-siŋam*	'mother's brother's wife, man's sister's son's wife'

This would have been used for a different-sex relationship between a nibling and an aunt/uncle. Sirva added final *am*, a formative associated with female referents in some other Sogeram kin terms.

*-si			***isaŋ, pafa**	***na-si**	***nɨ-si**	'same-sex older sibling (ssos), spouse's ssos, ssos's spouse'
GWS	MND		*a-saŋ*	*a-zen*	*Ø-zen*	
	NEN		*azɨŋ*	*aynar*	*yanɨr*	
	MNT		*tasaŋ*	*na-i*	*nɨ-i*	
	APA		*isaŋ*		*nu-si*	
NS	MUM		*ya-si*	*na-si*	*niŋu-si*	
	SIR		*pava*	*na-s*	*nɨ-si*	
ES	MAG		*isaŋ*	*na-sɨ(m)*	*nɨ-sɨ(m)*	(Aisi)
	AIS		*isam*	*na-sɨ(m)*	*nɨ-sɨ(m)*	
	KUR		*apava*	*na-s*	*no-s*	'older brother'

This term also referred to parallel cousins. In Mand, Apalɨ, and Aisi, the term can be extended to different-sex older siblings as well, suggesting the extension was possible in Proto-Sogeram. Meanings referring to spouse's sibling are found in Mand, Manat, Apalɨ, and Mum; meanings referring a sibling's spouse are in Mand, Apalɨ, and Mum. Two 1.POSS forms can be reconstructed based on diverse witnesses; what distinguished them is unclear. Proto-Greater West Sogeram changed the *i in the 1.POSS form > *a by analogy with the usual prefix *a-. The rest of the West Sogeram forms are difficult. Manat changed the *i in the 1.POSS form to a nursery syllable. Apalɨ and Kursav changed the 3.POSS prefix by analogy with the 3SG pronoun. Mum changed the 1.POSS form by analogy with the other forms. Aisi changed the final *ŋ in the 1.POSS form > *m and then added *m* to the other forms by analogy. The Magɨ 2.POSS and 3.POSS forms may thus be borrowed from Aisi.

*-sɨki		*a-sɨki	*na-sɨki	*nɨ-sɨki	'mother's father, fatherling's motherling, wife's father'
GWS	MNT	a-sɨh(at)	na-sɨh(at)	nɨ-sɨh(at)	'grandmother, wife's mother'
	APA	asi			'son-in-law'
NS	MUM	a-sɨhi	na-sɨhi	nɨ-sɨhi	cf. -sɨhat 'maternal grandmother'
	SIR	asi	na-sɨi	nɨ-sɨi	
ES	MAG			nɨ-siki	Archaic.
	AIS	a-siki	na-siki	nɨ-siki	
	KUR		na-sike	no-sike	

This was one of two 'grandfather' terms, the other being *-ñki. 'Grandfather/grandchild' meanings are found in every language but Apalɨ. Affinal meanings are only in Manat and Apalɨ, but given the polysemy of other grandparent terms I reconstruct 'wife's father' as part of the meaning. In most languages it means simply 'grandmother' the 'maternal grandmother' meaning is only found in Mum, but other meanings (Manat and Apalɨ) also specify a female linking relative, suggesting that the Mum meaning is archaic. Manat voiced *k > h, which may suggest that the added material on the end is -hat, not just -at. Apalɨ lost expected ^{t}h. The Sirva 1.POSS form is irregular. Kursav changed the 3.POSS prefix by analogy.

7.3 English – Proto-Sogeram finderlist

This list is intended as a reference to help readers find specific Proto-Sogeram forms. It presents all the meanings that have been reconstructed for Proto-Sogeram, the part of speech of the associated Proto-Sogeram form, and the Proto-Sogeram form itself.

act badly *v.* *ibra
afternoon *adv.* *kɨftiti
air *n.* *afɨr
anger *n.* *igif
appear (at) *svc.* *ipa mɨga
area *n.* *abra
area under *n.* *tɨkwɨ
arm *n.* *kuman

armpit *n.* *kwɨgɨs
arrow, kind of *n.* *kɨŋaN
axe *n.* *kakri; *kinaŋ
back *n.* *kut
bad *adj.* *idua
bag *n.* *faŋan
ball *n.* *muku
bamboo *n.* *sakai

banana *n.* *maniŋ
barter *v.* *ifra
be *v.* *=rɨ-
be afraid *v.* *tɨpa
be full *v.* *mɨta
bean *n.* *umai
become *v.* *ti
bee *n.* *muŋmi
before *kusai
betel pepper *n.* *kamura
betelnut *n.* *kari
bird *n.* *kapa
bird of paradise *n.* *kuyif
bite *v.* *isa
black *adj.* *tɨgiñ
black cockatoo *n.* *kwɨñaŋ
blood *n.* *mɨdɨ; *yagum
blow *v.* *kra
body *n.* *kadi
boil *v.* *kugra
bone *n.* *kañaŋ; *puzɨŋ
bow *n.* *kɨmi
bowstring *n.* *mazɨn
brain *n.* *mikuŋ
branch *n.* *makam
breadfruit *n.* *kasam
break (intr.) *v.* *kubru; *sɨkra
breast *n.* *aman
brother *n.inal.* *-muk
brush-turkey, collared *n.* *aŋam
brush-turkey, wattled *n.* *kɨñakuŋ
burn (intr.) *v.* *tua, tu-
burst *v.* *fɨku
butterfly *n.* *apapara
buttress root *n.* *pɨŋ
buy *v.* *tauka
call out *v.* *ura
call to (an animal) *v.* *mara
carry *v.* *i; *kapu
carry away *v.* *akwra

carry on shoulder *v.* *kɨbar, kɨbari-
cassowary *n.* *muyam
center *n.* *pat
centipede *n.* *kudar
cheek *n.* *mɨkum
chicken *n.* *ikakara
child *n.* *ñɨŋi
chin *n.* *akar
chop *v.* *ika; *kwaka
close *v.* *sɨdia, sɨdi-
cloud *n.* *kamu
coconut *n.* *kuimaŋ
cold *kɨmri
come *v.* *aya, fai-
come down *v.* *mɨga
come out, across *v.* *ipa
come up *v.* *yaka
completely *adv.* *sɨkan, sɨkansɨkan
cook *v.* *kugra
cordyline *n.* *mirkwa
cough *n.* *mɨti
co-wife *n.inal.* *-kun
crocodile *n.* *mafra
crooked *adj.* *kina, kinakina
cross-cousin *n.inal* *midaŋ, -mida
cry *v.* *irɨka
cry out *v.* *agwa
cut *v.* *fɨka; *ika; *kwaka; *mɨgra
daughter-in-law *n.inal.* *-b, -nab
dawn *vac.* *fɨr kama
day *adv.* *iŋar
day before yesterday *adv.* *añɨkwriñ
decoration (festival) *n.* *kazɨŋ
detach *v.* *tɨka
die *v.* *kɨmu
dig *v.* *mapa
distribute *v.* *tabra
do *v.* *ada, adɨ-; *sɨ-
dog *n.* *upri
dove species *n.* *sɨkif

earthquake *n.* *mumim
eat *v.* *ña
edge *n.* *irañ
eel *n.* *kɨbaram
egg *n.* *maga
exceed *vac.* *ir wara
exchange *v.* *ifra
eye *n.* *tamkan
family *n.* *sif
far *ataŋ
fasten *v.* *kaka
fat *n.* *sɨdaŋ
father *n.inal.* *-ŋti, -fan
father's younger brother *n.inal.* *-ifi
fear *v.* *tɨpa
feces *n.* *su
fetch water *v.* *isi
fight *n.* *kira; *sagam
fill *v.* *tɨki
finish *v.* *fɨkara
fire *n.* *af
firelight *n.* *mira
first *kusai
firstborn *n.* *kiman
fish *n.* *yau
fly *v.* *fumra
flying fox *n.* *karif
focus particle *adv.* *agi
fog *n.* *kamu
food *n.* *ñaŋña
foot *n.* *tadam
footprint *n.* *kiwañ
forest *n.* *sura
frog *n.* *kukasa; *naŋram
garden *n.* *kuar
get *v.* *mɨŋa
get up *v.* *kɨpa
give *v.* *igwa, igw-
go *v.* *wa, u-
go bad (of food) *v.* *ibra

go down *v.* *mɨgu, mɨgw-
go in *v.* *ipu
go up *v.* *yaku, yakw-; *tai
good *adj.* *arum; *ibɨd
grandfather, maternal *n.inal.* *-sɨki
grandfather, paternal *n.inal.* *-ñki
grandmother, maternal *n.inal.* *-fai
grandmother, paternal *n.inal.* *-pɨki
grass *n.* *sɨs
ground *n.* *fɨr
ground possum *n.* *igɨn
grow *v.* *kukra
hair *n.* *mɨnɨ; *sɨs
hair, white *n.* *mukɨr
hand *n.* *kuman
hear *v.* *idar, idarɨ-
heart *n.* *ubaŋ
hide (intr.) *v.* *ipra
hit *v.* *ifu
handle *v.* *maru
hold *v.* *i; *mɨŋa
hook *n.* *kag
house *n.* *uram
husband *n.inal.* *-mum
jaw *n.* *kaban
jump *v.* *kupra
just *adv.* *kap
knot *n.* *kugɨ
land *n.* *fɨr
later *adv.* *mɨni
laugh *n.* *arɨN
leaf *n.* *asɨŋ; *faga
leave *v.* *mita
leg *n.* *tadam
liver *n.* *mapɨn
loincloth *n.* *kaura
long *adj.* *kutaŋ
look *v.* *tɨku, tɨkw-
look for *v.* *fVkra
louse *n.* *iman

male *adj.* *maka
man *n.* *kuram
maybe *adv.* *waka
middle *n.* *arɨka
millipede *n.* *kamɨŋawa
mist *n.* *figau
moon *n.* *takun
morning *adv.* *ikudɨ
morning star *n.* *ufia
mosquito *n.* *ñagur
mother *n.inal* *-mkam, -mɨŋ
mother's brother *n.inal.* *-kaf, -f, -fɨ
mountain *n.* *apar
mouth *n.* *sɨbɨ
mushroom *n.* mɨraŋ
name *n.* *ibi
navel *n.* *sibirɨm
near *adv.* *kɨñam
neck *n.* *nagum
nephew *n.inal.* *iwi, -mku
new *adj.* *kɨki
niece *n.inal.* *iwi, -mku
night *n.* *kɨfɨr
nose *n.* *mu
one *adj.* *pam
only *adv.* *paka; *pam
open *v.* *idua, idu-
paddle *v.* *mata
paint tree *n.* *kɨñakw
parrot species *n.* *iran; *urir
path *n.* *kubɨ
peel *v.* *tɨka
penis *n.* *mɨgɨn
perceive *v.* *idar, idarɨ-; *iga
period of time *n.* *mut
pick (from plant) *v.* *maka
piece *n.* *sɨka; *tɨm
pierce *v.* *kui
pig *n.* *sabaN
place *n.* *abra; *si

plant *v.* *kur, kurɨ-
plate *n.* *kunaŋ
pot *n.* *sɨgi
pull *v.* *magra
put *v.* *tama
put in pot *v.* *imu
red *n.* *yagum
reed sp. *n.* *sukan
remove *v.* *kubra
ripe *adj.* *mɨdɨ
roast *v.* *kra
root *n.* *kɨdɨr
run *v.* *kaŋra
sago *n.* *makin
sago grub *n.* *kukɨ
saliva *n.* *kibañ
salt *n.* *tutɨm
sand *n.* *kasɨñ; *mia
sap *n.* *mɨrɨm
say *v.* *wa, u-
scratch *v.* *fɨr, frɨ-
see *v.* *iga; *tɨku, tɨkw-
sharpen *v.* *tagwa, tagw-
sharpness *n.* *irañ
shoot *v.* *kui; *kur, kurɨ-
shore *n.* *saban
sibling, same-sex older *n.inal.* *isaŋ, pafa, -si
sibling, same-sex younger *n.inal.* *ñama, -ra
sickness *n.* *kadi
side (of body) *n.* *madɨŋ
sister (of male ego) *n.* *mɨr
sister-in-law *n.inal.* *-fa
skin *n.* *pɨsa
sleep *n.* *abɨta; *aku
slice *v.* *fɨka
small *adj.* ñɨŋi
smoke *n.* *sɨ
snake *n.* *sar; *takwɨ

son *n.* *ña
sorcerer *n.* *marɨk
sore *n.* *fim
speak *v.* *aba
spear *n.* *kɨsar
SPECIFIC *mu
speech *n.* *kia
spin *v.* *ir, irɨ-
spirit *n.* *sudɨ
stand *svc.* *tagwa tama
star *n.* *tidɨ
starling *n.* *siar
stay *v.* *kɨña, kɨñɨ-
step on *v.* *tagwa, tagw-
stomach *n.* *kwɨmka
stone *n.* *taba
straight *sɨrɨfɨr
stump *n.* *pɨdum
sugar *n.* *akɨru
sulphur-crested cockatoo *n.* *kayagi
sun *n.* *ina; *iŋar
sweat *n.* pubiŋ
swell *v.* *kukra
sword grass *n.* *mɨda
tail *n.* *tam
take *v.* *pia, pi-
take off *v.* *kubra
tear *v.* *taka
thing (a certain) *phrs.* *(mu) kɨm
think *vac.* *mi tama
thought *n.* *mi
three days away *adv.* *sikɨñ
throat *n.* *agu

throw *v.* *kapra
tie *v.* *kaka; *tɨbu
together *adv.* *kaba
tomorrow *adv.* *amur
tongue *n.* *mir
tooth *n.* *maka
tree *n.* *tar
true *adj.* *kada
turn *v.* *ir, irɨ-
two days away *adv.* *añɨr
unripe *adj.* *kaur
very *adv.* *kada; *sɨku
Victoria crowned pigeon *n.* *kubin
village *n.* *kayabra
vine *n.* *sumɨñ
vomit *v.* *miŋra
vulva *n.* *takam
walk *v.* *kɨda
watch *v.* *kikra
weight *n.* *pɨm
wet *adj.* *pɨta
what *pro.* *atɨ
whistle *n.* *kugiŋ
white *adj.* *ugam
who *pro.* *ni, nini
wife *n.inal.* *abi, -nabɨr
wind *n.* *afɨr
wing *n.* *abiŋ
woman *n.* *naudi
yam *n.* *kuza
yellow *adj.* *kuga
yesterday *adv.* *amɨr

Chapter 8
Conclusion

In the preceding chapters I have reconstructed aspects of the phonology, lexicon, verbal and nominal morphology, and grammar of Proto-Sogeram (PSOG). I proposed that the comparative method can be applied to grammatical constructions, when these are properly understood, and the application of these ideas was reasonably successful. Because of the nature of grammatical borrowing, though, a method had to be devised that emphasized the reconstruction of partially schematic constructions, that is, constructions that contain some amount of directly specified phonological material. This meant that in certain domains—notably the noun phrase—the method was relatively unsuccessful. There simply isn't enough morphology, in the grammars of the Sogeram languages, that is associated with the relative order of head noun and attributive noun, or head noun and adjective, in order to enable a secure reconstruction. Consequently, even in cases of nearly perfect unity among daughter language constructions, my reconstruction has had to remain tentative, if it can be proposed at all. But in other domains, where grammatical constructions contain more morphology, the effort has been much more fruitful. Several constructions could be reconstructed with a fair amount of certainty, including verbal clause negation, serial verb constructions, nonverbal predicate structure, switch reference, and clause chain nominalization.

In comparative reconstruction the historical linguist is always limited to making those reconstructions that are allowed by the data. Because the methodology I employed made more stringent requirements of the data than other methods for reconstructing syntax, one might reasonably have supposed that the data simply wouldn't be good enough for much to be reconstructed. It is reassuring to see that this was not the case.

In addition to the fairly novel domain of syntactic reconstruction, I also engaged in a great deal of more traditional reconstruction. The success of the comparative method in this case will not surprise many, I expect, but it is still good to see that it was able to reconstruct the phonology, twelve paradigms of verbal agreement suffixes, several other pieces of verbal morphology, inalienable possession prefixes, a complex system of demonstratives, five sets of pronouns, and 324 words. All of this is summarized below, in a sketch of the grammar of Proto-Sogeram. I then provide two constructed Proto-Sogeram texts as an illustration of the language in §8.2.

8.1 Proto-Sogeram grammar sketch

In this section I present an outline of Proto-Sogeram grammar, to the extent that I have been able to reconstruct it. This section is intended as a summary and a reference; I offer no arguments for the reconstructions I present here, but rather refer to the sections where argumentation can be found. I also do not distinguish between very secure reconstructions and highly speculative ones.

8.1.1 Phonology (Chapter 3)

Proto-Sogeram had eighteen consonants, which are presented in Table 53. Where the orthographic symbol I use differs from the phonetic symbol, the orthographic symbol is given in <angled brackets> on the right.

Table 53: PSoG consonant inventory.

	bilabial	alveolar	palatal	velar	labio-velar
voiceless plosive	*p	*t		*k	*kʷ <kw>
voiceless prenasalized plosive	*ᵐp <b>	*ⁿt <d>		*ⁿk <g>	*ⁿkʷ <gw>
voiceless fricative	*ɸ <f>	*s			
voiceless prenasalized fricative		*ⁿs <z>			
nasal	*m	*n	*ɲ <ñ>	*ŋ	
liquid		*r			
glide			*j <y>		*w

One case of allophonic variation can be pointed out. The bilabial fricative *f was voiceless word-initially and voiced elsewhere:

*f >   *[ɸ] / #__
     *[β] / elsewhere

The Proto-Sogeram vowels are presented in Table 54.

Table 54: PSoG vowel inventory.

	front	central	back
high	*i	*ɨ	*u
low		*a	

In addition to these four simple vowels, a syllable nucleus could be composed of either of the diphthongs *ai or *au.

It is unclear whether *w and *y were consonants in their own right, or allophones of the high vowels *i and *u. It does seem that when *i and *u were followed by an open syllable, an epenthetic *[j] or *[w] was inserted between them and the following vowel. That is, *i.V and *u.V were realized as *[i.jV] and *[u.wV].

The prenasalized stops, *r, *ŋ, and the vowel *ɨ, did not occur in word-initial position, and it is unclear if *ɨ occurred in word-final position. Every consonant could occur word-finally.

A few kinds of consonant clusters were permitted. One consisted of a non-alveolar plosive, or *f, plus *r. This type of cluster was allowed word-initially (if the plosive was non-nasal) and medially. Another cluster was a non-homorganic sequence of a nasal and a plosive; these clusters were restricted to word-medial position.

Word-final consonant clusters were not allowed, but *ai and *au could be followed by consonant codas (as in *kaur 'unripe'). This suggests that these vowel sequences should be analyzed as diphthongs rather than as sequences of two vowels in which the *a served as the nucleus and the high vowel took its consonantal allophone, since the latter analysis would require positing a complex coda in forms like *kaur.

8.1.1.1 Vowel elision (§4.1.1)

When a verb ending in a vowel was combined with a vowel-initial suffix, the vowel of the suffix usually elided the vowel of the verb root. This process can be described in some detail, and in fact verbs can be broken into five classes based on their interaction with verb suffixes: *a*-root, *u*-root, *i*-root, *kw*-root, and C-root verbs. The first three ended in the segments *a, *u, and *i, respectively; *kw*-root verbs ended in one of the labiovelar consonants *kw or *gw; and C-root verbs ended in any other consonant.

Verb suffixes began with either *i, *ɨ, *u, or a consonant. No verb suffixes beginning with *a have been reconstructed. This produces twenty possible combinations of a verb class with a suffix-initial segment, and the outcomes for nineteen of these are presented in Table 55. It is not known what resulted from the combination of an *i*-root (like *tɨki 'fill') with a *u-initial suffix (like *-u '2SG.IMP').

A-roots, *u*-roots, and *i*-roots all underwent vowel elision except in two circumstances. When an *a*-root (like *tama 'put') was combined with a *u-initial suffix (like *-u '2SG.IMP'), both vowels were preserved (*tama-u). And when an *i*-root (like *tɨki 'fill') was combined with a *ɨ-initial suffix (like *-ɨba 'IRR.INF'), the root vowel elided the suffix vowel instead of vice versa (*tɨki-ba).

Table 55: Verb class behavior.

	First segment of suffix			
	*i	*ɨ	*u	*C
a-root	*i	*ɨ	*au	*aC
u-root	*i	*ɨ	*u	*uC
i-root	*i	*i	?	*iC
kw-root	*kwi	*ku	*ku	*kuC
C-root	*Ci	*Cɨ	*Cu	*CɨC

Kw-roots retained their root-final labiovelar consonant (represented by *kw in the table, although *gw behaved similarly) when followed by an *i-initial suffix, but changed it to a *ku or *gu sequence when followed by a suffix that began with *ɨ, *u, or a consonant. And C-roots remained unchanged before vowel-initial suffixes but added an epenthetic *ɨ before consonant-initial suffixes.

8.1.2 Parts of speech

Proto-Sogeram had at least six parts of speech: nouns, verbs, adjectives, adverbs, pronouns, and demonstratives. These are described below.

We know that word classes usually exhibit prototype structures and often have fuzzy boundaries. Proto-Sogeram was not unusual in this respect, and a few words blurred the line between various word classes. Thus, for example, *kada was both an adjective meaning 'true' and an adverb meaning 'very,' and *iŋar was a noun meaning 'sun' and an adverb meaning 'day(time)'.

8.1.2.1 Nouns

Nouns could head a noun phrase, which could serve as the subject or object of a clause, or as an oblique argument. They could also modify another noun attributively (§6.2.1). Proto-Sogeram nouns can be further divided into two subclasses: inalienably possessed nouns and common nouns.

Inalienably possessed nouns were a small, closed class of kin terms (§5.1). They were distinguished by the fact that they were obligatorily inflected to show the person of their possessor. This was usually done with the possessive prefixes *a- '1.POSS,' *na- '2.POSS,' and *nɨ- '3.POSS,' but some nouns had suppletive forms for a given person category, such as *-mku 'nephew, niece,' which had the suppletive 1.POSS form *iwi. Inalienably possessed nouns were also distinguished by the fact that they could take the accusative enclitic *=ŋ (§5.2.2), which did not attach to noun phrases headed by common nouns. (This enclitic probably also attached to proper nouns, although no proper nouns can be reconstructed for Proto-Sogeram.)

Common nouns were simply those nouns that were not inalienably possessed. They had no defining characteristics that distinguished them from inalienably possessed nouns, aside from the fact that they lacked those characteristics that defined inalienably possessed nouns. Note that some forms, such as *ña 'son' and *mɨr 'sister of male ego', were not inalienably possessed in spite of belonging to the semantic class of kin terms.

8.1.2.2 Verbs (Chapter 4)

Verbs usually served as the main predicate of the clause, and could be inflected for subject agreement as well as tense, aspect, mood, and switch reference. As mentioned above, Proto-Sogeram verbs can be grouped into five classes based on their morphophonological behavior: *a*-roots, *u*-roots, *i*-roots, *kw*-roots, and C-roots (§4.1.1).

Verbs could also remain uninflected in serial verb constructions (§4.2). When in their uninflected form, some verb roots had a different root shape, although most did not. This special uninflected root always involved the addition of an *a to the end of the inflected root (§4.2.1).

8.1.2.3 Adjectives (§6.1.1) and adverbs (§6.1.2)

Adjectives could modify nouns attributively or serve as predicates on their own (§6.3.3). Both of these functions could also be performed by nouns, but Proto-Sogeram adjectives can be distinguished from nouns because attributive adjectives followed their head noun (§6.2.2), while attributive nouns preceded it.

A separate class of adverbs also existed. Like adverbs in many languages, Proto-Sogeram adverbs comprised a fairly heterogeneous set of words which fulfilled a variety of functions. They could modify various constituents of the clause (with meanings like 'only' and 'very') or the clause itself (with meanings ranging from 'tomorrow' to 'completely').

8.1.2.4 Pronouns (§5.2)

Pronouns were a small, closed class of words that distinguished singular and plural number as well as first, second, and third person. As shown in Table 56, they came in subject, object, oblique, possessive, and emphatic forms.

As this table shows, the non-subject forms were composed of a root and a suffix or enclitic. The possessive *-kw only attached to pronouns, and hence is analyzed as a suffix; the object, oblique, and emphatic morphemes also attached to other noun phrases and are analyzed as enclitics. In the singular forms the

Table 56: PSOG pronouns.

	Subject	Object	Oblique	Possessive	Emphatic
1SG	*ya	*ya=ŋ	*ya=d	*ya-kw	*ya=bi
2SG	*na	*na=ŋ	*na=d	*na-kw	*na=ba
3SG	*nɨ, *nu	*nɨ=ŋ, nu=ŋ	*nɨ=d, nu=d	*nɨ-kw	*nɨ=ba
1PL	*ara	*ar=ɨŋ	*ar=d	*ar-kw	*ar=bV
2PL	*nara	*nar=ɨŋ	*nar=d	*nar-kw	*nar=ba
3PL	*nɨra	*nɨr=ɨŋ	*nɨr=d	*nɨr-kw	*nɨr=ba

pronominal root was identical to the subject root, but in the plural forms the root used differed from the subject root in the deletion of a final *a. Note also that the 3SG often varied between *nu and *nɨ, although in the possessive and emphatic pronouns only *nɨ was used. The significance of this variation is unclear.

The subject pronouns were used as subjects (§5.2.1). The object pronouns were composed of the bound pronominal roots and the accusative enclitic *=ŋ, and functioned as objects (§5.2.2). The oblique pronouns were formed with the oblique enclitic *=d (§5.2.3). This enclitic usually marked constituents that occurred within a larger noun phrase and modified the head noun. This modification could take various forms, including the marking of possession (§6.2.3). So the oblique pronouns either indicated that their referent was the possessor of the head noun, or was a relevant for the interpretation of the head noun in some other way. The possessive pronouns were formed with the suffix *-kw and indicated possession (§5.2.4); how this possession differed from that expressed by the oblique pronouns is not clear. Finally, the emphatic pronouns were formed with an enclitic with two allomorphs, *=ba and *=bi (§5.2.5). The latter was used in the 1SG, the former in the second and third person, and it is unclear which was used in the 1PL. Emphatic pronouns conveyed contrastive and individuating focus, and could serve as the subject of a clause.

8.1.2.5 Demonstratives (§5.3)

Demonstratives in Proto-Sogeram distinguished three deictic distances: near, mid, and far (§5.3.1). The roots could be used by themselves, in which case they marked a referent that was already topical (§5.3.2). They could also be reduplicated to convey contrast (§5.3.3). Both of these forms—the simple root and the reduplicated root—could then take a number of suffixes and enclitics which marked case or information structure. The forms are presented in Table 57.

Note that there is a fourth demonstrative root in this table, the interrogative demonstrative root *aba-. This form took the same suffixes as the other demonstrative roots to form question words, although only one such pairing can be directly reconstructed: *aba=ñ [QD=LOC] 'where' (§6.3.2).

Table 57: PSoG demonstratives.

	ND	MD	FD	QD
bare	*in	*ka	*adu	
contrastive	*in~in	*ka~ka	*adu~du	
topic/object	*inɨ-n	*ka-n	*adu-n	
oblique	*inɨ=d	*ka=d	*adu=d	
locative 1	*inɨ=ñ	*ka=ñ	*adu=ñ	*aba=ñ
locative 2	*inɨ-bV	*ka-bV	*adu-bV	
focus	*inɨ-kw	*ka-kw	*adu-kw	

Note also that some of the affixes on demonstratives are suffixes while others are clitics. The clitics are forms that could attach to a noun phrase or a pronoun without a demonstrative there to host them; the suffixes are forms that only attached to demonstratives.

The topic/object forms with the suffix *-n served three functions: they marked accusative case on noun phrases headed by common nouns; they marked the subjects of nonverbal predicates (§6.3.3); and they marked left-peripheral topics for verbal predicates (§5.3.5). The latter two functions are, in reality, a single, left-peripheral topic function.

The oblique forms in *=d indicated that their referent functioned as an oblique argument of some kind in the clause—the exact semantics are difficult to reconstruct (§5.3.4). They could also mark noun phrases functioning attributively to modify a head noun within a larger noun phrase (§6.2.3).

The two locative forms in *=ñ (§5.3.6) and *-bV (which ended in either *a or *u; §5.3.7) marked locations. It is not clear how they differed.

The focus forms with the suffix *-kw marked individuation or contrast (§5.3.8).

Finally, the unaffixed middle demonstrative *ka had an additional function that it did not share with the unaffixed near or far demonstratives: it could topicalize a medial clause. In this construction, it followed a medial clause (whether same-subject or different-subject) and indicated that its event was topical or important for the event of the upcoming clause (§5.3.2).

8.1.3 Noun phrase structure (§6.2)

Several aspects of the noun phrase can be reconstructed. The order of constituents was as follows:

$\quad$ *N_{ATTR} N_{HEAD} ADJ DEM CLITIC

That is, the attributive noun (or noun phrase) came first (§6.2.1), followed by the head noun, the adjective (§6.2.2), the demonstrative, and the enclitic. All of these elements, including the head noun, were optional. Possessors could either precede or follow the head noun (§6.2.3). While their order with respect to the attributive noun and the adjective cannot be reconstructed, it is clear that they preceded the demonstrative and enclitic.

8.1.3.1 Enclitics and demonstratives

There was a good deal of interaction between the demonstrative and the enclitic at the end of the noun phrase. Four noun phrase enclitics can be reconstructed, as shown in Table 58.

Table 58: PSoG noun phrase enclitics.

gloss	form	pronoun	demonstrative
ACC	*=ŋ	yes	no
OBL	*=d	yes	yes
LOC	*=ñ	no	yes
EMPH	*=bi/=ba	yes	no

Each of these enclitics could attach to noun phrases that did not contain demonstratives. Some could also attach to pronouns (indicated in the 'pronoun' column) or to noun phrases that did contain demonstratives (the 'demonstrative' column). As I discuss below, these forms also sometimes behaved differently depending on whether the noun phrase to which they were attaching was headed by a common or an inalienably possessed noun.

Accusative *=ŋ was used to form the object pronouns (§5.2.2). It could also attach to noun phrases headed by inalienably possessed nouns to mark them with accusative case. But it did not mark common nouns; this function was instead performed by the topic/object demonstratives in *-n (§5.3.5). Consequently, *=ŋ did not occur on demonstratives.

Oblique *=d formed the oblique pronouns (§5.2.3) as well as the oblique demonstratives (§5.3.4). This enclitic could also attach to a noun phrase headed by any noun, whether common or inalienably possessed.

The locative enclitic *=ñ did not attach to pronouns, but did attach to demonstratives (§5.3.6). It could also attach directly to a noun phrase, although only one headed by a common noun. This enclitic had two allomorphs: it was realized as *=ñ when it attached to a vowel, and as *=i when it attached to a consonant.

Finally, the emphatic enclitic *=bi/=ba marked contrastive and individuating focus on subject noun phrases (§5.2.5). It attached to pronouns but not to demonstratives, where focus was marked by the demonstrative suffix *-kw (§5.3.8).

It should be noted that none of these enclitics attached to a noun phrase in which a demonstrative was already hosting another suffix. In other words, the occurrence of any of the demonstrative suffixes presented in Table 57 above (*-n 'TOP/ACC,' *=bV 'LOC,' or *-kw 'FOC') blocked the co-occurrence of any of these enclitics. Contrastive reduplication of the root did not function this way, so *ka~ka=ñ 'MD~CTR=LOC,' for example, was well-formed (§5.3.3).

8.1.4 Verb morphology (Chapter 4)

Proto-Sogeram had very rich verb morphology, and a great deal can be reconstructed. Proto-Sogeram made a morphological distinction between medial and final verbs. Final suffixes marked subject agreement and a wide range of TAM categories (§4.3). Medial suffixes marked switch reference and relative tense, but received absolute TAM information from their final verb (§4.4). The sections below present eleven final verb categories, including six tenses, one aspect, and four moods. One of these moods, the irrealis (§4.3.10), could also be used medially. Four other medial categories can be reconstructed: two same-subject suffixes, a different-subject paradigm, and a reduplicative simultaneous suffix. Finally, three verb suffixes can be reconstructed that are not easily classified as medial or final: a nominalizer (§4.5.1), a participle (§4.5.2), and an infinitive (§4.5.3).

Verb morphology generally conformed to the following template (§4.3):

Root TAM Agreement

The verb root was followed first by a TAM suffix and then by a subject agreement suffix. For some categories, such as the immediate past and the imperative, there was no TAM suffix; rather, the TAM category was inferable because no other category took those agreement suffixes without a TAM suffix. There were seven different sets of agreement suffixes, presented in Table 59, each of which was used in a subset of the TAM categories.

Note that there was no 3PL agreement suffix (§4.1.3). It is unclear whether Proto-Sogeram 3PL subjects were marked with the 2PL agreement forms—which had marked a syncretic combination of 2PL and 3PL in Pre-Proto-Sogeram—or with a special plural serial verb construction that used the 3SG suffix.

Table 59: PSOG verb agreement suffixes (§4.3).

Name	1SG	2SG	3SG	1PL	2PL	TAM categories
Set I	*-in	*-na	*-i	*-rɨŋ	*-ra	Immediate past, historic past, DS realis
Set II	*-n	*-na	*-r, *-i	*-urɨŋ	*-ra	Today past, recent past, far past
Set III	*-n	*-na	*-ri	*-rɨŋ	*-ra	Future
Set IV	*-n	*-na	*-i	*-rɨŋ	*-ra	Habitual
Set V	*-ŋ	*-na	*-r, *-i	*-rɨŋ	*-ra	Counterfactual, Irrealis
Set VI	*-ŋ	*-u		*-ɨmɨri	*-mar	Imperative
Set VII	*-ñ	*-na	*-d	*-rɨŋ	*-ara	Prohibitive

8.1.4.1 Immediate past (§4.3.1)

The immediate past tense was formed with the Set I agreement suffixes and no tense suffix, as shown in Table 60. The time reference of this tense included the present moment and also extended a few hours into the past.

Table 60: Immediate past tense suffixes.

	SG	PL
first person	*-Ø-in	*-Ø-rɨŋ
second person	*-Ø-na	*-Ø-ra
third person	*-Ø-i	

8.1.4.2 Today past (§4.3.2)

The today past tense was formed with the suffix *-iamɨ and the Set II agreement suffixes, as shown in Table 61. Note that the 3SG suffix was *-i, not *-r. This tense referred to events that took place on the day of the speech act, but before the time reference of the immediate past.

Table 61: Today past tense suffixes.

	SG	PL
first person	*-iamɨ-n	*-iam-urɨŋ
second person	*-iamɨ-na	*-iamɨ-ra
third person	*-iam-i	

8.1.4.3 Recent past (§4.3.3)

The recent past tense, shown in Table 62, was formed with the suffix *-gɨ and the Set II agreement suffixes (with *-r, not *-i, in the 3SG). The time reference of this tense preceded that of the today past, although it is unclear how far into the past it extended.

Table 62: Recent past tense suffixes.

	SG	PL
first person	*-gɨ-n	*-g-urɨŋ
second person	*-gɨ-na	*-g-ra
third person	*-gɨ-r	

8.1.4.4 Far past (§4.3.3)

The far past was formed with two tense suffixes: *-ma, which is used in the historic past, and *-gɨ, used in the recent past. These were combined with the Set II agreement suffixes; the forms are given in Table 63. The time reference of this tense lay between those of the recent past and the historic past.

Table 63: Far past tense suffixes.

	SG	PL
first person	*-ma-gɨ-n	*-ma-g-urɨŋ
second person	*-ma-gɨ-na	*-ma-g-ra
third person	*-ma-gɨ-r	

8.1.4.5 Historic past (§4.3.4)

Table 64 gives the forms for the historic past, which was formed with the suffix *-ma and the Set I agreement suffixes. This tense referred to everything before the far past, although it is not clear exactly where the boundary between the two was, or how flexible it was.

Table 64: Historic past tense suffixes.

	SG	PL
first person	*-m-in	*-ma-rɨn
second person	*-ma-na	*-ma-ra
third person	*-m-i	

8.1.4.6 Future (§4.3.5)

The future tense was formed with the suffix *-iba and the Set III agreement suffixes, as shown in Table 65. Note that in the 1SG the suffix changed to *-ibia. This was the only future tense, and as such referred to all future events.

Table 65: Future tense suffixes.

	SG	PL
first person	*-ɨbia-n	*-ɨba-rɨŋ
second person	*-ɨba-na	*-ɨba-ra
third person	*-ɨba-ri	

8.1.4.7 Habitual (§4.3.6)

The habitual aspect, shown in Table 66, was formed with the suffix *-itia and the Set IV agreement suffixes. This verb form signified that an event occurred habitually, but did not appear to combine that aspectual meeting with any tense meaning.

Table 66: Habitual aspect suffixes.

	SG	PL
first person	*-ɨtia-n	*-ɨtia-rɨŋ
second person	*-ɨtia-na	*-ɨtia-ra
third person	*-ɨtia-i	

8.1.4.8 Imperative (§4.3.7)

The imperative mood was formed with only the Set VI agreement suffixes and no TAM suffix. The forms are given in Table 67; note that there are no third person forms. It is unclear whether this is because they did not exist in Proto-Sogeram or simply because they cannot be reconstructed. The imperative verb forms were used to give positive commands.

Table 67: Imperative mood suffixes.

	SG	PL
first person	*-ŋ	*-ɨmɨri
second person	*-u	*-mar
third person		

8.1.4.9 Prohibitive (§4.3.8)

Proto-Sogeram had a dedicated prohibitive, or negative imperative, paradigm of verb suffixes, shown in Table 68. It was formed with the prohibitive suffix *-ɨmɨ and the Set VII agreement suffixes. These forms were used to give negative commands.

Table 68 Prohibitive mood suffixes.

	SG	PL
first person	*-ɨmɨ-ñ	*-ɨmɨ-rɨŋ
second person	*-ɨmɨ-na	*-ɨm-ara
third person	*-ɨmɨ-d	

8.1.4.10 Counterfactual (§4.3.9)

The counterfactual paradigm is given in Table 69. It was formed with a suffix *-ɨfɨ (in the first person and 2SG) or *-ɨfa (in the 3SG and 2PL) and the Set V agreement suffixes. It was used to refer to hypothetical events or other events that did not happen. In this function it overlapped somewhat with the semantic range of the imperative, prohibitive, and irrealis moods, and it is not clear exactly how semantic space was carved up among these different forms.

Table 69: Counterfactual mood suffixes.

	SG	PL
first person	*-ɨfɨ-ŋ	*-ɨf-rɨŋ
second person	*-ɨfɨ-na	*-ɨfa-ra
third person	*-ɨfa-r	

8.1.4.11 Irrealis (§4.3.10)

The irrealis mood was formed with the suffix *-ɨt and the Set V agreement suffixes, as shown in Table 70. This verb paradigm was unique in that it could function both medially and finally. When functioning finally it had irrealis meaning, but it is unclear how this meaning differed from the meaning of the counterfactual verbs forms. When it functioned medially, the irrealis paradigm had different-subject meaning. Importantly, it could only perform this medial function in irrealis clause chains—that is, clause chains that ended in a semantically irrealis TAM category such as the imperative, future, or counterfactual.

Table 70: Irrealis mood suffixes.

	SG	PL
first person	*-ɨt-iŋ	*-ɨt-rɨŋ
second person	*-ɨt-na	*-ɨt-ra
third person	*-ɨt-i	

8.1.4.12 Same-subject (§4.4.1)

Proto-Sogeram had two same-subject switch reference suffixes, *-i and *-ta, which distinguished immediately sequential actions from actions that were separated by an interval of time. The suffix *-i indicated that the action of the following verb was immediately sequential to the action of the marked verb, while *-ta indicated that an interval of time elapsed between the marked verb and the following verb.

8.1.4.13 Different-subject realis (§4.4.2)

The different-subject realis forms are given in Table 71. As mentioned above, in irrealis clause chains Proto-Sogeram used the irrealis mood forms as different-subject markers. But in realis chains, these forms were used. They were formed with the suffix *-ɨka and the Set I agreement suffixes.

Table 71: Different-subject realis suffixes.

	SG	PL
first person	*-ɨk-in	*-ɨka-rɨŋ
second person	*-ɨka-na	*-ɨka-ra
third person	*-ɨk-i	

8.1.4.14 Different-subject simultaneous (§4.4.3)

The different-subject verb forms, both irrealis and realis, could be reduplicated to indicate that the action of the marked verb and the action of the following verb occurred simultaneously. The reduplicative suffix copied the whole word, and was probably a separate phonological word.

8.1.4.15 Nominalization and participle (§4.5.1, §4.5.2)

Proto-Sogeram had a reduplicative nominalizing suffix that derived nouns from verbs. This suffix copied the whole verb root to create nominal forms that could function both as common nouns and as adverbial forms that modified the main predicate. A few verbs formed their nominalizations irregularly, with a suffix *-ŋ instead of by reduplication, but it is not clear which verbs behaved this way.

Proto-Sogeram had another derivational suffix, the participial *-m which derived adjectives from verbs.

8.1.4.16 Irrealis infinitive (§4.5.3)

The final verbal category that can be reconstructed for Proto-Sogeram is the irrealis infinitive. This was formed with the suffix *-ɨba—the same suffix that was used to form the future tense—and no agreement suffix. The specific kind of irrealis meaning that this form conveyed, as well as its grammatical function, are difficult to reconstruct.

8.1.5 Clause structure

Several aspects of Proto-Sogeram clause structure can be reconstructed. The grammar of verbal and nonverbal clauses was quite different, so I discuss them in separate sections below. In addition, verbal clauses could contain fairly complicated serial verb constructions, so I devote a separate section to them.

8.1.5.1 Verbal clauses

The order of arguments in Proto-Sogeram verbal clauses was SOV (§6.3), although the placement of oblique arguments remains somewhat unclear. Polar questions were formed by appending the enclitic *=bi to the clause. Content questions were formed with dedicated question words that were left *in situ*. Some of these were simple question words, such as *atɨ 'what'; others, like *aba=ñ [QD=LOC] 'where' were built on the interrogative demonstrative root *aba, which took the same suffixes and enclitics as other demonstratives but formed question words (§6.3.2).

Verbal clauses were negated by placing the negative particle *ma before the verb. It may have also been possible to place *ma after the verb in an emphatic negation construction, although this is not clear (§6.3.1).

8.1.5.2 Serial verb constructions (§4.2)

Proto-Sogeram verbs could be combined in serial verb constructions (SVCs). These constructions consisted of a number of uninflected verbs followed at the end by a verb that carried all the inflection for the SVC, whether medial or final. Many verbs—particularly if they were not *a*-root verbs—had slightly different stem shapes when they were uninflected serial verbs (§4.2.1). For example, 'go up' was *yakw- when bound but *yaku when free, 'give' was *igw- when bound but *igwa when free, and 'close' was *sɨdi- when bound but *sɨdia when free. Free forms commonly differed from their bound counterparts in the addition of a final *a.

Three distinct types of SVCs can be reconstructed: aspectual (§4.2.2), orientation (§4.2.3), and causative (§4.2.4). In aspectual SVCs, the final verb of the SVC did not contribute its normal lexical semantics to the SVC, but contributed aspectual or other grammatical meaning instead. At least four verbs occurred in this position, and these are presented in Table 72 along with the meaning that they contributed to their SVC.

Table 72: Aspectual SVCs.

Verb	Lexical sense	Meaning
*kɨda	walk	habitual
*kiña	stay	stative
*tɨku	see	conative ('try to V')
*tama	put	completive

Orientation SVCs differed from others in that they allowed other parts of speech to intervene between the serialized verbs. Orientation SVCs consisted of an initial intransitive verb—usually a verb of motion or posture—that oriented the subject of the clause to the rest of the predicate. The other verbs in the SVC were not necessarily intransitive, though, and if they had objects or other arguments these came between the orientation verb and the other verbs.

Finally, causative SVCs consisted of a two-verb pair in which the first verb described a causative action and the second verb described the result. The subject of the first verb was the subject of the whole clause, but the subject of the second verb was the affected entity. This distinguished causative SVCs from other SVCs, since in other SVCs every verb had the same subject. Two verbs can be reconstructed to the causative position: *mɨna 'get' and *igwa 'give,' although the latter may only have occurred in one causative SVC: *igwa ña [give eat] 'feed'. Examples of the kind of causative SVC that *mɨna 'get' occurred in include *mɨna yaku [get go.up] 'lift,' *mɨna kɨmu [get die] 'kill,' and *mɨna ibra [get go.bad] 'ruin'.

8.1.5.3 Nonverbal clauses (§6.3.3)

Nonverbal clauses were composed of only a topic and a predicate, as Proto-Sogeram did not have a copula. The topic, if it contained a demonstrative, was marked with the topic/object suffix *-n, which also marked accusative arguments in verbal clauses. The predicate did not necessarily receive case marking, but inalienably possessed nouns may have been optionally marked with the emphatic focus enclitic *=bi/=ba (§5.2.5).

Because nonverbal predicates only consisted of the topic and the predicate, they were not normally marked for tense or other verbal categories. However, if tense, switch reference, or some other verbal category was desired, nonverbal predicates could contain the verb *kɨña 'stay' at the end of the predicate. In this construction *kɨña simply meant 'be' and functioned only to carry verbal morphology. Speakers could also use *ada 'do' in this construction to convey a more inceptive meaning of 'become'.

Negation of nonverbal clauses could be accomplished in three ways. In the first, the whole nonverbal predicate was followed by the negative word *maka 'none,' as in (410). This construction simply negated the nonverbal predicate.

(410) *[TOP PRED.VERBAL maka]$_S$ 'TOP is not PRED'

In the second, the topic was directly followed by the negative word *maka 'none,' with no intervening predicate, as in (411). In this construction *maka functioned as the nonverbal predicate and had a negative existential interpretation, signaling that there was none of the topic.

(411) *[TOP maka]$_S$ 'There is no TOP'

The last nonverbal negation construction was composed entirely of the negative word *manat 'no'. This word functioned pro-clausally—it took the place of an entire clause—and it negated the expected result of a preceding clause. In this construction the preceding clause was marked with different-subject switch reference morphology, as in (412).

(412) *[[V-DS]$_S$ [manat]$_S$] 'V happened but the expected result did not'

Pro-clausal *manat was probably also used when listing alternatives, in sentences with meanings like 'Will they come or not?' The grammar of this construction, however, cannot be reconstructed as accurately.

Like other nonverbal predicates, negative nonverbal predicates could occur with *kɨña 'stay' to carry verbal morphology.

8.1.6 Clause combining (§6.4)

Three constructions involving multiple clauses can be reconstructed: clause chaining, clause chain nominalization, and quoted speech.

8.1.6.1 Clause chaining and switch reference (§6.4.1)

Proto-Sogeram clauses were frequently combined into what are called clause chains. These constructions are widespread among Papuan languages (Roberts 1997; Foley 2000, 2018). In Proto-Sogeram they consisted of one or more medial clauses (clauses in which the verb carried medial morphology) followed by a final clause (one in which the verb carried final morphology). The final clause carried the TAM information that governed the whole chain; the medial clauses were marked only for switch reference and relative tense.

Switch reference marking worked as follows. Each medial verb carried a switch reference suffix that indicated whether its own subject was the same as, or different from, the subject of the following verb. If the suffix was same-subject, it did not mark person or number information; if it was different-subject, it agreed with the person and number of its own subject while signaling an upcoming change of subject (but not signaling what the person or number of the upcoming subject would be).

Switch reference markers also distinguished some relative tense categories—that is, they specified certain facts about the temporal relationship between their clause and the following clause. If the switch reference marking was same-subject, it distinguished between immediately sequential events (indicated with *-i 'SS.SEQ') and events separated by an interval of time (indicated with *-ta 'SS.DELAY'). If the switch reference marking was different-subject, it distinguished between sequential events (indicated with a normal DS-marked verb) and simultaneous events (indicated by full reduplication of the DS-marked verb).

Different-subject medial clauses also made an additional, mood-related distinction. If the final clause of the chain was semantically realis, the realis different-subject suffix *-ɨka was used. If the final clause was irrealis, though, the irrealis suffix *-ɨt was used as a different-subject suffix.

8.1.6.2 Clause chain nominalization (§6.4.2)

Proto-Sogeram possessed a subordination construction in which a clause or clause chain was followed by a demonstrative. This demonstrative subordinated the preceding chain, and the construction functioned as a noun phrase in the matrix clause. The case marking on the demonstrative indicated what role the subordinate chain played in the matrix clause.

The subordinate chain was grammatically identical to a matrix chain; it was not distinguishable from a normal matrix clause chain either morphologically or syntactically. Naturally, because it served as a noun phrase, it referred, but its referent was pragmatically inferred rather than syntactically marked. It could refer to one of its arguments (whether core or oblique), to the location where its event took place, or to its event as a whole.

The subordinating demonstrative could take the topic/object suffix *-n or the locative enclitic *=ñ. It could also be the unaffixed middle demonstrative *ka. It is likely that a wider array of case markers could function as subordinators, but this cannot be securely reconstructed.

8.1.6.3 Quoted speech (§6.4.3)

Quoted speech itself did not receive special grammatical marking, but Proto-Sogeram did use different verbs before and after quotes, which I refer to as pre-quote and post-quote verbs. The pre-quote verb in Proto-Sogeram was *aba 'speak'. When it introduced a quote, it took final morphology and occurred under a separate, final intonational contour. The post quote verb was *wa 'go, say,' and it could take either medial or final morphology as the situation warranted. It occurred under the same intonational contour as the preceding quoted material.

8.2 Texts

In the tradition begun by August Schleicher (1868), I have composed two short texts in Proto-Sogeram, which are presented below. Like Schleicher's original work, this is done "partly to demonstrate that cohesive sentences ... can, albeit with difficulty, be constructed, partly for pleasure" (Schleicher 1868: 206).[22] The first is an adaptation of Schleicher's original fable; the second is a version of an indigenous Papuan story I encountered a number of times during my fieldwork. In both cases the story is followed by commentary on the constructions and lexemes employed in the narrative.

8.2.1 Schleicher's Fable

Below is a rendition of Schleicher's Fable, also known as "The Sheep and the Horses". Unfortunately, in spite of my best efforts, I have been unable to reconstruct several key terms, including 'sheep,' 'wool,' 'horse,' and 'wagon'. Indeed, my failure in this regard has been so complete that I have had to significantly revise the story in order to be able to tell it in Proto-Sogeram. The sheep is now a pig; the horses are dogs. The wool and the wagon are gone, the latter having become an unfortunate cassowary. As a consequence of these lexical replace-

---

[22] My translation from the German "Theils um darzuthun, dass, wenn auch mit mühe, zusammenhangende sätze ... gebildet werden können, theils animi causa".

ments, the conversation between the protagonists has also undergone a considerable degree of transformation. Nevertheless, the outline of the story remains the same, and I hope this remains a suitable homage to the practitioners of syntactic reconstruction who have gone before me, and to whom I owe so much.

*Inɨn sabaŋ kia. Sabaŋ mu wa apar kañ tagwa tami tɨku mɨgwɨki uprɨ kɨña kwrɨ. Kɨñɨ muyam kaka wa kɨña kwrɨ. Kaka wa kwrɨki igi pam kan abi. Narɨŋ tɨkukin ka, mapɨn yakw pɨm adi wi. Muyam kan kaka uta uta uta mɨnɨtra naŋti ñɨti narɨŋ ma igwa ñɨbari wi. Puzɨŋ paka igubari wi. Uki uprɨ kaka abi. Ara tɨkurɨŋ ka, mapɨn pɨm adi wi. Kuram kɨpi ñaŋña mi tami ka, naŋ mɨnɨ ifi fɨki kri ñɨbari wi. Wa tamɨki sabaŋ kaka tɨpa kaŋri sura mɨgwi.

Inɨ-n	*sabaŋ*	*kia.*	*Sabaŋ*	*mu*	*wa*	*apar*	*ka=ñ*	*tagwa*
ND-ACC	pig	speech	pig	SPEC	go	mountain	MD=LOC	step.on
tam-i	*tɨku*	*mɨgw-ɨk-i*		*uprɨ*	*kɨña*	*kwr-i.*	*Kɨñ-i*	*muyam*
put-SS.SEQ	look	go.down-DS-3SG		dog	stay	PL-3.IPST	stay-SS.SEQ	cassowary
kaka	*wa*	*kɨña*	*kwr-i.*	*Kaka*	*wa*	*kwr-ɨk-i*	*ig-i*	*pam*	*ka-n*
tie	go	stay	PL-3.IPST	tie	go	PL-DS-3	see-SS.SEQ	one	MD-ACC
ab-i.		*Nar=ɨŋ*	*tɨku-k-in*	*ka,*	*mapɨn*	*ya-kw*	*pɨm*
speak-3SG.IPST		2PL=ACC	see-DS-1SG	MD.TOP	liver	1SG-POSS	weight
ad-i	*w-i.*		*Muyam*	*ka-n*	*kaka*	*u-ta*
do-3SG.IPST	say-3SG.IPST		cassowary	MD-ACC	tie	go-SS.DELAY
u-ta	*u-ta*	*mɨŋ-ɨt-ra*	*na-ŋti*	*ñ-ɨt-i*	*nar=ɨŋ*
go-SS.DELAY	go-SS.DELAY	get-IRR-2PL	2.POSS-father	eat-IRR-3SG	2PL=ACC
ma	*igwa*	*ñ-ɨba-ri*	*w-i.*	*Puzɨŋ*	*paka*	*igu-ba-ri*	*w-i.*
NEG	give	eat-FUT-3SG	say-3SG.IPST	bone	only	give-FUT-3SG	say-3SG.IPST
U-k-i	*uprɨ*	*ka~ka*	*ab-i.*	*Ara*	*tɨku-ka-rɨŋ*	*ka,*	*mapɨn*
say-DS-3SG	dog	MD~CTR	speak-3SG.IPST	1PL	see-DS-1PL	MD.TOP	liver
pɨm	*ad-i*	*w-i.*	*Kuram*	*kɨp-i*	*ñaŋña*	*mi*
weight	do-3SG.IPST	say-3SG.IPST	man	get.up-SS.SEQ	food	thought
tam-i	*ka,*	*na=ŋ*	*mɨŋ-i*	*if-i*	*fɨk-i*	*kr-i*
put-SS.DELAY	MD.TOP	2SG=ACC	get-SS.SEQ	hit-SS.SEQ	cut-SS.SEQ	roast-SS.SEQ
ñ-ɨba-ri	*w-i.*		*Wa*	*tam-ɨk-i*	*sabaŋ*	*ka~ka*	*tɨpa*	*kaŋr-i*
eat-FUT-3SG	say-3SG.IPST		say	put-DS-3SG	pig	MD~CTR	fear	run-SS.SEQ
sura	*mɨgw-i.*
forest	go.down-3SG.IPST

> 'This is the pig story. A pig went and stood on a mountain and looked down at some dogs. The dogs were chasing a cassowary. The pig watched them and spoke to one. "When I see you it makes me sad (lit. 'my liver is heavy')," it said. "You'll chase and chase the cassowary and catch it, but your owner will eat it and won't give you any," it said. "He'll only give you bones," it said. The dog replied. "When we see you, it makes us sad," it said. "When the man thinks of food (lit. 'puts a food thought'), he'll take you, kill you, cut you up, cook you and eat you," it said. When it had said this, the pig fled down into the forest.'

This story is told using the immediate past tense as a historical present. The place of articulation for the final nasal in *sabaN 'pig' cannot be reconstructed; the velar nasal *ŋ is a guess. The way Proto-Sogeram handled 3PL subject agreement on verbs is also unknown. I have chosen to use a serial verb construction ending in a hypothetical plural verb *kwra, based on a reflex in Manat. A word for 'chase' cannot be reconstructed, so I use the serial verb construction *kaka wa 'tie go,' inspired by a Sirva compound verb. An expression for sorrow cannot be reconstructed, so I have invented a verb adjunct construction *pɨm ada 'weight do' that takes the liver as its subject, based on similar expressions in several languages.

8.2.2 How the Ancestors Got Sago

This is, it seems, a fairly widespread story in the Madang region. I encountered it in the villages of Paynamar, Musak, and Panim, while conducting fieldwork on, respectively, Manat, Aisi, and Panim. Manat and Aisi are Sogeram languages; Panim is a distantly related Madang language of the Croisilles group. Another version of the story, from the Kire-speaking village of Giri, was encountered by John Z'graggen (1992: 98–99). As Kire is a Ramu language and is unrelated to the three others, the provenance of this story is uncertain. This presentation should therefore not be interpreted as an assertion that the story was told by speakers of Proto-Sogeram, although of course it may have been.

The outline of the story is the same in all four cases, though many of the details vary. In general it runs as follows.

> Long ago, our ancestors did not process sago the way we do today. They used to just drill a hole in a sago palm, put a basket underneath it, and edible sago would just fall into the basket. But then someone did something to the sago palm and it closed up. Now getting sago is hard work. We have to cut the tree down, split it open, scrape the pith out, and wash it before we can eat it.

In Giri the one responsible for closing the sago palm was a child who, mistaking the sago flowing out of the tree for a snake, shot it with a toy bow. In Panim it was the flying fox, who watched people getting sago the old way and devised the new way. He convinced the other birds[23] of the superiority of his way, and the innovation spread from them to people. And in the Sogeram languages it was a dog. In Manat the dog licked at the flowing sago. In Aisi the master forgot to feed the dog so, after spying on its master, the dog scratched at the sago tree in an attempt to procure food for itself. In both cases the dog's actions shut the sago tree forever.

Because the rendering below is in Proto-Sogeram, I have chosen to follow the Sogeram examples as closely as possible. Sometimes, where appropriate vocabulary is not available (as with 'drill,' 'basket,' and 'wash'), I have made minor changes.

> *Inɨn makin kia. Kusai, añki arkw makin ma adɨtiara. Sura kañ kap uta, fɨki, faga tamɨkara ñaŋña ka mɨgɨtiai. Mɨgɨkimɨgɨki kuar uta, abañ abañ uta, faitiara. Faikara mɨta kiñɨki mɨŋɨtiara. Añki arkubɨr kan ada kɨdamara. Mɨni kuram mu kɨpi upri mɨŋi makin kad umi. Ikudɨ ma igwa ñami. Ka adi makin fɨki faga tami kuar umi. Kuar uki, upri kaka kɨñi, ñaŋña mɨgami kan kikri makin kan frɨmi. Frɨki sɨkan sɨdimi. Ñaŋña nɨkw ma mɨgami. Ka adɨki, kuram ka fai tɨkwɨki manat. Ñaŋña maka kiñɨki makin kan kwakɨki mɨgaki fri ifi ñami. Ka adɨmi ka, iŋar inɨñ arba iki fri ifi ña kɨdarɨŋ.

Inɨ-n	makin	kia.	Kusai,	a-ñki		ar-kw	makin	ma
ND-ACC	sago	speech	before	1.POSS-grandfather		1PL-POSS	sago	NEG

ad-ɨtia-ra.	Sura	ka=ñ	kap	u-ta,	fɨk-i,	faga
do-HAB-2/3PL	forest	MD=LOC	just	go-SS.DELAY	cut-SS.SEQ	leaf

tam-ɨka-ra	ñaŋña	ka	mɨg-ɨtia-i.	Mɨg-ɨk-i~mɨgɨki
put-DS-2/3PL	food	MD.TOP	come.down-HAB-3SG	come.down-DS-3~SIM

kuar	u-ta,	aba=ñ	aba=ñ	u-ta,	fai-tia-ra.
garden	go-SS.DELAY	QD=LOC	QD=LOC	go-SS.DELAY	come-HAB-2/3PL

Fai-ka-ra	mɨta	kiñ-ɨk-i	mɨŋ-ɨtia-ra.	A-ñki
come-DS-2/3PL	be.full	stay-DS-3SG	get-HAB-2/3PL	1.POSS-grandfather

ar-ku=bi	ka-n	ada	kɨda-ma-ra.	Mɨni	kuram	mu
1PL-POSS=EMPH	MD-ACC	do	walk-HPST-2/3PL	later	man	SPEC

kɨp-i	upri	mɨŋ-i	makin	ka=d	u-m-i.	Ikudɨ
get.up-SS.SEQ	dog	get-SS.SEQ	sago	MD=OBL	go-HPST-3SG	morning

ma	igwa	ña-m-i.	Ka	ad-i	makin	fɨk-i	faga
NEG	give	eat-HPST-3SG	MD.TOP	do-SS.SEQ	sago	cut-SS.SEQ	leaf

---

[23] In Panim, as in many folk taxonomies in the area (such as Kalam; cf. Majnep & Bulmer 1977), flying foxes and other bats are grouped taxonomically with birds.

tam-i	kuar	u-m-i.		Kuar	u-k-i,	upri	ka~ka
put-SS.SEQ	garden	go-HPST-3SG		garden	go-DS-3SG	dog	MD~CTR

kiñ-i,	ñaŋña	miga-m-i		ka-n	kikr-i	makin
stay-SS.SEQ	food	come.down-HPST-3SG		MD-ACC	watch-SS.SEQ	sago

ka-n	fri-m-i.	Fr-ik-i	sikan	sidi-m-i.	
MD-ACC	scratch-HPST-3SG	scratch-DS-3SG	completely	close-HPST-3SG	

Ñaŋña	ni-kw	ma	miga-m-i.	Ka	ad-ik-i,	kuram
food	3SG-POSS	NEG	come.down-HPST-3SG	MD.TOP	do-DS-3SG	man

ka	fai	tikw-ik-i,	manat.	Ñaŋña	maka kiñ-ik-i	makin
MD.TOP	come	look-DS-3SG	no	food	none stay-DS-3SG	sago

ka-n	kwak-ik-i	miga-k-i	fr-i	if-i	
MD-ACC	chop-DS-3SG	come.down-DS-3SG	scratch-SS.SEQ	hit-SS.SEQ	

ña-m-i.	Ka	adi-m-i	ka,	iŋar	ini=ñ	ar-ba
eat-HPST-3SG	MD.TOP	do-HPST-3SG	MD.TOP	day	ND=LOC	1PL-EMPH

ik-i	fr-i	if-i	ña	kida-riŋ.
chop-SS.SEQ	scratch-SS.SEQ	hit-SS.SEQ	eat	walk-1PL.IPST

'This is the sago story. Before, our ancestors didn't process sago. They used to just go to the forest, cut (a sago palm), put a container (there) and food would fall down. As it fell they'd go to the garden, or go wherever, and come back. When they came back it'd be full and they'd take it. Our ancestors used to do that. (Some time) later, a man took his dog and went (looking) for sago. In the morning he didn't feed (his dog). He went and cut sago, put a container (there) and went to his garden. But the dog stayed, watched the food coming down, and scratched the sago tree. Then it closed up completely. Its food didn't come down (anymore). Then, the man came back and looked, but alas! There was no food, so he chopped the sago down, scraped it (out), pounded it and ate it. Because of that, now we also cut it, scrape it (out), pound it and eat it.'

This story is told using the historical past. Here I treat the 2PL agreement suffix as a 2/3PL suffix, which may have been how 3PL agreement was marked in Proto-Sogeram. This decision results in the verb *fai 'come' being combined with the habitual suffix *-itia and the different-subject realis suffix *-ika. It is not known how the combination of verb-final *ai and suffix-initial *i was handled, but Proto-Sogeram i-root verbs, when combined with a suffix-initial *i, retained their *i and elided suffix-initial *i. I have assumed that *fai behaved the same way. No verb can be reconstructed for processing sago, so I simply use *ada 'do'. The word for basket also cannot be reconstructed, so I use *faga 'leaf'. The use of question words like *abañ 'where' for expressions like 'wherever' is widespread in the Sogeram languages, but it has not been directly reconstructed. It is likely that the combination of the 1PL possessive pronoun *arkw with the emphatic enclitic *=bi would result in the same *kw > *ku change that is seen with *kw*-root verbs, but that is not certain.

References

Aikhenvald, Alexandra Y. 2006. Serial verb constructions in typological perspective. In Alexandra Y. Aikhenvald & R. M. W. Dixon (eds.), *Serial verb constructions: A cross-linguistic typology*, 1–87. Oxford: Oxford University Press.

Aikhenvald, Alexandra Y. 2010. *Imperatives and commands*. Oxford: Oxford University Press.

Andersen, Henning. 2001. Actualization and the (uni)directionality of change. In Henning Andersen (ed.), *Actualization: Linguistic change in progress* (Current Issues in Linguistic Theory 219), 225–248. Amsterdam: John Benjamins.

Andersen, Henning. 2006. Synchrony, diachrony, and evolution. In Ole Nedergaard Thomsen (ed.), *Competing models of linguistic change: Evolution and beyond* (Current Issues in Linguistic Theory 279), 59–90. Amsterdam: John Benjamins.

Baker, Mark. 2008. The macroparameter in a microparametric world. In Theresa Biberauer (ed.), *The limits of syntactic variation*, 351–373. Amsterdam: John Benjamins.

Balles, Irene. 2008. Principles of syntactic reconstruction and "morphology as paleosyntax": The case of some Indo-European secondary verbal formations. In Gisella Ferraresi & Maria Goldbach (eds.), *Principles of syntactic reconstruction* (Current Issues in Linguistic Theory 302), 161–186. Amsterdam: John Benjamins.

Barðdal, Jóhanna. 2013. Construction-based historical-comparative reconstruction. In Thomas Hoffmann & Graeme Trousdale (eds.), *The Oxford handbook of Construction Grammar*, 438–457. Oxford: Oxford University Press.

Barðdal, Jóhanna. 2015. Syntax and syntactic reconstruction. In Claire Bowern & Bethwyn Evans (eds.), *The Routledge handbook of historical linguistics*, 343–373. New York: Routledge.

Barðdal, Jóhanna, Valgerður Bjarnadóttir, Serena Danesi, Tonya Kim Dewey, Thórhallur Eythórsson, Chiara Fedriani & Thomas Smitherman. 2013. The story of 'woe'. *Journal of Indo-European Studies* 41(3–4). 321–377.

Barðdal, Jóhanna & Thórhallur Eythórsson. 2012a. Reconstructing syntax: Construction grammar and the comparative method. In Hans C. Boas & Ivan A. Sag (eds.), *Sign-Based Construction Grammar*, 257–308. Stanford: CSLI Publications.

Barðdal, Jóhanna & Thórhallur Eythórsson. 2012b. 'Hungering and lusting for women and fleshly delicacies': Reconstructing grammatical relations for Proto-Germanic. *Transactions of the Philological Society* 110(3). 363–393.

Barðdal, Jóhanna & Spike Gildea. 2015. Diachronic construction grammar: Epistemological context, basic assumptions and historical implications. In Jóhanna Barðdal, Elena Smirnova, Lotte Sommerer & Spike Gildea (eds.), *Diachronic Construction Grammar* (Constructional Approaches to Language 18), 1–50. Amsterdam: John Benjamins.

Barðdal, Jóhanna & Thomas Smitherman. 2013. The quest for cognates: A reconstruction of oblique subject constructions in Proto-Indo-European. *Language Dynamics and Change* 3(1). 28–67.

Barðdal, Jóhanna, Thomas Smitherman, Valgerður Bjarnadóttir, Serena Danesi, Gard B. Jenset & Barbara McGillivray. 2012. Reconstructing constructional semantics: The dative subject construction in Old Norse-Icelandic, Latin, Ancient Greek, Old Russian and Old Lithuanian. *Studies in Language* 36(3). 511–547. doi:10.1075/sl.36.3.03bar.

Barker, Fay & Janet Lee. 1985. *Waskia diksenari: Waskia, Tok Pisin, English* (Dictionaries of Papua New Guinea 7). Ukarumpa: Summer Institute of Linguistics.

Berghäll, Liisa. 2006. Negation in Mauwake, a Papuan language. *A man of measure: Festschrift in honour of Fred Karlsson on his 60th birthday. Special supplement to SKY Journal of Linguistics* 19. 269–281.

Berghäll, Liisa. 2015. *A grammar of Mauwake* (Studies in Diversity Linguistics 4). Berlin: Language Science Press.

Blust, Robert. 1996. The Neogrammarian hypothesis and pandemic irregularity. In Mark Durie & Malcolm Ross (eds.), *The comparative method reviewed: Regularity and irregularity in language change*, 135–156. New York: Oxford University Press.

Boerger, Brenda H. & Gabrielle Zimmerman. 2012. Recognizing Nalögo and Natügu as separate languages: Code-splitting in ISO 639-3. *Language and Linguistics in Melanesia* 30(1). 95–132.

Bohnemeyer, Jürgen, Nicholas J. Enfield, James Essegbey, Iraide Ibarretxe-Antuñano, Sotaro Kita, Friederike Lüpke & Felix K. Ameka. 2007. Principles of event segmentation in language: The case of motion events. *Language* 83(3). 495–532.

Bowern, Claire. 2008. Syntactic change and syntactic borrowing in generative grammar. In Gisella Ferraresi & Maria Goldbach (eds.), *Principles of syntactic reconstruction* (Current Issues in Linguistic Theory 302), 187–216. Amsterdam: John Benjamins.

Braine, Martin D. S. 1976. Children's first word combinations. *Monographs of the Society for Research in Child Development* 41(1). 1–104. doi:10.2307/1165959.

Brooks, Joseph. 2018. *Realis and irrealis: Chini verb morphology, clause chaining, and discourse*. University of California, Santa Barbara Ph.D. dissertation.

Bybee, Joan. 2001a. *Phonology and language use* (Cambridge Studies in Linguistics 94). Cambridge: Cambridge University Press.

Bybee, Joan. 2001b. Main clauses are innovative, subordinate clauses are conservative: Consequences for the nature of constructions. In Joan Bybee & Michael Noonan (eds.), *Complex sentences in grammar and discourse: Essays in honor of Sandra A. Thompson*, 1–17. Amsterdam: John Benjamins.

Bybee, Joan. 2006. From usage to grammar: The mind's response to repetition. *Language* 82(4). 711–733.

Bybee, Joan. 2010. *Language, usage and cognition*. Cambridge: Cambridge University Press.

Bybee, Joan & David Eddington. 2006. A usage-based approach to Spanish verbs of 'becoming'. *Language* 82(2). 323–355.

Campbell, Lyle & Alice C. Harris. 2002. Syntactic reconstruction and demythologizing 'Myths and the prehistory of grammars'. *Journal of Linguistics* 38(3). 599–618. doi:10.1017/S0022226702001706.

Capell, Arthur. 1951. Languages of Bogia District, New Guinea—1. *Oceania* 22(2). 130–147.

Capell, Arthur. 1952. Languages of Bogia District, New Guinea—2. *Oceania* 22(3). 178–207.

Carrington, Lois. 1996. *A linguistic bibliography of the New Guinea area*. Canberra: Pacific Linguistics.

Carroll, Matthew. 2016. *The Ngkolmpu language, with special reference to distributed exponence*. Australian National University Ph.D. dissertation.

Chafe, Wallace. 1976. Givenness, contrastiveness, definiteness, subjects, topics, and point of view. In Charles N. Li (ed.), *Subject and topic*, 25–56. New York: Academic Press.

Chang, Will, Chundra Cathcart, David Hall & Andrew Garrett. 2015. Ancestry-constrained phylogenetic analysis supports the Indo-European steppe hypothesis. *Language* 91(1). 194–244. doi:10.1353/lan.2015.0005.

Clark, Ross. 2011. Birds. In Malcolm Ross, Andrew Pawley & Meredith Osmond (eds.), *The lexicon of Proto Oceanic: The culture and environment of ancestral Oceanic society*, vol. 4: Animals, 271–370. Canberra: Pacific Linguistics.

Colburn, Mike. n.d. Erima grammar essentials. Unpublished ms, Summer Institute of Linguistics.

Craig, Colette. 1991. Ways to go in Rama: A case study in polygrammaticalization. In Elizabeth Closs Traugott & Bernd Heine (eds.), *Approaches to grammaticalization II* (Typological Studies in Language 19), vol. II: Focus on Types of Grammatical Markers, 455–492. Amsterdam: John Benjamins.

Croft, William. 2001. *Radical Construction Grammar: Syntactic theory in typological perspective*. Oxford: Oxford University Press.

Croft, William. 2008. On iconicity of distance. *Cognitive Linguistics* 19(1). 49–57. doi:10.1515/COG.2008.003.

Dąbrowska, Eva. 2000. From formula to schema: The acquisition of English questions. *Cognitive Linguistics* 11(1–2). 83–102.

Daniels, Don. forthcoming. The history of tense and aspect in the Sogeram family. *Journal of Historical Linguistics*.

Daniels, Don. 2010. A preliminary phonological history of the Sogeram languages of Papua New Guinea. *Oceanic Linguistics* 49(1). 163–193.

Daniels, Don. 2014. Complex coordination in diachrony: Two Sogeram case studies. *Diachronica* 31(3). 379–406.

Daniels, Don. 2015. *A reconstruction of Proto-Sogeram: Phonology, lexicon, and morphosyntax*. University of California, Santa Barbara Ph.D. dissertation.

Daniels, Don. 2016. Magɨ: An undocumented language of Papua New Guinea. *Oceanic Linguistics* 55(1). 199–224.

Daniels, Don. 2017a. A method for mitigating the problem of borrowing in syntactic reconstruction. *Studies in Language* 41(3). 577–614.

Daniels, Don. 2017b. Gants is a Sogeram language. *Language and Linguistics in Melanesia* 35. 82–93.

Daniels, Don. 2019. Using phonotactics to reconstruct degrammaticalization: The origin of the Sirva pronoun *be*. *Diachronica* 36(1). 1–36.

Daniels, Don, Danielle Barth & Wolfgang Barth. 2019. Subgrouping the Sogeram languages: A critical appraisal of historical glottometry. *Journal of Historical Linguistics* 9(1). 92–127. doi:10.1075/jhl.17011.dan.

Daniels, Don & Joseph D. Brooks. forthcoming. The history of *=a: Contact and reconstruction in northeast New Guinea. *Journal of Language Contact*.

Davies, John. 1981. *Kobon*. Amsterdam: North Holland Publishing Company.

Donohue, Mark. 2005. Configurationality in the languages of New Guinea. *Australian Journal of Linguistics* 25(2). 181–218.

Dyen, Isidore, Joseph B. Kruskal & Paul Black. 1992. An Indoeuropean classification: A lexicostatistical experiment. *Transactions of the American Philosophical Society* 82(5). 1–132. doi:10.2307/1006517.

Eberhard, David M., Gary F. Simons & Charles D. Fennig (eds.). 2019. *Ethnologue: Languages of the world*. Twenty-second edition. Dallas: SIL International. http://www.ethnologue.com.

Epps, Patience. 2007. Grammatical borrowing in Hup. In Yaron Matras & Jeanette Sakel (eds.), *Grammatical borrowing in cross-linguistic perspective* (Empirical Approaches to Language Typology 38), 551–565. Berlin: Mouton de Gruyter.

Epps, Patience. 2013. Inheritance, calquing, or independent innovation? Reconstructing morphological complexity in Amazonian numerals. *Journal of Language Contact* 6(2). 329–357. doi:10.1163/19552629-00602007.

Evans, Nicholas. 2007. Insubordination and its uses. In Irina Nikolaeva (ed.), *Finiteness: Theoretical and empirical foundations*, 366–431. New York: Oxford University Press.

Evans, Nicholas & Honoré Watanabe. 2016. *Insubordination*. Amsterdam: John Benjamins.

Fillmore, Charles J. 1982. Frame semantics. In The Linguistic Society of Korea (ed.), *Linguistics in the morning calm: Selected papers from SICOL-1981*, 111–137. Seoul: Hanshin.

Fillmore, Charles J. 1988. The mechanisms of Construction Grammar. *Proceedings of the fourteenth annual meeting of the Berkeley Linguistics Society*, 35–55.

Fillmore, Charles J. 2013. Berkeley Construction Grammar. In Thomas Hoffmann & Graeme Trousdale (eds.), *The Oxford handbook of Construction Grammar*, 111–132. Oxford: Oxford University Press.

Fillmore, Charles J., Paul Kay & Mary Catherine O'Connor. 1988. Regularity and idiomaticity in grammatical constructions: The case of *let alone*. *Language* 64(3). 501–538. doi:10.2307/414531.

Foley, William A. 2000. The languages of New Guinea. *Annual Review of Anthropology* 29. 357–404.

Foley, William A. 2018. The morphosyntactic typology of Papuan languages. In Bill Palmer (ed.), *The languages and linguistics of the New Guinea area: A comprehensive guide*, 895–937. Berlin: De Gruyter Mouton.

Fox, Anthony. 1995. *Linguistic reconstruction: An introduction to theory and method*. Oxford: Oxford University Press.

François, Alexandre. 2015. Trees, waves and linkages: Models of language diversification. In Claire Bowern & Bethwyn Evans (eds.), *The Routledge handbook of historical linguistics*, 161–189. New York: Routledge.

Fried, Mirjam & Jan-Ola Östman. 2004. Construction Grammar: A thumbnail sketch. In Mirjam Fried & Jan-Ola Östman (eds.), *Construction Grammar in a cross-language perspective* (Constructional Approaches to Language 2), 11–86. Amsterdam: John Benjamins.

Gasaway, Eileen, Patricia M. Lillie & Heather Sims. 1992. Girawa grammar. Unpublished ms, SIL International.

Geeraerts, Dirk. 1997. *Diachronic prototype semantics: A contribution to historical lexicology*. Oxford: Clarendon Press.

Geeraerts, Dirk. 1999. Diachronic prototype semantics: A digest. In Andreas Blank & Peter Koch (eds.), *Historical semantics and cognition* (Cognitive Linguistic Research 13), 91–107. Berlin: Mouton de Gruyter.

Gildea, Spike. 1998. *On reconstructing grammar: Comparative Cariban morphosyntax* (Oxford Studies in Anthropological Linguistics 18). Oxford: Oxford University Press.

Gildea, Spike. 2000. On the genesis of the verb phrase in Cariban languages: Diversity through reanalysis. *Reconstructing grammar: Comparative linguistics and grammaticalization* (Typological Studies in Language 43), 65–105. Amsterdam: John Benjamins.

Givón, T. 2000. Internal reconstruction: As method, as theory. *Reconstructing grammar: Comparative linguistics and grammaticalization* (Typological Studies in Language 43), 107–159. Amsterdam: John Benjamins.

Goldberg, Adele E. 1995. *Constructions: A Construction Grammar approach to argument structure*. Chicago: University of Chicago Press.

Goldberg, Adele E. 1999. The emergence of the semantics of argument structure constructions. In Brian MacWhinney (ed.), *The emergence of language*, 197–212. Mahwah, NJ: Lawrence Erlbaum.

Goldberg, Adele E. 2006. *Constructions at work: The nature of generalization in language*. Oxford: Oxford University Press.

Goldberg, Adele E. 2013. Constructionist approaches. In Thomas Hoffmann & Graeme Trousdale (eds.), *The Oxford handbook of Construction Grammar*, 15–31. Oxford: Oxford University Press.

Goldberg, Adele E. & Johan van der Auwera. 2012. This is to count as a construction. *Folia Linguistica* 46(1). 109–132. doi:10.1515/flin.2012.4.

Goldberg, Adele E., Devin M. Casenhiser & Nitya Sethuraman. 2004. Learning argument structure generalizations. *Cognitive Linguistics* 15(3). 289–316.

Haiman, John. 1979. Review of: Papuan Languages and the New Guinea Linguistic Scene by S. A. Wurm. *Language* 55(4). 894–903. doi:10.2307/412750.

Haiman, John. 1980. The iconicity of grammar: Isomorphism and motivation. *Language* 56(3). 515–540. doi:10.2307/414448.

Haiman, John (ed.). 1985. *Iconicity in syntax: Proceedings of a symposium on iconicity in syntax, Stanford, June 24–6, 1983* (Typological Studies in Language 6). Amsterdam: John Benjamins.

Hamp, Eric P. 1976. Why syntax needs phonology. In Sanford B. Steever, Carol A. Walker & Salikoko S. Mufwene (eds.), *Papers from the parasession on diachronic syntax, April 22, 1976*, 348–364.

Hanke, August. 1909. *Grammatik und Vokabularium der Bongu-Sprache (Astrolabebai, Kaiser-Wilhelmsland)* (Archiv Für Das Studium Deutscher Kolonialsprachen 8). Berlin: Georg Reimer.

Hardin, Barbara. 2002. Maia grammar essentials. Unpublished ms, Summer Institute of Linguistics.

Hardin, Barbara, Eunice Loeweke, Jean May, Mavis Price, Susan Richardson, Edwin Richardson & Linda Weisenburger. 2007. Maia - English - Tok Pisin dictionary. Unpublished ms, Summer Institute of Linguistics.

Harris, Alice C. 1985. *Diachronic syntax: The Kartvelian case*. New York: Academic Press.

Harris, Alice C. 1990. Alignment typology and diachronic change. In Winfred P. Lehmann (ed.), *Language typology 1987: Systematic balance in language*, 67–90. Amsterdam: John Benjamins.

Harris, Alice C. 2008. Reconstruction in syntax: Reconstruction of patterns. In Gisella Ferraresi & Maria Goldbach (eds.), *Principles of syntactic reconstruction* (Current Issues in Linguistic Theory 302), 73–95. Amsterdam: John Benjamins.

Harris, Alice C. & Lyle Campbell. 1995. *Historical syntax in cross-linguistic perspective*. Cambridge: Cambridge University Press.

Harris, Kyle. n.d. Nend texts. Electronic files, Pioneer Bible Translators.

Harris, Kyle. 1990. Nend grammar essentials. In John R. Roberts (ed.), *Two grammatical studies* (Data Papers on Papua New Guinea Languages 37), 73–156. Ukarumpa: Summer Institute of Linguistics.

Haspelmath, Martin. 1998. Does grammaticalization need reanalysis? *Studies in Language* 22(2). 315–351. doi:10.1075/sl.22.2.03has.

Haspelmath, Martin. 2008. Reply to Haiman and Croft. *Cognitive Linguistics* 19(1). 59–66. doi:10.1515/COG.2008.004.

Haspelmath, Martin. 2016. The serial verb construction: Comparative concept and cross-linguistic generalizations. *Language and Linguistics* 17(3). 291–319. doi:10.1177/2397002215626895.

Heine, Bernd. 1997. *Possession: Cognitive sources, forces, and grammaticalization* (Cambridge Studies in Linguistics 83). Cambridge: Cambridge University Press.

Heine, Bernd & Tania Kuteva. 2003. On contact-induced grammaticalization. *Studies in Language* 27(3). 529–572. doi:10.1075/sl.27.3.04hei.

Heine, Bernd & Tania Kuteva. 2005. *Language contact and grammatical change*. Cambridge: Cambridge University Press.

Heine, Bernd & Kyung-An Song. 2011. On the grammaticalization of personal pronouns. *Journal of Linguistics* 47(3). 587–630. doi:10.1017/S0022226711000016.

Hepner, Mark. 2002. Bargam dictionary. Unpublished ms, SIL International.

Hepner, Mark. 2006. Bargam grammar sketch. Unpublished ms, SIL International.

Hetzron, Robert. 1976. Two principles of genetic reconstruction. *Lingua* 38(2). 89–108.

Hoffmann, Thomas & Graeme Trousdale. 2013a. Construction Grammar: Introduction. In Thomas Hoffmann & Graeme Trousdale (eds.), *The Oxford handbook of Construction Grammar*, 1–12. Oxford: Oxford University Press.

Hoffmann, Thomas & Graeme Trousdale (eds.). 2013b. *The Oxford handbook of Construction Grammar*. Oxford: Oxford University Press.

Hooper, Joan. 1976. Word frequency in lexical diffusion and the source of morphophonological change. In William Christie (ed.), *Current progress in historical linguistics*, 96–105. Amsterdam: North Holland.

Ingram, Andrew. 2001. *Anamuxra: A language of Madang Province, Papua New Guinea*. University of Sydney Ph.D. dissertation.

Ingram, Andrew. 2003. The morphosyntax of classifiers in Anamuxra: Details of a multiple classifier system. *Anthropological Linguistics* 45(2). 129–168.

Ingram, Andrew. 2010. Wordhood in serial verb constructions: Evidence from Anamuxra. In John Bowden, Nikolaus P. Himmelmann & Malcolm Ross (eds.), *A journey through Austronesian and Papuan linguistic and cultural space: Papers in honour of Andrew Pawley* (Pacific Linguistics 615), 481–498. Canberra: Pacific Linguistics.

Järvinen, Liisa & Poh San Kwan. 2007. Mauwake–English and English–Mauwake dictionary. Unpublished ms, SIL International.

Kalyan, Siva & Alexandre François. 2018. Freeing the Comparative Method from the tree model: A framework for Historical Glottometry. In Ritsuko Kikusawa & Lawrence Reid (eds.), *Let's talk about trees: Genetic relationships of languages and their phylogenic representation*, 59–89. Osaka: National Museum of Ethnology.

Kaspruś, Aloys. n.d. Wordlists. Unpublished ms.

Kaspruś, Aloys. 1942. The languages of the Mugil District, NE-New Guinea. *Anthropos* 37/40. 711–778.

Kay, Paul & Charles J. Fillmore. 1999. Grammatical constructions and linguistic generalizations: The What's X doing Y? construction. *Language* 75(1). 1–33. doi:10.2307/417472.

Kerr, Harland B. 1973. The Proto Kainantu kinship system of the East New Guinea Highlands. In Howard McKaughan (ed.), *The languages of the Eastern Family of the East New Guinea Highland Stock*, 769–799. Seattle: University of Washington Press.

Klamer, Marian & Antoinette Schapper. 2012. 'Give' constructions in the Papuan languages of Timor-Alor-Pantar. *Linguistic Discovery* 10(3). 174–207.

Kleef, Sjaak van. 2007. *Siroi-English dictionary, English-Siroi dictionary.* Unpublished ms, SIL International.

Koch, Harold. forthcoming. Teknocentric kin terms in Australian languages. In Zhengdao Ye & Helen Bromhead (eds.), *Meaning, life and culture.* Canberra: ANU Press.

Koch, Harold. 1996. Reconstruction in morphology. In Mark Durie & Malcolm Ross (eds.), *The comparative method reviewed: Regularity and irregularity in language change*, 218–263. New York: Oxford University Press.

Kroonen, Guus. 2013. *Etymological dictionary of Proto-Germanic.* Leiden: Brill.

Kulick, Don. 1992. *Language shift and cultural reproduction: Socialization, self, and syncretism in a Papua New Guinean village.* Cambridge: Cambridge University Press.

Lambrecht, Knud. 1994. *Information structure and sentence form: Topic, focus, and the mental representations of discourse referents.* Cambridge: Cambridge University Press.

Lane, Jonathan. 2007. *Kalam serial verb constructions* (Pacific Linguistics 589). Canberra: Pacific Linguistics.

Lang, Ranier. 1976. Review of: *Papuan languages and the New Guinea linguistic scene* by S. A. Wurm. *Language and Linguistics in Melanesia* 9(1). 72–80.

Langacker, Ronald W. 1987. *Foundations of Cognitive Grammar, vol I: Theoretical prerequisites.* Stanford: Stanford University Press.

Lightfoot, David W. 1979. *Principles of diachronic syntax* (Cambridge Studies in Linguistics 23). Cambridge: Cambridge University Press.

Lightfoot, David W. 1980. On reconstructing a proto-syntax. In Paolo Ramat (ed.), *Linguistic reconstruction and Indo-European syntax: Proceedings of the colloquium of the 'Indogermanische Gesellschaft,'* 27–45. Amsterdam: John Benjamins.

Lightfoot, David W. 2002a. Myths and the prehistory of grammars. *Journal of Linguistics* 38(1). 113–136.

Lightfoot, David W. 2002b. More myths. *Journal of Linguistics* 38(3). 619–626.

Lillie, Patricia M. 1999. *Girawa dictionary.* Unpublished ms, SIL International.

MacDonald, Lorna. 1990. *A grammar of Tauya.* Berlin: Mouton de Gruyter.

MacDonald, Lorna. 2013. *A dictionary of Tauya* (Pacific Linguistics 638). Berlin: De Gruyter Mouton.

Majnep, Ian Saem & Ralph Bulmer. 1977. *Birds of my Kalam country (Mñmon yad Kalam yakt).* Auckland: Auckland University Press, Oxford University Press.

Matisoff, James A. 2002. Genetic versus contact relationship: Prosodic diffusibility in South-East Asian languages. In Alexandra Y. Aikhenvald & R. M. W. Dixon (eds.), *Areal diffusion and genetic inheritance: Problems in comparative linguistics*, 291–327. Oxford: Oxford University Press.

McElhanon, Kenneth. 1975. Isolates: Morobe District: Wasembo (or Gusap). In Stephen A. Wurm (ed.), *Papuan languages and the New Guinea linguistic scene* (Pacific Linguistics C 38), 897–902. Canberra: Pacific Linguistics.

McElhanon, Kenneth & C. L. Voorhoeve. 1970. *The Trans–New Guinea Phylum: Explorations in deep-level genetic relationships.* Canberra: Pacific Linguistics.

Næss, Åshild & Mathias Jenny. 2011. Who changes language? Bilingualism and structural change in Burma and the Reef Islands. *Journal of Language Contact* 4(2). 217–249. doi:10.1163/187740911X589253.

Newmeyer, Frederick J. 1992. Iconicity and generative grammar. *Language* 68(4). 756–796. doi:10.2307/416852.

Nguyen, Noël, Sophie Wauquier & Betty Tuller. 2009. The dynamical approach to speech perception: From fine phonetic detail to abstract phonological categories. *Approaches to phonological complexity* 193–217.

Osthoff, Hermann & Karl Brugmann. 1878. *Morphologische Untersuchungen auf dem Gebiet der indogermanischen Sprachen*. Leipzig: Hirzel.

Pawley, Andrew. 1966. *The structure of Karam: A grammar of a New Guinea highlands language*. University of Auckland Ph.D. dissertation.

Pawley, Andrew. 1995. C. L. Voorhoeve and the Trans New Guinea Phylum hypothesis. In Connie Baak, Mary Bakker & Dick van der Meij (eds.), *Tales from a concave world: Liber amicorum Bert Voorhoeve*, 83–123. Leiden: Leiden University.

Pawley, Andrew. 1998a. The Trans New Guinea Phylum hypothesis: A reassessment. In Jelle Miedema, Cecilia Odé & Rien A. C. Dam (eds.), *Perspectives on the Bird's Head of Irian Jaya, Indonesia: Proceedings of the conference, Leiden, 13–17 October 1997*, 655–690. Amsterdam: Rodopi.

Pawley, Andrew. 1998b. A neogrammarian in New Guinea: Searching for sound correspondences in the Middle Ramu. Unpublished ms, Australian National University.

Pawley, Andrew. 1999. Chasing rainbows: Implications of the rapid dispersal of Austronesian languages for subgrouping and reconstruction. In Elizabeth Zeitoun & Paul Jen-kuei Li (eds.), *Selected papers from the 8th International Conference in Austronesian Linguistics*, 95–138. Taipei: Academica Sinica.

Pawley, Andrew. 2001. The Proto Trans New Guinea obstruents: Arguments from top-down reconstruction. In Andrew Pawley, Malcolm Ross & Darrell Tryon (eds.), *The boy from Bundaberg: Studies in Melanesian linguistics in honour of Tom Dutton*, 261–300. Canberra: Pacific Linguistics.

Pawley, Andrew. 2005. The chequered career of the Trans New Guinea hypothesis: Recent research and its implications. In Andrew Pawley, Robert Attenborough, Jack Golson & Robin Hide (eds.), *Papuan pasts: Cultural, linguistic and biological histories of Papuan-speaking peoples*, 67–107. Canberra: Pacific Linguistics.

Pawley, Andrew. 2006a. Madang languages. In Keith Brown (ed.), *Encyclopedia of language and linguistics*, vol. 7, 429–432. 2nd edn. Boston: Elsevier.

Pawley, Andrew. 2006b. Trans New Guinea languages. In Keith Brown (ed.), *Encyclopedia of Language and Linguistics*, 17–21. 2nd edn. Boston: Elsevier.

Pawley, Andrew. 2012. How reconstructible is Proto Trans New Guinea? Problems, progress, prospects. In Harald Hammarström & Wilco van den Heuvel (eds.), *History, contact and classification of Papuan languages (Special issue of Language and Linguistics in Melanesia)*, 88–164.

Pawley, Andrew & Ralph Bulmer. 2011. *A dictionary of Kalam with ethnographic notes*. Canberra: Pacific Linguistics.

Pawley, Andrew & Harald Hammarström. 2018. The Trans New Guinea family. In Bill Palmer (ed.), *The languages and linguistics of the New Guinea area: A comprehensive guide*, 21–195. Berlin: De Gruyter Mouton.

Pelkey, Jamin. 2011. *A Phula comparative lexicon: Phola, Phuza, Muji, Phowa, Azha*. SIL International.

Petruck, Miriam R. L. 1997. Frame semantics. In Jef Verschueren, Jan-Ola Östman, Jan Blommaert & Chris Bulcaen (eds.), *Handbook of pragmatics*, 1–13. Amsterdam: John Benjamins.

Pierrehumbert, Janet. 2001. Exemplar dynamics: Word frequency, lenition, and contrast. In Joan Bybee & Paul J. Hopper (eds.), *Frequency and the emergence of linguistic structure* (Typological Studies in Language 45), 137–157. Amsterdam: John Benjamins.
Pires, Acrisio & Sarah G. Thomason. 2008. How much syntactic reconstruction is possible? In Gisella Ferraresi & Maria Goldbach (eds.), *Principles of syntactic reconstruction* (Current Issues in Linguistic Theory 302), 27–72. Amsterdam: John Benjamins.
Priestley, Carol. 1986. First Koromu dictionary. Unpublished ms, Summer Institute of Linguistics.
Priestley, Carol. 2008. *A grammar of Koromu (Kesawai), a Trans New Guinea language of Papua New Guinea*. Australian National University Ph.D. dissertation.
Priestley, Carol. 2018. *Koromu (Kesawai): Grammar and information structure in a Papuan language*. Berlin: Mouton de Gruyter.
Reesink, Ger. 1987. *Structures and their functions in Usan: A Papuan language of Papua New Guinea* (Studies in Language Companion Series 13). Amsterdam: John Benjamins.
Roberts, John R. 1987. *Amele*. London: Croom Helm.
Roberts, John R. 1990. Modality in Amele and other Papuan languages. *Journal of Linguistics* 26(2). 363–401.
Roberts, John R. 1997. Switch-reference in Papua New Guinea: A preliminary survey. In Andrew Pawley (ed.), *Papers in Papuan linguistics no. 3* (Pacific Linguistics A 87), 101–241. Canberra: Pacific Linguistics.
Rosch, Eleanor. 1978. Principles of categorization. In Eleanor Rosch & Barbara Lloyd (eds.), *Cognition and categorization*, 27–48. Hillsdale, NJ: Lawrence Erlbaum.
Ross, Malcolm. 1988. *Proto Oceanic and the Austronesian languages of western Melanesia* (Pacific Linguistics C 98). Canberra: Pacific Linguistics.
Ross, Malcolm. 1995. The great Papuan pronoun hunt: Recalibrating our sights. In Connie Baak, Mary Bakker & Dick van der Meij (eds.), *Tales from a concave world: Liber amicorum Bert Voorhoeve*, 139–168. Leiden: Department of Languages and Cultures of South-East Asia and Oceania, Leiden University.
Ross, Malcolm. 1997. Social networks and kinds of speech-community event. In Roger Blench & Matthew Spriggs (eds.), *Archaeology and language I: Theoretical and methodological orientations*. London: Routledge.
Ross, Malcolm. 2000. A preliminary subgrouping of the Madang languages based on pronouns. Unpublished ms, Australian National University.
Ross, Malcolm. 2005. Pronouns as a preliminary diagnostic for grouping Papuan languages. In Andrew Pawley, Robert Attenborough, Jack Golson & Robin Hide (eds.), *Papuan pasts: Cultural, linguistic and biological histories of Papuan-speaking peoples*, 15–65. Canberra: Pacific Linguistics.
Ross, Malcolm. 2007. Calquing and metatypy. *Journal of Language Contact* 1(1). 116–143.
Ross, Malcolm. 2008. A history of metatypy in the Bel languages. *Journal of Language Contact* 2(1). 149–164. doi:10.1163/000000008792525255.
Ross, Malcolm. 2015. The argument indexing of Early Austronesian verbs: A reconstructional myth? In Dag T. T. Haug (ed.), *Historical linguistics 2013: Selected papers from the 21st International Conference on Historical Linguistics, Oslo, 5–9 August 2013*, 257–279. Amsterdam: John Benjamins.
Ross, Malcolm & John Natu Paol. 1978. *A Waskia grammar sketch and vocabulary* (Pacific Linguistics B 56). Canberra: Pacific Linguistics.

Round, Erich R. 2010. Syntactic reconstruction by phonology: Edge Aligned Reconstruction and its application to Tangkic truncation. In Rachel Hendery & Jennifer Hendriks (eds.), *Grammatical change: Theory and description* (Studies in Language Change 6), 65–81. Canberra: Pacific Linguistics.

Rucker, Diane J. 1983. Anjam grammar essentials. Unpublished ms, Summer Institute of Linguistics.

Schleicher, August. 1853. Die ersten Spaltungen des indogermanischen Urvolkes. *Allgemeine Monatsschrift für Wissenschaft und Literatur* 1853. 786–787.

Schleicher, August. 1868. Fabel in indogermanischer Sprache. In Adalbert Kuhn & August Schleicher (eds.), *Beiträge zur vergleichenden Sprachforschung auf dem Gebiete der arischen, celtischen und slawischen Sprachen*, vol. 5, 206–208. Berlin: Dümmler.

Schmidt, Johannes. 1872. *Die Verwandtschaftsverhältnisse der indogermanischen Sprachen*. Weimar: Hermann Böhlau.

Seržant, Ilja A. 2015. An approach to syntactic reconstruction. In Carlotta Viti (ed.), *Perspectives on historical syntax*. Amsterdam: John Benjamins.

Slade, Benjamin. 2008. How (exactly) to slay a dragon in Indo-European? PIE *bheid-{h3égwhim, kwr̥mi-}. *Historische Sprachforschung* 121. 3–53.

Stanley, Evan R. 1923. *Report on the salient geological features and natural resources of the New Guinea Territory, including notes on dialectics and ethnology*. Report to the League of Nations on the Administration of the Territory of New Guinea for 1921–22.

Stefanowitsch, Anatol & Stefan Th. Gries. 2003. Collostructions: Investigating the interaction of words and constructions. *International Journal of Corpus Linguistics* 8(2). 209–243. doi:10.1075/ijcl.8.2.03ste.

Suter, Edgar. 1997. A comparative look at the dual and plural forms of verb inflections and pronouns in Northeast New Guinea Papuan languages. *Language and Linguistics in Melanesia* 28. 1–39.

Sweeney, Mike. n.d. Mum texts. Electronic files, Pioneer Bible Translators.

Sweeney, Mike. 1994a. A description of the phonology of the Katiati (Mum) language. Unpublished ms, Pioneer Bible Translators.

Sweeney, Mike. 1994b. A study of the life and culture of the Mum (Katiati) people. Unpublished ms, Pioneer Bible Translators.

Tomasello, Michael. 1992. *First verbs: A case study of early grammatical development*. Cambridge: Cambridge University Press.

Tupper, Ian D. 2012. *A grammar of Pamosu*. La Trobe University Ph.D. dissertation.

van der Auwera, Johan. 2009. The Jespersen Cycles. In Elly van Gelderen (ed.), *Cyclical change* (Linguistik Aktuell/Linguistics Today 146), 35–71. Amsterdam: John Benjamins.

Voltmer, Brad. 1998. Grammar essentials: Saep language, Papua New Guinea. Unpublished ms, Summer Institute of Linguistics.

von Mengden, Ferdinand. 2008. Reconstructing complex structures: A typological perspective. In Gisella Ferraresi & Maria Goldbach (eds.), *Principles of syntactic reconstruction* (Current Issues in Linguistic Theory 302), 97–119. Amsterdam: John Benjamins.

Wade, Martha. n.d.a. Apalɨ dictionary. Electronic files, Pioneer Bible Translators.

Wade, Martha. n.d.b. Apalɨ texts. Electronic files, Pioneer Bible Translators.

Wade, Martha. 1987. A tentative phonological analysis of the Apalɨ (Emerum) language. Ms, Pioneer Bible Translators.

Wade, Martha. 1989. A survey of the grammatical structures and semantic functions of the Apalɨ (Emerum) language. Ms, Pioneer Bible Translators.

Wade, Martha. 1991. An overview of the culture of the Apalɨ speaking people. Ms, Pioneer Bible Translators.
Wade, Martha. 1993. Language convergence or divergence: The case of the Apalɨ (Emerum) language. *Language and Linguistics in Melanesia* 24(1). 73–93.
Wade, Martha. 1997. Switch reference and control in Apalɨ. *Language and Linguistics in Melanesia* 28(1). 1–16.
Walkden, George. 2013. The correspondence problem in syntactic reconstruction. *Diachronica* 30(1). 95–122. doi:10.1075/dia.30.1.04wal.
Walkden, George. 2014. *Syntactic reconstruction and Proto-Germanic* (Oxford Studies in Diachronic and Historical Linguistics 12). Oxford: Oxford University Press.
Wells, Margaret A. 1979. *Siroi grammar* (Pacific Linguistics B 51). Canberra: Pacific Linguistics.
Willis, David. 2011. Reconstructing last week's weather: Syntactic reconstruction and Brythonic free relatives. *Journal of Linguistics* 47(2). 407–446. doi:10.1017/S0022226710000381.
Wurm, Stephen A. (ed.). 1975. *Papuan languages and the New Guinea linguistic scene* (Pacific Linguistics C 38). Canberra: Pacific Linguistics.
Z'graggen, John A. 1971. *Classificatory and typological studies in languages of the Madang District* (Pacific Linguistics C 19). Canberra: Pacific Linguistics.
Z'graggen, John A. 1975a. *The languages of the Madang District, Papua New Guinea* (Pacific Linguistics B 41). Canberra: Pacific Linguistics.
Z'graggen, John A. 1975b. The Madang-Adelbert Range subphylum. In Stephen A. Wurm (ed.), *Papuan languages and the New Guinea linguistic scene* (Pacific Linguistics C 38), 569–612. Canberra: Pacific Linguistics.
Z'graggen, John A. 1980a. *A comparative word list of the Southern Adelbert Range languages, Madang Province, Papua New Guinea* (Pacific Linguistics D 33). Canberra: Pacific Linguistics.
Z'graggen, John A. 1980b. *A comparative word list of the Mabuso languages, Madang Province, Papua New Guinea* (Pacific Linguistics D 32). Canberra: Pacific Linguistics.
Z'graggen, John A. 1980c. *A comparative word list of the Northern Adelbert Range languages, Madang Province, Papua New Guinea* (Pacific Linguistics D 31). Canberra: Pacific Linguistics.
Z'graggen, John A. 1980d. *A comparative word list of the Rai Coast languages, Madang Province, Papua New Guinea* (Pacific Linguistics D 30). Canberra: Pacific Linguistics.
Z'graggen, John A. 1992. *And thus became man and world*. Edinburgh: Pentland Press Ltd.

Index

accusative. *See* object
adjective 57, 153–155, 213, 216, 218, 219, 231, 251, 305, 308, 309, 312, 319
adverb 57, 112, 148–153, 156, 187, 213, 216, 251, 308, 309, 318
agreement 41, 60, 93, 95, 116, 120, 121, 124–131, 134–136, 139, 140, 142, 146, 147, 155, 156, 217, 223, 224, 305, 309, 313–319, 325, 327
Aisi 4–6, 11, 46, 49, 50, 76–84, 91, 116, 117, 121, 122, 125, 128–135, 139–144, 148, 151, 152, 155, 157, 161, 163–169, 176, 177, 183–186, 189, 190, 200, 203–205, 207, 209–211, 215, 221, 223–226, 229, 230, 237, 240, 242, 245, 246, 326
Anamuxra 10, 39, 41, 51, 92, 95, 128, 133, 139, 156, 163, 175, 176, 177, 226, 230, 252
Apalɨ 2, 4, 6, 10, 39, 43, 47, 50, 52–54, 58, 68, 69, 73, 79, 91, 92, 97, 99, 101, 103–105, 107, 111, 114, 119, 127–135, 138, 143, 144, 150, 152, 155, 163, 165, 183, 185, 195–197, 202, 205, 220, 224, 230
arbitrariness 18, 22–24, 29, 34, 114
aspect 9, 13, 45, 89, 129, 131, 132, 142, 174, 242–246, 305, 311, 313, 319, 320
– completive 102, 106, 107
– habitual 102–104, 120, 129, 239, 316
– imperfective 102, 104
– stative 102, 104, 105

borrowing 22–25, 34, 37, 43, 44, 57, 60, 66, 68, 83, 114, 132, 249, 252, 305

causative 96, 116, 320
child language 20, 21
clause 27, 28, 34, 37, 98, 108, 109, 112–115, 119, 137, 140, 143, 144, 146, 150, 156, 183, 188–197, 202, 203, 210, 213, 223, 308–311, 319

– chain 26, 305, 317, 318
– nonverbal. *See* predicate
– subordinate 26, 37, 44, 188–190, 194, 197, 230, 240–246
cognate 6, 7, 14, 16, 17, 19, 24, 30, 39, 41, 43, 44, 47, 58, 64, 68, 71, 72, 77, 86, 92, 94, 95, 98, 104, 110, 114, 115, 117, 122, 123, 127–129, 133, 134, 139, 141, 143, 150, 151, 156, 160–163, 175, 176, 181, 189, 190, 192, 195, 202, 209, 213, 219, 249, 291, 294
comparative method 2, 9, 14–17, 19, 22–24, 37, 42, 46, 305
construction 11, 20–28, 33, 36–38, 53, 89, 94, 96, 125, 177, 181, 195, 217, 218, 227, 233, 238, 242, 244, 245, 248, 249, 305, 319, 321, 323, 325
Construction Grammar 19, 20, 26, 33, 34
contact. *See* borrowing
correspondence 22–25, 37, 47, 52, 54, 55, 63, 77, 160, 198, 234, 292

demonstrative 27, 154, 159, 165, 168, 169, 179, 182, 183, 213, 218, 229, 230, 238, 240, 242–246, 305, 310, 312, 319, 320, 322
diachrony 22, 31, 34
– diachronic identity. *See* cognate
– diachronic stability 18
different-subject 76, 95, 103, 130, 136, 137, 140, 238, 239, 313, 317, 321, 322, 327
– realis 141, 318
– simultaneous 144, 152, 318
directionality 19, 22, 23, 25, 30, 36, 37
dual 41, 92, 163, 213

East Sogeram 43, 48, 70, 76, 115, 133, 140, 152, 179, 228, 252

family tree. *See* subgrouping
focus 177, 179, 181, 182, 184, 189, 196, 198, 200, 209, 211, 216, 310, 311, 313, 321
future 18, 19, 39, 120, 123, 128, 129, 133, 137, 155, 239, 249, 252, 316, 317, 319

https://doi.org/10.1515/9783110616217-010

Gants 2, 4, 9, 27, 43, 76–78, 85–87, 97, 98, 101, 104, 108, 113, 122, 123, 126, 135, 139, 144, 147, 165, 167, 171, 177, 183, 191, 237, 243
glottometry. *See* subgrouping
gradience 15
grammaticalization 21, 25, 95, 104, 108, 155, 161, 181, 219
– parallel 25
Greater West Sogeram 43, 54, 115, 125, 152, 177, 182, 235, 251, 292

iconicity 24, 27, 28, 35, 115
infinitive
– irrealis 155–157, 319
inheritance hierarchy 26

Kalam 8, 11, 41, 226, 252
Kursav 2, 5, 6, 9, 43, 76–78, 84, 85, 91, 97, 104, 133, 137, 139, 141, 143, 144, 147, 148, 151, 163–165, 177, 183, 191, 195, 197, 207, 226, 237, 242, 243, 249

lexicon 1, 15, 19, 22, 23, 25, 27, 31, 33, 44, 49, 53–56, 59, 60, 71, 92, 100, 305
linkage 40, 43
locative 26, 27, 173, 184, 196, 199, 202, 204, 216, 230, 242–244, 311, 312

Madang 2, 8–11, 38, 41, 51, 93, 96, 141, 223, 226, 252, 253, 325
Magɨ 4, 5, 76–82, 97, 110, 118, 128–131, 134, 142, 143, 161, 167, 171, 221
Manat 4, 11, 47–49, 54–57, 64, 68–70, 91, 95, 102, 106, 107, 112, 117, 122, 123, 125, 126, 132, 138, 139, 142, 145, 147, 149, 152, 153, 155, 163–166, 170, 176–181, 183, 185–187, 192, 199, 200, 202, 205, 207, 208, 223, 224, 230, 234–236, 240, 246, 248, 249, 251, 325, 326
Mand 2, 4, 6, 11, 46, 49, 54–61, 92, 93, 120–125, 129, 131, 140, 142, 148, 153, 154, 155, 160–165, 170, 171, 176, 178, 179, 182, 184, 187, 192, 199, 201, 208, 209, 211, 219–223, 226, 230, 234, 236, 245, 246, 252

Minimalism 31
mood 102, 120, 136, 137, 239, 309, 313, 316–318
– counterfactual 120, 121, 317
– imperative 120, 239, 316
– interrogative 182
– irrealis 137, 318
– prohibitive 120, 317
Moresada 10, 39, 47, 92, 163, 209
Mum 2, 4–6, 10, 49, 52, 68–75, 118, 122, 127, 132, 133, 138–146, 148, 155, 160, 161, 165–167, 169, 171, 173, 179, 184–186, 188, 194, 195, 206, 207, 209, 220, 223, 242, 243, 246

negation 113, 223, 232–237, 319, 321
Nend 4, 6, 10, 11, 46, 48, 51, 54–58, 61–64, 97, 105, 117, 120–124, 127, 129–136, 139, 140, 149, 155, 160, 163, 164, 169, 170, 172, 178, 179, 181, 184, 186, 195, 197–199, 201, 204, 211, 220, 223, 226, 230, 235, 236, 240, 251
nominalization 148
– clause chain 240, 305, 322
– verbal 44, 305
noun 2, 26, 57, 112, 148, 151–154, 156, 159, 161, 172, 174, 180, 187, 192, 213–216, 218, 220, 226, 231, 251, 253, 291, 305, 308, 309, 318, 321
– attributive 217–219, 305, 308, 309, 312
– inalienably possessed 159, 168, 169, 180, 200, 213, 251, 253, 291, 308, 309, 312, 321
– phrase 26, 153, 162, 165, 168, 169, 171, 174, 179–182, 184, 191, 193, 194, 198–200, 204, 207, 210, 213, 217, 219, 221, 238, 240–246, 305, 308, 309, 311, 322
North Sogeram 43, 48–50, 54, 66, 68, 115, 125, 140, 152, 185, 252

object 13, 22, 27, 28, 30, 37, 108–110, 112, 114, 115, 118, 162, 165, 169, 170, 172, 174, 175, 177, 178, 184, 198, 221, 230, 240–242, 308–312, 320, 323
onomatopoeia 16, 18, 35
orthography 5, 6, 45, 50, 87, 88, 306

participle 60, 132, 133, 152, 153, 156, 313, 318
past 92, 95, 98, 100, 103, 106, 108, 120, 239, 246, 313, 314, 325, 327
– far 120, 124, 125, 127, 143, 315
– historic 95, 120, 126, 129, 315
– immediate 103, 121–123, 142, 239, 314
– recent 123, 125–127, 129, 315
– today 120, 123, 125, 126, 314
– yesterday 124
phonotactics 45, 51
plural 41, 90, 92, 93, 107, 108, 122, 139, 142, 155, 160, 163–167, 171, 177–179, 310, 325
present 104, 108, 123
possessor 159, 170, 172, 173, 175, 215, 217, 220, 308, 310, 312
predicate, nonverbal 44, 180, 181, 187, 189, 190, 193, 200–203, 230, 311, 321
productivity 21, 30, 96, 246, 247
pronoun 9, 39, 41, 57, 92, 93, 159, 160, 161
– emphatic 177–182
– object 165–169
– oblique 169–174
– possessive 175–177
– subject 162–165
Proto-Germanic 16, 33
Proto-Madang 9, 41, 92, 93, 96, 163
Proto-Oceanic 18, 24, 35

quoted speech 238, 247, 321, 323

reanalysis 21, 29, 30, 57, 211
reconstruction 14, 33, 48, 50, 57, 89, 98, 105, 114, 115, 117, 121–124, 128–135, 139, 140, 142, 145, 153, 155, 159–164, 169, 175, 182, 184, 185, 193–195, 204, 207, 211, 213, 216, 218, 219, 223, 226, 230, 234, 237, 239, 245, 249, 251
– morphological 1, 24, 30, 37, 89
– phonological 1, 11, 44, 45, 157
– syntactic 1, 22–24, 28, 89, 115, 213, 223, 305, 324
reduplication 46, 75, 144, 148, 149, 151, 152, 183, 184, 195, 313, 319, 322
regularity 22–25, 30, 34, 35, 52, 67, 165

same-subject 140, 238, 239, 313, 318, 322
sign
– Saussurean 15
– schematic 20, 33
– signified 15, 18
– signifier 15, 18
Sirva 5–7, 9, 11, 49, 52, 67, 68–73, 75–77, 85, 92, 93, 95, 97, 98, 101, 109, 116, 122, 127, 132, 136, 141, 145, 147, 148, 151, 152, 160, 166–169, 176, 177, 179–181, 183, 185, 189, 194–197, 206, 207, 219, 221, 225, 228, 234, 242, 243, 247, 325
stops 5, 47, 52, 61, 66, 69, 76, 86, 132, 149
– labiovelar 48, 49, 69
– prenasalized 6, 46, 48, 51, 58–60, 62, 228, 307
– voiceless 59, 65, 67, 69, 77, 148, 150, 151
subgrouping 9, 13, 38, 39, 54, 164, 227, 251, 252
synchrony 9, 14, 16, 26, 59, 65, 84, 122, 132, 141, 154, 162, 177, 181, 187, 252

tense 31, 39, 60, 89, 92, 98, 100, 103, 104, 108, 119, 121, 123–128, 131, 155, 157, 231, 239, 309, 313–316, 319, 321, 322, 325
token, linguistic 14, 16, 17, 30
topic 27, 89, 91, 182, 184, 187–197, 200, 210, 213, 223, 230, 233, 240–242, 244, 310, 311, 320–323, 328
tradition of speaking 16–18, 30, 32, 37
Trans New Guinea 8, 39, 41, 46, 119, 141, 183, 223, 238, 252, 253
type, linguistic 16, 30

verb 2, 9–11, 21, 27, 28, 41, 44, 47, 49, 53, 55, 57, 60, 69, 89, 180, 193, 202, 203, 213, 214, 223, 227, 238, 239, 247, 249, 252, 253, 305, 307–309, 313, 316–319, 323, 325, 327
– final verb 49, 89, 90, 104, 119, 227, 313, 320
– medial verb 103, 119, 137, 148, 225, 239, 322
– root 89–92, 96–101, 307, 319, 327

– serial verb 27, 28, 53, 94, 96, 309, 313, 319, 325
– uninflected 90, 94, 96–101, 109–111, 114, 115, 144, 227, 252, 309, 319

wave model. *See* subgrouping
West Sogeram 6, 43, 46–48, 53, 58, 63, 66, 68, 94, 124, 125, 130, 131, 133, 134, 140, 143, 144, 152, 160, 166, 211, 224, 234

www.ingramcontent.com/pod-product-compliance
Lightning Source LLC
Chambersburg PA
CBHW031753220426
43662CB00007B/393